The Brooklyn Bridge

The Brooklyn Bridge

A Cultural History

RICHARD HAW

RUTGERS UNIVERSITY PRESS
NEW BRUNSWICK, NEW JERSEY, AND LONDON

Library of Congress Cataloging-in-Publication Data

Haw, Richard, 1968–
   The Brooklyn Bridge : a cultural history / Richard Haw.
     p. cm.
   Includes bibliographical references and index.
   ISBN 0-8135-3587-5 (hardcover : alk. paper)
  1. Brooklyn Bridge (New York, N.Y.)—History.   I. Title.
   TG25.N53H39 2005
   624.2'3'097471—dc22

                                                           2004021378

A British Cataloging-in-Publication record for this book is available from the British Library.

Manufactured in the United States of America

Book design by Karolina Harris

Frontispiece photograph by Michael Iacovone

For Erica, for everything

Contents

Acknowledgments

All books are in essence collaborative, and it is my great pleasure to acknowledge here the many debts I have accumulated over the years.

This book is a product of two different environments and two different groups of people. It was begun at Leeds University in the United Kingdom and finished in New York. At Leeds, I was lucky enough to receive financial support from the Douglas Grant and Joseph Wright graduate scholarships, and even luckier to find myself in the company of Nick Bandu, Ben Caines, Ian Copestake, Tara Deshpande, Rachel Fairbrother, Ingrid Gunby, Mel Kersey, Eric Langley, Michael MacDonald, Gillian Roberts, Chris Rook, Anja Schmidt, Rob Stanton, David Stirrup, Caroline Sumpter, Rob Ward, Andrew Warnes, Steve Watson, Colin Winborn, Louise Winfield, and Jayne Wood. I couldn't ask for better friends, and I will always remember my times with them as some of my very best.

After arriving in New York, I was lucky to land in the English department at John Jay College of Criminal Justice. My new colleagues quickly became firm friends, and I would especially like to thank Valerie Allen, Ed Davenport, Betsy Gitter, Ann Huse, Pat Licklider, John Matteson, Mark McBeth, Adam McKible, Alexander Schlutz, Tim Stevens, Anya Taylor, and Cristine Varholy for their generosity and unfailing good humor. As much as anyone, my students at John Jay have monitored my often stumbling attempts to stop being so British and to start becoming a New Yorker. Their encouragement, as much as any, makes me feel I can make it.

In New York, Jay Albanese, Dan Backer, Kenny Faltischek, Jeanne Finnerty, Evan Garcen, Mike Guinan, Ed Hanna, Mary Hart, Mike Iacovone, Eric Jones, Eric Katz (and the Velvet's Underdogs subvention fund), Sophi Kravitz, Dan Markunas, Jesse Meyer, Lisa Modifica, Valerie Ogar, Alex Racine, Paula Reynolds, Selene Telles, and Dave Waters all told me to shut up about the bridge and buy a round. I couldn't appreciate them more or be more in their debt.

I have leaned on the skill, goodwill, and patience of numerous librarians and archivists in putting this book together. I would especially like to thank the staffs at the Brotherton Library in Leeds; the special collections department at the Archibald S. Alexander Library, Rutgers University; the New-York Historical Society (especially Jill Reichenbach); the Library of Congress; New York City's Municipal Archives; the Lloyd Sealy Library at John Jay; and the many hundreds of librarians who have aided me throughout the

New York Public Library and Brooklyn Public Library systems. Equally deserving of special mention are Polly Armstrong at Stanford University's special collections; Karen Becker at Gorney Bravin + Lee; Jacalyn Blume at Harvard's Schlesinger Library; Tori Counter at the Autry Museum of the American West; Ruth Jansen at the Brooklyn Museum of Art; Linda McCurdy at Duke University's special collections; Gil Pietrzak at Pittsburgh's Carnegie Library; Alix Reiskind at Harvard's Frances Loeb Library; and Eva Waters from the studio of Ellsworth Kelly.

I am very grateful to Daniela Gioseffi, Cynthia Hogue, and Ken Siegelman for permission to quote from their poetry. They are copyright: Daniela Gioseffi, "To the Brooklyn Bridge," from her booklet "The Brooklyn Bridge Poetry Walk, June 25, 1972," copyright © 2004 by Daniela Gioseffi, reprinted by permission of the author. "Crossing Brooklyn Bridge," by Cynthia Hogue, was published in *The Southern Review* (1994), copyright © by Cynthia Hogue, and collected in *The Never Wife*, by Cynthia Hogue (MAMMOTH books, 1999), copyright © by Cynthia Hogue. Used by permission. "Heaven's Gate," copyright © 2003 by Ken Siegelman. Used by permission. The lines from Sujata Bhatt, Charles Reznikoff, Harvey Shapiro, and Andrei Voznesenski are copyright: Sujata Bhatt, "Walking Across the Brooklyn Bridge, July 1990," from *Monkey Shadows*, Carcanet Press Limited, 1991. Copyright © 1991 by Sujata Bhatt. Reprinted by permission of Carcanet Press Limited. *Rhythms*, from *The Complete Poems of Charles Reznikoff*, by Charles Reznikoff. Reprinted by permission of Black Sparrow Books, an imprint of David R. Godine, Publisher, Inc. Copyright © 1976 by Charles Reznikoff. Harvey Shapiro, three poems from *The Sights Along the Harbor: New and Collected Poems*, Wesleyan University Press, 2006. "National Cold Storage Company," originally published in *Battle Report* © 1966, and "In Brooklyn Harbor" and "The Bridge (for John Wissemann)," originally published in *Lauds and Nightsounds* © 1978, by Harvey Shapiro. Reprinted by permission of Wesleyan University Press. "New York Airport at Night," from *Antiworlds and the Fifth Ace: Poetry by Andrei Voznesensky.* © 1966, 1967 by Basic Books, Inc. © 1963 by Encounter Ltd. Copyright renewed. Reprinted by permission of Basic Books, a member of Perseus Books, L.L.C. For help with copyrights, I would especially like to thank Kim Radowiecki at Wesleyan University Press.

Chapter 1 first appeared in *New York History,* and I would like to thank Daniel Goodwin at the New York State Historical Association for both his interest in my work and permission to republish. A part of the Introduction first appeared in the *Journal of American Studies,* and the ideas behind Chapter 2 were first worked out in an essay published in *Dreams of Paradise, Vi-*

sions of Apocalypse, ed. Jaap Verheul (VU University Press, 2004). I am grateful to the editors of both publications for permission to reclaim my work.

No one writing about the Brooklyn Bridge can ignore the work of David McCullough and Alan Trachtenberg, and I would like to acknowledge my debt to them. To this list I wish to add Hugh Wilford, who long ago stimulated my interest in American intellectual history, as did Alistair Stead, a man whose ability to answer almost any question (no matter how busy) with authority has always come with a smile. In my research on Yun Gee, I was guided by Li-lan and Tunghsiao Chou, both of whom showed great warmth and tolerance. At John Jay, Gerald Markowitz and Jacob Marini generously made time to answer questions from someone with whom they had only a passing acquaintance. At Rutgers University Press, Melanie Halkias was quick to pick up the phone when she heard of my project. Her belief in this book has been constant and, for a first-time author, more than a little welcome. Also at Rutgers, I would like to thank Emily Adler, Marilyn Campbell, Alison Hack, Donna Liese, and Jessica Pellien for all their time and effort. Gretchen Oberfranc did a wonderful job with my manuscript — equally meticulous and thoughtful — and I thank her for her generosity and rigor. From near and far, David Nye has long followed the gestation of this book, and I thank him for his enthusiasm, advice, and friendship. Mick Gidley has supported and encouraged my studies for many years now. His influence has been profound, and I only hope that this book and I live up to his example.

My family has sustained me through different (!) periods in my life. To my parents, Gillian and Peter, my brother Chris and his wife, Becky, I owe more than I can say. In addition to them, a second family — Ben, Joyce, Marcia, Michele, and Stephen — welcomed me to New York with open arms and friendly faces. Old friends have been equally important. Long ago, Sean Body and Emma Lindley convinced a disgruntled twenty-three-year-old that a university somewhere would take him. Their faith and support were equaled by Sam and Tim Body, as well as David Essery and Richard Garratt. The depth of my gratitude seems hardly adequate to the breadth of their friendship over the years.

Finally, this book is dedicated to Erica Brody, with whom I have shared the last ten years of my life. She has read this book more times than anyone really ought, offering wise counsel at every step. Her friendship, humor, love, understanding, and encouragement have sustained my life and this project. For all of this and more, my love and thanks are unending.

Richard Haw
Brooklyn, 2004

It so happens that the work which is likely to be our most durable monument, and to convey some knowledge of us to the most remote posterity, is a work of bare utility; not a shrine, not a fortress, not a palace, but a bridge.

                             –Montgomery Schuyler, "The Bridge as a Monument," 1883

I doubt that anything manmade has entered the American imagination in quite as forceful and prominent a way.

                        –Arthur Miller, interviewed for the *New York Times Magazine,* 1983

The Brooklyn Bridge has remained celebrated and cherished, long after its technological achievements have been superseded. . . . Why has the Brooklyn span remained so alive in the popular culture?

                              –Philip Lopate, *Waterfront: A Journey around Manhattan,* 2004

The Brooklyn Bridge

Introduction

Culture, History, and the Brooklyn Bridge

It would not be unreasonable to say that the two greatest works of architecture in New York are things that are not buildings at all — Central Park and the Brooklyn Bridge.
— Paul Goldberger, *The City Observed*, 1979

Architecture, after all, is the most public and tangible expression of a civilization.
— John A. Kouwenhoven, *Made in America*, 1948

The Bridge
Still stands, getting ancient
With its freight of poetry.

— Harvey Shapiro, "In Brooklyn Harbor," 1978

At the close of World War II, an American serviceman is stationed in Germany. He is lovelorn and homesick. Chided by his peers, the young man is forced to reveal the treasured image of the "girl" he carries around in his wallet. It is a photograph of the Brooklyn Bridge. Although teased by his buddies, he is defiant: "Yeah, that's my pinup girl," he tells them. "Ain't she a beauty?" Upon returning to America, he runs from the transport depot and yells to a taxi driver, "Do you know the way to the Brooklyn Bridge?" Once there, he bursts into song and begins to stroll along the sunlit promenade.

These are scenes from the film *It Happened in Brooklyn* (1947), starring Frank Sinatra, and they lovingly evoke the place of the Brooklyn Bridge in the American imagination. Appearing at every level of culture, the bridge is a national obsession. For academic specialists and the general public alike, the bridge is the nineteenth century's most important and defining work of engineering, and, equally, the world's most famous and beloved span. It may very well be the most photographed structure on earth: the collections of the Library of Congress hold more images of the Brooklyn Bridge than of any other manmade structure — more, in fact, than of anyone or anything other than Niagara Falls.

From the Donaldson Brothers' attempt to publicize their "cable screw wire for boots and shoes" in 1875 to the television advertising campaigns of Ford, I.B.M., and Verizon in 2003, the bridge has been used to promote a

1. *It Happened in Brooklyn:* Frank Sinatra sings Sammy Cahn and Jule Styne's classic "The Brooklyn Bridge" (1947). From the author's collection.

plethora of now forgotten goods—Dr. Scott's Electro-medical Products, Royal Baking Powder, Lydia E. Pinkham's Vegetable Compound, Willimantic Six-Cord Spool Cotton, and Mulford, Cary and Conklin's Leather and Findings—as well as more familiar products: Chesterfield cigarettes, Coca-Cola, Maxwell House coffee, Kentucky Fried Chicken, Singer sewing machines, Vaseline, and Absolut vodka. For decades the span has been the official emblem of the two most "New York" of soft drinks: Manhattan Special and Dr. Brown's Cel-Ray Soda. In Italy, Brooklyn Bridge chewing gum has long been a leading brand. Currently, the bridge serves as the logo for the Brooklyn Savings Bank and New York's Independence Community Bank—having performed the same function for the now defunct Brooklyn Bank—and has provided the title to a national television show and a national magazine. It has been "sold" by such illustrious Americans as Mae West and Bugs Bunny, and used to sell America itself through countless postcards, posters, guidebooks, book covers, T-shirts, and souvenirs of all descriptions. In the Netherlands in 1979, Ed Schilders began to publish the bimonthly fanzine *Brooklyn Bridge Bulletin.* The publication was warmly received, as was the surprising nature of the enthusiast's fascination: remarkably, Schilders had never seen the bridge in person.

The bridge's international fame has been sustained by the arts. In film,

2. "The Great Willimantic Bridge": co-opting the bridge for commercial promotion. Willimantic Six-Cord Spool Cotton trade card (1883). From the author's collection.

3. Absolut Brooklyn advertisement (1994). © Richard Lewis, TBWA \ Chiat \ Day.

ABSOLUT BROOKLYN.

like the Eiffel Tower and Big Ben, its image instantly identifies the location. In 1899, Thomas Edison placed a camera on a Brooklyn-to-Manhattan elevated railroad and captured the journey. That same year, the American Mutoscope and Biograph Company took a camera up to the top of the bridge's New York tower and produced a motion-picture panorama of lower Manhattan. In 1921, the bridge was a cornerstone image in Paul Strand and Charles Sheeler's cinematic hymn to New York, *Mannahatta*. Subsequently, the bridge has appeared in countless films, from Josef von Sternberg's *The Docks of New York* (1928) and Raoul Walsh's *The Bowery* (1933) to such recent blockbusters as *The Siege* (1998), *Godzilla* (1998), *8mm* (1999), and *Kate & Leopold* (2001).

As in film, so in popular music. In early standards, such as Elf St. Moritz and John Vorsatz's "The Highway in the Air: A Ballad of the Brooklyn Bridge" (1883), George Cooper and J. P. Skelly's "Strolling on the Brooklyn Bridge" (1883), and Edward Harrigan and David Braham's "With Danny by My Side" (1891), and in later genres—Bobby Bare's country lament "The Brooklyn Bridge" (1961), Sonny Rollins's jazz masterpiece *The Bridge* (1962), Marilyn and Alan Bergman and Marvin Hamlisch's show tune "Just Over the Brooklyn Bridge" (1991), and Wyclef Jean's eclectic rap "No Airplay" (1999)—the bridge has found its celebrants.

Further, the bridge has made innumerable appearances in the visual and literary arts. Visual representations of the span have been the subject of exhibitions all over the United States, and the original design drawings have been shown at the Whitney Museum of American Art and the Smithsonian Institution. At the library of the Brooklyn Historical Society, "Brooklyn Bridge poetry" merits a file of its own. No other structure has a similar dossier. In 1983, Arthur Miller captured the essence of this cultural prominence: "I doubt that anything manmade has entered the American imagination in quite as forceful and prominent a way." [1]

Miller's observation is revealing. Despite the sheer physicality of the Brooklyn Bridge, its cultural history owes as much to the imagination as it does to historical events. A broad range of advertising executives, artists, filmmakers, historians, intellectuals, musicians, politicians, writers, and other participants in the to-and-fro of cultural commentary have contributed to the development of the bridge's image, which has subsequently taken its place among other canonized American icons: George Washington, Thomas Jefferson, Abraham Lincoln, the U.S. flag, the Grand Canyon, the Statue of Liberty, Niagara Falls, the Empire State Building, and the World Trade Center towers. As an American monument, somehow symbolic of the national mind, the bridge has been discussed and debated, characterized and represented, from its inception until the present. With each new voice, the bridge's image has grown, its cultural lexicon incorporating new concerns and new interpretations. As Merrill Peterson among others has shown, the intellectual and cultural play surrounding distinctive American icons creates further, secondary images: social and imaginative constructions standing at once in tandem and in dispute with one another.[2] The history of the Brooklyn Bridge has shown a similar capacity for cultural and symbolic metamorphosis.

As the bridge's *physical* construction began in 1869, a parallel process of *cultural* construction was also initiated. Their dual courses have resulted in two quite distinct Brooklyn Bridges: the physical bridge that stands astride the East River, linking Brooklyn with Manhattan, and the cultural bridge of the mind and the imagination. The first is arguably the world's most impressive and inspiring public structure, a dazzling monument to the public good, the common path, and the necessity of municipal fellowship. The second is a vast tapestry of representations, all subject to the vagaries of individual perception. Needless to say, fundamental tensions exist between these two Brooklyn Bridges, but also among the various, competing assessments that constitute the second, cultural bridge.

The effect is best understood through David Hockney's wonderfully astute photomontage *The Brooklyn Bridge, Nov. 28, 1982* (1982). Hockney's image both *shows* and *enacts* the cultural process, whereby a single central icon is recognized as a mosaic: a composite constructed from a variety of different, single images. Although in Hockney's creation we recognize the bridge in its entirety—we see the familiar lines of the bridge's Gothic arches, the magnificent cable structure, the oft-trod boardwalk, and even the feet of an observer—a closer inspection highlights a basic friction. Hockney's bridge, like the Brooklyn Bridge of culture, is fashioned from myriad juxtaposed images, each somehow in conflict yet also in accord with the others.

By tracing dominant modes of perception and representation, this book will explore the sometimes jarring trends and patterns that constitute the cultural history of the Brooklyn Bridge. I shall scrutinize the ways in which the bridge has been received, adopted, and interpreted as a preeminent American icon. My goal is a history not of the bridge per se, but of the *representation* of the Brooklyn Bridge from its opening ceremonies in 1883 to the blackout of 2003.[3]

I begin by exemplifying my argument. In trying to understand the relationship between the Brooklyn Bridge and the nature (and forms) of its representational history, we might usefully look at the case of Walt Whitman, the public figure most closely associated with the cities of New York and

4. The cultural icon: recognizing the bridge as a mosaic. David Hockney, *The Brooklyn Bridge, Nov. 28, 1982*, photographic collage, edition: 20, 109 × 58 in. © David Hockney.

Brooklyn during the period in which the Brooklyn Bridge was conceived, built, and opened. Whitman and the Brooklyn Bridge have long been conjoined in the public and private imagination. Author Christopher Morley found the bridge to be the best place to read and digest Whitman; critic Allen Keller thought it was the structure the poet had most persistently and energetically "glorified"; art historian Kenneth Clark believed that Whitman wrote "The Song of the Broad-Axe" (1856) with the Brooklyn Bridge in mind.[4] In her best-selling historical romance set in antebellum Brooklyn, *The Sunlit Field* (1950), Lucy Kennedy presents a fictional Whitman traversing the East River on one of his beloved ferries. In a "far off" voice the poet declares: "One day, there'll be a bridge across this river. Strong, so that men and horses and wagons can cross over. The bridge will make a relationship between the two cities. A wonderful feat to throw a bridge across a river! No living thing but man can do it! It's a mastering of the earth's materials — wood, iron and stone! It's a figuring out how to use them!"[5] The novelist Lucille Fletcher continued this trend eight years later. In *The Daughters of Jasper Clay* (1958), Fletcher created a character who felt intimately bound to the span for the simple reason that "Walt Whitman had loved this bridge."[6] The appropriation of Whitman reached its peak at the bridge's centennial in 1983, when journalists from across the United States seemed to rise up with one voice to proclaim the poet's total admiration for Brooklyn's grand old bridge. Some even followed Kennedy's lead and went so far as to declare that Whitman had predicted its construction.[7]

Since 1983, writers, critics, and historians have continued to link Whitman with the bridge. At the span's anniversary celebrations in 2003, *Time Out: New York* alluded to the Good Grey Poet when listing an official reading: "poets follow in the footsteps of Whitman and praise the bridge." A few years earlier, Ellen Fletcher noted that, to Whitman, the Brooklyn Bridge "was the work of engineering that completed Columbus's mission." In *The New Yorker*, Hendrik Hertzberg complained that "the George Washington Bridge has never really been given its due. The Brooklyn Bridge gets all the attention — the Walt Whitman poetry, the Joseph Stella painting, the David McCullough book, the Ken Burns documentary." Gloria Deák stated that "the grandeur of New York City's bridges has inspired lofty poetry — Walt Whitman and Hart Crane were two of the earliest bards to pay tribute."[8]

Writing in *Attaché*, an in-flight magazine aimed at travelers, Jim Collins made a claim that is common among tourist resources: "John Roebling's famous bridge . . . inspired poems by Walt Whitman."[9] On the Internet, the newyork.com tourist site asserts that "Walt Whitman said that the view from the walkway was 'the best, most effective medicine my soul has yet partaken.'"[10] Also on the Web, we find statements by reputable and seemingly reliable sources. From the New York City Department of Transportation: "The soaring lines of the Brooklyn Bridge have inspired countless architects, engineers, painters and poets to pursue their own expressions of creative excellence, among them . . . Walt Whitman."[11]

If we pause to consider Whitman's relationship with Brooklyn, the poet and the bridge would seem to be natural companions. "If there ever existed a city whose resources were undeveloped, whose capabilities were misunderstood, and undervalued," wrote Whitman in 1858, "it is Brooklyn."[12] Less than four years later, certain achievement had taken the place of "undervalued" potential. Taking aim at a period "twenty-five or thirty years ahead,"

Whitman extolled: "The child is already born, and is now living, stout and hearty, who will see Brooklyn numbering one million inhabitants! Its situation for grandeur, beauty and salubrity is unsurpassed probably on the whole surface of the globe; and its destiny is to be among the most famed and choice of the half dozen of the leading cities of the world. And all this, doubtless, before the close of the present century."[13]

The poet's predictions were on target. Although it may never have ranked among "the half dozen of the leading cities of the world," Brooklyn in the late nineteenth century grew remarkably. The city expanded out of Brooklyn Heights to include Williamsburg to the north, Coney Island and Gravesend to the south, and Canarsie and New Lots to the east. Its population, a mere 20,000 in Whitman's youth, would become the third largest in the Union, and it would top one million by the time Brooklyn was absorbed in the New York City consolidation of 1898, a fivefold increase from 1862, when Whitman was making his predictions. Taking advantage of sixty-five miles of natural shoreline, trade flourished in the city, and by 1880 Brooklyn was the fourth-largest industrial city in the United States. To commercial success was added significant municipal and cultural improvement. Brooklyn was home to the United States's first modern sewerage system (1858), urban redevelopment and civic pride were welded in the designs for Prospect Park (1867) and Eastern Parkway (1868), and transportation was improved through the construction of an elevated railroad (1885) and an electric trolley system (1890). By the century's end, Brooklyn was home to a Philharmonic Society (1857), an Academy of Music (1859), a Historical Society (1863), a free public library (1896, at the Pratt Institute), and an Institute of Arts and Sciences (1897, now the Brooklyn Museum).[14]

Yet, despite these significant advances, Brooklyn remained in the shadow of its illustrious cross-river neighbor for much of Whitman's lifetime. Where New York had its Central Park and Trinity Church, the archetypal bustling Broadway, and the aristocratic Fifth Avenue, Brooklyn was known by a more sedate epithet, "the city of homes and churches." The municipality's most famous attraction was neither a place nor a thing, but a preacher. People who would never travel to Brooklyn to see the city itself came to hear the words of Henry Ward Beecher, America's preeminent religious orator. But Brooklyn's identity and destiny were about to change. On May 24, 1883, the Great East River Bridge — the *Brooklyn* Bridge — was dedicated and declared opened to the public.

The opening of the bridge confirmed and announced what Whitman had long predicted. With an authentic world icon — the largest suspension bridge in existence and one of the most talked about engineering feats in an era obsessed with new technology—Brooklyn had finally come of age. In its own right, it was now an eminent and distinguished city, a legitimate destination for global and national travelers. The event should have been the crowning moment in Whitman's career as a Brooklyn booster. Unfortunately, it was not. And the answer to Whitman's complex relationship with the Brooklyn Bridge lies more in the realities of New York City history and the poet's own writings than in the imagination that presumes Whitman's love for all things Brooklyn.

In 1944 New York decided to remove the railroad tracks that ran across the bridge and to raze the transport terminals that stood at either end. The following year the bridge was reopened to pedestrians and automobile traffic at a grand ceremony. As Stanley Hyman subsequently reported, "the sponsors of the bridge's 'reunveiling' in 1945 were so certain Whitman must have written something about [the] Brooklyn Bridge that they recklessly announced that a poem by him would be read at the ceremony. They were unable to produce."[15] The sponsors, however, upheld their promise. Sandwiched between the addresses of Manhattan Borough President Edgar Nathan Jr. and New York Mayor Fiorello La Guardia was a public reading of Whitman's "historic verse," "Crossing Brooklyn Ferry."[16] Written thirteen years before construction began—and a full twenty-seven years before the bridge opened—"Crossing Brooklyn Ferry" makes no reference to a bridge between New York and Brooklyn, and neither does it envision one. Nevertheless, public recitals of this "historic verse" have become a standard commemorative practice. The poem enjoyed public readings at the bridge's rededication in 1954, at the span's seventy-fifth anniversary, and again at the centennial in 1983. In addition, "Crossing Brooklyn Ferry" was the only poem among those included in Daniela Gioseffi's much-publicized Brooklyn Bridge poetry walk of June 25, 1972, that made no reference to the bridge. The same can be said for the New York–based Poets' House's annual poetry walk across the Brooklyn Bridge, which has featured "Crossing Brooklyn Ferry" since the event's inauguration in 1995.

As the organizers of the 1945 re-unveiling ceremonies realized, Whitman wrote no poetry that celebrated the Brooklyn Bridge.[17] In fact, he barely wrote about the bridge at all. The span appears only twice in his voluminous literary output, and on both occasions the reference is fleeting. In "Song of the Exposition" (1876), the bridge is included with the Atlantic cable, the Pacific Railroad, the Suez Canal, and great railway tunnels in Europe and America (Mont Cenis, St. Gothard, and Hoosac) as an example of the "latest connections, works, the inter-transportation of the world." In the short prose piece "Manhattan from the Bay" (1878), Whitman briefly diverts his attention from "the broad water-spread" of life on the bay—"magnificent in size and power, fill'd with their incalculable value of human life"—to observe "the grand obelisk-like towers of the bridge, one on either side, in haze, yet plainly defin'd, giant brothers twain, throwing free graceful interlinking loops high across the tumbled current below."[18] This description, written a full five years before the bridge was completed, was Whitman's last reference to the bridge in his writing. From then on, the span's troubled construction elicited no response from him. He made no mention of the opening ceremonies—a truly national event—even though he was in good health and loved the raw spectacle of great public occasions.[19]

More puzzling, Whitman was remarkably silent about the early years of the bridge's construction. Between 1869, when the project began, and 1873, Whitman undertook five long trips to Brooklyn, ranging from five weeks to almost three months. Yet he failed to mention the bridge even once, although, by his own admission, he regularly traversed the East River from Brooklyn to New York. As he wrote on June 29, 1871, "I am daily on the water here."[20] Equally, his move to Camden in 1873 hardly accounts for his continued silence on the subject of the bridge. As "Manhattan from the Bay" suggests and his letters confirm, he subsequently visited New York on many occasions, continued to write of it, and corresponded with numerous friends in the area. From the completion of the bridge in 1883 until the poet's death in 1892, there is no evidence that Whitman ever set foot upon the structure.

So, despite the historical record, why has Whitman become inextricably linked with the Brooklyn Bridge? There are numerous answers to this question, the most persuasive of which concern the idealized nature of public memory as it relates to cultural history.[21] Throughout the twentieth century, those who invoked Whitman's unadulterated approval and concomitant love of the bridge relied heavily on flawed precedent, assumption, misreading, and specious evidence. The quotations used to support Whitman's affection for the bridge were taken from poems and prose pieces that had nothing to do with the bridge. On other occasions, history has simply been invented. Although Whitman's expressed interest in the bridge is at best marginal, his place in the bridge's cultural history has become central. In this respect, the poet's relationship to the bridge reflects what John Bodnar has called "official cultural expression." As he explains: "official culture relies on 'dogmatic formalism' and the restatement of reality in ideal rather than complex or ambiguous terms."[22]

As the foremost poet of democratic, progressive, optimistic, and exuberant nineteenth-century New York—and also, of course, the artist most closely associated with celebrating the rhapsodic American ideal of progress, union, and democracy—Whitman has become the "ideal" official spokes-man for the Brooklyn Bridge. That his written statements about the bridge produce an image at once "complex" and "ambiguous"—more antipathy than advocacy—has often seemed irrelevant. For writers wishing to provide direct evidence of Whitman's approval, such phrases as "The shapes arise!" (from "Song of the Broad-Axe," and used by Kenneth Clark and David Mc-Cullough, among many others) have often proved irresistible. Yet this line first appeared in 1856, when it was included in the second edition of *Leaves of Grass*. Although predating the legislation that established the New York and Brooklyn Bridge Company by eleven years, and predating the beginning of construction by thirteen years, the phrase fits the parameters of official cul-tural expression: if the words fit the "ideal," print them.

In direct contrast to Martin Filler's assertion in its centennial year that the Brooklyn Bridge has received "virtually unanimous critical acclaim,"[23] Whitman's legacy shows that strong tensions exist in our archive of responses to it. At no time was this ambivalence more obvious than in the forms, prac-tices, and rhetoric of the bridge's opening day. The bridge's dedication cere-mony was a glaring attempt to direct and define the terms through which the bridge would be discussed and represented. And it was a major success. As an event, it consecrated a language and a set of perceptions that continue to dominate cultural interpretations of the Brooklyn Bridge.

From the events of the opening day, this study proceeds through the bridge's representational history, employing a wide range of cultural media: commemorative practices, oratory, visual arts, guidebooks and travelogues, film, journalism, autobiography, imaginative literature, and structural, pop-ular, and critical history. Such important themes as national ideology, im-migration and tourism, technological iconography and urban perception, historical memory and commemorative ritual, and rededication and revi-sionism are considered in relation to the bridge. The analysis concludes with a brief assessment of the period from September 11, 2001, to the blackout of 2003—two events with deep implications for the Brooklyn Bridge. Along the way, I shall challenge much received wisdom, although I do not aim at dis-paragement. I examine the cultural history of the Brooklyn Bridge as a his-torian interested in how people have absorbed, made sense of, and sought to present the bridge.

In presenting the tensions in the bridge's cultural history, I shall focus on two broad forms of response. These I term expressions of assent and of dis-sent. By glorifying the Brooklyn Bridge as an exemplary American icon, as-senting voices have affirmed Filler's claim. Yet this assent has often involved a studied avoidance of physical, social, and economic context. Under the assenting gaze, the bridge is transformed from a bustling city spot to a depopulated, aestheticized showcase for American technological and economic progress; in effect, it is a perfect art object, an American version of Keats's "well-wrought urn." Dissenting voices, on the other hand, have criticized this approach and sought to contextualize the bridge as a profoundly *public*, communal place. By prioritizing the city's vast humanity over its technological iconography, they have fashioned a "vernacular"[24] image of the bridge that is essentially anthropocentric. In this respect, the dissenters have perhaps proved themselves more faithful than the assenters to the spirit of the bridge, and most especially to its unique central walkway. For it is only when we relate our public monuments to the human life that teems around them that we can approximate the raw optimism and happy acceptance of difference that has so often defined the promise of New York.

1 Manufacturing Consensus, Practicing Exclusion
Ideology and the Opening of the Brooklyn Bridge

This splendid structure thrown across the river . . . is not only good in itself but a sure promise of immeasurably greater good to come.

—*Brooklyn Daily Eagle*, May 24, 1883

The potter, and not the pot, is responsible for the shape of the pot.

—Alfred North Whitehead, *Symbolism*, 1927

On May 24, 1883, after fourteen years of arduous work, the Great East River Bridge between the independent cities of New York and Brooklyn was dedicated and declared open to the public. In accord with the auspicious nature of the event, the cities celebrated in grand style. A parade was staged, speeches were given, and the day ended with an hourlong fireworks display. President Chester A. Arthur and New York Governor Grover Cleveland attended the festivities, and the event was widely covered in the local, national, and international press. On the whole, these reports stressed the visible and voluble assent of the people; everywhere, joy and celebration, veneration and approval reigned. Subsequent commentators have echoed these sentiments.

Among historians, the opening of the Brooklyn Bridge has been regarded as a seminal event. The structure represented an unparalleled technological achievement and a remarkable municipal consensus. After the ravages of the Civil War, the dislocations of the troubled postwar economy, the political malfeasance of Tammany Hall, and the conflicts occasioned by new mass immigration, the bridge seemed to unite the two cities' diverse peoples and heal their open wounds.[1]

In truth, the bridge's dedication was a tightly controlled municipal event saturated with ideological considerations.[2] It is not unusual for urban populations to celebrate and commend the completion of public works, but in this case the construction had been highly controversial. From the onset in 1869, alarm, criticism, and protest accompanied the bridge project. John Roebling, the span's designer and the world's most trusted bridge builder, died as a result of a freakish accident only days into the construction. He was succeeded by his thirty-two-year-old son Washington, a qualified but

5. "The Grand Display of Fireworks and Illuminations: At the Opening of the Great Suspension Bridge between New York and Brooklyn on the Evening of May 24th 1883." Published by Currier and Ives (1883). Courtesy of the Library of Congress.

untested and relatively inexperienced engineer. During construction, hazardous working conditions claimed more than thirty additional lives, and scores of laborers suffered permanent disability.[3] In the political and financial arenas, the bridge's construction history was littered with fraud, delay, uncertainty, and mistrust. In the months leading up to the opening, criticism was widespread, and, just days before the opening, many of the city's newspapers reported that public confidence in the project was very low.[4] An unveiling ceremony might have reversed such doubts about a smaller, less visible structure. Yet the bridge had emerged over the course of fourteen years, and its appearance was new to nobody. In retrospect, the almost instantaneous rate at which universal approval replaced widespread denigration seems more than a little unusual.[5]

6. Worker injuries on the bridge: Harry Supple falls to his death. "Terrible Accident on the New York Tower of the East River Bridge," *New York Illustrated Times*, June 29, 1878. Courtesy of the Library of Congress.

The White City and Central Park

It is impossible to separate the opening of the Brooklyn Bridge from the context of its times. Begun in the aftermath of the Civil War, and continued through Reconstruction and the beginnings of the Gilded Age, the bridge's construction spanned an era of fluctuating cultural power. As one critic has observed, this period was characterized by "controversies over the meaning of America," by "struggles over reality, over the power to define as well as control it."[6] In addition, as debates raged over the meaning of America, the management of social order was both honed and refined. The drive for definition and control found its logical acme at Chicago's 1893 World's Columbian Exposition. Directed by architect and city planner Daniel Burnham, the exposition sought to present a constructed, idealized version of the modern city. Its guiding principle was the hegemony of commerce, technology, and middle-class culture, not the free expression of individual citizens. One of the White City's many functions was to legitimize its fictional self at the expense of the very real problems facing the surrounding metropolis. The purpose of the White City was to display a "distorted mirror"[7] to the emerging urban scene; the "idola" of the Great Basin and the Manufactures and Liberal Arts Building replaced the realities of labor unrest, ethnic conflict, political malfeasance, and overwhelming poverty.[8]

The means by which the Columbian Exposition controlled, displayed, and defined the American urban experience were not invented in a vacuum. Just as the creators of the exposition appropriated the physical elements of the city, so they also consolidated the management of order. The construction and maintenance of social stability had been an issue in America's cities since before the Civil War. With regard to New York, the nation's foremost urban environment and in many ways its most troubling, two events are especially important when one considers the sort of polarization not only perfected at Chicago's exposition, but also evident nationally throughout the era.

In 1859 New York's Central Park opened to the public. The park's design was chiefly the work of landscape architect Frederick Law Olmsted, who would go on to play a major role in the design of the White City. Olmsted envisioned Central Park as a transcendent, democratic space: a meeting ground for all New York. Yet his egalitarianism hid an ideological agenda. Embedded in his vision was a set of concerns that reflected his middle-class New England background, not the reality of life in New York. In "Public Parks and the Enlargement of Towns" (1870) Olmsted attacked the unhealthy influence of city streets. The function of public parks, he declared, was to eradicate the degrading stain of local urban culture and to educate the lower classes in the values and manners of their social betters. As Alan Trachtenberg notes, "Olmsted's park presented itself as a practical pedagogy: on the one side, all pastoral picture, composed views, nature artfully framed as spectacle, and on the other, firm regulation, clear rules, sufficient police."[9]

Olmsted's vision has received generally positive assessments from other critics, yet the centrality of his middle-class conceit can hardly be challenged. For many lower-class New Yorkers the streets provided a comforting familiarity that could not be replicated in the more alien environment of the park. Moreover, Olmsted failed to realize that a majority of poor New Yorkers — and especially those residing downtown — could not afford to travel to the park. As Charles Mackay, author of guidebooks and travelogues, illustrated in 1859, the park proved itself a pleasure ground for the upper classes, revealing "the worth and wealth" of the city: "one could hardly believe he was in a republican country to see the escutcheoned panels of the carriages, the liveried coachmen, and the supercilious air of the occupants of the vehicles. . . ." Exactly twenty years later, the park's reputation was unchanged. While visiting in 1879, Walt Whitman noted that the space embraced "the full oceanic tide of New York's wealth and 'gentility,'" and he privately wondered why it was not "more popular" and "free" to the city's common classes.[10]

New York's "search for order" was aided by the highly planned spectacle of Central Park, yet forces were also working in another direction. The city's unease over the visibility of the lower classes was palpable at this time, and the 1863 Civil War draft riots heightened anxiety over lower-class unrest. In response, the city made parade permits compulsory, instituted stringent laws of assembly, and augmented its law enforcement units. The increased visibility accorded the middle and upper class via the pastoral environment of Central Park was matched by the decreased visibility of the poor. The city's lower classes stayed "hidden" until the late nineteenth century, when Jacob Riis published *How the Other Half Lives: Studies among the Tenements of New York* (1890).[11] They inhabited the shadows of New York's slum regions, while more prosperous citizens strolled in the sunshine of the park. These two halves of the city could not be kept apart indefinitely, however, especially during important civic occasions. Nevertheless, every effort would be made to enforce their separation when the Brooklyn Bridge was finally opened in 1883.

The People's Day and the Irish Boycott

The opening of the Brooklyn Bridge was a symbolic event. Its main subject was a transfer of power; its principal actors, purportedly, were the bridge trustees and the general public. In service to these ideals, May 24 was officially designated "The People's Day." After years of political infighting and financial shenanigans, the people, it seemed, were to take center stage, a fact reiterated by every one of the day's speakers. Time and again, the American people were praised as wise and courageous builders. For the Reverend Richard C. Storrs, chief pastor of Brooklyn's Church of the Pilgrims and one of the opening's principal orators, "the real builder of this surpassing and significant structure has been the people."[12] Such claims were elaborated throughout the press, as references to an idealized populace abounded. The official report confirms:

> From the announcement by the Trustees . . . it was evident that the popular demonstration would be on a scale commensurate with the magnificence of the structure and its importance to the people of the United States. The evidences of widespread and profound interest in the event were early and unmistakable. They were not confined to the metropolis and its sister city on the Long Island shore, nor yet to the majestic Empire State. The occurrence was recognized as one of National importance; and throughout the Union . . . the opening ceremonies were regarded with intelligent concern and approval.[13]

Deliberately phrased to echo earlier glories, the report uses such key words and phrases as "announcement," "national," "popular demonstration," "intelligent concern and approval" to place the bridge within the American civil religion of revolution and, especially, public readings of the Declaration of Independence.

The press also alluded to this wider, national significance. For the *New York Herald*, the twenty-fourth of May was as much "the nation's day" as "the people's day,"[14] in essence, an event that deserved equal status with America's annual celebration of national liberty. The *New York World* even went so far as to describe the bridge as "a shortcut to life, liberty and the pursuit of happiness."[15] In stone and steel, the bridge reverberated with the qualities of the American people. Forged in the crucible of freedom, liberty, and equality, the Brooklyn Bridge, declared Storrs, "takes the aspect, as so regarded, of a durable monument to Democracy itself."[16]

Despite these constant references to the general public, the ceremonies that opened the Brooklyn Bridge were conspicuous for their lack of municipal inclusion. In fact, evidence of calculated exclusion pervades the historical record. The report of a special committee of the Common Council of Brooklyn reveals that the bridge trustees had initially decided *against* a public celebration. The committee noted that "the opening of the Bridge is to be attended by some ceremonies, apparently private in character, access to which is debarred to the public and to be granted to the few by an arbitrary selection to be exercised by the Trustees of the Bridge."[17] Given that the board of trustees was composed solely of local officials and wealthy industrialists, it takes little imagination to realize how "private" and "arbitrary" such a ceremony would have been.[18] Ultimately, however, festivities were planned, although no reason is provided for this decision. One suspects that Brooklyn's desire for national exposure was influential, and that politicians backed away from the untenable position of condoning a private celebration of a public work. But the turnaround would prove to be less radical than it might seem. In nearly all particulars, the opening celebrations were more private than public.

When the day's orators spoke so generously of the people who had toiled for so long to build the bridge, they conveniently forgot that just weeks earlier worker objections to the opening had been dismissed outright. On the eve of the ceremonies, *Puck* magazine ran a story that imagined the following day's events. It described a grand celebration and a magnificent procession. The object of this celebration, however, was not the opening of the bridge, but the sixty-fourth birthday of Queen Victoria. Mention of the bridge was reserved for a wonderfully offbeat conclusion: "In the evening, just after the display of fire-works, a few citizens, in the exuberance of their delight at the glorious day's proceedings, wended their way to a neighboring creek to see a small bridge opened. It was a dull affair, and not of the slightest importance."[19] *Puck's* purpose was satire, of course, but such ridicule rarely exists without reason.

Beyond the continuing objections to the bridge's building and financing, one of the most virulent expressions of protest concerned the date on which it was to be opened. Many workers were insulted by the choice of May 24, Queen Victoria's birthday, and none more so than those of Irish descent. Although the bridge's laboring staff included African Americans, Germans, Poles, and Italians, the majority were poor Irish navvies. These Irish Americans had long endured the project's appalling working conditions, and they were justifiably proud of their work. Yet they felt betrayed by the trustees' decision to open on the British monarch's birthday, and a genuine sense of outrage swept the community. Their indignation only increased when their objections were flatly ignored.

Evoking Samuel Adams's anti-British, revolutionary coterie and, perhaps more specifically, its slogan of "no taxation without representation," Irishmen formed an association called the Sons of Liberty to protest the resolution, and the group's views were aired in the press. Only a few days before the scheduled opening, the main spokesman for the Sons of Liberty, Civil War veteran P. J. Gallagher, unleashed a furious attack on the organizers: "it was England that gave the rebels their Alabamas, who sunk our ships and tried to drive our flag from the seas . . . I would like to see this English toadyism knocked off of that bridge."[20] The *Brooklyn Daily Times* labeled the protesters "fiery and untamed lunatics," but New York Alderman John Fitzpatrick adopted their cause. He offered a resolution to change the date and met with the bridge trustees. His proposal to move the ceremony back one week to coincide with Memorial Day was popular with the public at large. The trustees, however, deemed the coincidence unimportant and declared themselves happy with their original decision.[21] In protest, New York's Irish population boycotted the bridge's opening.[22]

For historian Craig Steven Wilder, the absence of Irish participants at the festivities constitutes one of the most striking aspects of the day. A consideration of the Irish presence in the New York region broadens this significance. The total population of just less than 2 million in 1883 included more than 275,000 individuals born in Ireland and another 250,000 of Irish descent. As Wilder continues, these "Irish working-class hacks . . . didn't make a lot of money and . . . never got a lot of credit."[23] Certainly, they received no credit from the bridge trustees, despite having performed much of the hard labor that went into erecting the bridge. Moreover, this working-class embargo was not only ideological, it was also physical.

Exclusion, Coercion, and the Politics of the American Parade

Gallagher's closing retort to the bridge trustees contained a major irony: "I hope that no working men will go near the bridge on opening day." [24] With or without a boycott, the day's organizers saw to it that no workingmen were able to get near the bridge on May 24. Nearly one hundred years earlier, in 1797, George Warner warned that oppression based on social difference would dominate the United States if "tradesmen, craftsmen, and the industrious classes consider themselves *too little consequence* to the body politic." [25] By 1883, social difference had indeed segregated New York, and the industrious classes were hardly to blame. [26] Workers were absent from the opening-day festivities not because they lacked the self-esteem to attend; they were barred by decisions made by influential people behind closed doors.

Just days before the opening, the *Herald* wrote: "The Mayor [Seth Low of Brooklyn] is opposed to a long and unwieldy procession, and he has declined many proffers from social and trade organizations to assist by turning out with banner and music. Such bodies have been requested . . . not to insist on a place in the line of march to pass over the bridge." [27] The report of the special committee of the Common Council authenticates this official mandate. Although "a suggestion was made that a procession of the citizens and tradesmen would be a desirable feature of municipal celebration," the idea was "finally deemed unadvisable and abandoned." [28] This decision is not elaborated upon, and one might speculate that the trustees questioned the structure's load-bearing capacity. Yet the chief engineer's report delineated the bridge's more than adequate strength; moreover, the trustees planned to open the bridge to the general public at midnight following the opening ceremonies. [29] At that time, many more people than could be contained within a single parade would have been expected to cross. Evidently, the trustees, and especially Mayor Low, sought to exercise a large measure of control over content and participation at the festivities.

On opening day, reactions to the physical appearance of Brooklyn itself were prominent in the press reports. For the city's newspapers, the visible and voluble support of Brooklynites was perfectly highlighted by the pride and energy with which they had adorned their city. Bunting flew from every available support, each house was illuminated, and the entire population seemed to be on the streets. The message was presented simply: the united people of Brooklyn had, of their own free will and in glorification of the completed structure, risen up overnight and expressed their approval through a marvelous display of civic decoration. The *Brooklyn Daily Eagle*, for example, captured the tremendous amount of local pride when it observed that Brooklyn met the opening day as "a transformed city."[30]

Yet the reality of civic celebration is rarely so straightforward: the reactions that seemed voluntary were in fact compulsory. What we find in Brooklyn's appearance on May 24, 1883, is an early example of what Daniel Boorstin has termed a "pseudo-event."[31] Just as the date of the opening ceremonies was strictly determined, so was the appearance of Brooklyn. A resolution was passed by the Common Council directing the citizens of Brooklyn to "close their places of business . . . and to decorate their houses, and in the evening to cause them to be illuminated. . . . It is especially desired that all buildings on the City Hall Square and the streets leading thence to the Bridge, be brilliantly illuminated." For "the owners of shipping and the warehouses along the river," the region must be made "beautiful with bunting and with fire-works."[32] The council focused on buildings lining the parade route and on Brooklyn's image from either Manhattan or the bridge—in essence, only the areas visible to tourists, reporters, and official guests. We do not know the extent to which the whole of Brooklyn was decorated; reports of the day stressed only the parade route and the riverside area. It would seem likely that in many poorer neighborhoods, without the funds for such a transformation, the streets remained bare. Yet their lack of participation would not have been an issue. To present civic unity, those in power need only control the areas that are visible.

The presentation of civic unity is often defined by public turnout. A majority of the press reports about the ceremonies observed that the turnout in Brooklyn had been far higher than that in Manhattan. The presence of such a large number of Brooklynites on the streets was understood to constitute proof of assent. To reverse the question, though, is instructive: what else were Brooklynites to do on this day? In Manhattan the day was given no special consideration, and a majority of residents made their way to work as usual. In Brooklyn, a public holiday was declared, closing municipal offices and city schools, in addition to businesses, stores, bars, and other private concerns. To all intents and purposes, the city was shut down. This situation led to some consternation. On the eve of the bridge's opening, an irate Brooklyn storekeeper, apparently "echoing the voices of many," wrote to the *Eagle* to berate the city for its actions. Not only were traders losing a day's profit, but the council was also imposing a "fast day appearance" on the city.[33] Again, however, this complaint illustrates how officials manipulated the city's appearance. In the parts of the city not affected by the celebrations, a "fast day appearance" would no doubt have predominated, providing all the more reason for citizens to throng to those areas decorated for festivity. With access to the bridge denied and the queues for the ferry service interminably long, Brooklynites were stranded in a city whose public services and leisure businesses were all closed for the day.[34]

As a civic occasion, the opening of the Brooklyn Bridge stands in the same historical tradition as the Grand Federal Procession in Philadelphia in 1788 and the opening ceremonies of the Erie Canal in 1825 and the Croton Aqueduct in 1842. Although these occasions marked genuine national pride, the civic rituals were framed by concerns over municipal definition and display. The Federal Procession was over a mile and a half long and showcased many of the city's trades and occupations. Likewise, at the celebrations for the Erie Canal and the Croton Aqueduct, the parades were both long and inclusive.[35]

By comparison, the Brooklyn Bridge parade was surprisingly short. Composed of President Arthur, Governor Cleveland, their respective staffs, and two branches of the New York state militia, the parade highlighted only the loftiest levels of government and their military wing. No workers—from engineers through craftsmen to manual laborers—were included. Moreover, they were not invited to either the formal ceremonies or the official speeches. Describing a similar situation at Chicago's World's Columbian Exposition ten years later, James Gilbert notes that there was "no place for workers in the White City, no evidence of their presence."[36] Few more striking parallels exist between the two late-nineteenth-century phenomena. At the time of optimum publicity, those who had built the bridge were excluded from view. Consequently, they received none of the attention and no direct acclaim.

A look at comparable civic occasions helps to contextualize the bridge's opening-day parade. In 1867 in St. Louis, work began on a structure equal in all regards to that being planned in New York. Technologically and symbolically, the Eads Bridge matched the significance of the Brooklyn Bridge. It was the first bridge to span the Mississippi River, the first to employ steel, and the first to subject workers to the miseries of "caisson disease." When the Eads Bridge opened in 1874, the accompanying procession stretched for fifteen miles. A throwback to the celebrations of the early national and Jacksonian periods, the St. Louis parade included representatives from the entire spectrum of the city's working population. From high officials to manual laborers, all were able to celebrate publicly.[37]

This democratic inclusion was not replicated in New York nine years later. Instead, the opening conformed to a burgeoning national trend highlighted by Susan Davis. In her work on Philadelphia's nineteenth-century parades, Davis has traced the gradual disappearance of workers as a recognizable presence in civic ceremonies. The rise of the modern market economy transformed independent craftsmen into dependent wage earners, and with this change in economic standing came a change in civic, visual status: from prominence, through subservience, to disappearance.[38]

The declining presence of workers in the civic parades of the late nineteenth century can be attributed to the growing antagonisms between capital and labor. Increasingly, tradesmen and manual workers used the municipal parade as an arena in which to voice objections to modern economic practices. At New York's 8-Hour Day March of 1871, paraders walked beside a large cannon while a banner declared, "Peaceably if we can; Forcibly if we must." Likewise, the Knights of Labor used banners to proclaim their working-class principles at Philadelphia's centennial celebration of the U.S. Constitution.

For the officials in charge of the Brooklyn Bridge festivities, the previous year's "Monster Demonstration" organized by the Central Labor Union would have loomed large. This event marked the inauguration of Labor Day as a public holiday and was both comprehensive — encompassing a majority of the city's working classes — and chaotic.[39] The parade organizers would have realized that to allow labor a visible place in such an atmosphere would mean granting it a voice. As T. J. Jackson Lears reminds us: "a lack of expressed grievances may not mean genuine consensus; the most effective use of power may be to prevent grievances from arising in the first place." At the opening of the Brooklyn Bridge, restricted participation led to restricted debate.[40]

Accessing the Physical Bridge

The connections between symbolic import and material culture are important in any assessment of the Brooklyn Bridge. Although the opening implied the transfer of the bridge from its trustees to the people of New York and Brooklyn, the public did not participate. Excluded from the formal business, they were also barred from the day's more informal events, the most important of which was the afternoon promenade.

At the opening of the Eads Bridge, the public was invited to saunter across the span after the official procession had finished. Citizens were also able to raise their voices in appreciation at the opening of the Golden Gate Bridge in 1937, when pedestrians were allowed to stroll across after the opening ceremonies. On May 24, 1883, only a select group of prominent and influential New Yorkers — all invited as guests of the bridge trustees — enjoyed the experience of walking the bridge. The trustees' original desire for a celebration "access to which is debarred to the public and to be granted to the few by an

7. *Puck* lampoons the opening of the Brooklyn Bridge. On the "People's Day," "The Dude Brigade," "Tammany Heelers," "Political Tramps," and the Free and Accepted Masons stroll along the bridge, protected by policemen whose truncheons are emblazoned with the names of newspapers. "The Grand Opening March over the Brooklyn Bridge," *Puck,* May 23, 1883. From the author's collection.

arbitrary selection to be exercised by the Trustees of the Bridge" was, it seems, honored. Ironically, this private viewing was free and took place immediately *after* the bridge had been officially presented to the people. Individuals wishing the cross at midnight, when the bridge was opened to the general public, were required to pay a toll. As one newspaper noted with no small sense of outrage, "The big bridge is open . . . and now to any man or woman . . . the serial highway is free — after the payment of a one-cent fare."[41]

For the fortunate few allowed to cross on the opening day, direct experience of the bridge was facilitated by the paucity of fellow walkers. Unencumbered by the general public, they were able to meander at leisure and undisturbed. For the privileged few, the experience of the "technological sublime" was a reality.[42]

For the general public, the experience was far less inspiring. As W. H. Hickerson recounted fifty years later, celebrators were corralled into holding pens as they awaited access to the bridge. Hickerson himself was "marooned" for more than six hours and sustained three broken ribs in the process.[43] Another person who managed to cross just after midnight complained of the "unwholesome position" among those "willing to throttle the police and pound one another to mince-meat." In the "helter skelter," the bridge seemed "phantom-like and awful." That everyone managed to "escape from some terrible calamity was deemed almost miraculous."[44] The sense of unease and physical danger grew dramatically during the next few days.

On the day after the opening, the *New York Sun* decried the prevalence of public disorder on the bridge. Certain men, it seems, were conducting horse races across the span and felling frightened pedestrians. Others complained that several individuals had passed their time on the bridge by dropping rocks onto passing boats. One wonders how these men found the space to conduct such activities. Other sources noted that "crushes" were an almost constant occurrence when crossing the bridge. (Never slow to note the irony in any situation, *Puck* offered the following advice: "To keep cool while people are being crushed to death on the Bridge — why, don't go *over* but *under* it [in a ferry].") In such close quarters, an untold number of pickpockets flourished.[45] Protests over the conditions on the bridge appeared daily. "Seeing the rough sport," one woman "became almost hysterical. . . . 'I'm going home,' she said. 'I know I'll get killed here.'"[46] And from another source: "when you see a man with his coat torn off of him and a lady with her hat jammed over her eyes it is pretty safe to say that they have crossed the bridge. That noble structure has thus far been ruled by the mob."[47]

On the opening day, the general public was unable to experience the bridge as material culture, as a physical structure that could carry them from one shore to the other. Thereafter, the experience of walking the bridge was dominated by fear, worry, and conflict. The sort of violent disorder displayed a week later — when twelve people died during the fateful Memorial Day panic — was not an aberration but a logical extension of the previous week's chaos. For historian David Nye, crowds play an important role in the experience of the technological sublime; yet once a gathered throng becomes a lawless mêlée, one doubts that the sublime response is still possible. Even though fear constitutes a dominant trope of the sublime experience, it must not intrude to the point of actual and imminent physical danger.[48]

For members of the general public in 1883, fear coexisted with wonder as they trod across the bridge's wooden boards. Their perceptual experience, unlike that of the few individuals fortunate enough to cross on the afternoon of the twenty-fourth, or of the millions of visitors who have encountered the sublime spectacle in the years since, was ambiguous and troubled. Literally, in the aftermath of its opening, the public understood the bridge to be a potential deathtrap. These perceptions in the public consciousness ensured

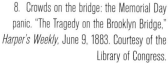

8. Crowds on the bridge: the Memorial Day panic. "The Tragedy on the Brooklyn Bridge," *Harper's Weekly*, June 9, 1883. Courtesy of the Library of Congress.

that the experience of the bridge as a sublime public monument would, for the moment, remain textual rather than physical.[49]

Oratory as Ritual of Assent

The principal texts of the bridge's inauguration are the opening-day speeches. Their legacy is strong, and, as cultural material, they constitute the prism through which the event is most often interpreted. Not surprisingly, none of the speakers had actually worked on the bridge. Instead, those who spoke for the bridge, and defined its significance, were all of a type. Chosen from the ranks of the influential, they echoed one another's sentiments. No competing or challenging voices were heard, and the image presented was so wholly unified that one wonders if the speakers collaborated. The force with which they laid claim to the bridge — and defined America through it — represents one of the most important aspects of the day.

In the speeches, the physical structure "Brooklyn Bridge" and the symbolic construction "America" were used almost interchangeably. For Mayor Seth Low, the bridge "is distinctly an American triumph. American genius designed it, American skill built it, and American workshops made it. . . . Courage, enterprise, skill, faith, endurance — these are the qualities that have made the great Bridge."[50] The other speakers—Abram Hewitt, the Reverend Storrs, and William Kingsley—continued this theme. For Hewitt, a prominent industrialist and former bridge trustee, the achievements of American progress were evident in the transformation from the "once green monotony of forest hills" to the "splendors" of the now "vast metropolis." As the foremost example of this progress, the bridge represented "the sum and epitome of human knowledge," and gave illustrative and undeniable proof that America had succeeded in its errand.[51] Storrs also placed the bridge at the heart of American progress. America's mastery over nature was praised repeatedly as proof of the nation's greatness. For Storrs, the bridge showed "what multitudes, democratically organized, can do if they will." For the Brooklyn businessman Kingsley, former publisher of the *Brooklyn Daily Eagle* and president of the board of trustees, it cemented the "union, growth and greatness" of "American enterprise and of American genius."[52]

According to Alan Trachtenberg, the opening ceremonies "baptized Brooklyn Bridge into its role as a ready-made symbol: text, type, sign and agent of 'progress,' of the American way." Taken together, the day's events constituted an American "ritual of assent." A means of social reaffirmation, the ritual of assent finds its form in the cultural continuity of the American experience and its voice in an overarching confirmation of national merit. As Sacvan Bercovitch observes: "Technology and religion, politics and art, individualism and social progress, spiritual and economic values—all the fragmented aspects of thought, belief, and behavior in this pluralistic society flowed into *America* . . . and then, in a ritual fusion of process and control, outward again to each self-reliant unit of culture."[53] We see this process at the bridge's opening. As the orators spoke, the entirety of American history flowed into the exemplary image of the Brooklyn Bridge.

The essence of the American ritual of assent was captured shortly after the bridge's opening in William Conant's essay "Will New York Be the Final World Metropolis?" Conant begins: "The metropolis is the chief organ through which both expression and effect are given to the genius and character of a nation. . . . It is the heart, whose vital pulsations gather and redistribute the vital currency from and to the remotest veinlets. It is the alimentary center where the national wealth is digested, mobilized, and infused into the circulation to nourish every fiber of the system."[54] The substance of Conant's essay is obvious from its title, and the answer to his question is a resounding yes. "New York," he argues, "seems as if planned at the creation for the ultimate center of the world."[55] The impetus for both the question and the answer are, for Conant, contained within the physical and philosophical aspects of the city's new bridge. Here the various elements of America flow into New York and then, in Bercovitch's "ritual fusion of process and control, outward again to each self-reliant unit of the culture." At the heart of this image of New York lies the Brooklyn Bridge.[56]

Abram Hewitt

More than any other speech given that opening day, Hewitt's has attracted the most discussion. The press reports both highlighted and endorsed it.[57] The chief function of the speech was to "explicate the bridge as an emblem of the forces at work in modern America."[58] Hewitt accomplished this task by addressing two of the most crucial questions in American society at the time: financial corruption and labor relations. Allegations of fraud and dishonesty had plagued the bridge project since its inception. Although it was not possible for Hewitt to claim absolute honesty in the bridge's construction, a serviceable scapegoat was available in the figure of William "Boss" Tweed. During his trial in 1873 for embezzlement and municipal fraud, Tweed openly declared that he had been given large amounts of stock and $60,000 in cash to facilitate the necessary legislation. The bribery was a matter of public record, yet Hewitt was able to turn this fact to his advantage. As the entirety of American history flowed into the image of the Brooklyn Bridge, Hewitt directed the entirety of public corruption into the image of Tweed. By foisting the blame for all fraud onto the vanquished Tweed, Hewitt was able to claim absolute propriety for the subsequent history: "The methods by which the Ring proposed to benefit themselves were clear enough, but its members fled before they succeeded in reimbursing themselves for the preliminary expenses they had defrayed. With their flight a new era commenced. . . . no fraud was committed, and none was possible."[59] Although Hewitt's speech was riddled with inaccuracies, the facts were subservient to the message: with the flight of Tweed, a new era had dawned for the United States, and honest public administration was its keynote. For Hewitt, all was now sound in the American polity; reform was not needed because it had already occurred. The bridge stood as a testament to progressive government and proved beyond doubt that those steering the American ship were honest.[60]

Hewitt also sought to reassure the many Americans worried about the deteriorating relations between capital and labor. In the process, he illustrated how remuneration and working conditions had steadily improved with the passage of time. Using the building of the pyramids as his example, and through an explication of manpower and cost, he came to the following conclusion: in 1883 dollars, even after inflation had been factored in, the workers on the pyramids had earned the equivalent of two cents per day, whereas the workers on the bridge earned an average of $2.50 per day. Although this

9. Financial corruption: "How Kingsley and Fowler Amused Themselves in Spending the Money for Bridging the East River." *Frank Leslie's Illustrated Newspaper*, July 5, 1873. Collection of The New-York Historical Society, neg. # 76436.

conclusion might seem ridiculous to a twenty-first-century reader, it was not thought so at the time. The *New York Times*, for example, regarded the comparison as "highly instructive."[61] Hewitt drew a clear message from his illustration:

> This comparison proves that through forty centuries . . . hardships have been steadily diminished; that all the achievements of science, all the discoveries of art, all the inventions of genius, all the progress of civilization, tend by a higher and immutable law to the steady and certain amelioration of the condition of society. It shows that, notwithstanding the apparent growth of great fortunes, due to an era of unparalleled development, the distribution of the fruits of labor is approaching from age to age to more equitable conditions, and must, at last, reach the plane of absolute justice between man and man.[62]

Social parity, in this view, is an evolutionary process. It will undoubtedly happen, and, significantly, it will happen *naturally*. Ideologically, these are the words of a millionaire industrialist seeking to soothe the worries of labor and provide expert assurance of future comfort. Hewitt's interpretation of current conditions denied the country's social climate and sponsored the ideal of "official public memory."[63] Gone were the scandals and tensions of the Gilded Age; society was in a process of amelioration. With faith in existing systems of government, business, and technological invention, America was a nation poised on the brink of equity. Furthermore, this process was impervious to individual or class protests. Like the Puritan errand, it would flow from "a higher and immutable law," not the messy business of human history.[64]

Trachtenberg has written that the Brooklyn Bridge "was completed at a moment of crisis in American life, a moment of perceived threat to the system of meaning or ideology by which many Americans took their bearings and imagined their relations to the real world. . . . At such a moment the bridge seemed to promise that the old ideology would remain intact, would prevail."[65] This promise was not inherent but affected, forged onto the bridge as it entered into the public's myriad consciousnesses. In less than two months, the Brotherhood of Telegraphers would strike to protest working conditions at New York's Western Union Telegraph Company. A year later, strike action would sweep through Jay Gould's expansive railroad network, and troops would be dispatched to the streets of Cincinnati. In just two more years the Haymarket affair in Chicago would divide the nation. At this time of national crisis, the men responsible for the bridge's opening manufactured an image that blurred the realities of life in America and sponsored a wholly conservative vision. At the day's speeches, amelioration was less the promise than the desired effect.

Reporting the Weather

Ironically, almost no one heard the speeches given at the bridge's opening. Delivered without amplification, the speakers' words were mostly lost to the poor acoustics of the cavernous Brooklyn trolley terminal. Amid such conditions, the audience grew restless and ambivalent. Hewitt did not even finish his speech, instead directing his audience to seek its continuation in the press. Despite the great significance attached to the speeches, their importance was not in their delivery but in their circulation. As the *New York Tribune* claimed, while rather mixing its verbs, "the only way to hear the speeches will be through the newspapers."[66]

The orators knew they were speaking to a far larger audience than the one assembled before them. Before the speeches started, noted the *Herald*, printed copies were handed out to the press.[67] Subsequently, they were reprinted verbatim in a majority of the city's newspapers. If Brooklyn's physical appearance can be seen as evidence that the opening day was a pseudo event, then the day's speeches only strengthen the claim that the event's organizers were concerned with the production of a central, manufactured image. Equally *planned* and *planted*, the pseudo event is undertaken with the "express purpose and convenience of being reported" and is designed "to create a thicket of unreality which stands between us and the facts of life."[68] A pseudo event turns on the idea of "self-fulfilling prophecy." This method of sculpting public opinion was also important in the early republican era when, as one critic notes, "rhetoric functioned as a self-fulfilling prophecy, in that its local details, such as the smiling faces, were meant to inspire what they described."[69] In other words, the ability to report an event translates into the ability to construct it.

Of all the major histories of the opening day, only Trachtenberg's fails to mention the weather. Although this detail might seem trivial at first, it points to an important factor in our understanding of the opening. So many historical accounts of the event begin by evoking the day's perfect weather that there would seem little reason to doubt that fact.[70] The reality, however, is more complicated.

In contrast to many of the day's reports, the *Daily Graphic* observed: "A strong southwestern breeze sprang up . . . and clouds soon began to obscure the sun, which from time to time made spasmodic efforts to conquer, and then seemed to give up the struggle in disgust, and many were the fears expressed that after all the Bridge would be opened amid a rainstorm."[71] The *Eagle* wrote along similar lines: "it is true that the weather was not literally all that could have been desired, for the wind was anything but balmy." By the evening's edition, however, the *Eagle*'s judgment had altered. Certainly the weather might have improved, but, more important, the rhetoric had inspired a reassessment: "Nature celebrates the great event by giving us a day of surpassing loveliness. A clear, bracing atmosphere, a genuine Yankee blue sky across which battalions of snowy clouds are chasing each other . . . and a vivid sunshine that lacks all suggestion of Summer's sultry heat, are conditions so appropriate as to excite the thought that the gods themselves have caught the inspiration of the occasion."[72] A similar sentiment is found in the *Herald*: "the fondest hope never suggested a more beautiful combination of sun and sky, of air and water, than that which made yesterday a thing of radiant beauty. A million people desired a pleasant day, a million people felt content when the sun pushed aside the curtains of the sky."[73]

These descriptions imply divine intervention. The benevolence of the day's weather became a response of the deity to both the American people and America's achievement. The *Sun* even noted that "the weather yesterday was thoroughly American weather—a bright blue sky, warm sunshine."[74] Here the meteorologically perfect becomes American and itself flows into the image of the bridge. The weather emerges as a constructed, ulterior way to attach meaning to the bridge. If, for the orators, a "higher and immutable law" was bringing about the steady amelioration of American society, the gift of a perfect day could only have been sanctioned from above.[75]

Nourishing the Image

Although it is impossible to read public opinion directly from newspapers, it is through the press that we can begin to understand the ways in which experience is processed, repackaged, and presented to the wider population.[76] In this regard, it is difficult to overemphasize the role of the media in our understanding of civic occasions. In the early national period, according to David Waldsteicher, newspaper editors "emerged as key mediators in [the] nexus of public space, oratory and print culture."[77] With the rise of the penny press in the 1830s, this influence increased immeasurably. By 1883, 540 newspapers and magazines, almost 40 of which were dailies, were published in the New York metropolitan region.[78] Understandably, all of these publications devoted a great deal of space to the bridge opening; extras appeared almost hourly and sold out just as quickly. Magazines commissioned special articles, and editorials flowed from every source. In addition, reports of the opening dominated the headlines in Philadelphia, Boston, Richmond, Washington, Chicago, Albany, and even in the major capitals of Europe.

From the Revolutionary period onward, claims Simon Newman, "many Americans were taking part in or watching [decisive national] events [but] even more were reading about them in local or more distant newspapers."[79] At the opening of the bridge, only the military and the government took part, while most onlookers were relegated to peripheral locations affording poor views. In addition, some of the day's most important events—the orations, the opportunity to walk the bridge, and the exclusive receptions at the houses of Washington Roebling and Seth Low—were witnessed only by a select few.[80] As many newspapers pointed out, direct experience of the day's events would be available only through the press. The same holds true for those of us wishing to view the occasion from a historical distance. For Raymond Schroth, the job of the newspapers at the opening was to "nourish" the day's speeches. Although this purpose was achieved through a variety of differing tropes and strategies, three are especially significant. All were comparative, with the first two being historical.[81]

Hewitt began his speech by evoking the image of Manhattan as found by

Henry Hudson — "waiting till commerce should come and claim its own." [82] For Hewitt, the city that now stood upon Manhattan Island represented a successful transformation in both landscape and population: the "wild" and "savage" had been displaced by the "commercial" and "civilized." This view was echoed in the press, as the *Eagle* appraised the untamed American continent and its native peoples:

> If the purpose were set before one to show at a glance the difference between this continent as the white man found it and what he has made it, ingenuity would be taxed to find a happier illustration than the bridge in contrast with the Indian dependence for passage from island to island upon his ruddy canoe. The distance from the wigwam to the palace is not so great as from the Red man's sole means of communication to the highway [now] suspended in midair. . . . The Indian represents the barbarism which recognized in every gulf, stream and hill a reason for separate tribal existence and local hatreds. The bridge represents the intelligence which will yet make a brotherhood of all nations. [83]

Here the bridge again subsumes the history of America into itself as a culmination of benevolent progress. It is the representation of the union of the states and the visible proof of the passage from "savagery" to "civilization."

For the second historical comparison, attention was turned to the Old World. In his speech, Hewitt derived further lessons from the pyramids of Egypt: "[They] were built by the sacrifices of the living for the dead. They served no useful purpose, except to make odious to future generations the tyranny which degrades humanity to the level of the brute." [84] Comparisons with the building of the pyramids appeared in a majority of the reports and represented the primary focus for historical precedent. For Hewitt and the press, both structures were characteristic of their ages, yet their achievement and meaning were entirely separate. Although the Egyptians could not have raised a Brooklyn Bridge, America, "if it were so minded," could build pyramids. Here the stress was laid on *inclination*. America is not "minded" to build pyramids; Egypt was not "minded" to produce large works of public utility: "[The pyramids] recall the magnificence of a tyrannical dynasty, the vast influence of a hierarchy buttressed by superstition and the practical enslavement of millions of industrious people. The bridge is a monument to the skill of a free people, to the arts of peace, to liberal thought and to the spirit which makes the promotion of the common welfare the chief end of government." [85]

In a section devoted to other major bridges throughout history, the *Eagle* offered further comparisons: "There are bridges in the Old World which one

10. "Held in a Vise." *Frank Leslie's Boys' and Girls' Weekly*, January 27, 1883. Compare this image with the *Brooklyn Daily Eagle*'s historical comparison on opening day: "How grandly does our noble bridge, standing clear and guiltless of concealment against the sky, contrast with the bridges that stand dark and gloomy, only eloquent of hidden ways and deeds." Courtesy of the Department of Special Collections, Stanford University Libraries.

crosses with a shudder as one remembers the crimes and sorrows which their dark arches recall." Gathered from the pages of Charles Dickens, most of these "crimes and sorrows" lacked historical reliability, but reportorial accuracy was not a strong aspect of the opening day. And this lapse applied to the bridge itself. The bridge's construction devastated the "pleasant residential neighborhood" of Old Ferry, transforming it into a "Brooklyn Bowery . . . haunted by vagabonds and derelicts."[86] If not yet evident to the *Eagle*, the decline was already apparent to those working in popular culture. Just four months earlier, for example, *Frank Leslie's Boys' and Girls' Weekly* featured a very Dickensian image on its front cover: in the dead of night beneath the Brooklyn Bridge three criminals hoist a body in a sack over a railing.[87] Despite this turnaround in the neighborhood's character, the *Eagle*'s rhetoric never wavered: "How grandly does our noble bridge, standing clear and guiltless of concealment against the sky, contrast with the bridges that stand dark and gloomy, only eloquent of hidden ways and deeds."[88]

David Nye has written that "the [sublime] encounter leaves observers too deeply moved to reflect on the historicity of their experiences." Here Nye has in mind Edmund Burke's contention that the power of the sublime "is that state of the soul, in which all its motions are suspended. . . . In this case the mind is so entirely filled with its object, that it cannot entertain any other, nor by consequence reason on that object which employs it."[89] Both Burke and Nye are interested in the direct experience of the sublime encounter, yet what we witness in the reporting of the opening day is a separation between experience and rhetoric. If the day's orations, supplemented by press reports, inscribed the bridge with meaning, they also marked the occasion's "historicity." While observers stood emotionally in thrall to the experience of the bridge, the city's press editors mediated the interpretational void with a historical image of the bridge that conformed to the one presented in the day's speeches. If the public was unable to reflect on the historicity of the bridge, then others could. The bridge authenticated the history and culture of America as a unified ideal; in the words of the *Eagle*, it "unfolds a prospect for the future dazzling in its brilliant possibility."[90]

Russia

Even as newspaper reports nourished the image of the bridge with historical comparisons, history itself provided the opening day with an interesting coincidence. As the *Brooklyn Union* noted in a sub-headline, the twenty-fourth of May 1883 was a day of "two celebrations." In Moscow, Alexander III was officially crowned tsar of Russia. Although third in the list of significant strategies that aimed to define the meaning of the Brooklyn Bridge, the reporting of this event is perhaps the most important because the occasion provided the press with a direct point of national and ideological comparison.[91]

The relationship between the United States and Tsars Alexander II and Alexander III is worthy of note. Throughout his reign, Alexander II initiated a number of innovative reforms. Known as the Tsar-Liberator, he freed the Russian serfs two years before the Emancipation Proclamation ended slavery in the United States. The frequent comparisons with Abraham Lincoln extended to his death: Alexander II was assassinated in March 1881 in a plot executed by the revolutionary organization known as the People's Will. Coincidentally, U.S. President James A. Garfield would be assassinated by a disgruntled office seeker just four months later. An affinity between the nations would have seemed natural at this time. Yet the countries regarded each other as menacing competitors.[92]

No such tensions were apparent in 1871, when the future tsar embarked upon an extensive tour of the United States. Upon his arrival in New York, the city held a Broadway parade to honor the royal visitor. Subsequently, the tsarevich was fêted with an extravagant banquet at Delmonico's before he journeyed west on a hunting trip with William "Buffalo Bill" Cody and General Philip H. Sheridan. Fresh from their western jaunt, Alexander and Cody headed to New Orleans for Mardi Gras. Again the tsarevich was honored, and the elite krewe (parade organization) Rex was created to mark his presence at the carnival. By the time of Alexander III's coronation, however, all feelings of affection had dissipated. An important transformation had taken place: Tsarevich Alexander had become Tsar Alexander. He no longer represented privilege and youth, but embodied institutional monarchy. This change in representational import was crucial.[93]

In his opening-day speech, the Reverend Storrs made his opinions about Russian society perfectly clear when he contrasted St. Petersburg with New York and Brooklyn. The latter were built through "the arts of peace," whereas the Russian city had been created "by the will of an autocrat [Peter the Great], to give him a new center of empire, with a nearer outlook over Europe; its palaces rising on artificial foundations, which it cost, it is said, 100,000 lives in the first year to lay."[94] In the pages of the *Eagle*, the tyranny of Russian monarchy was updated. The rhetoric is worth quoting at length to demonstrate both its strength and its fervor:

> Two great cities of the world were *en fête* to-day, and it was difficult to help contrasting them and their peoples and the occasions of their holidays. One was Brooklyn; the other Moscow. In this latter city . . . the populace have come together (or been brought together, rather) to shout in ecstasy over a further riveting of their chains. Their huzzas for the man whom they are compelled to regard as God's vice regent, are purchased; the food they eat and the liquor they drink are doled out to them as royal bounty; the genuflexions they make as their imperial master rides by are ordered as to number and as to degree of humility by the hated, and feared police; their wretched lives and their stunted liberties are in danger if they dare refuse the most groveling homage to one whose race has ever strangled their aspirations, imprisoned their bodies and enchained their souls. . . .
>
> In Brooklyn a free people have determined to celebrate the completion of one of the greatest improvements of civilization devised by man. Of their own sovereign will they throng about the bridge and hail as conquerors those before whose genius and patience unparalleled difficulties and dangers of engineering have been dissipated as the mist disappears before the steady rays of the sun. Their cheers are not bought or compelled; their presence is voluntary; their gratulation is sincere; the great work is their own.[95]

In almost the same breath, the newspaper turned its attention to the potential for labor protests at the opening. In a bizarre incongruity, it noted that "the men who are the [labor] leaders are being closely watched by detectives in citizens' clothing and if they start any demonstration they will be quickly silenced in a forcible manner."[96] Such declarations clarify the lack of public inclusion at the opening of the Brooklyn Bridge. Suppression of free speech was by no means unique to Russia. It had happened very publicly in the great railroad strikes of 1877 and would appear again during Chicago's 1886 Haymarket affair. Yet the United States at the opening of the Brooklyn Bridge was not a series of historical incidents: a sometimes soaring, sometimes stuttering historical phenomenon. Bolstered by the events of the day, it became a nation united and succeeding in its errand.

Conclusions

In formulating and presenting opinion on opening day, the orators and the press failed to canvass the public. Although championed as leading actors in the bridge's construction and celebration, the general population instead served as the day's audience. Its job was to do the listening, not the talking; to take note, not to spell out. Although references to democracy abounded, the active participation of the people—the defining ideal of democracy—was denied. In the period leading up to the opening, opinions about the bridge were solicited from a variety of sources. One gentleman believed that there had been "a big steal somewhere"; another felt that the "novelty of the bridge will soon wear away." In the *Daily Times* someone complained that the bridge—"more a nuisance than a blessing"—would increase, rather than alleviate, congestion.[97]

By the opening, however, individual members of the general population had been incorporated into an unspeaking homogenous crowd. Time and again we are told that the crowd cheered, yet no individuals are named or described. By contrast, those upon whom suspicion had rested for so long took center stage and rendered their own unchallenged interpretation of the era, the nation, and the bridge. To borrow a phrase from Mary Ryan, at the bridge's opening the trustees drew "a portentous line of exclusion across the landscape of democracy."[98]

The organizers responsible for the day engineered an image of the bridge as the American symbol *par excellence*. Public opinion was neutralized, and officials wove an exemplary narrative of the American errand that "naturally" culminated in the towering icon of the bridge. This image did not conform to the state of American society, but posited an ulterior, almost mythic, state-

11. *Finis Coronat Opus:* where the end is good, all is good. *Daily Graphic,* May 24, 1883. Milstein Division of United States History, Local History and Genealogy, The New York Public Library, Astor, Lenox and Tilden Foundations.

of-the-union address. Its message was that through commerce and a belief in the existing forms of American polity, the nation would continue from glory to glory. As union and completion were stressed, divisive recent history and individual dissent were both dispelled. Concomitantly, the trauma-tic and suspicious, not to mention corrupt, process through which the bridge, and American society, had recently traveled became subsumed into the structure's marvelous sublimity. America had arrived at this historical point with this visual image, and the character of the country was reduced to a form of single-issue binary politics. As the entirety of the American experi-ence flowed into the culminating image of the bridge, the nation's citizens were presented with a ballot. To approve of the Brooklyn Bridge was to ap-prove of America, the Gilded Age, and the status quo; as the *Daily Graphic* proudly proclaimed on the front cover of its opening-day special edition: *Fi-nis Coronat Opus,* where the end is good, all is good.[99]

The unity proclaimed at the opening of the Brooklyn Bridge was not a spontaneous expression of assent; rather, it was a statement formulated, shaped, and staged by a group of influential New Yorkers. Tirelessly repeated by the press and sanctioned by subsequent historians, it has found its way into our shared cultural memory. With each new addition to our historical understanding, the manufactured assent of the opening day has become canonized as the dominant interpretation. What we witness at the opening of the Brooklyn Bridge follows Albert Boime's observation that "the history of each [U.S.] icon reveals that privileged members of the American hierarchy, bent on maintaining their economic and social class advantages, attempted to appropriate the symbols of America almost from their inception and use them to stimulate an illusion of inclusivity." [100]

Rereading the opening day from a historical distance, we find little in the way of democratic practice or public input. Instead, we discover a tightly controlled municipal event characterized by segregation and omission. At the opening ceremonies, an ideological curtain was drawn over the Brooklyn Bridge and an exclusive social agenda was reworded to spell civic consensus. The unity proclaimed both then and now represents an ideology of manufactured assent: while consensus was preached, exclusion prevailed.

2 "The Eyes of All People Are upon Us"
Tourists, Immigrants, and the Brooklyn Bridge

New York City includes some of the grandest places on earth — from the Brooklyn Bridge and Central Park to the more conventional architectural gems of Empire State and Flatiron. But my New York shall be two absolutely ordinary places, central to the lives of people I loved, and who made my life possible in the most literal sense — a grim and undistinguished workplace that was not to be my grandmother's pyre and a wretched house, cynically built for profit but destined to be the foundation of hope for a young couple starting at the bottom in a land of opportunity.

— Stephen Jay Gould, interviewed in *New York* magazine, 2000

The various kinds of urban perspectives held by the residents of a city are constructed from spatial representations resulting from membership in particular social groups.

—Anselm L. Strauss, *Images of the American City*, 1961

When John Winthrop wrote "A Model of Christian Charity" in 1630, he established a major trope in American cultural expression. Described as the "Ur-text of American literature,"[1] Winthrop's essay crucially linked two different cultural ideas. Not only did he stress the need to establish a harmonious community at once ordered, stable, and unified through the model of Christian brotherhood — the archetypal "city upon a hill" — but he also noted that "the eyes of all people are upon us." Leaving his native England behind, Winthrop had many reasons to focus on the future. Failure was a prospect, and should it visit the colony, exhorted the future governor, "we shall be made a story and a by-word throughout the world."[2] The union of entity ("the city upon a hill") and audience ("the eyes of all people") was vital. Judgment on the colony, it seems, would come from the external observing community and not from its inhabitants.

The continual redeployment and reappropriation of Winthrop's model attests to its prominence in American communal thought. Nevertheless, this influence began to assert itself only in the years immediately preceding the opening of the Brooklyn Bridge.[3] The nation's utopian imagination was at its most active during the late nineteenth century, and Winthrop's paradigm was recalled time and again in the literature of the period. In such works as Edward Bellamy's *Looking Backward* (1888) and William Dean Howells's *A Traveler from Altruria* (1893), a harmonious and benevolent community is contrasted with a corrupt society marked by inequality and social chaos. Placed in judgment over these two worlds is the mediating figure of an external observer.

By contrast with these fictions, however, municipal attainment of Winthrop's dream proved far more elusive—always imminent, never grasped. Regardless, anyone following the reported events of May 24, 1883, might well have been forgiven for thinking that the wait was over. Guided by "a higher and immutable law," the Brooklyn Bridge was regarded as the crowning monument in the creation of America's new, industrial "city upon a hill."

Winthrop's model sought to change the New World landscape *rhetorically*. Recent scholarship suggests that Winthrop wrote and delivered his essay prior to emigration, not en route to the New World, and that the text was circulated after his departure.[4] The difference is crucial. If delivered mid-Atlantic, the address represents a declaration of moral and civic values: an internal manifesto for a new settlement. If delivered before an assembled crowd at Southampton, Yarmouth, or Cowes and popularized postdeparture, Winthrop's essay reached a wider audience and can be read as orientated as much to those who *might* travel as to those who *were* traveling to the New World. The disastrous efforts to colonize Roanoke in 1587 and Jamestown in 1607 still lingered in the English memory, and general unease surrounded New World settlement.[5] To counter these misgivings, Winthrop combined the devices of practical promotion with the appeal of spiritual beckoning. His vision was an early form of public relations, seeking to persuade in much the same way that a modern guidebook or tourist brochure does.

Like Winthrop's essay, the ceremonies at the opening of the Brooklyn Bridge performed a symbolic coup d'état. Against a backdrop of doubt, civic inequity, and the chaos of rapid urbanization, they promoted the exemplary city of union, social harmony, and progress. Nationally heralded, the opening celebrations also stressed the external, global community. One newspaper stated that "the world over[,] people are wondering about the bridge," and a periodical noted that "the undertaking was looked upon throughout the civilized world."[6] This outward projection of social achievement also contained a genuine, exuberant civic boosterism. A sign placed in the window of Abraham and Wechsler's new Brooklyn department store typified the local pride: "Babylon had her hanging garden, Egypt her pyramid, Athens her Acropolis, Rome her Athenaeum; so Brooklyn has her Bridge."[7] The placard illustrated the event's triumphalism and captured one of the day's basic sentiments: the bridge would enshrine New York and Brooklyn as world cities.

Winthrop's model was essentially predictive, and with hindsight we can make the same claim for the messages expressed at the bridge opening.[8] The *Daily Graphic* wrote that New York "must inevitably become the great city of the world," and when William Conant wondered, "Will New York Be the Final World Metropolis?" his answer was a resounding yes.[9] This predictive quality also extended to reactions from outside the United States. The *Daily Times* anticipated that visitors would "marvel" at the new bridge. The *Brooklyn Daily Eagle* turned its attention to individuals seeking to make their home in America: "May it stand firm forever as 'westward the star of empire takes its way,' may the sight of it inspire the emigrant who seeks a home here with new hopes and energy, telling him as he gazes at it in silent wonder that in America industry rises upward to the clear blue sky and spans with enterprise and ambition the river of life."[10]

The importance of the global community was also recognized in more thoughtful judgments. Amid the pomp and self-congratulation of the opening day, the architectural critic Montgomery Schuyler published his essay "The Bridge as a Monument," a frank and forthright assessment of the structure's architectural achievement. Schuyler's purpose was not to commend and glorify, but to inquire critically. He began by looking to the future. Unlike Conant and his "final world metropolis," Schuyler envisioned a far different future, one in which New York might lay in devastation, a "forsaken city." Imagine a lone traveler from a distant land — Thomas Macaulay's celebrated New Zealander — stumbling upon a scene in which the bridge's towers were all that remained of the once great city. The massive suspension cables, that "web of woven steel," had long since "rusted into nothingness under the slow corrosion of the centuries." The bridge's builders and "the generation for which they wrought may have been as long forgotten as are now the builders of the Pyramids," Schuyler continued. "It is not unimaginable that our future archeologist, looking from one of these towers upon the solitude of a mastless river and a dispeopled land, may have no other means of reconstructing our civilization than that which is furnished him by the tower on which he stands." Schuyler then asks: "What will his judgment of us be?"[11]

Schuyler's assessment was predicated on a simple idea: what might the bridge symbolize to an outsider, someone unfamiliar with America? If one had to see America *through* the bridge, what would one see? The answer to this question would not have to await the city's ruin. With the opening of the bridge, New York and Brooklyn found themselves with a legitimate object of global fascination. And if one objective of the opening ceremonies was to "sell" the bridge to foreign tourists, the results did not disappoint. Foreign visitors arrived in droves, eager to see the bridge and report their impressions to audiences back home. Patiently, Americans waited to see what "the eyes of all people" made of the Brooklyn Bridge and the new, industrial "city upon a hill" it symbolized.[12]

Tourism in Nineteenth-Century America

In the first half of the nineteenth century, many well-known European political and cultural figures traveled to the United States to see the new republic for themselves and to pass judgment. Mostly, their verdicts were expressed through published journals and reports, which formed a growing collection of detailed travelogues, critical summaries, and cultural analyses. These accounts were important for the young nation; they could provide external approval, a broad confirmation of the American errand.[13] Yet often they were highly critical and dismissive. The derogatory remarks expressed, for example, by Basil Hall (1829), Frances Trollope (1832), and Charles Dickens (1842) mortified and troubled Americans. By the late nineteenth century, however, foreign criticism was on the wane, and approval was in the ascendancy. At the same time, Americans had become a more confident people and better able to take foreign criticism in stride.[14] The negative opinions of Sir Henry Lepel Griffin (1884) and William T. Stead (1898), among others, were often lost in an ocean of positive reports. Consequently, such critics were labeled cranks and dismissed.[15]

Several factors contributed to this turnaround. In the early nineteenth century, European liberals and reformers like William Cobbett and Jeremy Bentham were attracted by American democracy, as was Alexis de Tocqueville.[16] Yet Tocqueville's *Democracy in America* (1848) was something of an anomaly. The American democratic experiment found few serious commentators during the early nineteenth century. Instead, most of the era's foreign observers judged the new nation along cultural lines: the United States lacked history and tradition, manners and taste, civilization and erudition. By the late nineteenth century, however, the American political system had begun to replace culture as the subject most often discussed by overseas writers. Prior to the American Civil War, the idea of American freedom had often seemed somewhat hollow. As Samuel Johnson famously asked, "how is it that we hear the loudest *yelps* for liberty among the drivers of Negroes?"[17] For foreign observers, the Civil War seemed to consign the contradictions of freedom and slavery to the dustbin of history.

The second half of the nineteenth century also coincided with Europe's own renewed struggles for fuller democracy. Such a historical confluence fueled an intense curiosity about American society. Europe's widening political liberalism was reflected in such important events as Britain's first and second Reform Acts (1832 and 1867), the second French Revolution (1848), and Garibaldi's rise in Italy (1860). Where the concept of European social equality was raised, however, it was never fully realized. As Eric Hobsbawm reminds us, "the (British) industrial revolution . . . swallowed the (French) political revolution."[18] To many intellectuals, the American democratic model—freed from slavery's incongruities—provided hope for a Europe torn by international conflict, rapid industrialization, and contested internal power relations.

Comfort and convenience also played their part in the rise of positive foreign opinion. Travel to the United States was facilitated by faster, cheaper trans-Atlantic voyages, an enhanced interstate and intercity transportation network, and lavish accommodations with modern plumbing. Travelers with the financial means and leisure time could cross the Atlantic, see much of the East, some of the South or West, and return home all in a matter of weeks. During the late nineteenth century, ease of travel brought many more visitors to America than ever before: for the first time, Europeans en masse began to judge the American experience firsthand. Not only could foreigners travel comfortably to and around America, they wished to do so.

Case Studies from Around the World

Travelers from all over the globe arrived in New York to view the new bridge. From Britain came Alexander Graham Bell, inventor of the telephone, Lord Chief Justice Charles Russell, and Edward Aveling, Karl Marx's miscreant son-in-law. Cuban radical and nationalist José Martí reported on the bridge's opening during a brief stay in New York, and future Nobel laureate Bjørnstjerne Bjørnson wrote home to Norway that the bridge was the emblem of America, "the bold spirit, the tremendous abilities, the grand vision of the future of that nation."[19] A journalist sent by *Dianshizhai Huabao*, a popular Shanghai picture magazine, reported that "the scale and strength of construction are . . . unprecedented in the world since ancient times." German newspaper publisher Nicolaus Mohr included a full-page image of the bridge in his book *Excursions Through America* (1883) and described the structure as "truly one of the wonders of the world."[20]

Nor were such responses confined to the bridge's first years. The Soviet poets Sergei Esenin and Vladimir Mayakovsky both discovered the bridge in the 1920s. Esenin, who visited with his wife, Isadora Duncan, expressed some distinctly uncomradely emotions: "if one looks at the merciless might of . . . the Brooklyn Bridge suspended between two towns, at a height of more than a twenty-story building above the ground, no one could regret that wild Hiawatha no longer hunts his deer here. And no one would regret that the hand of the builders of this culture was sometimes cruel."[21] Mayakovsky, usually a scrupulous ideologue, found himself heckled at a meeting of American communists. Apparently, his poetic tribute — "Yeah, / Brooklyn Bridge . . . / It's something that!"—was a little too enthusiastic for his audience. He subsequently amended the piece to appease his working-class critics.[22]

The creation and reception of Mayakovsky's poetry are revealing. In "A Skyscraper Dissected" (1925), the poet welded iconography and context to form an intricate disquisition on the public blight caused by private, corporate architecture. In "The Brooklyn Bridge" (1925), however, he took a different approach to the monumental architecture of New York, one that explicitly ignored the many ruined lives of those who built it. As Edward Brown notes, "the flight of the poet's imagination, unencumbered by a social theme, was not what the audience wanted."[23] Yet his critics were mistaken. Mayakovsky's ode was replete with social themes, although perhaps not explicitly. The Soviet poet saw the bridge as a constructivist ideal, a commentary on the past and a conduit to the future. In the stone archways he saw "rooted conservatism," in its cables, "radical uplift." The effect was dialectical, revolutionary. It foretold the liberation of mankind through the application of material force.[24]

Mayakovsky saw a bridge to a socialist future, but his audience did not recognize themselves on it. Instead they saw the exaltation of a structure built under a corporate hierarchy without regard for workers' lives. The difference was crucial. Mayakovsky envisioned the future in a national physical icon, in stone and steel, not in the lives of working New Yorkers. The poet's critics faulted him for prioritizing the symbolic over the material, the abstract over the tangible, and, in so doing, ignoring the context of the bridge's creation. Ironically, this reading placed him in league with the heartless Esenin: neither expressed regret over the fact that "the hand of the builders of this culture was sometimes cruel."

If Mayakovsky failed to articulate his concern for working Americans, Esenin simply did not care. And neither, it seems, did Bjørnson. Having long admired America, Bjørnson visited the country in the early 1880s to "confirm his image of an ideal America." Which is exactly what he did — though not among his Norwegian compatriots who had emigrated to this land of promise. Despite spending almost eight months in the United States, Bjørnson rarely strayed far from his comfortable base at the home of James Russell Lowell in Cambridge, Massachusetts. America's Norwegian immigrants, he felt, could tell him little about American society, and he spared them little concern. Instead, he enjoyed the company of America's cultural elite: Ralph Waldo Emerson, Walt Whitman, Henry Wadsworth Longfellow, William

Dean Howells, and former president Ulysses S. Grant. When studying a nation, he explained, one should "begin with the most advanced states, and in those with the most advanced individuals." This pronouncement angered his fellow Norwegians both at home and in the United States. When his reports and interviews were reprinted in Norway, he was chided for his limited travels, constant use of superlatives, and remarkable naïveté. The America he portrayed, it seems, did not correspond to that described by the many Norwegian Americans who were also writing home. In the Brooklyn Bridge, Bjørnson discovered "the bold spirit, the tremendous abilities, the grand vision of the future of that nation," but he seemed unwilling to look for it in his fellow Norwegians. Like Mayakovsky, he saw the country's future in a physical structure, not in its people.[25]

Nicolaus Mohr's visit to the United States in 1883 traversed a similar line. If America's cultural elite had embraced Bjørnson, the country's industrial elite courted Mohr. To secure additional financing for his North Pacific Railroad, Henry Villard, its president, selected a number of prominent guests from America's Eastern Seaboard, Britain, and Germany to accompany him on an all-expenses-paid journey across the country.[26] Although Mohr, as a potential investor and promoter, had exceptional reasons for his trip, his descriptions of the country, along with those of his traveling companion, Lord Russell, are typical.[27] It was a brief sojourn, and, as Klaus Lanzinger notes, Mohr's impressions "dovetailed surprisingly well into the pattern of European travelers who wrote about the United Sates."[28]

Mohr's trip was tightly orchestrated, and he had little time to himself. Mohr laments having to leave the bridge as he is rushed off to visit yet another New York attraction. On Villard's itinerary, Mohr was swept from icon to icon and from elite hotel to exclusive club. Not surprisingly, his impressions of America were wholly positive, and his endorsement sings out the triumphs of American progress. Like the speakers on opening day, Mohr indulged a vision free from wider social concerns. As Lanzinger explains, "Urban crowding, ever-spreading slums, air contamination, sweatshops, stark poverty, crime and intemperance—all these were urban phenomena in the 1880s, stirring the first reformers into action. But Mohr and the American elite with whom he associated closed their eyes to these evils. . . . Mohr not only saw the American city through the rose-tinted glasses of his day—and class—but even tried . . . to do justice to American cultural achievements."[29]

Just as the rhetoric of the opening-day speeches surfaced in many of the day's newspapers, it also greeted tourists and infused the pages of their travelogues. Wined and dined by America's industrial elite, Mohr returned to

Germany to write his narrative. His excitement at the scale and success of U.S. industry found its way into the pages of his newspaper, the commercially influential *Weser Zeitung*. Likewise, returning tourists flooded the European book market with tales of American progress, the prime symbol of which was often the Brooklyn Bridge. As an icon, the bridge validated the march of American industry not only at home, but across the Atlantic as well.

Tourists and Guidebooks

Mohr did not simply wander across the United States in 1883; he was steered. And in composing his chronicle, Lanzinger argues, Mohr "relied heavily on observations in guidebooks."[30] Mohr's travelogue illustrates the impact of a new cultural form on the opinions of foreign observers. As an unprecedented number of domestic and foreign sightseers began to explore the United States in the late nineteenth century, a tourist industry emerged to help shape and interpret their itineraries. As a number of critics have pointed out, the tourist is the recipient of "a planned . . . self-conscious and contrived national image"; for this passive observer, experience is organized and supplied, not discovered.[31] Paradoxically, greater access to and increased interest in the United States resulted in a more prescribed and restricted travel experience. As Richard Rapson notes, American travelogues written between 1870 and 1922 are often brief and superficial. Their discussions of democracy, equality, and progress generally take place in Fifth Avenue hotels, on ferry rides around Manhattan, on Wall Street, and on the Brooklyn Bridge. The reliance on organized tourism meant that foreign observers writing between 1870 and 1922 seldom strayed to where "the other half lived."[32]

The nucleus of tourism is the selection of icons — or images — that best express a regional or national ideal, a function that makes the history of tourism vital in considering the formation of American cultural identity.[33] As the example of Mohr illustrates, the principal organizing force of this new tourism was the guide and the guidebook. For the tourist, the guidebook provided an image already cataloged and classified. Selection and presentation were, and remain, paramount. Through the guidebook, a region is exemplified, ranked, and projected. As Dean MacCannell notes, sightseers do not in any empirical sense *see* a place or region; instead, they survey a selection of symbolic markers.[34] At the turn of the twentieth century, the Brooklyn Bridge was arguably New York's most important symbolic marker. In this respect, New York as a tourist site was formulated and presented in much the same terms invoked on the bridge's opening day. The images by which the city was exemplified were transplanted from the rhetoric of speeches and newspapers into the "objective" guidebook. Within the pages of these volumes, the city was redefined as a series of sights and landmarks. Implicit was the assumption that certain areas were more representative than others.[35]

The symbolic cartography of guidebooks presents an ideal image of the city while simultaneously insulating visitors from the everyday world in which they are traveling. The sightseer proceeds within a hermetically sealed tourist environment.[36] Rapson notes that many British visitors to New York received their primary impressions of the city from the individuals they met and the experiences they had within the city's fashionable hotels and restaurants. Novelist Abraham Cahan captured this contradiction wonderfully. Recollecting an East Houston Street café, he remarked that "people from uptown . . . came there ostensibly to see 'how the other half lived,' but . . . only saw one another eat and drink in freedom from the restraint of manners."[37]

In many of the era's guidebooks, an announcement greets the reader: the tourist who wishes to sample the city in its most favorable light should trust the guidebook absolutely. *A Visitor's Guide to the City of New York* (1901) begins: "we will suppose that the visitor is wide-awake and wants to see what is really best worth his attention, with too short a time for selection."[38] The desire to delineate the city on behalf of its visitors is also revealed in a pamphlet issued the same year: "if the stranger follows this book as a guide he will miss little of interest in and about New York."[39] *Rand, McNally & Co.'s Handy Guide to New York City* (1896) calmly addresses the anxieties of visitors new to the city: "An arrival in New York for the first time is an ordeal to which many persons look forward with justifiable dread. What shall they do first . . . how shall they find the proper way—how escape the mischievous misleading of some sort, and unnecessary expenses? These questions occur to many inexperienced travelers; and it is the purpose of this book to answer them."[40]

Although it is not uncommon for a visitor to rely on a guidebook when first entering a foreign city, the advice proffered merits analysis. A majority of guides provided a comprehensive itinerary, yet it is often fleeting—as regards the amount of time one should devote to each sight—and confined to the more wealthy areas of the city. Monuments, religious buildings, upscale shops, and civic institutions are prioritized, as are the homes of the rich. For the journey between recommended stops, visitors are advised to use specific routes so as not to stray into undesirable territory.[41] *A Visitor's Guide to the City of New York* counsels those wishing to visit the Washington Monument to "stop short of the shabby buildings" standing to the south and east. *New York (Illustrated)* (1901) discreetly raised the issue of "slumming." After warning about potential dangers, it noted that Chinatown "should only be visited with a recognizable guide." The services of such a person are also essential for the examination of a flophouse: "one might entertainingly end the day's sightseeing by visiting the Mills Hotel. . . . An inspection of [which] is usually one of the features of an evening's 'slumming.'"[42] Not surprisingly, a visit to the Brooklyn Bridge is highly recommended. *McCoy's Centennial Illustrated, How to See New York and Its Environs* (1876) featured a picture of the bridge on its cover even though the span was still seven years from completion.[43] In *Rider's New York City* (1916), the bridge "is one of the essential sights of the city," and the first American Baedeker declared that "the view from the raised promenade in the middle of the bridge is one which no visitor should miss."[44]

Turn-of-the-century guidebooks went beyond identifying what was and was not worth seeing in New York; they also specified how to act in the city. Beginning with Robert Ogden's *New York City, and How to See It* (1876), instruction was often codified within the guidebook title itself.[45] The aim was to relate a system of conduct, taking care to describe the "how" along with the "what" to see in the city. M. F. Sweetser's *How to Know New York* (1895) employs an informative tone to broach the topic of New York's ethnic neighborhoods. In essence, Sweetser imparts the sort of pseudo-scientific racism found at the "ethnological" displays popular at contemporaneous world's fairs.[46] *How to Know New York* specifies the physical and social characteristics of Germans, Italians, African Americans, Chinese, and Jews, while naming the best streets on which to view their daily lives. The descriptions seem better suited to a museum than a place where people live and work. Discussing the Lower East Side, Sweetser notes that "wondrously preserved Semitic people are found in great numbers."[47] He portrays the city's ethnic neighborhoods as displays or viewing attractions. Yet, as interesting as they might be as diversions, he goes to some lengths to counsel against interaction with the subjects on view.

The concern to insulate the tourist from the city's ethnic residents also surfaces in other guidebooks. The Rand McNally *Handy Guide* cautions against talking to immigrants, and *Rider's New York City* advises against approaching anyone in the street not wearing a uniform, "for a large majority of New Yorkers today are of foreign birth or extraction."[48] Although *Rider's* strongly warns against personal interaction in the city, it does make one exception. The financial desperation of Russian immigrants can lead to some rewards for the tough negotiator: "many bargains can be picked up . . . by the collector who has a moderate knowledge of the hallmarks of the genuine antique."[49] The message seems obvious: one should steer clear of the city's ethnic neighborhoods, unless, of course, one could benefit financially.

Tourism further cemented a familiar New York trope: the concept of the city as a duality of "sunshine and shadow." In essence these accounts presume the existence of two cities, separate, unequal, and ignorant of each other. For visitors to New York after the opening of the Brooklyn Bridge, interaction was not advised and rarely attempted. Their New York was the guidebook city, the city of sunshine, the city projected during the bridge's opening day.

Sublime Awe, National Unity, and the "Totalizing Impulse"

The trajectory of nineteenth-century American tourism follows the country's reevaluation of the parameters of the national sublime. In the nineteenth century, Americans reimagined the romantic ideal of the sublime first to include and then to prioritize the technological over the natural.[50] The ramifications of this shift were profound. Anxious over a perceived lack of institutional and cultural traditions, Americans found historical validity in their country's natural landscape. By projecting the question of history away from "culture" and onto "nature," Americans were able to claim for themselves an important domestic tradition. Logically, this new focus resulted in the creation of national "sacred places."[51] Where Britain had the Tower of London and France had Chartres Cathedral, for example, the United States had Niagara Falls, the Hudson Valley, the White Mountains of New Hampshire, and the Rocky Mountains, each of which promoted the idea of national unity and mythic history.

America's "sacred places" mirrored the properties of spiritual renewal and national unity found in Winthrop's "city upon a hill." And as technology began to intrude into the American landscape, it also found a place in the "sacred" act of national sightseeing. By the late nineteenth century, according to historian William Irwin, "the American version of the Grand Tour featured requisite visits to the Brooklyn Bridge, massive factories, subways, and great industrial cities."[52] When the actress Sarah Bernhardt visited New York in 1883, the idea of renewal was epitomized for her in the Brooklyn Bridge. After a trying experience at New York's Customs House upon her arrival in America, Bernhardt recalled:

> I was so nervous and upset that I wanted to go somewhere far away, to have some fresh air, and to stay out for a long time. A friend offered to take me to see the Brooklyn Bridge.
>
> "That masterpiece of American genius will make you forget the petty miseries of our red-tape affairs," he said gently and we set out for Brooklyn Bridge.
>
> Oh, that bridge! It is insane, admirable, imposing, and it makes one feel proud. Yes, one is proud to be a human being when one realizes that a human

brain has created and suspended in the air, fifty yards from the ground, that fearful thing. . . . I returned to the hotel reconciled with this great nation. I went to sleep tired in body but rested in mind, and had such delightful dreams that I was in a good humor the following day.[53]

Among personal testimonies of tourist arrivals in New York, Bernhardt's response is archetypal. The rigors of arrival and entry are calmed through a visit to the bridge. Ultimately, "reconciliation" with the "great nation" is achieved. As the sacred transcends the profane by bringing one closer to God, so the Brooklyn Bridge brings one closer to the American nation.

Twelve years after Bernhardt, the French writer Paul Bourget had much the same reaction. Bourget's trip to the bridge convinced him of the genius of American technology: "A bridge connects New York with Brooklyn, overhanging an arm of the sea. Seen from afar, this bridge astounds you like one of those great architectural nightmares given by Piranesi in his weird etchings. . . . [The] indisputable evidence of its height confuses the mind. But walk over it . . . and you will feel that the engineer is the great artist of our epoch, and you will own that these people have a right to plume themselves on their audacity, on the *go-ahead* which has never flinched."[54] Like Bernhardt, Bourget employed the rhetoric of the technological sublime. At once astounding and fearful, the bridge challenged the limits of the imagination and impressed upon the viewer the "sublime" and "sacred" nature of American technological progress.

The trope was a familiar one in late-nineteenth-century descriptions of American cities. Although, according to Richard Rapson, most "highly vocal visitors" were left "awed and speechless,"[55] the point of a travel narrative is to give expression to such indescribable sights, and we can detect a sense of sublime awe overriding all other considerations. On the bridge John Kirkwood felt "exalted above the other ways" and "tempted to linger long." For Joel Cook, the scene was "bewitching" and presented the city in its "unrivalled glories." William Glazer saw the bridge as "one of the most wonderful products of our wonderful civilization."[56] These responses all invoke the rhetoric of the sublime, and together they provide a chorus to the anthem intoned on opening day and echoed by Bjørnson, Mohr, and Esenin: the singularity of the sublime vista inexorably subverts the politics of the whole. As Donald Pease notes, "like the modernist dogma of the new, the American myth of revolution converted into an endlessly repeatable sublime ritual, turned into a tacit form of control."[57]

In *Land of the Dollar* (1897), British journalist and travel writer G. W. Steevens regarded the city of New York as chaotic, reptilian, and savage. In it "nothing is given to beauty," and "confusion takes the hindmost and the foremost, the topmost and the whole jumble." Yet from the Brooklyn Bridge, the city appears ordered; it becomes "rosy" and takes on a type of "softness." Magically, "from that point the low, red houses sloping up from the waterside looked like a carpet for the giants to tread upon."[58] Although Steevens's is a standard tourist response to the bridge/city axis, it is also pointedly ideological. Bathed in the hues of imagination, the city is transformed through what Hana Wirth-Nesher calls a "totalizing impulse."[59] Furthermore, Steevens's view is validated as the city's only authentic and rightful image. In a complex reversal, the chaos of the streets is made to seem unreal, and the imaginative reconfiguration of the city from the bridge is legitimized. Here, the symbolic trope of "sunshine" is literally "rosy" and "softening." The "shadow" of the streets vanishes in a single, totalizing image of the city. The diversity of its people, places, buildings, and beliefs flow into the guidebook image of the city seen from the bridge.

H. G. Wells Looks at American Technology

After a twenty-year romance with the abstract principles of democracy and the concrete results of technological progress, the ideal of America's fundamental correctness began to corrode with the dawn of the twentieth century. Perhaps in response to the prodding of America's own native reformers, the ideals of liberalism and equality so unanimously saluted in previous years began to be tested on the streets. There, visitors found no sense of widespread liberty. With disdain, Eliza Humphreys wrote in 1910: "In coming to America, I had pictured a land of freedom and true citizenship: I had never pictured such inequalities and contradictions as confront one on every side. Has the land which claims freedom as a nation's birthright, only erected the Goddess of liberty as witness to a falsified creed?"[60] The practical liberty of the nation's population *as a whole* became a key issue. In 1926 Douglas Woodruff considered Americans to be "the least free of all people," chiefly because "propaganda more than anything else informs the views of the people."[61] During the era of the Brooklyn Bridge's opening, Lord Bryce had characterized America as "all made of a piece"; by the early twentieth century, the dominant tone was decidedly that of James Muirhead's *America, the Land of Contrasts.*[62]

Criticism focused on the amount of wealth concentrated in so few hands. Elijah Brown loathed what he called New York's "insane worship of money." Under the prevailing economic system, he continued, the nation's future looked bleak indeed. Likewise, Alexander Francis characterized the city's

power brokers as "an ever-growing circle of wolves."[63] Yet, even as they recognized and abhorred the widespread social inequality, observers continued
to be fascinated by the physical city. Unable to see the built city and the economic city as two halves of a whole—that the "sunshine" created the
"shadow"—Philip Bourne-Jones bemoaned the "aristocracy of great wealth"
that had "out-Heroded Herod," while praising the city's architecture, especially the Brooklyn Bridge.[64] Travelogues of this era display a fundamental
adherence to the rhetoric of industrial progress and a simultaneous vilifi-
cation of industrial fortunes. Many seemed unable to conceive that both out-
comes might result from the same process. As *Outlook* magazine lamented
in 1904, "The stranger's New York, is a surface New York."[65]

One might expect such economic and social concerns to dominate the
thoughts of an avowed socialist like H. G. Wells. Unfortunately, the record
of his first trip to the United States—*The Future in America* (1906)—shows
Wells at his least incisive. Always somewhat beguiled by new technologies,
Wells allowed his usually acute cultural commentary to dissipate before the
scale of U.S. industrial development. On numerous levels, Wells's travelogue
represents one grand "totalizing" vision, with all of American society symbolized by the achievements of its engineers.

Later in life, Wells would become disillusioned with the United States,
but in 1905 he was entranced.[66] "The great thing is the mechanical thing,"
he notes early in his visit, and his mood advances toward giddy elation. During a railroad journey, Wells lapses into the type of rhetoric displayed at the
bridge's opening: "How quickly things had come! 'Progress, progress,' mur-
mured the wheels, and I began to make this steady, swift and shiningly
equipped train a figure . . . of that big onward sweep that is moving us all together." As he continues, Wells grasps for appropriate language: "this great
American symphony, this symphony of Growth"; "the enormous scale of this
American destiny"; and "Growth Invincible."[67]

Wells's techno-euphoria reached its zenith during his stay in New York. To
a large degree its expression in *The Future in America* bears comparison with
the thoughts and photographs of Wells's American friend Alvin Langdon
Coburn. A great admirer of Coburn, Wells hung a number of Coburn's New
York photographs in the dining room of his home in Kent, and in 1910 he
wrote a glowing foreword to Coburn's book on the city. Coincidentally,
Coburn was also in New York in 1905, taking photographs of skyscrapers and
bridges. Both the writer and the photographer were dazzled by the tall buildings and overwhelmed by the sight of New York from the harbor, especially
the league-long bridges that spanned the East River. In his photographs,

12. A "magnificent Martian-like monster." Alvin Langdon Coburn, "Brooklyn Bridge," 1912. Courtesy George Eastman House.

Coburn emphasized the grandeur of the Brooklyn Bridge and exaggerated its scale in comparison with the city's skyline. For Wells, "the large Brooklyn suspension bridge" was significantly "more impressive than the skyscrapers":

> I have never troubled to ask who built that, its greatness is not in its design, but in the quality of necessity one perceives in its inanimate immensity. It *tells,* as one goes under it up the East River, but it is far more impressive to the stranger

to come upon it by glimpses . . . one sees parts of Cyclopean stone arches, one gets suggestive glimpses through the jungle growth of business, now of the back, now of the flanks of the monster, then as one comes out on the river one discovers, far up in one's sky, the long sweep of the bridge itself.[68]

Likewise, Coburn confessed an innate "kinship" with "the mind that could produce" such an edifice and called the bridge a "magnificent Martian-like

57

monster." Yet, for both men, this "monster" was no figure of fear — no atrocity — but an enormous object of adoration.[69]

Wells's response to the Brooklyn Bridge and Coburn's photographs are infused with the technological sublime. Their swift dismissal of the general public also echoes the rhetoric that accompanied the bridge's opening.[70] Wells describes a group of workers marching home on the bridge much as Esenin would eighteen years later: with their "unmeaning faces . . . the individuals count for nothing."[71] For a socialist, this is an odd statement, yet it typifies Wells's writings on New York. Recalling Edmund Burke and David Nye, we recognize that Wells's mind is "so entirely filled with its [technological] object, that it cannot . . . reason on that object which employs it."[72] Coexisting with Wells's techno-euphoria is an almost total failure to "reason on" the city. As regards the mass of new immigrants flooding into the country, for example, the city's ability to absorb them seems to outweigh the fate of the individual: "In one recorded day this month 21,000 immigrants came into the port of New York alone; in one week over 50,000. This year the total will be 1,200,000 souls, pouring in, finding work at once, producing no fall in wages." And on the question of personal wealth, Wells's view replicates Abram Hewitt's projection of parity and equality: "There can be little doubt to any one who goes to and fro in America that, in spite of the huge accumulation of property in a few hands . . . there is still no general effect of impoverishment. To me, coming from London to New York, the crowd in the trolley-cars and subways and streets seemed one of exceptional prosperity."[73] For Wells to base his judgment of the status of the population of New York solely on the individuals he found in "trolley-cars and subways" seems no different from a tourist basing an appraisal of the country on the quality of its hotels. Again Wells's reasoning is suspended, and the city's economic disparities remain unnoticed.[74]

For Rapson, "the most persistent crime committed by writers in the name of analysis has been to personify the nation on the basis of one or a few personal interviews with 'typical Americans.'"[75] Wells is guilty of this lapse of judgment even as he bases his evaluation of America on technology. For many admirers — both then and now — Theodore Roosevelt represents a "typical American," and Wells clearly thought so. After an interview with the then president, Wells commits what can only be described as a crime of prophecy: "Never did a president before so reflect the quality of his time. The trend is altogether away from the anarchic individualism of the nineteenth century, that much is sure, and towards some constructive scheme which, if not exactly socialism, as socialism is defined, will be, at any rate, closely analogous to socialism."[76]

En route to New York, Wells complained about America's concept of its own future. It was certain to be impressive, that much Wells understood. But he was annoyed by the "volley of rhetorical blank cartridge[s]" — "so empty is it of all but sound" — that Americans themselves often used to explain their vision. In the American character, he bemoaned, alacrity took precedence over understanding. Ultimately, however, Wells is guilty of the same crime.[77] In describing "this great American symphony, this symphony of Growth," Wells himself resorted to "rhetorical blank cartridge[s]." In *The Future in America*, Wells imbued American technology with the type of official, "totalizing" opinion found at the opening of the Brooklyn Bridge. Technological icons become autonomous social forces, and their example becomes inherent, not rhetorical. As Harold Beaver has wryly observed, "for a confessed futurist, he got things decidedly wrong."[78]

Henry James's New York Nightmare

A majority of tourists stood spellbound upon the Brooklyn Bridge. Some were horrified. Federico García Lorca came to New York shortly before the stock market crash of 1929 and left in disgust ten months later. The poems he wrote about the experience, published as *Poet in New York* (1940), present one of the most malignant visions the city has ever inspired.[79] To Peter Conrad, Lorca's New York "is a body in diseased extremism, and his images are its lesions." For other critics, it is a living variation on James Thompson's "The City of Dreadful Night" or Yeats's "Second Coming."[80] Instead of Yeats's "rough beast," however, Lorca evokes vipers, cobras, and other reptilian images of nightmare to populate New York. They are the city's soul made manifest. They spring forth from the city's guts and prowl the streets as a menacing, relentless force. Like many poets, Lorca recognized the Brooklyn Bridge as New York's cynosure, yet there is no triumph or exhilaration in his evocation of it, only loathing and exhaustion: the bridge is the hub of a vile, unending panorama. In "Sleepless City (Brooklyn Bridge Nocturne)," Lorca gazes at Manhattan — an "incredible crocodile resting beneath the tender protest of the stars" — and understands: modernity has ripped mankind from its natural moorings. Business and technology have formed a twenty-four-hour-a-day nightmare. Unable to tap into the regenerative forces of sleep, "brokenhearted fugitive[s]" with "bitter inflamed wounds" stare lidless at their fate: "Out in the World, no one sleeps. No one, no one. / No one Sleeps." In such a place, the bridge is incomprehensible — a boy weeps because he cannot understand the bridge — it is merely a platform upon which to track the progress of a disease.[81] Unlike Bernhardt, Lorca finds neither national unity nor spiritual renewal at the Brooklyn Bridge; rather, it is a place to realize the city's savage, exhausting, and cancerous nature.

Lorca's response is arresting, but it is not the most visceral the bridge has aroused. Arriving in New York City after a twenty-one-year absence, Henry James was appalled by what he saw. Consequently, *The American Scene* (1907), James's record of his return and a valuable counterpoint to Wells's *The Future in America* and Coburn's photographs, has often been read by critics as a response to the present rooted heavily in past experience.[82] James himself saw "absolutely *no* profit in scanning or attempting to sound the future" during his stay in America.[83] Nevertheless, the future takes on a significant role in James's travelogue. His New York plays host to a battle between progress and conservation, between the new city of economic consumption and the regenerative city of historical tradition. For James, the former is outstripping the latter, and a lasting victory is close. When he contemplates the consequences of this defeat, his fear turns to panic at the thought that those forces "that speak loudest for the economic idea"[84] will have the final advantage and be projected forward. It is here that James enters the future and becomes most predictive.

Approaching the city from the bay, James writes:

The aspect the power wears then is indescribable; it is the power of the most extravagant of cities, rejoicing . . . in its might, its fortune, its unsurpassable conditions. . . . This appearance of the bold lacing-together, across the waters, of the scattered members of the monstrous organism . . . does perhaps more than anything else to give the pitch of the vision energy. One has the sense that the monster grows and grows, flinging abroad its loose limbs even as some unmannered young giant at his "larks," and that the binding stitches must for ever fly further and faster and draw harder; the future complexity of the web, all under the sky and over the sea, becoming thus that of some colossal set of clockworks, some steel-souled machine-room of brandished arms and hammering fists and opening and closing jaws. The immeasurable bridges are but the horizontal sheaths of pistons working at high pressure, day and night, and subject, one apprehends with perhaps inconsistent gloom, to certain, to fantastic, to merciless multiplication. In the light of this apprehension . . . the breezy brightness of the Bay puts on the semblance of the vast white page that awaits beyond any other perhaps the black overscoring of science.[85]

Here, James's responses to the city coalesce into a composite image. Although the paragraph begins with sublime exhilaration, the mood soon deteriorates. As the scene comes together, the dominant forces of modernity gather. Symbolically, technology and finance create the storm; the Brooklyn Bridge provides the magnetism. From the present, James shifts to the future.

The image "grows and grows" and "must forever fly further and faster" into "the future complexity of the web": New York is advancing, gaining momentum. James's key image is of a "colossal set of clockworks." Like time itself, the city is moving inexorably onward; like clockwork, its historical trajectory is governed by an internal mechanism. Even though a human hand may have set the mechanism in motion, there is no longer any human agency in the process. New York's bridges have become autonomous "steel-souled machine-room[s] of brandished arms and hammering fists and opening and closing jaws"; they are the "pistons" *driving* modernity through the city and eating away at its past. Transformed into a science fiction nightmare, New York's internal clock is ticking. The city's destiny supposes the victory of the machine over humanity. As certain as time's arrow, scientific advancement promises "the black overscoring" of human life and culture.

James's choice of the Brooklyn Bridge as the centerpiece of his dystopian image is informed by his own biography. He left America for his long, self-imposed exile in Europe three months after the bridge's opening. By placing the bridge at the center of his critique, James draws a historical connection to the length of his absence. Moreover, if the bridge can be seen as a center, it also functions as a foundation. It marks the beginning of James's dark prophecy. James placed the span at the heart not only of his visual impression but also of his conceptual image of New York's prevailing forces. The bridge enables James to make sense of the city and place it within an evolving chronology. He does this by returning to the origins of its spiritual timetable. In his account of Western civilization, Kenneth Clark felt that "all modern New York, heroic New York, started with Brooklyn Bridge."[86] For James, the opposite is true. New York has become an anticivilization. Its citizens have ceded control to the indifference of technological progress, and what appears as heroism is revealed as the folly of trusting too deeply in the machine. Diametrically opposed to the rhetoric of the bridge's opening, James saw technology, finance, and the Brooklyn Bridge as the components of a nightmare, not a harmonious civic Eden. New York's industrial landscape is governed by technological and economic determinism, and set to the mechanical rhythms of perpetual motion.

The promise implicit in James's New York is akin to that found in late-twentieth-century science fiction classics. In James Cameron's *The Terminator* (1984), Katsuhiro Otomo's *Akira* (1984–1985), Greg Bear's *Blood Music* (1985), and the Wachowski brothers' *The Matrix* (1999), the forces of technology have displaced the agency of organic life. James believed that this process had already begun, and he foresaw that once the machine is set in motion, it cannot be undone. Its nature is the kinetic relentlessness of

13. Kinetic modernism. John Marin, *Brooklyn Bridge,* 1913. Etching and dry-point, platemark; 29.2 × 22.9 cm (11½ × 9 in.). Museum of Fine Arts Boston, Gift of C. Adrian Rubel. Photograph © Museum of Fine Arts, Boston.

consumption, and its end point is hellish, not paradisiacal. For James, all modern New York, all nightmarish New York, started with the Brooklyn Bridge.

In a radio interview, documentary filmmaker Ken Burns dismissed James's reaction to the bridge. As one voice in a larger chorus of positive appreciations of the bridge, it represented "such a tiny, tiny minority" as to be virtually worthless. "Come on, Henry," Burns concluded, "get a life here."[87] Notwithstanding Burns's unwillingness to sanction the validity of opposition, James's contribution to the bridge's cultural history *is* important. His image of kinetic modernism reminds us of John Marin's watercolors and etchings from the 1910s, and of the strenuous attempts of the Polish immigrant Max Weber to codify New York's new urban environment in the same decade.

Shortly after James's death in 1916, the French artist Albert Gleizes added the bridge to his ongoing portrait of New York. Cubist in style and heavily abstracted, Gleizes's *On Brooklyn Bridge* (1917) is a terrifying explosion of energy, of metal, lights, and stone. It is difficult to determine whether Gleizes's canvas is a celebration or a condemnation, an evocation of modern vitality

14. A terrifying explosion of energy, of metal, lights, and stone. Albert Gleizes, *On Brooklyn Bridge (Sur Brooklyn Bridge)*, 1917. Oil on canvas, 63¾ × 51 in. (161.8 × 129.5 cm). Solomon R. Guggenheim Museum, New York. © 2004 Artist Rights Society (ARS), New York / ADAGP, Paris.

or its predicted collapse into chaos and destruction. The influence of James's response extends to other visual depictions of the bridge, yet only rarely to those produced by other visitors. James's image of alienation, a modernist battleground and a technological hell, instead resurfaced in the work of another major group for whom New York Harbor was familiar ground: the millions of new immigrants who poured into New York in the early years of the twentieth century. They sought a home in America, not an edifying vacation: a Promised Land of religious freedom, financial opportunity, and racial and social liberty.[88]

Positive Immigrant Symbolism and Its Alter Ego

At the centennial of the Brooklyn Bridge in 1983, reporter Bill Prochnaw rhapsodized about the city's collective decision to take "time out today to celebrate an immigrant story — an American story really — about people who came here in steerage and poverty, carrying dreams, visions, hope and little else. For decades they came in waves, and their first sighting of the dream was a misty torch in New York harbor. Then they saw the vision, the soaring gothic arches and the gleaming cables of a bridge that told them that here anything was possible, and the gap could be spanned."[89] Twenty years later, Brooklyn poet laureate Ken Siegelman celebrated the bridge's 120th anniversary with "Heaven's Gate," a poem that proposed an intrinsic link between the bridge and the immigrant experience. "Just in reach of some divinity," Siegelman wrote:

> She was always less a passageway
> From island to island,
> Than a portal through time and space;
> Much the way that Heaven's Gate
> Was seen by immigrants in tenements and clapboard shacks
> Crowded into cobble streets on either side
> that fell inside her shadow. . . .[90]

These observations would seem to support the forecasts made at the bridge's opening that the span would "inspire the emigrant who seeks a home here with new hopes and energy."[91] One such immigrant, artist Louis Lozowick, made a career by celebrating the precise order and perfect symmetry of America's cities, and especially its bridges.[92] In addition, numerous writers have championed the Brooklyn Bridge's role as a positive immigrant symbol, and one can hardly forget the childlike fascination and awe shown by Austrian immigrant Helmut (played by Armin Mueller-Stahl) as he drives over the bridge in Jim Jarmusch's film *Night on Earth* (1991). "Beautiful," he murmurs, as if no other words are necessary or adequate.[93]

Yet the overall picture is not nearly so clear. In Prochnaw's paean to the immigrant experience, the bridge functions in tandem with the Statue of Liberty. Although the latter is often regarded as the immigrant symbol *par excellence*, its conception owed nothing to such ideas. During the mass immigration from 1880 to 1920 the statue was rarely used to symbolize benevolent welcome. Rather, it was predominantly imagined as a defenseless maiden under attack from malevolent foreigners or as a sword-wielding warrior fighting off the rising immigrant tide. As Albert Boime notes, "it was only after immigrant ships dwindled to minuscule numbers that the Statue of Liberty began to be intensively promoted as a mythical shrine to the memory of the immigrant experience."[94] Similar inconsistencies in historical memory can be found in the cultural history of the Brooklyn Bridge.

The origins of the bridge's positive symbolism for immigrants can be found at the opening day. New Americans were lavishly praised for their contributions to the national errand, and their virtues were extolled. At the same

15. Skyscrapers, "el" tracks, and the Brooklyn Bridge: celebrating the precise order and perfect symmetry of America's cities. Louis Lozowick, *New York*, 1925. Oil on canvas, 30³/₁₆ × 22³/₁₆ in. Walker Art Center, Minneapolis, Gift of Hudson D. Walker, 1961.

time, and in accord with the nature of the opening, the immigrant experience was simplified and redefined. Just as William Tweed became the repository for all corruption — and the bridge for American progress — so the life of John Roebling was hailed as the epitome of immigrant success. In light of the ideological content of the day, this appropriation of the bridge's designer is not surprising. His biography reads like a textbook on American achievement.[95] Fleeing Germany's turmoil, bureaucracy, and social inequality, Roebling arrived in America in 1831, two years into the presidency of Andrew Jackson, and his career combined elements of both the Jacksonian hero and the American success story. Upon arrival, he set about farming in the outer reaches of Pennsylvania; later, as a wire-rope manufacturer and bridge builder, he coupled great leadership with remarkable innovation and an iron will. His accomplishments epitomized the American ideal of the self-made man. And as Sacvan Bercovitch notes, "to be *self-made* in America was more than to make one's own fortune; it was to embody a cultural metaphysics."[96]

With Roebling as the mediating figure, observers across the decades have forged links between the immigrant, the American success story, and the Brooklyn Bridge. This triumvirate lies at the heart of Prochnaw's tribute. Yet the reality of nineteenth-century immigration is much more problematic. The early 1880s mark the dividing line between what have become known as the eras of "old" and "new" immigration.[97] During the period of old immigration, Oscar Handlin noted, questions over the nature of the American character were rarely asked:

> Americans of the first half of the century had assumed that any man who subjected himself to the American environment was being Americanized. Since the New World was ultimately to be occupied by a New Man, no mere derivative of any extant stock, but different from and superior to all, there had been no fixed standards of national character against which to measure the behavior of newcomers. The nationality of the new Republic had been supposed fluid, only just evolving; there had been room for infinite variation because diversity rather than uniformity had been normal.[98]

Toward the end of the nineteenth century, however, new immigration had altered the concept of American national character. "A note of petulance" and "impatience" greeted this wave of newcomers, as anxiety over assimilation and Americanization grew. The drive for national cohesiveness was reflected in the desire for uniformity, and distrust became the watchword of diversity.[99]

The opening of the Brooklyn Bridge marked the end of one era and the beginning of another within the history of American immigration. If the bridge's dominant narrative does contain an immigrant story, it is not one of steerage and poverty. Roebling arrived as a university-trained engineer, in good standing with the country's predominant religion, and with sufficient funds to purchase a sizable amount of land in western Pennsylvania.[100] Yet by the time of the bridge's opening, the nature of both the "individual received" and the "receiving society" had changed dramatically. The experience of America's new immigrants—those who *did* journey in steerage and poverty—would find little relevance in the old immigrant story of Roebling, and their responses to America would reflect these circumstances.

Mario Maffi has declared that the culture of America's new immigrants "seems ever to accompany Mainstream America as its *alter ego.*"[101] This sense of dichotomy, which has led to a reevaluation of many traditional immigrant symbols, can be extended to the Brooklyn Bridge. For example, the social reformer Jacob Riis, writing just seven years after the bridge's opening, crucially inverted much of the rhetoric of the opening day. He too described the city as a beacon; but rather than beckoning with the glow of opportunity and achievement, his New York glimmered with a deadly attraction, "like a lighted candle to a moth."[102] Where the opening-day celebrants reveled in the creation of a new sacred space, Riis posited a far less edifying set of landmarks. To the inhabitants of the Lower East Side, Potter's Field and the alcoholic cells at Bellevue Hospital provided the only opportunities for travel. Discussing the city's most visible and famous landmarks, he wrote: "Out of forty-eight boys twenty had never seen the Brooklyn Bridge that was scarcely five minutes walk away, three only had been in Central Park. . . . The street with its ash-barrels and its dirt, the river that runs foul with mud, are their domain."[103] In their circumscribed conditions, New York's new arrivals were unlikely to see a positive symbol in the Brooklyn Bridge, as the opening-day speakers supposed they must. For these immigrants, food, work, and lodging took precedence over sightseeing. When they could spare some thought for the bridge, they forged a vision that stands as the alter ego of the one broadcast by the *Eagle* in 1883 and perpetuated by Prochnaw a century later.[104]

Arrival and Passageway

On the eve of the centennial of the Brooklyn Bridge, David McCullough wrote: "for millions of new Americans arriving by ship, [the bridge] was the first thing to be seen of the New World, its twin towers rising like triumphant gateways. 'You see great ships passing beneath it and this indisputable evidence of its height confuses the mind,' wrote a man from France. 'But walk over it . . . and you will feel that the engineer is the great artist of our epoch, and you will own that these people have a right to plume themselves in their audacity.'"[105] This testimony would seem to support the idea of the bridge as a positive symbol for immigrants. Yet the author of these words, quoted earlier in this chapter, was not a "new American" but the French novelist Paul Bourget.[106] Bourget visited America in 1895 as a leisure-class tourist and enjoyed the society of the country's cultural elites.

In contrast, the eponymous hero of Edward King's *Joseph Zalmonah* (1893)—a recent immigrant living in poverty on the Lower East Side—anticipates his wife's arrival as he walks upon the Brooklyn Bridge. His thoughts are not on the American engineer but on the cruelty and oppression that await his wife. Against Bourget's triumphant exclamation of America's rightful audacity, Zalmonah cries out "a welcome to slavery and sorrow! A welcome to living death."[107]

Henry Roth presents another paradigmatic account of reunion and arrival in *Call It Sleep* (1934) as Albert Schearl greets his wife, Genya, at Ellis Island.[108] For Genya, the popular conception of America as "the Golden Land" seems borne out by the sight of the Statue of Liberty and the Brooklyn Bridge, yet her unease is palpable. In contrast to her guarded optimism is Albert's more experiential attitude: "The man had evidently spent some time in America and . . . it might have been thought that he had spent most of his time in lower New York, for he paid only the scantest attention to the Statue of Liberty or to the city rising from the water or to the bridges spanning the East River."[109] Confronted with the prime symbols of American promise, Albert remains unmoved: "'And this is the Golden Land.' She spoke in Yiddish. The man grunted, but made no answer." Experience, it seems, has taught Albert to question and doubt the symbols by which Americans represent their country. When juxtaposed against New York's opulent landmarks, Albert's physical appearance shocks Genya: "You must have suffered in this land . . . you're thin. Ach! Then here in the new land is the same old poverty. You've gone without food. I can see it now. You've changed." Within an instant, Genya's ideal of the golden land is challenged, and she is forced to confront a new, unanticipated reality. Neither the Statue of Liberty nor the Brooklyn Bridge can uphold the image of promise when juxtaposed with the everyday hardships of immigrant life. On the way home, Genya's optimism is reduced to a single repeated phrase: "I'm sorry Albert, I'm sorry."[110]

As Wirth-Nesher implies, the prologue to *Call It Sleep* charts an important shift in visual perception. Arriving in the "Golden Land," the wife soon finds herself on the way to "Bronzeville."[111] Even this image is eroded, as the bronze of Brownsville ultimately gives way to the muddy shores of the Lower East Side. At one point her son David gazes out at the Brooklyn Bridge and imagines a train gliding across "like a trickle of gold." The image is distant and elusive; much closer is the "stinkin' heap" of the shore.[112] The trajectory here is the inverse of that enshrined by Emma Lazarus. The immigrant as "wretched refuse" may approach the "Golden Door," but the opening leads only to a place of literal refuse. Although certainly "yearning to breathe free," the members of the Schearl family are forced to breathe "the festering stench of the city's iron entrails."[113] Even as the Brooklyn Bridge remains golden, the door entered by the Schearl family is tarnished.

In keeping with comfortable notions of exodus and the promised land, some critics have remarked that the profile of the Brooklyn Bridge takes on the contours of a portal or gateway.[114] Harold Gorde has contended that, for New York's immigrants, the bridge represented a passageway from the congested regions of lower Manhattan to spacious Brooklyn. According to Cleveland Rodgers, the opposite was true: the bridge symbolized a gateway to Broadway, Wall Street, Columbia University, or salubrious Park Avenue.[115] To Alfred Kazin and Boris Todrin, the bridge—from provincial Brooklyn to cosmopolitan Manhattan—symbolized immigrant access to a world of social and intellectual betterment. For both Rose Cohen and Harry Roskolenko, however, the bridge was a route to worry and fear, not to accomplishment. For Roskolenko, the bridge meant "crossing into the unknown Gentile world of other woes, fears and disguises." Cohen "was in constant fear of meeting strangers" while walking the bridge, and she would "turn back."[116]

In her study of the life and literature of American urban environments, Sidney Bremer has formulated the idea of the "sheltering home." In contrast to the widely believed image of the "evil city," Bremer asserts that the local urban neighborhood has, for many dwellers, represented a wholly positive urban space replete with mutual dignity, strength, community, and spiritual renewal.[117] Roskolenko and Cohen illustrate the geographic relationship between Bremer's prime example of the "sheltering home," New York's Lower East Side, and the Brooklyn Bridge. "Scarcely five minutes walk away," the bridge leads away from their positive urban space. What emerges in Roskolenko and Cohen is the concept of the bridge as a frontier, a frontier that is particularly European, not American. The bridge represents an environment of hostility and estrangement: a barrier, not a passageway.[118]

Work in the Promised Land

The building of technologically innovative structures in the nineteenth century attracted two classes of people: workers and tourists.[119] Although the public was banned from the construction site of the Brooklyn Bridge, entry was often granted to those with the requisite influence. Through his connections within the office of the trustees, the popular author Thomas Knox was able to arrange such a visit. In *Underground; or Life Below the Surface* (1875), Knox detailed the life of those who toiled outside of, and below, society's gaze. Although his title might seem to imply an exposé, Knox intended no such thing. Accompanied by a guide, this tourist failed to interact with the men he saw "below the surface," and his tone is consistently condescending. In effect, his visit was a form of pseudo slumming, and his book offers a glimpse into the life of the squalid for those who disdained direct contact.

Knox's tourist status is highlighted even before he enters the Brooklyn caisson to review the undertaking. During the descent, he seems somewhat surprised to find "no velvet-covered seats, as are generally found in hotel elevators." He describes the air inside the caisson as neither "impure nor unpleasant" and states that the scene in general was a "very novel one." His attitude toward the workers is at best offhand. He remarks matter-of-factly that a worker who was looking pale died shortly after his visit, and he blames another worker's stupidity and carelessness for the severe injuries suffered in an accident. The curiosity that impelled Knox's visit is well satisfied after an hour.[120]

Most of the men who ventured down into the caissons did so not to satisfy some curiosity but to meet pressing financial necessity, and they often returned day after day until physically injured or psychologically broken. Sinking the caissons was backbreaking labor conducted in intense heat and stultifying compressed air. The threat of "caisson disease"—now better known as the bends—was constant, and many workers were crippled by it. Accompanied by "an unearthly and deafening screech,"[121] the passage into compressed air was a physical and mental ordeal. The scene that Knox found "very novel" was in fact a subterranean hell for those who worked there, as assistant chief engineer E. F. Farrington makes clear:

> Inside the caisson everything wore an unreal, weird appearance. There was a confused sensation in the head, like "the rush of many waters." The pulse was at first accelerated, then sometimes fell below the normal rate. The voice sounded faint, unnatural, and it became a great effort to speak. What with the flaming lights, the deep shadows, the confusing noise of hammers, drills, and chains, the half-naked forms flitting about, with here and there a Sisyphus rolling his stone, one might, if of a poetic temperament, get a realizing sense of Dante's inferno.[122]

It was work for the desperate, the poor, and those who frankly knew no better. As a result, a steady stream of recent immigrants—mainly Irish, with some Germans, Chinese, Italians, and African Americans—supplied the labor. Unlike the self-made John Roebling, these immigrants were barely mentioned on opening day.

For many immigrants, McCullough has written, "the bridge was a first big chance to take hold in American life."[123] Although McCullough is perhaps overly positive, the statement does contain an important point: a job on the Brooklyn Bridge provided a swift lesson in the nature and practices of American life. Many of these lessons are dramatized in Frank Harris's *The Bomb*

(1909), a fictional re-creation of the events surrounding the Haymarket riot of 1886.[124] The novel's subject is Rudolph Schnaubelt, and the action follows his emigration from Germany to New York and on to Chicago.[125]

Upon arrival in New York, Schnaubelt is forced to labor in the bridge caisson. As opposed to Knox's distanced sightseeing, Harris is concerned with *work*, the antithesis of tourism,[126] and his scenes have the immediacy of Farrington's descriptions. After working through excruciating pain, Schnaubelt witnesses the fate of a fellow worker: "I never saw anything so horrible as the poor, twisted, writhing form of the unconscious giant. Before we could lift him on a mud-barrow and carry him away to the hospital he was bathed in blood, and looked to me as if he were dead." His political conscience is awakened by a fellow worker who claims that "it isn't men's work they buy . . . but men's lives, damn them!" Increasingly, the workers are imagined as "convicts." After witnessing another violent encounter with the bends, a weakened and sick Schnaubelt refuses to continue in the caisson.[127]

In the world of *The Bomb*, the blame for such degrading employment is placed squarely on the management. Although working conditions could easily have been improved, Harris editorializes, they remained subhuman.[128] For Schnaubelt, working on the bridge is a formative experience. His understanding of American labor—and the ambivalence of those who direct it—informs his journey toward Chicago's Haymarket Square. One imagines that in Harris's mind, each of the real individuals involved in that bloody affair had undergone an experience similar to that of his fictional Schnaubelt. The novel depicts the violence at the Haymarket as a justifiable reaction to the wicked and debasing treatment of immigrant laborers. Unlike the immigrant experience of his fellow German, John Roebling, disappointment and devastation mark Schnaubelt's life in America.

Tenure and Justice

The positive immigrant symbolism forecast at the opening of the Brooklyn Bridge and affirmed at its centennial finds its alter ego in the history of American responses to new immigration. From the early 1880s to the late 1920s, new immigration and American nativism rose reciprocally. In addition, this period was bracketed by two important events. For John Higham, the Haymarket affair represented "the most important single incident in late nineteenth century nativism,"[129] and its correlative was found during the late 1920s at the trial of Nicola Sacco and Bartolomeo Vanzetti. Both events were sensational local crimes that influenced national opinion; in both cases, due process of law—conclusive evidence, impartial judgment—became subsumed behind the "un-American" foreignness of those accused.

16. The inspiration for the setting of *Winterset?* George Bellows, *The Lone Tenement*, 1909. Chester Dale Collection. Image © Board of Trustees, National Gallery of Art, Washington, DC.

The events in Chicago and Boston marshaled the nation's antiforeign senti-ment and focused attention on the position of immigrants in American so-ciety. Those convicted were judged on their ethnicity, not on their actions. And both incidents have been linked to the Brooklyn Bridge in the national literature.

Just as the Haymarket affair provides the backdrop to *The Bomb*, so the trial of Sacco and Vanzetti lies at the heart of Maxwell Anderson's verse drama *Winterset* (1935). Mio, the play's central character, is the son of Ital-ian immigrant Bartolomeo Romagna, who many years earlier was tried and executed for a crime he did not commit.[130] In the wake of the execution, Mio travels the country, seeking to exonerate his father. In the meantime, a col-lege professor who has researched the case publishes his discovery that a key witness—Garth Esdras—was not called to give evidence. The search for Garth brings Mio to New York.

Anderson highlights Mio's social situation early in the play: "Talk about the lost generation, I'm the only one fits that title. When the state executes your father, and your mother dies of grief, and you know damned well he was innocent, and the authorities of your home town politely inform you they'd consider it a favor if you lived somewhere else—that cuts you off from the world—with a meat-axe."[131] Mio's estrangement is reflected on the stage. The scene is set along the East River shore on "an early, dark December morning." A derelict tenement is bordered by a rocky outcropping and by "sheds . . . built by waifs and strays for shelter." "Loaded with typhus rats," the area is a poisonous wasteland, populated by the desperate and the down-trodden. Anderson depicts a cruel environment, an unjust immigrant "hooverville." Bremer's "sheltering home" is far away indeed.[132]

The stage is dominated by the underside of the Brooklyn Bridge: "a gigantic span starts from the rear of the stage and appears to lift over the heads of the audience and out to the left."[133] The bridge's soaring arch serves as a counterpoint to the East River shore. It symbolizes progress, attainment, and a passageway out of the cruel confines below. Throughout, the bridge extends a measure of hope, the means by which to escape the play's dispiriting locale. Yet from beginning to end, the bridge is out of reach. As Mio moves closer to the truth, he is pursued. And as the violent conclusion approaches, the bridge emerges as the only means of escape. With exit blocked left and right, Mio contemplates fleeing up through the tenement and onto the bridge. "How many floors has this building?" he asks. "It's not as high as the bridge," is the reply. Meanwhile, Esdras (Garth's father) ventures to call for outside help, yet his attempts to escape via the bridge are foiled. The pursuers are stationed there, and the bridge—physically and symbolically—is slippery:

> He would not let me pass.
> The street's so icy up along the bridge
> I had to crawl on my knees—he kicked me back
> three times—and then he held me there.[134]

For Mio and Esdras, the bridge cannot be reached; it looms above them throughout, tantalizingly near, yet unattainable. Like the bridge in *Call It Sleep*, it is distant and elusive; much closer and more pressing are the poverty and violence of the immigrant enclave. The gulf between the juxtaposed urban spaces—the bridge and the tenement slum—is insurmountable. In *Winterset*, the immigrant is cut off—"with a meat-axe"—from the world symbolized by the Brooklyn Bridge.

The stage's visual dichotomy permeates the entire drama. Thematically, the play concerns the relationship between nativist prejudice and legal justice. Just as the bridge is unattainable for those who live below, so is the ideal of equal justice before the law. Early in the play, Garth tells his sister

Miriamne: "everybody knew Romagna wasn't guilty! But they weren't listening to evidence in his favor. They didn't want it."[135] Public opinion is more important than a fair hearing. According to Mio's friend Carr, justice is a matter of finance, not legal rights or evidence: "It's something you can buy. In fact, at the moment I can't think of anything you can't buy, including life, honor, virtue, glory, public office, conjugal affection and all kinds of justice, from the traffic court to the immortal nine. Go out and make yourself a pot of money and you can buy all the justice you want. Convictions obtained, convictions averted. Lowest rates in years."[136] Like the bridge's roadway, social and legal justice would seem to be available to all; but in reality, they are not. As Esdras states: "we ask for truth / and justice. But this truth's a thing unknown . . . and as for justice, / who has seen it done?"[137]

Although the immigrants beneath the bridge have not seen justice done, they *are* introduced to its agent. The professor's published findings arouse not only Mio but also Judge Gaunt, who presided over Romagna's trial and execution. Now old and infirm, Gaunt is a crucial figure in the drama. A respected Boston Brahmin, he is the only character who comes from the outside world. Equally, he is defined by his strong nativism. Responding to Mio's anger, the judge declares: "there was murder in your sire, / and it's to be expected!"[138] The judge's name calls attention to the withering of the nation's third estate; it is impoverished and malnourished.

Gaunt highlights the play's juxtaposition of "above" and "below." As Mio argues, by "deciding who's to walk above the earth / and who's to lie beneath,"[139] the judge is involved in legal, but also social and economic, segregation. His system of trickle-down justice fails to penetrate society's lower levels. As he says, "a vendor of fish / is not protected as a man might be / who kept a market."[140] Cut off from the promise of the bridge, Anderson's immigrants are denied as well the shelter of the American legal system, which dispenses social justice via economic privilege and nativist sentiment.

Winterset reverses the contention that "for those that lived below, the bridge meant hope."[141] Set in the cold, barren misery of winter, the play depicts a total absence of hope. Although Mio finally reconnects with the world — his thirst for revenge is supplanted by his love for Miriamne — the advance is negated. Gunned down ruthlessly in the final act, neither Mio nor Miriamne attains the heroic transcendence of classic tragedy. Instead the drama's conclusion seems to share the pathetic futility of Horace McCoy's *They Shoot Horses, Don't They?* (1935), published the same year. In both theme and tone, Anderson's imaginative re-creation proclaims the judgment of his generation's intellectuals and of later historians: justice was crucified at the trial of Sacco and Vanzetti.[142] Unlike the effusive optimism that percolates through Israel Zangwill's *The Melting Pot* (1909), no new sermon on the mount emerges from Anderson's drama. In place of a coming "city upon a hill," *Winterset* bespeaks an American Golgotha with no hope of rebirth. Unable to reach the bridge, Mio's American life ends in senseless death.

Spiritual Renewal

Writers seeking to extol the Brooklyn Bridge as an exemplary site of spiritual renewal have most often cited the immigrant painter Joseph Stella. According to numerous critics, Stella's New York canvases, and especially his many renditions of the bridge, represent a dazzling celebration of urban life and "an affirmative vision of the spiritual potential of the new civilization."[143] Yet Stella's paintings are rarely so unambiguous. In context, they remind us more of Henry James than of such high priests of futurism as F. T. Marinetti, Umberto Boccioni, and Giacomo Balla.

In *Brooklyn Bridge* (1919), later reworked as *Old Brooklyn Bridge* (1940), Stella depicted a frenzied urban landscape, with the bridge at its center. The painting's vibrancy, however, verges on chaos and lawlessness. In many respects it replicates the "psychovisual disorientation" that characterized Stella's earlier *Battle of the Lights, Coney Island* (1913).[144] The sense of confusion and disarray are reinforced by Stella's modernist style. His appropriation of futurism's "lines of force" suggests pain, not strength. Modeled on the bridge's cables, these lines are tapered to acute angles and resemble sharpened implements of torture: needles, skewers, and knives. Together they fracture the painting's visual plane, and the result denies the frequent claim that Stella saw the bridge in terms of a cathedral. Against the synthesized unity of a cathedral, the visual plane of Stella's *Brooklyn Bridge* is broken; it resembles not stained but smashed glass.

The splintered enmity of Stella's canvas is reflected in its color scheme. Suffused in a series of cold blues, the image suggests icy hostility, not warmth and affection. The predominance of blue is broken near the bottom of the painting by a roughly triangular mass of bright red. The feature hints at the mouth of a tunnel, yet also a set of barred teeth. Coupled with two white circles directly above, whose outward lines seem to be appropriated from the cartographic symbol for a viewpoint, these teeth form the lower half of a skull. This bloodthirsty shape stands directly before the bridge, as if blocking the way. Positioned between its "eyes" are a red and an amber light. Significantly, there is no green light.[145]

In his later *The Bridge (Brooklyn Bridge)* (1922), the final panel in the monumental *New York Interpreted (The Voice of the City)*, Stella placed the bridge front and center. Its towers fill and dominate the canvas. In the 1919

17. The frenzied urban landscape. Joseph Stella, *Old Brooklyn Bridge,* 1940. Oil on canvas, 193.67 × 73.35 cm (76¼ × 68¼ in.). Museum of Fine Arts Boston, Gift of Susan Morse Hilles in memory of Paul Hellmuth. Photograph © Museum of Fine Arts, Boston.

and 1940 paintings, however, the bridge is remote: small and ill defined. In terms of perspective, the bridge is in the background, swamped by its kinetic surroundings. Surprisingly, there are three towers, not two, and as each rendition retreats further into its surroundings, the image grows fainter. The effect is almost filmic; as if replicating the separate frames of a motion picture or a flipbook, the bridge grows smaller, receding into the distance away from the viewer. Within the landscape of *Brooklyn Bridge,* attainment seems ever postponed. Although the bridge is visually present, it is physically inaccessible.

Sources for Stella's ambivalence can be found in his background. Born in the mountain village of Muro Lucano, Italy, in 1877, Stella emigrated to New York in 1896. He spent the next ten years in and out of art school and on the congested streets of the Lower East Side. His first professional assignment complemented his own experience of the United States. In 1905, *Outlook* magazine commissioned Stella to produce a series of pencil and charcoal sketches of immigrants at Ellis Island. The following year he helped illustrate Ernest Poole's *The Voice of the Street* (1906), a documentary novel about immigrants living in poverty in lower Manhattan.[146]

Stella's first major breakthrough came with a national tragedy. On December 6, 1907, an explosion at a colliery in Monongah, West Virginia, took the lives of almost 350 miners, roughly half the town's working population. Stella traveled with reporter Paul Kellogg to document the tragedy, the worst in U.S. mining history, for the social reform magazine *Charities and the Commons*. Stella was shocked by the misery he found among the townspeople, mainly poor recent immigrants. Kellogg recounts how they were wretched "for the fate met by their brother workers, and for the destitute condition in which so many families had been left. To-day, to-morrow, and God knows when, these laborers are to be grave diggers. That is the new mission imposed upon them."[147]

Through the influence of his brother Antonio, a tireless campaigner for immigrant rights, Stella secured further work with *Charities and the Commons*.[148] During 1908, he worked on the magazine's groundbreaking *Pittsburgh Survey*, producing more than one hundred sketches and drawings of the miserable living and working conditions of poor immigrants. Although Stella was deeply affected by their suffering, his revulsion was tempered by a fascination with modern industrial iconography. For contemporary observers, Pittsburgh was "hell with the lid off"; for Stella, it "was like the stunning realization of some of the most stirring infernal regions sung by Dante."[149] Like the great poet's *Inferno*, however, this hell held an aesthetic dimension. Stella later assessed his Pittsburgh drawings in an autobiographical essay: "In them the artist succeeded to portray the spasm and the pathos of those workers condemned to a very strenuous life, exposed to the constant MENACE OF DEATH. Besides he discovered for himself the aesthetic beauty of Pittsburgh and surroundings as a landscape, beauty lying in the arabesque forms given by the structures of those huge volcano-like steel mills, emerging from the fluctuating waves of smoke and fog, with an eloquent mystery."[150]

Strangely, Stella's Pittsburgh work does not conform with his avowed appreciation of industrial aesthetics. A majority of his sketches were of "Pittsburgh types": workers contemplating their lives, often with heads bowed as

18. "Hell with the lid off": Pittsburgh's industrial blight. Joseph Stella, *Pittsburgh*, 1908. Carnegie Library of Pittsburgh.

if in defeat or scarred by their labors. In others, for example *Painter's Row, Spring 1908* or *Pittsburgh* (both 1908), Stella depicts a landscape of industrial blight. In this time and place, Stella's affirmation is played out in his writing, not his art. Even as his images bespeak the destructive effects of industrialism on the lives of working-class immigrants, his written thoughts suggest the possibility of aesthetic transcendence. This process required Stella to reconfigure the industrial landscape, from social problem to visual sublimity. And to accomplish this feat, he was forced to remove that which defined the city: its working residents. In effect, he vacillated between the reality of steel work ("the constant MENACE OF DEATH") and the drama of steel production ("those huge volcano-like steel mills"). Stella's Pittsburgh work held resolution in abeyance. He would continue his search for spiritual renewal in the industrial landscape of New York.

In his written work, Stella was much less kind to New York City than to Pittsburgh. He described Brooklyn as "that horrible city, an industrial inferno . . . a place to run away from with both feet flying. . . . This is America of the iron fists and steel nerves."[151] Equally, Manhattan was a "Shakespearian nightmare [the] Alma Mater of the derelict of all the world." Its skyline was like a "gigantic jaw of irregular teeth, shiny black like a bulldozer . . . like bandages covering the sky, stifling our breath, life shabby and mean, provincial, sometimes shadowy and hostile like an immense prison where the

ambitions of Europe sicken and languish."[152] In spite of these bleak charac-
terizations, Stella maintained an equivocal relationship with New York. As
the five panels of *New York Interpreted (The Voice of the City)* suggest, his
search for spiritual regeneration was ongoing.

The drama of Stella's quest is played out in "Brooklyn Bridge (a page of
my life)" (1928), a short essay in which he reflects on the bridge's place in his
imagination and his struggle to capture the city through it. For numerous
critics, the essay depicts a journey toward spiritual renewal and peace via the
healing symbolism of the bridge. Unquestionably, Stella begins by depicting
the dark wilderness of an artist's mind and ends with "the luminous dawn of
a NEW ERA." Yet the source of the artist's regeneration is not necessarily the
city or the bridge itself. Stella plainly states that "from the sudden unfolding
of the blue distances of my youth in Italy, a great clarity announced
PEACE."[153] In addition, this regeneration leads Stella toward what he calls
"my new art . . . the new-born tree of my hopes." The manifestation of this new
art is not a gloriously positive image of New York or the Brooklyn Bridge, but
more plausibly his pastoral masterpiece, *The Tree of My Life* (1920).[154] In
these terms, Stella's struggles to depict the chaotic forces surrounding the
bridge are resolved through personal memory. As he recalls the peace and
harmony of his rural childhood, resolution is achieved; the result is a bucolic
"tree of life," not an urban celebration. To express "the luminous dawn of a
NEW ERA," Stella turned his back on New York—the "Alma Mater of the
derelict of all the world"—and returned to the innocent lyricism of his rural
homeland.[155]

The most frequently quoted sections of Stella's Brooklyn Bridge essay in-
volve his religious imagery. Standing on the bridge, Stella felt "deeply
moved, as if on the threshold of a new religion or in the presence of a new
DIVINITY." This experience certainly would seem to point to a positive vision
of a modern "city upon a hill." Yet it might be a mistake to take this "new divinity" entirely at face value, as a sign of affirmative religious fervor. Just
three years earlier in another prose piece about his experiences in Pittsburgh,
Stella used the phrase very differently: "A new divinity, more monstrous and
cruel than the old one, dominates all around and the phantom like black
man of the crane, impossible as Fate . . . subduing the brutal force of the
metal impresses one as the high Priest performing the rites of this new religion."[156] This "new divinity" is radically different from the one imagined by
many of Stella's critics. His "new religion" provides no harmonious code for
living, but instead offers a cruel and brutal energy forged for destruction. In
this light, Stella's Brooklyn Bridge epiphany is more the realization of futility than spiritual renewal. Faced with the "new divinity" of technological

modernism, the value of Stella's rural home is evoked and championed as the rightful source of renewal.

The chronology of Stella's thoughts on New York is revealing. As Thomas Ferraro notes, Stella's career encompassed three distinct phases: "progressive realism, vanguard modernism, and folk classicism."[157] The transition from one phase to the next was accompanied by a period of tension and competition. Stella's vanguard modernism triumphed over his progressive realism, and he never returned to the character sketches of his early artistic life. Equally, his folk classicism existed alongside his vanguard modernism for many years. As *The Tree of My Life* shows, along with *The Virgin* (1922) and *The Apotheosis of the Rose* (1926), Stella's work in the 1920s involved a strenuous effort to resolve his commitment to vanguard modernism. "Brooklyn Bridge (a page of my life)" dramatizes both this struggle and its resolution. It marks the period when Stella turned his back on vanguard modernism and sought renewal and regeneration in folk classicism. By the time he wrote the piece in 1928, his fascination with New York was virtually over. He would return to the city only in the dystopian nightmare of *American Landscape* (1929).[158]

American Landscape is Stella's final artistic statement on the Brooklyn Bridge and New York's urban industrial landscape. A caustic New York, seen through the bridge's cables, appears wracked with decay, and the bridge itself is askew: the lines of its cables flow unnaturally outward as if forcibly pulled in opposite directions. Robert Saunders and Ernest Goldstein have written that the bridge of *American Landscape* "is no longer an open door; it is a closed gate." And they link these ideas to Stella's immigrant status: "although Stella glorified New York City in his painting, he was never at home here. As an immigrant, he felt he was an outsider. This bridge is a barrier to the city. He was outside looking in. Yet, when he was inside, the walls of the city seemed like a prison."[159]

Like Lorca, Stella sought spiritual renewal in the urban industrial landscape of New York. For more than thirty years, he struggled to reach the same conclusions the Spanish writer formulated within ten months. Stella's search for spiritual renewal in the city would always be confounded. After finishing *American Landscape*, he departed for Europe and stayed away from America for much of the next ten years, returning only for important shows and to renew his passport in 1938. He would never make another important artistic statement about industrial New York. After holding the dichotomies of industrialism in balance for so long, Stella opted for flight. Physically, Lorca returned to Spain; emotionally and spiritually, Stella returned to his rural

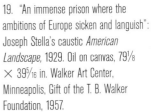

19. "An immense prison where the ambitions of Europe sicken and languish": Joseph Stella's caustic *American Landscape*, 1929. Oil on canvas, 79⅛ × 39⁵⁄₁₆ in. Walker Art Center, Minneapolis, Gift of the T. B. Walker Foundation, 1957.

homeland in southern Italy. Neither found spiritual renewal in the Brooklyn Bridge or in the new industrial "city upon a hill" it heralded.

Failure

John Winthrop's model was haunted by the potential for failure. Unless the Bay Colony could achieve comprehensive unity under the auspices of human brotherhood, it would never become the "city upon a hill." Although Winthrop could scarcely have anticipated the ethnic plurality that would later define the country, his prophecy speaks directly to modern America. Around the turn of the century, nativism atomized the social landscape, defining its various elements as entirely separate and distinctly unequal. Yet even within the immigrant experience of racial prejudice, few ethnic groups met with the hatred poured upon arrivals from Far East Asia.

Yun Gee was born in the Chinese province of Guangdong in 1906. He was a talented and ambitious child, and in 1921 the fifteen-year-old Gee followed his father, Gee Quong On, a merchant and entrepreneur, to San Francisco to further his education. Gee would later prove himself an accomplished musician, teacher, poet, and dancer, but his true vocation was painting. Gee held his first solo exhibition at the Modern Gallery in downtown San Francisco in 1926, and later in that decade his art was shown at the esteemed Salon des Indépendants in Paris. He showcased several paintings in the prestigious exhibition "Murals by American Painters and Photographers," which inaugurated the new location of New York's Museum of Modern Art in 1932. During all of this time, Gee lived through what Anthony Lee describes as "perhaps the most sustained and racist ghettoizing of any Chinese American citizenry" in the nation's history.[160]

Even well before the Chinese Exclusion Act of 1882, severe racial aggression was a daily issue for Chinese Americans. In 1924, three years after Gee's arrival, U.S. race relations were made significantly worse with the passage of the Johnson-Reed Immigration Reduction Act. Described as "the Nordic victory,"[161] the law ended Asian immigration entirely, reduced total immigration to 150,000 people, and reserved more than 50 percent of acceptances for Irish, British, and German applicants. Such legislation not only institutionalized racial intolerance, it legitimized local practice. For Gee's generation, the Chinatowns throughout the nation were ghettoes in the true sense of the word. Effectively, they were sealed-off communities, kept in check by social and economic segregation and heavily policed. For most Chinese Americans, to venture outside of Chinatown was to experience the full force of racial hatred and intolerance; spurious arrest, verbal abuse, and physical intimidation made paranoia, fear, and emotional distress constant companions.[162]

Despite San Francisco's racial landscape, Gee enjoyed an active life both inside and outside of its Chinatown. He studied at the California School of Fine Arts (now the San Francisco Art Institute) from 1924 to 1926, helped establish the Modern Gallery in 1926, and later founded the Chinese Revolutionary Artists' Club. Through the painter Otis Oldfield, his teacher at the School of Fine Arts and ultimately a lifelong friend, Gee was introduced to San Francisco's radical avant-garde: poet Kenneth Rexroth, muralist Victor Arnautoff, painter John Ferren, and sculptor Ruth Cravath, among others. Through the art world, Gee was able to escape San Francisco's racial prejudice, though by no means entirely. As an artist, he was accepted and praised; as an individual on the streets, he was a victim of the sort of intolerance experienced by his fellow immigrants. In San Francisco, Gee found himself suspended between two worlds, neither fully ghettoized nor wholly accepted by the wider society. Clearly, Gee achieved success in San Francisco, but when he left the city in 1927, something must have lingered in his psyche. Gee returned to San Francisco only once before his death in 1963, to attend his father's funeral in 1958.

Gee traveled to Paris in 1927 under the patronage of Prince and Princess Achille Murat. Intending to further his artistic education, he was drawn to the city's vibrant art scene and its rich tradition. Gee enjoyed great acclaim there, exhibiting twice at groups shows at the Salon des Indépendants and holding a solo show at the Galerie Bernheim-Jeune. In 1930, he married the poet Princess Paule de Reuss. The union was a tempestuous one, however, and Gee's unhappiness was compounded when the princess's family promptly disowned her. Shortly after his marriage, Gee left Paris and his wife for New York. Yet it was more than Gee's difficulties with the de Reuss family that hastened his return to the United States: the Great Depression crippled the world art market and forced many collectors and patrons to close their checkbooks. Moreover, Paris was hardly the egalitarian utopia Gee had hoped it would be. Rising anti-Chinese sentiment in Paris, it seems, made everyday life painful. "Paris is a liberal city," he later stated, "only that liberality is limited to certain nations among which are not the United States and China."[163]

Gee settled in New York, where he resided for most of the rest of his life (he spent three years in Paris in the late 1930s). Although he enjoyed two solo shows—at the In Tempo Gallery (1931) and at the Balzac Gallery (1932)—and was able to place nine paintings in the Brooklyn Museum's

"Paintings, Sculpture and Drawings by American and Foreign Artists" exhibition (1931), Gee did not prosper. Social conditions in New York's Chinatown were, it seems, far worse than anything he had experienced in San Francisco or Paris. In his poem "Sensation," written five years after his return to America, Gee describes the physical sensibility of the racialized individual in New York. On the subway, in an elevator, on a bus, in a train—in fact, whenever he is on the move around the city—Gee is faced with alarming, active hatred. Eventually, unable to understand the unprovoked animosity of a "man who bares his teeth to me," Gee decides he must have "an unclean expression" and examines himself in the mirror. The hatred of others has tapped a well of anger within Gee and prompted an emotional reciprocation: in the mirror, he finds that his own teeth are bared.[164]

Anger dominated Gee's reaction to New York and to the city's art world. Despite small successes, Gee felt he was judged not on "the subject of my work, but [by] my race." Purportedly, his work was turned down by the Whitney Museum because its collections already included "one Oriental." As Gee later stated with some bitterness, "I was no longer an Artist. I was an Oriental from China Town, and I suppose the interpretation of such a person was that he was only a Launderer or a Restaurateur."[165] After just two years in New York, Gee was suffering from depression and drinking heavily; he also painted his most significant extant work, *Wheels: Industrial New York* (1932).

Bathed in garish, apocalyptic sunlight, the milieu of *Wheels* is feverish and ominous. Thematically, Gee incorporates synchronist and futurist techniques to produce an abjuration—not an affirmation—of the modern urban environment. Visually, the painting depicts two worlds: the manmade and the human. The skyline dominates the painting's upper half, and in the foreground a group of polo players rides in a circle. Between these two realms are a smattering of derelict buildings and a bizarre image of the Brooklyn Bridge. More metaphor than literal illustration, the bridge seems to synthesize both worlds. Perhaps a visual reference to the "Chinese families who aided in making America grow"[166]—who surrendered their bodies to the idea of American progress—the bridge's towers seem composed of two giant femur bones, while the cables appear to be ligaments and sinew.

The painting's most evocative feature is its foreground. Clustered in a circle, the polo players seem to be in constant motion. The Sisyphean connotations of incessant repetition are obvious—a theme reinforced by the painting's title—yet a sense of benign futility is missing. The riders seem frenzied; they are deformed, brutal, and menacing. Their polo mallets look like weapons, and their helmets seem forged for battle, not play. As Lewis

20. The apocalyptic city. Yun Gee, *Wheels: Industrial New York*, 1932. Private collection, USA. Photo credit: Kevin Ryan.

Kachur notes, the riders seem "more like horsemen of the apocalypse than sportsmen of leisure."[167] Yet it would be wrong to lose sight of Gee's sporting analogy. Drawing upon his Asian background, Gee would have viewed the nature of sports as being more "ritual" than "record."[168] As such, the activity depicted in the foreground becomes intrinsic to the social world pictured to its rear. Although initially the painting may seem to contemplate two separate worlds, they are indeed one. Gee's "industrial New York" is governed by the ritual gamesmanship of perpetual, cyclical violence.[169]

In Gee's art, autobiography is never far from the surface. As Anthony Lee notes: "For Gee, the experience of being a racialized person in a profoundly unequal society was, on a daily basis, a constant companion for him, a small trauma that accompanied him everywhere he went, a chain of traumas that accrued with each passing day, and a gigantic trauma out of which he fashioned his life. The constant negotiation with the pain and loss brought about simply because he was Chinese American was not something easily portioned. Instead it organized his life and work."[170] The image of the modern city found in *Wheels* is certainly emblematic of Gee's American experience. Upon closer inspection of the painting, we see just below the bridge's roadway a small, seemingly Asian male with his arms extended upward. Although for one critic this figure is "enigmatically suspended in mid-air,"[171] it would seem more plausible that he is jumping from the span. Faced with the daily experience of ritualized violence, the figure seems to have reached the very ends of desperation, leaving only suicide as a means of escape.[172]

Located just a short walk from New York's Chinatown, the Brooklyn Bridge clearly spoke to the painter. Yet its message was not that predicted by the *Eagle* or argued by Prochnaw or Siegelman. It did not inspire Gee with new hopes. Instead, the bridge confirmed that for Asian American immigrants the gap between citizenship and acceptance was large indeed, that it was easier, perhaps, to bridge the East River than it was to span national ethnic divides.

Destruction

Born in Italy in 1906, the artist O. Louis Guglielmi emigrated to New York with his family in 1914 and lived in East Harlem until he began to work for the federal Works Progress Administration (WPA) in the early 1930s. As an Italian American, Guglielmi was disturbed by the prejudice that had condemned Sacco and Vanzetti. In *Memory of Charles River* (1936) he painted the two anarchists with their heads mounted on a plaque as if they were the spoils of a big-game hunt. In *A Muted Street* (1942), Guglielmi blended elements of the Ashcan School with the sensibilities of Edward Hopper. In the shadow of the Brooklyn Bridge, a young woman sits on the ledge of an upper-floor window. Yet the scene below is not the chaotic orgy of life found in William Glackens's *Patriots in the Making* (1907) or George Bellows's *Cliff Dwellers* (1913). Instead, Guglielmi's street is more akin to those created by Hopper. As much a soundscape as a cityscape, it is muted, devoid of life. The young woman's relationship to life also seems tenuous: she seems to ignore the scene below while preparing to jump.

Many of Guglielmi's cityscapes feature the Brooklyn Bridge, and their mood and tone are often bleak. In *South Street Stoop* (1935), according to John Baker, "all the strength and elegance of Brooklyn Bridge . . . cannot lessen the poverty and despair that exist in its shadow." In *Wedding in South Street* (1936), melancholy, not festivity, dominates the canvas. Storm clouds

21. "A hundred dead, a thousand violated bodies. Valencia, Madrid, Barcelona, Guernica. Yesterday Toledo, the Prado—tomorrow, Chartres—New York—Brooklyn Bridge is by the process of mental geography a huge mass of stone, twisted girders and limp cable." O. Louis Guglielmi, *Mental Geography*, 1938. From the collection of Barney A. Ebsworth.

gather behind the bridge, and the wedding party stands quietly hunched over. For Baker, the mood seems "more appropriate to a funeral than a wedding."[173]

The Great Depression provided the backdrop for much of Guglielmi's work, yet his most radical depiction of the Brooklyn Bridge came as a response to the Spanish Civil War. *Mental Geography* (1938) depicts the bridge in ruins, its cables twisted and torn loose. The walkway has been violently ruptured; the tops of both towers are smashed. A woman sits slumped on a girder with a bomb protruding from her back. The sky is a haunting, unnatural purple. When first shown, the painting was accompanied by a caption written by Guglielmi: "Headlines, eloquent loudspeakers of fascist destruction scream out the bombing of another city, another moment of human achievement, a debris of mutilation. A hundred dead, a thousand violated bodies. Valencia, Madrid, Barcelona, Guernica. Yesterday Toledo, the Prado—tomorrow, Chartres—New York—Brooklyn Bridge is by the process

87

of mental geography a huge mass of stone, twisted girders and limp cable." [174] In 1943, he commented further: "I pictured the destruction after an air raid; the towers bomb-pocked, the cables a mass of twisted debris. I meant to say that an era had ended and that the rivers of Spain flowed to the Atlantic and mixed with our waters as well." [175]

Clearly, Guglielmi is warning of the dangers posed by fascist aggression — and the threat is by no means confined to Europe. The image of Spain's rivers mixing with those of the United States implies a reciprocal flow of national ideals. [176] Undoubtedly, Guglielmi feared that dictatorial nationalism would pollute the waters of American democracy. And for an immigrant, this fear was natural. The painter was eighteen years of age when President Calvin Coolidge signed the Johnson-Reed Immigration Act, legislation that fundamentally challenged America's image as a tolerant, safe haven. Fearing for the future of the melting pot, Guglielmi saw a trans-Atlantic trend, with xenophobic nationalism outpacing the ideal of ethnic pluralism. Indeed, for Guglielmi and other immigrants, "an era had ended." The intolerance of nativism had seemingly replaced the tolerance of difference. With America's legacy of liberty and equality in peril, Guglielmi articulated his social and ethnic fears through the visualization of a coming apocalypse. And by using the image of the Brooklyn Bridge, Guglielmi delivered his warning to America in its own cultural language. [177]

Conclusions

H. G. Wells, among many others, failed to understand that humanity tends to invent "symbols in which to invest passion and authority, then forgets that symbols are inventions," as Joyce Carol Oates described the process. [178] Against Wells, many observers chose to judge the Brooklyn Bridge on the society it heralded, not on the scale of its technological achievement or its abstract symbolism. Even as icons *become* symbols, icons themselves are essentially blank. Yet to ignore the meanings that have been inscribed upon them presents a further trap. The true history of these social symbolic phenomena more fittingly lies somewhere between projection and reception. Where one can read the bridge as an exemplary national icon — fusing social progress and sublime technology — it also supports a profoundly antithetical vision. It is within this polarity that the structure is best understood.

Few people have been able to stand on the bridge and see as the painter Max Weber did: "I was on the old Bridge . . . and thought of this pile throbbing, boiling, seething, as a pile after destruction, and this noise and dynamic force created in me a peace the opposite of itself. Two worlds I had before me . . . I lived in both!" [179] Weber's dual response is perhaps the most exact. Waldo Frank famously declared that "we go forth all to seek America. And in the seeking we create her."[180] Just as America has sought and (re)created itself, each new wave of arrivals has done the same. The "creations" so revealed have often failed to confirm the promise projected at the Brooklyn Bridge's opening. Where some predicted a new industrial city upon a hill, others discovered a nativist Babylon. Even within America's most sublime icons there lurks an eminently negative judgment.

3 The View of the Bridge
Perspective, Context, and the Urban Observer

Above the congestion and pollution of their cores American cities began to present soaring skylines. . . . They were the result of chance and of competition for rentals or prestige waged under the most lenient conditions of *laissez faire* and with almost no concern for anything other than economic gain. Yet they were not always ugly. From the Brooklyn Bridge the tip of Manhattan Island began to take on its handsome aspiring shape. . . . But whatever the promise from afar, as soon as one went ashore into the deepening canyons, the appearances were less amiable. . . . Vast areas of the city with the shining front towers were slums where immigrants managed to cling to a little of their traditional culture but which, all too often, were . . . foci of infection threatening the whole city with disease and crime.

— John Burchard and Albert Bush-Brown, *The Architecture of America*, 1961

A striking landscape is the skeleton upon which many . . . races erect their socially important myths.

— Kevin Lynch, *The Image of the City*, 1960

Brooklyn Bridge belongs first to the eye.

— Alan Trachtenberg, *Brooklyn Bridge*, 1965

In a 1913 interview with Djuna Barnes, fifth-generation Brooklynite Joseph Dowling captured the feel of New York in the late nineteenth century: "And the changes that I've seen. . . . Why, I helped build the Brooklyn Bridge. I stood under the bed of the East River and bossed men — foreman with human lives under me — and Lord, how the city grew when she started. I'd go down it seemed between tea and dinner, and when I came back up they had built a block."[1] Disorientation was by no means an experience unique to the newest arrivals in New York at the turn of the century. Even for longtime residents, a sense of dislocation was a constant feature of life in the emerging metropolis. In the post–Civil War era, New York was defined by massive development and protean change.

As the city marched inexorably uptown, buildings were raised, then razed, and then raised again. Anticipated by the Brooklyn Bridge — principally through height and the use of steel — physical construction in the city erupted. The development of the steel-framed skyscraper facilitated New

York's "creative destruction," a confusing process of physical revolution that altered the city's landscape both daily and forever.[2] During Dowling's youth, New York possessed no legitimate skyscrapers—when completed, the towers of the Brooklyn Bridge were the tallest structures in North America—yet by the time of his interview forty years later, Manhattan was home to more than four hundred skyscrapers, and the East River had been bridged three more times. This transformation was mirrored by the city's population, which more than tripled between 1870 and 1913. By 1913, for example, the city's Jewish residents outnumbered the population of the entire city in 1870. Nor was this explosive growth confined to one ethnic or racial group: people from all over the globe poured into New York.[3]

Amid this bewildering change, a revolutionary cultural medium emerged. The documentary history of modern American cities owes much to photography. Moreover, the new technologies of photography and structural engineering evolved in tandem. Both sought to subject the American landscape to the work of industrial culture; both turned on questions of spatial organization and visual representation. Instinctively, the new pictorial form found a natural affinity with the new structural phenomena being showcased across the nation. As photography bespoke the influence of new technology—new ways of seeing and experiencing—its practitioners rushed to the nation's burgeoning cities. From Albert S. Southworth and Josiah J. Hawes's early daguerreotypes of Boston, through George R. Fardon and Eadweard Muybridge's San Francisco panoramas and Robert Newell and John Moran's Philadelphia cityscapes, to the urban images of Henry R. Koopman in Chicago and George François Mugnier in New Orleans, photographers strove to capture and present the new modern environment. Nowhere was this mission more keenly felt than in New York City. As the city marched uptown, as buildings and neighborhoods were created and demolished at a staggering rate, the camera was there to document every stage and each new detail.[4]

Photographers sought to document the city in all its physical aspects; yet they also attempted to assimilate and accustom residents to the new city rising around them. This sense of civic brokerage was mirrored in the world of literature. Kin to the tourist guidebook and the immigrant press, a new American literature emerged in the last half of the nineteenth century. With a reportorial tone, it sought to keep readers in step with the rapid changes in landscape and urban relations, to provide a legible image of the new, modern city. Exemplified by such diverse works as Horatio Alger's *Ragged Dick; or, Street Life in New York* (1868), James McCabe's *Lights and Shadows of New York Life* (1872), Stephen Crane's New York City sketches (1892–1896), and Hutchins Hapgood's *Types from City Streets* (1910)—not to mention the

mass of articles that appeared almost daily in New York's printed media—
this new urban literature sought to provide order and stability through cate-
gorization and explanation: in short, to make sense of an increasingly fragmented urban milieu.[5]

Despite their obvious differences, photographic and literary accounts of
late-nineteenth-century and turn-of-the-century New York can be seen as
first-person narratives. Both types of representation sought to relate the cultural city of personal experience to the spatial, architectural city of visible
perception. In essence, they relied on a similar cultural agent: the individual
consciousness of a single urban observer. This character—at once seeing,
recording, processing, and describing—dominates the visual and conceptual history of both New York City and the Brooklyn Bridge. It is only by analyzing the perspectives and concerns of these individuals that we can begin
to understand how the bridge has been interpreted and presented as part of
an evolving urban, cultural, and ideological landscape—how, in fact, the
view of, and from, the bridge has been formulated and developed.

The Birth of the View

The most important years in the construction of the Brooklyn Bridge
were 1876 to 1878. Early in the nation's centennial year, the two great towers were completed, and on August 25, E. F. Farrington took the historic first
trip across the East River in a boatswain's chair. After seven years of toil, a
man was finally able to pass from Brooklyn to New York *above* the East River.
Both literally and symbolically, the focus of work had shifted from the un-
seen, hellish operation below the East River to the visible, *evident* work of
linking the towers. Farrington's ride captured the imagination of New Yorkers. They turned up for the celebration in large numbers and cheered each
leg of Farrington's journey. At last, the public could begin to see the work taking shape above their heads and could envision a successful completion.[6]

Soon thereafter, however, problems beset the bridge. The wire spinning
that seemed so promising became the focus of a vicious public battle over
specification and supply. A number of fatal accidents further alarmed the
public, and the unease became palpable in June 1878 when a cable strand
broke loose from the New York anchorage. Dragging a massive cast-iron anchorage shoe, the strand flew five hundred feet to the base of the New York
tower before taking off again over the tower and plunging into the East River,
narrowly missing a passing ferry. Disconcerted by these events, City Comp-
troller John Kelly quickly began to withhold money from the project.
Throughout, a debate raged about the mental fitness and physical health of
the bridge's chief engineer, Washington Roebling, an invalid and a recluse

since suffering a devastating attack of the bends four years earlier. The mood was captured in the *Brooklyn Union*: "It has become the deepest of mysteries . . . where the chief engineer is, and what is his condition. For aught any public act or appearance of his may indicate, he may have been dead or buried for six months. He is surrounded by clouds impenetrable. . . . We declare the great East River Bridge in peril, because it has no head, because its wires of control run into somebody's closely guarded sickroom."[7]

Worse news greeted the bridge in 1878. Unbeknown to the engineers, substandard wire rope had been woven into the main cables. This massive deceit rocked public confidence: not only had the bridge been defrauded, but its structural integrity was now in doubt. With costs far exceeding the original estimate, a fresh start was impossible. To compensate, it was decided that an additional 150 wires would be woven into each cable. Although this decision was a sound engineering solution, the faulty wire continued to haunt public opinion.

The cable spinning was completed on October 5, 1878, and, in contrast to Farrington's ride across the river two years earlier, the "event was marked by no demonstrations."[8] The excitement so evident at the beginning of the cable spinning had dissipated, leaving only a residue of public consternation. Anxiety was compounded in November, when work on the bridge was halted indefinitely because Kelly refused to honor Manhattan's financial obligation. For all practical purposes, the bridge concern was bankrupt. With construction at a standstill and amid continuing doubts about the bridge's structural safety, leadership, and financial future, New Yorkers began to regard the bridge with disparagement.

However bleak this period may seem, numerous cultural documents created at the time show the bridge in a different light. Many stressed the venture's heroic achievement, while others imbued the bridge with an exemplary national message. To the degree that these documents originated and illustrated ways of looking at (and specifically from) the bridge, two are especially significant: an image, Joshua H. Beal's five-plate photographic panorama from the Brooklyn tower (1876); and a magazine article, *Appletons' Journal*'s "Up Among the Spiders; or, How the Great Bridge Is Built" (1878). Their legacy in the continuing life of the bridge would prove to have a greater impact than the construction's mundane historical details.

In early 1876, Joshua Beal ascended the recently completed Brooklyn tower, set up his camera, and began to photograph lower Manhattan. The resultant panorama was a seminal event in the representation of both the Brooklyn Bridge and New York City.[9] Although lithographs featuring bird's-eye views had proliferated for almost thirty years, Beal's image had a unique

22. Building the monumental city. Joshua Beal, "Panoramic View of NYC, Lower Manhattan from Brooklyn Bridge Tower," 1876. Collection of The New-York Historical Society, neg. # 32185.

vantage point and medium.[10] In contrast to the meticulous photographic record of the bridge's early construction, Beal's image was the first to focus on the bridge in relation to the city and its evolving landscape.[11] Equally important was the medium itself. Although popular, the lithographs that dominated earlier New York views compared poorly with photographs. Artistically rendered by hand, their lack of authenticity was continually reinforced by their obviously unattainable vantage point. Photographs, on the other hand, offered firsthand testimony; they were the product of an objective machine and were understood, as Peter Hales points out, "as empirical truth."[12]

This "empirical truth" was presented through what Hales has termed "grand style urban photography." Central to this new approach was the context of rapid and bewildering change. As Hales notes, the mediating influence of photography became

more crucial with the Civil War and post–Civil War transformation of the orderly, comprehensible "walking city" into the sprawling, uncontrolled urban-industrial matrix. Here the commodity of growth so prized by earlier urban entrepreneurs and their visual messengers became not a promise of future urban grandeur but a threat to order, sense, and the civilized ideal as well. In this ambiguous area, the stylistic developments of urban photography from earlier eras gained new force and relevance. Photographers became deeply involved in the process of finding order in the urban chaos, of imposing or creating that order if they had to.[13]

Like the speakers at the opening of the Brooklyn Bridge, grand-style urban photographers were civic boosters. They promoted order and amelioration amid the chaos of massive redevelopment. In essence, they lent "empirical truth" to the message delivered through print and rhetoric at the bridge's opening.

Beal's attempt to produce a grand-style urban vision was challenged by three forces. First, the primitive technology of the camera made it impossible for him to capture the entirety of Manhattan; his panorama ends at Pier 39, leaving the image of the city incomplete. Second, the smog that hung over the city tended to obscure details rather than idealize them. And third, the sheer chaos of the downtown urban matrix failed to suggest purpose and order.[14]

Yet it is also important to notice the context of Beal's photographic series. All along the East River are myriad wharves and shipping vessels, which illustrate not only the importance of commerce, but also its scale. This activity is mirrored in the city itself. In common with previous attempts to depict New York (and other American cities), Beal's panorama—ending at around Houston Street—stresses Manhattan's business district.[15] Interspersed through this downtown area are a number of prominent new buildings, whose upward reach resonates with the aspirations of their builders. Both Trinity Church and St. Paul's Chapel represent the culture and values of the Episcopalian Church, the preferred religious denomination of New York's elite and business classes. The Central Post Office and the Western Union Telegraph Building connote the networks of communication so important to westward expansion. Finally, along with the Western Union Telegraph Building, the Tribune Building bespeaks the power and importance of new American industries. Although not yet fully ordered, the city in Beal's panorama is defined by the growth of civilization, culture, and commerce.

An assessment of the visual trajectory that led up to Beal's series helps us to gauge how grand-style urban photography validated claims made in other media. More than thirty bird's-eye panoramas appeared in New York in the 1870s, and the vast majority of them featured the Brooklyn Bridge completed and in operation.[16] *Harper's Monthly,* for example, printed a lithograph depicting the completed bridge a full thirteen years before it was opened. Again, the image focused on Manhattan's business enclaves,

23. Expansive optimism. *Harper's Weekly*, November 19, 1870. Courtesy of the Library of Congress.

24. Exaggerating the size of the bridge. *New York and Brooklyn, with Jersey City and Hoboken Water Front*, 1877. Published by Currier and Ives. Courtesy of the Library of Congress.

especially Printing House Square, and the city surrounding the bridge. Commenting on the print, John Kouwenhoven notes that the bridge, the orderly streets, and the commercial activity of the harbor are intrinsically linked in an image of "expansive optimism."[17]

Similar images were used on the covers or as frontispieces to guidebooks, including James McCabe Jr.'s *Lights and Shadows of New York Life* (1872), *McCoy's Centennial Illustrated, How to See New York and Its Environs* (1876), and L. P. Brockett's *Handbook of the United States, and Guide to Emigration* (1879). In the 1870s Currier and Ives produced numerous prints that further emphasized the commercial life of the city and vastly exaggerated the size of the bridge.[18] Following this path, Beal's panorama confirmed the era's confident ambition. What the earlier views projected, Beal confirmed.

Beal's series bares comparison with John Gast's 1872 painting *American Progress*. According to Merritt Roe Smith, this portrayal of America's heroic westward march "associates progress with technological change [and] clearly conveys the dominant culture's attitude toward . . . improvement."[19] The painting depicts a large swath of the American continent, from the Eastern Seaboard, across the Great Plains, and to the Rocky Mountains. Under instruction from his patron, George Crofutt, Gast made the railroad and the telegraph his principal images of technology. Pictured in the upper right-hand corner is New York, the source of these new technologies. The sun shines over the city, which is surrounded by commercial shipping and dominated by a large suspension bridge located at just the point where the construction of the Brooklyn Bridge was taking place.[20] Both the telegraph and the railroad predate the bridge, of course; yet within Gast's painting these forces — and by implication, the forces directing westward expansion and America's sense of its own Manifest Destiny — seem to flow out of the East, the main icon of which is the Brooklyn Bridge.[21]

The idea that America is defined by home-grown technological innovation featured prominently in the opening-day speeches for the Brooklyn Bridge and constitutes the main focus of Beal's panorama. Even if the details of Manhattan are somewhat obscured, the bridge itself takes over the foreground in perfect focus. It towers over the city, with its topmost point extending into the horizon over New Jersey. Everything about the bridge bespeaks new monumentality, and the image carries an implicit message: the bridge is *the* visual symbol of the emerging, commercial city. Furthermore, Beal presents, as empirical truth, an important cultural trend. By juxtaposing the new bridge with the older city, his panorama highlights a developing civic history. In its technological iconography, Beal's photography is prophetic. The panorama provides visual evidence to confirm the larger narrative of

25. The Brooklyn Bridge and America's heroic westward march. John Gast, *American Progress*, 1872. Oil on canvas, 17¾ × 21½ in. Museum of the American West Collection, Autry National Center, Los Angeles.

26. Forty years before the poet Benjamin Low contemplated it, William Louis Sonntag Jr. painted "That blue . . . track-way to the West./In steel and stone." Sonntag, *Brooklyn Bridge*, 1895. Watercolor with tempera. Museum of the City of New York, 54.63.

American progress. It realizes earlier predictions while mapping out "the shape of things to come."

Beal's bridge is a key element in the evolving history of the urban self-image. Grand-style urban photographers understood the city as a series of monumental structures; they characterized it through its façades, not its faces.[22] As in much of the urban photography of this period, Beal's city is eerily silent and still; there is no evidence of workers, nor any tools, materials, or refuse.[23] As would happen on the opening day, labor is factored out of the picture. The bridge is offered as an example of New York's technological and commercial progress, and, inferentially, of the power of those who direct it. By denying the human context and prioritizing the built environment, Beal established an important legacy for future images of the Brooklyn Bridge.

In the bridge's centennial year, a former president of the American Society of Civil Engineers observed that "the bridge gave nineteenth-century Americans a new perspective on themselves and the world."[24] From his position atop the Brooklyn tower, Beal certainly provided New Yorkers with a new perspective on their city, yet he adopted longstanding conventions as he did so. Best illustrated through nineteenth-century American landscape painting, this perspective has been analyzed extensively by Albert Boime. Like Hales's "grand style," Boime's "magisterial gaze" refers to a specific way of seeing, a metonymic image that encapsulates the social and political character of the era. It is distinguished by an Olympian perspective — an elevated viewpoint and a downward sight line — that fosters the ideas of mastery, possession, and dominance. The magisterial gaze is both personal and distinctly ideological. By embracing "past, present and future, synchronically plotting the course of empire," it is commensurate with the national ideology of Manifest Destiny. These landscapes are encoded with elite interpretations of American progress as defined by conquest and acquisition. In short, such landscapes are replete with the values of America's dominant classes.[25]

In its accentuation of the monumental products of American technological growth and, by implication, "the shape of things to come," Beal's photographic panorama can certainly be read as an urban "magisterial gaze." Yet the full extent of this phenomenon is best illustrated through the second important document noted earlier. In January 1878, *Appletons' Journal* published Charles Carroll's "Up Among the Spiders; or, How the Great Bridge Is Built." The article describes a visit to the Brooklyn construction site and a journey up and over the towers to New York on a wooden-slated footbridge. The piece begins with a paean to the merits of wire rope: "When the great bridge is finished, the word ['wire'] will be lifted into a new and unhoped-for glory. . . . All the momentous interests, the great throng of life and wealth . . .

PUBLISHED BY CURRIER & IVES
Red Hook Point   Staten Isd.   Ellis Isd. Bedloes Isd.   East River   Hudson River   Jersey City   116 NASSAU ST. NEW YORK.
Governors Isd.   Hoboken.

THE HARBOR OF NEW YORK.
From the Brooklyn Bridge Tower - Looking south-west.

27. From the bridge tower: the magisterial gaze. *The Harbor of New York*, n.d. Published by Currier and Ives. Museum of the City of New York, The Gerald LeVino Collection, 57.100.24.

will depend utterly on it." Not only are "life" and "wealth" linked, they are also tied to both technological progress and the country's "momentous interests."[26] Carroll's most interesting sentiments, however, are expressed from the height of the towers.

Upon ascending, Carroll begins to assert his domination and superiority over the scene. Looking down upon a ferry struggling against the tide, he remarks, "what does that insane ferry-boat mean by sidling off, crab-fashion, in that imbecile way? . . . Must I preach you a lesson of charity here in mid-ether?" Upon reaching the New York tower, Carroll's "magisterial gaze" is confirmed:

When I was a college senior, I remember I was restless till I ventilated in an essay my notion that the studious thinkers and observers really knew more about things, in a higher sense, than the fellows in the tug and thick of the fight. The man who can give the best description of a battle is the one who sits in the tower with his map and field-glass, not the private, musket in hand, amid the smoke and the carnage. And so, when you wish to give a clear account of any complex matter, social, political, or otherwise, where relations are more important than detail, if you can manage to lift yourself . . . to a good focal position, the better for you—and your hearer.[27]

This assessment—at once "social" and "political"—prioritizes the privileged over the common. Those at the top of society are imbued with a greater understanding of social relations. The importance of "relations" here is contained within the negation of "detail." In the context of the article, detail is represented by the "*heads*" and the "dots of white faces" seen swarming around the East River shore. Conversely, "relations" are those dynamic social forces of energy and power that order the urban scene. They speak of commerce and progress, not the city's common, human element. With annoyance, Carroll descends: "we come down upon the squalid tenements of Front Street, and catch involuntary glimpses of the dirt and misery which exude from its attic windows and alleys." This barely concealed distaste for New York's "details" prompts a wish that ascent above the mundane city will be possible again one day.[28]

Beal and Carroll both worked in the tradition of Hales's "grand style" and Boime's "magisterial gaze." Furthermore, both illuminate the subtitle appended to Carroll's article. Visually and symbolically, they are concerned with "how the great bridge is built." Both are ideologically framed to construct a specific image and an implicit story. Although presented within a documentary framework, both are selective in context. They seek to prioritize the monumental façade of the modernizing city at the cost of the human context of work, conflict, housing, and poverty. They mark an important stage in the commercial and technological course of empire.

The Evolving Grand Style

Beal's perspective was fashionable among subsequent photographers. Just seven years after Beal climbed the Brooklyn tower, an anonymous photographer retraced his steps; the Manhattan of 1883, however, is noticeably changed. The New York tower no longer dominates the panorama; its status is contested by a number of buildings to the rear.[29] Likewise, an Otis Elevator Company photograph of lower Manhattan, taken in 1908 from the Brooklyn tower, highlights the city's continuing radical transformation, but with one new detail.[30] As Beal's panorama seemed to foretell, and as the 1883 image showed in progress, the city's monumental size had caught up with that of the Brooklyn Bridge by 1908. At 268 feet, the bridge's New York tower dominates Beal's scene. The spire of Trinity Church, a mere two feet lower, is also visible. By 1908, Trinity is conspicuous by its absence, and a backdrop of new, tall buildings—epitomized by the 612-foot Singer Building just a block north of Trinity—looms over the bridge itself. The Otis photograph provides visual confirmation of an important new phenomenon: New York had developed a skyline.

The iconography of New York was transformed to an unprecedented degree by the formation, rise, and scope of its skyline. The city's building codes were stripped of height restrictions by 1892, and in 1896 the *New York Journal* published Charles Graham's *Skyline of New York* as a pictorial supplement. A year later the architectural critic Montgomery Schuyler wrote the first critical treatment of the phenomenon for *Harper's Weekly*.[31] Accompanying Schuyler's article was an illustration in which R. H. Robertson's thirty-story Park Row Building towers over all surrounding buildings, including the once dominant Brooklyn Bridge. A scant sixteen years later, Cass Gilbert's sixty-story Woolworth Building made a minnow of Robertson's former giant. In a skyline view of 1915, the Park Row Building is barely visible behind the middling height of the Western Union Building.[32] The rise of the skyscraper continued unabated until 1931. By that time, the Empire State Building—three times the height of the once impressive Park Row Building—dominated the skyline.

The evolution of New York's skyline had profoundly ideological implications. The new tall buildings represented anything but the "tombstones of capitalism," as painter George Ault described them during the Jazz Age.[33] By the 1920s, skyscrapers and the skyline were New York's preeminent cultural icons, and the degree to which they defined the city itself was remarkable. The products of both corporate and speculative capitalism, skyscrapers characterized, displayed, and celebrated a particular cultural landscape. At the heart of this landscape was an image of the city that prioritized technological progress, commercial achievement, and financial dominance. The skyline's increasing authority as New York's defining image illustrated and legitimized the social vision of the city's controlling classes.[34] Skyscrapers stood not as tombstones, but as ubiquitous and distinct logos, the successful trademark of the capitalist brand. As Schuyler observed, the city's skyline "is not an architectural vision, but it does, most tremendously, 'look like business.'"[35]

Aesthetics are only a minor concern in skyscraper design. Significantly more important are economic height, rentable space, and investment return. As structures, they are designed not from the outside in, but from the inside out. Within this framework, as Carol Willis emphasizes, they are not simply "*representations* of big business," but function as "*businesses themselves.*" Not merely the *visible symbols* of capitalist America, they are its *visible enactment.*[36]

Photographers of the early twentieth century were faced with a conundrum: how to reconcile their liberal politics and artistic idealism with the emergence of what the architect Sheldon Cheney called "the perfect business-machine."[37] Quite simply, many chose to ignore the clash. Although the skyscraper developed alongside antitrust legislation and the Progressive reform movement, many visual artists blocked such conflicts from view.[38] Instead of focusing on the social ramifications of the skyline, many proposed and developed a distinctly aesthetic image of the city. Devoid of social reality, such images were ideological by omission: they presented the city emptied of its economic and political implications. Best exemplified by Alfred Stieglitz and the Photo-Secession movement, these photographers inadvertently followed the traditions of the urban grand-style photographer. In their images, attention remained focused on technological and financial progress: the monumentality of the urban environment was extolled at the expense of its human and social context.[39]

It has been argued that Stieglitz's photographs, along with the writings of social activist and critic Randolph Bourne, belong to the vanguard of cultural radicalism that constituted the "lyrical left."[40] Certainly, Stieglitz was an important cultural radical, but his position within a left-wing intellectual tradition must be questioned. In 1910, Bourne began publishing distinctly left-leaning articles in the *Columbia Monthly,* and Stieglitz was busy photographing the New York cityscape. The resultant images — most notably "The City of Ambition" (1910), but also the related "The City across the River" and "Lower Manhattan" (both 1910) — are certainly lyrical and compositionally radical, yet it is almost impossible to construe them as politically leftist. "The City of Ambition" represents one of the defining urban images of the period, but its perspective belongs more to the earlier grand style than to the emerging traditions of reform, or progressive, photography, perhaps best exemplified by Lewis Hine.[41]

In many respects, "The City of Ambition" is the exemplary image of civic boosterism. Stieglitz's New York is a city busy with its own commercial ambition: the archetypal "city on the make." The photograph foregrounds financial trade and technological accomplishment. The plumes of smoke that characterize the image link the port, the warehouse, and the skyscraper in a chain of commercial energy.[42] It is a city in motion, a city at work, an urban environment pursuing its ambition. Yet there are no people going about this work; it involves no human presence. Like the new tall buildings, Stieglitz's photograph acts out and celebrates the business process while omitting the city's social reality. Within a historical trajectory, the photograph is the

28. A city on the make. Alfred Stieglitz, "The City of Ambition," 1910. The Metropolitan Museum of Art, Alfred Stieglitz Collection, 1949 (49.55.15).

optical equivalent of the city's vast splendors projected by Abram Hewitt at the bridge's opening, and the visual accompaniment to Calvin Coolidge's dictum that "the business of America is business."[43]

Although Stieglitz's "The City of Ambition" does not depict the Brooklyn Bridge, it does illustrate a significant development in the visual history of the bridge. In essence, the photograph resembles a cropped version of the 1908 image from the Brooklyn tower commissioned by the Otis Elevator Company. Both the left side of the 1908 image and Stieglitz's 1910 photograph portray a monumental cityscape infused with clouds of steam and dominated by the recently constructed Singer Building. Yet there is one crucial difference: whereas the Otis photographer looked out from atop the Brooklyn tower, Stieglitz gazed up at the city from the water. This changed perspective illustrates a broader trend. As the ever-taller buildings increasingly dwarfed the bridge, the tower view was abandoned. No longer able to overlook the city, photographers more often sought a position at its feet. As Alan Trachtenberg notes, such changes are important to the photographic medium: "decisions that may seem wholly technical or aesthetic . . . are decisions that implicate cultural perception and ideological determination." They are "embodiments of implicit propositions concerning reality."[44]

This shift, from above to below, served the trend that made a fetish of the skyline. For Boime, the magisterial gaze can be contrasted with what he terms the "reverential gaze." Traditionally the viewpoint of northern European artists, the reverential gaze "moves upward from the lower picture plane and culminates on or near a distant mountain peak. . . . The reverential gaze signified the striving of vision toward a celestial goal in the heavens, starting from a wide, panorama base. . . . The convergence of the line of vision on the celestial focal point metaphorically implied the yearning for the unity of the German nation under God."[45] As New York's skyline continued to rise, the urban gaze of those photographers who would record it became increasingly reverential. In the same year that Schuyler declared that the skyline "does, most tremendously, 'look like business,'" Lincoln Steffens was lamenting the passing of Trinity Church as a visible symbol of the city. The loss of Trinity in the skyline underscored the fact that "the enterprise of business . . . had surpassed the aspiration of religion."[46] Here the skyline is the agent in a spiritual reconfiguration: the godhead of traditional religious belief is replaced by the religion of commerce and technology. This visual and symbolic process was completed in the Woolworth Building (1913). Not only was the building described as "the cathedral of commerce," but it was given that distinction by a Brooklyn minister, Samuel Parkes Cadman. In his speech at the Woolworth's opening ceremonies, Cadman noted approvingly

29. The reverential gaze. George Hall, "Bridge Promenade," 1892. Courtesy of the Library of Congress.

that, just as religion had dominated the medieval world, so commerce dominated modern New York.[47] In effect, Cadman sanctioned the decline of religion in favor of commerce and technology. And so the flame of inspiration was passed within the tradition of the reverential gaze.

The visual history of the Brooklyn Bridge is dominated by the reverential gaze. In the early years of the twentieth century, the Detroit Publishing Company marketed a number of photographs that show the bridge from the perspective of its terminals. The visual trajectory leads the eye along the curving path of the trolley lines and toward the bridge. The bridge itself exists high above the city, as Hales notes, representing "both a monumental symbol of American civilization" and an "end itself."[48] An even more direct demonstration of the reverential gaze can be seen in images taken from the promenade, in which the cables of the bridge lead the eye away from the promenade and up to the height of the towers.[49] In George Hall's "Bridge Promenade" (1892), for example, the bridge's New York tower fills the entire the frame.[50] The few people who walk upon the promenade are dwarfed and

30. Commanding the scene. John Taylor Arms, *The Gates of the City*, 1922. Etching. Graphic Arts Collection, National Museum of American History, Smithsonian Institution. Photograph number 96-300.

seemingly inconsequential. The bridge's cables extend out past the limits of the frame and command the scene. The strength and power implicit in the network of cables lead the eye from all directions toward the bridge's central cornice. The photograph impels the viewer, in an act of reverence, away from the human and toward the technological.

Hall's thematic composition was adapted in numerous photographs, paintings, and etchings. For example, John Taylor Arms's etching *The Gates of the City* (1922) is identical to Hall's photograph, except for two changes. First, where Hall captured a few people dwarfed by the bridge, Arms shows the bridge alone, almost entirely uninhabited. Second, the etching's title encourages the viewer to look beyond the promenade and toward the city behind the bridge. Here the reverential gaze is directed toward two subjects: the heights of the bridge tower, then further, the skyline visible through the Gothic arches. This coupling relates the bridge to the skyline, not to its patrons. It presents a quintessential image of the city: monumental, aesthetic, and reverential, yet also desocialized and depopulated.[51]

Hall and Arms typify how a majority of artists have approached the bridge. Traditionally, the opportunity to portray one's fellow bridge users has been shunned. Instead, the governing image taken *on* the bridge is often that *from* the bridge. Arguably initiated by Karl Struss's "Cables" (1912), and repeated by Emil Otto Hoppé (1919), Christopher Nevinson (1921), Rudolph

31. Perspective: the city through the cables of the bridge. Karl Struss, "Cables—New York Skyline through Brooklyn Bridge," 1912. Printed by Phil Davis; platinum print. Image/sheet, 11.4 × 9.4 cm (4½ × 3¹¹/₁₆ in.); mount, 30.5 × 22.8 cm (12 × 9 in.). Museum of Fine Arts, Boston, Gift of Richard Germann. Photograph © Museum of Fine Arts, Boston.

Simmon (1924), Ludwig Reiner (1925), Helen Blumenschein (1932), Andreas Feininger (1940), and numerous anonymous photographers, this perspective sees the city through the cables of the bridge.[52] Occasionally, a single individual gazes through the cables—a reverential surrogate perhaps, or an appreciative witness to the city's monumentality—yet most often the scene is deserted.

Not only do the cables provide an aesthetic element, but they also forge stronger links between the bridge and the skyline. New York's discovery of steel—first used in the cables of the Brooklyn Bridge—was the central force

32. The bridge as a New York street. Childe Hassam, *A Winter Day on Brooklyn Bridge*, 1892. Reproduced in *Harper's New Monthly Magazine*, April 1893. From the author's collection.

behind the development of the skyscraper. Without the technique of steel-frame construction, the height of New York's buildings would have remained at around fourteen stories, or only a quarter of the height of the Woolworth Building. Consequently, by framing the skyline within a network of cables, artists and photographers linked the bridge's technological innovation to real estate development and the corporate economy. This "mirroring" process is stressed further in Hoppé's "Lower Manhattan from Brooklyn Bridge." The cables of the bridge in this photograph echo the bare steel frame of a new building being constructed on the skyline. This juxtaposition presents a stylistic unity: the commercial and technological city in monumental accord.

Childe Hassam painted two seemingly related yet entirely distinct images of the bridge: *A Winter Day on Brooklyn Bridge* (1892) and *Brooklyn Bridge in Winter* (1904). The former — remarkable for the manner in which it almost entirely ignores the bridge's cables — is akin to Hassam's earlier *Rainy Day, Boston* (1885) or *Une Averse, Rue Bonaparte* (1887). Employing diagonal sight lines to prescribe distance, illustrious architecture, and a flurry of street activity, Hassam anticipates the social dimension of the Ashcan School.[53] Unlike Hall's "Bridge Promenade," created in the same year, *A Winter Day* shows the bridge playing second fiddle to the foot traffic that battles through the winter storm. Hassam's later painting—a broad panorama—is entirely different. It showcases a new, evolving response to the modern city. Hassam considered the New York skyscraper to be "a wildly formed architectural freak." Yet in certain circumstances he found these buildings to be "truly beautiful." For this transformation to occur, one needed to "stand off at a proper angle to get the right light on the subject." To stand too close to a skyscraper would be akin "to sticking your nose in the canvas of an oil painting." Hassam believed the skyline to be more a work of art than an aspect of social history, and his ideological predisposition is broadened by his accent on perspective: to view the city in "the right light," he wrote, one must retreat from its everyday business.[54]

Like many good artists, Hassam did not always follow his own theories, but his stated framework was widely accepted, especially by photographers.[55] Exemplified by George Hall's "Vista of Bridge from Brooklyn Side" (1893), John Strauss's "The Bridge" (1903), Jessie Tarbox Beals's "The Bridge at Dusk, New York" (1910), Alvin Coburn's "Brooklyn Bridge, New York" (1912), Karl Struss's "Brooklyn Bridge, Nocturne" (1912), Weegee's frontispiece to *Naked City* (1930s), Reginald Marsh's *Pretty—Isn't It?* (1930s), and Andreas Feininger's "The Skyline with the Brooklyn Bridge" and "The Brooklyn Bridge as Seen from Brooklyn" (both 1940), in addition to countless illustrations published in guidebooks, newspapers, and other media, this focus incorporates the bridge and the Manhattan skyline in a panoramic view from the Brooklyn shore.[56] Here the bridge is less a platform from which to view the skyline than it is an integral aspect of the skyline itself. Where Struss, Hoppé, and Nevinson linked the bridge to the skyline through its cable structure, these panoramas insert the bridge into the heart of the physical and visual skyline. By drawing back from their subject, photographers and artists stressed size, strength, and monumentality over social, economic, and political context. In the process, they contributed to an ideological trend noted by Sam Warner: "the skyline quieted and pacified and avoided conflict inherent in the structure of the ideology by transforming new social facts into traditional art objects."[57]

Often this aestheticization—especially in such images as Karl Struss's photograph "Brooklyn Bridge, Nocturne" (1913), Edward Redfield's painting *Brooklyn Bridge at Night* (1909), and Joseph Pennell's watercolor *Brooklyn Bridge* (1926)—took the form of a profound romanticism. Its effects were to subdue the factual nature of the city and promote an exemplary, idealized image in which commercial speculation was legitimized as daring adventurism. This romanticism functioned in tandem with the reverential gaze. As they stare up from the Brooklyn riverfront, through the bridge, and to the

33. Retreating from the city: the panorama from Brooklyn. Jessie Tarbox Beals, "The Bridge at Dusk, New York," 1910. The Schlesinger Library, Radcliffe Institute, Harvard University.

34. The dramatic skyline. Anonymous, "New York: View with Brooklyn Bridge," undated. Courtesy of the Frances Loeb Library, Harvard Design School.

35. An integral part of the skyline. Reginald Marsh, *Pretty – Isn't It?* 1930s. Crayon and ink drawing. Courtesy of the Library of Congress.

skyline, these images evoke the modern godhead of the New York skyline: portrayed are the modern American triumvirate of technology, transportation, and business.[58] Within this reverential framework, the beholder's sight line ascends to the divine in the form of the Bankers Trust Building (finance), the City Investing Building (speculation), the Singer Building (manufacture), and the Woolworth Building (commerce). In this context, the bridge within the skyline takes up its role as commercial expedient, an aspect of the vast transportation network that supports and sustains the country's financial accomplishments. Visually, these panoramas fulfill C. C. Martin's opening-day claim: "it is earnestly urged upon all citizens and visitors to

36. The romantic bridge. Karl Struss, "Brooklyn Bridge, Nocturne," 1913. Printed by Phil Davis; platinum print. Image/sheet, 9.3 × 11.5 cm (3¹¹⁄₁₆ × 4½ in.); mount, 30.5 × 22.8 cm (12 × 9 in.). Museum of Fine Arts, Boston, Gift of Richard Germann. Photograph © Museum of Fine Arts, Boston.

37. The glory of New York. Joseph Pennell, *Brooklyn Bridge*, ca. 1926. Watercolor. Courtesy of the Library of Congress.

remember that the bridge is a great business thoroughfare, and when necessary everything else must be sacrificed to the demands of business."[59]

In effect, many urban photographers and artists developed an image of the bridge remarkably similar to that envisioned at the bridge's opening. By focusing on the bridge in relation to, and as an aspect of, the New York skyline, they involved themselves in commercial iconography, not community values. In the realm of painting, Benjamin Eggleston's *Brooklyn Bridge* (1927–1930) presents an extreme version of this trend.[60] Here the bridge is only a very marginal presence. Despite Eggleston's title, the canvas is more accurately described as an image of the New York skyline, and especially the Woolworth Building. Like Hewitt's opening-day speech, it embraces as its subject the now vast splendors of a city dominated by corporate and technological accomplishment; ignored are the social realities of many of its citizens.

John Jakle has written that the preference for viewing the skyline from a distance aids in "removing trivial detail and emphasizing broad patterns."[61] Not only does this tendency permeate the images of the bridge noted above, but it also encourages a continuation of the attitude toward individuals expressed by Charles Carroll in "Up Among the Spiders": the city's "relations" take precedence over its "detail." As Hales has remarked, the forces inherent in the built environment promote a "glittering civilization" while expunging "all traces of economic, and social, discord."[62] Complicit in the ideology of civic boosterism, such images tell a specific story: the key to the civilization fashioned in New York can be found in the monumentality of its skyline, not in the lives of its inhabitants.

Writing the Grand-Style Bridge

The grand-style urban vision flourished outside the visual realm as well as within it. Writers also transformed the bridge into a purely aesthetic icon. In such books as *New York Sketches* (1902), *A Loiterer in New York* (1917), *The Book of New York* (1917), and *New York: The Nation's Metropolis* (1921), for example, the structure is presented through the eyes of an individual on an unpopulated Brooklyn Bridge.[63] Like the photographer's camera, the writer's gaze is a romantic filter that supports the claim that the view from the bridge is entirely aesthetic, not social, political, or economic. In these texts, the bridge and the skyline confirm Marcel Duchamp's claim that "New York is itself . . . a complete work of art."[64]

On the rare occasions when the city's human context found its way into literary renditions of the bridge, it was greeted by a profound ambivalence. While gazing out at the span, H. G. Wells concluded that the "unmeaning faces" of the individuals he saw counted "for nothing." In 1923, Sergei Esenin felt no regret "that wild Hiawatha no longer hunts his deer here" or "that the hand of the builders of this culture was sometimes cruel."[65] Charles Reznikoff's poetry provides the logical extension of this theme:

On Brooklyn Bridge I saw a man drop dead.
It meant no more than if he were a sparrow;
For tower on tower behind the bridge arose
The buildings on Manhattan, tall white towers
Agleam with lights; below, the wide blue bay
Stretched out to meet the high blue sky
   and the first white star.[66]

The reflections of Wells, Esenin, and Reznikoff all illustrate a specific way of seeing. Ultimately, the lives and deaths of the city's population become insignificant when placed against the backdrop of the built environment. For other writers, ambivalence toward the neighborhoods in the vicinity of the bridge developed into active distaste. In Marrion Wilcox's 1894 poem

"North and South from the Brooklyn Bridge," the poet is exhilarated by the view from the bridge, yet revolted by the surrounding area: "A poisonous forest of houses as far as the eye can see, / And in their shade / All crime is made."[67] In prose, Don Marquis offered a similar sentiment:

> We used to walk over the Brooklyn Bridge, that song in stone and steel . . . at dusk, when the tides of shadow flood in from the lower bay to break in a surf of glory and mystery . . . against the tall towers of Manhattan. Seen from the middle arch of the bridge at twilight, New York with its girdle of shifting waters and its drift of purple cloud and its quick pulsations of unstable light is a miracle of splendor and beauty that lights up the heart like the laughter of a God.
>
> But descend. Go down into the city. Mingle with the details. The dirty old shed from which the "L" trains and trolleys put out their jammed and mangled thousands . . . the pasty streets stink like a paperhanger's overalls; you are trodden and over-ridden by greasy little profiteers . . . you are encompassed round about by the ugly and the sordid, and the objectionable is exuded upon you from a myriad candid pores; your elation and your illusion vanish like ingenuous snowflakes that have kissed a hot dog sandwich on its fiery brow, and you say: "Beauty? Aw, h-l! What's the use?"[68]

For Marquis, as for Charles Carroll, the city's "details" ruin the exemplary image of the city from the bridge.

Marquis also wrote poetry in honor of the bridge. In "From the Bridge" (1915) he raised the thorny question of context, yet found an easy resolution for the skyline's inherent contradictions. The beauty of the result nullifies the sordid means of creation:

> Held and thrilled by the vision
>   I stood, as the twilight died, . . .
>   Built by a lawless breed;
> Builded of lust for power,
>   Builded of gold and greed.
>
> Risen out of the trader's
>   Brutal and sordid wars—
> And yet, behold! a city
>   Wonderful under the stars.[69]

In common with "From the Bridge," Marquis's "The Towers of Manhattan" (1917) unfolds at twilight, stressing the city as a heightened aesthetic experience. While he stands "on the middle arch of the bridge," Marquis rhapsodizes, "before me apparelled in splendor, / Banded with loops of light, / Clothed on with purple and magic / Rose the tall towers of Manhattan."[70] Richard Le Gallienne's "Brooklyn Bridge at Dawn" (1905) strikes a similar chord. His bridge has "not yet a soul" upon it. Equally, he reconfigures the bridge's relation to context; the realism of creation is cast as the stuff of dreams: "Who, seeing thus the bridge a-slumber there, / Would dream such softness, like a picture hung, / Is wrought of human thunder, iron and blood?"[71]

In discussing the "image of the city," Kevin Lynch notes that no urban feature "is experienced by itself, but always in relation to its surroundings." He also believes that the city should be "seen in all lights and in all weathers."[72] Marquis and Le Gallienne, however, use only the surrounding skyline as context, and their city exists only at dawn or dusk. This perspective is the essence of romanticism, yet both authors are able to sidestep the inherent dichotomy. The "reality" of the bridge is found in the romantic gaze. Context is that which requires a leap of the imagination.

The presentation of Le Gallienne's poem set a cultural precedent. Published alongside two photographs by Alvin Langdon Coburn, it represents one of the first attempts to describe the bridge simultaneously through poetry and photography. In this respect, it anticipated the text that would most influence the image of the bridge for historians of American culture, Hart Crane's use of Walker Evans's photographs in his epic poem *The Bridge* (1930).

Walker Evans and Hart Crane: A Grand-Style Corroboration

Walker Evans has often been credited as a pioneer in the photography of the Brooklyn Bridge. He began to photograph the bridge extensively in 1929, and he produced more images of the structure than any previous photographer. For Trachtenberg, the originality of Evans's images "lies in part in their decisive break with the conventional distant and lateral views in standard commercial and 'serious' photographs. . . . Here the bridge is seen freshly, not merely looked at; it emerges . . . as *someone's* palpable experience."[73] Certainly Evans's photographs are among the most striking depictions of the Brooklyn Bridge; yet stylistically and thematically, they represent the culmination of a tradition rather than a break.

Although "distant and lateral views" predominated in the first decades of photographic representations of the bridge, they were by no means the only images. Moreover, Evans himself produced numerous photographs taken through the cables toward the Manhattan skyline and on the promenade upward and toward the bridge towers.[74] Not only do these images follow the established viewpoint, but they are also, unlike Hassam's A *Winter Day*, explicitly depopulated. Here, in contrast to his work for the Farm Security Administration, where Evans explicitly documented the interaction between traditional local culture and modern industrial civilization,[75] the local culture of both New York City and the Brooklyn Bridge remains outside of the photographic frame, and thus outside of Evans's vision. Instead, Evans gazes with reverence at the towers and toward the skyline.

A similar set of concerns haunts Evans's photographs from beneath the bridge. This perspective is Evans's most original. Yet here, too, commercial traffic is highlighted over human activity; a passing tugboat represents the only example of local culture.[76] Despite positioning himself beneath the bridge, Evans does not focus on life below the bridge.[77] The viewpoint — up toward the bridge's underside and onward to the skyline — is remote. In these images, Evans looks *away* from the social conditions of those living and working beneath the bridge. As described only a few years later by writers for the Works Progress Administration, the neighborhood around the bridge was "a slum . . . a sort of Brooklyn Bowery, with flophouses, small shops, rancid restaurants, haunted by vagabonds and derelicts."[78] We see not even a hint of these conditions in Evans's photographs. Instead, he provides the visual counterpart to a claim made by the *Eagle* on opening day: "how grandly does our noble bridge, standing clear and guiltless of concealment against the sky, contrast with the bridges that stand dark and gloomy, only eloquent of hidden ways and deeds."[79] By ignoring the real life beneath the bridge, Evans was free to construct an undiluted, aestheticized image of the bridge and the skyline. However original in perspective, Evans's views from underneath the bridge — "standing clear" of their context — are the counterpart of those he took on the promenade.

Although photographs exist as independent cultural objects, it is difficult to assess them outside their published context. Evans's photographs of the Brooklyn Bridge first appeared as a visual accompaniment to Hart Crane's epic poem *The Bridge,* and the two evocations of the structure are best considered alongside each other.[80] Crane grappled with the bridge's cultural meaning more than any other writer. It took him almost a decade to write the poem, and the effort drove him to exhaustion, depression, and perhaps even death: shortly after the publication of his epic, Crane took his own life. He

Opposite: 38. "Standing clear and guiltless of concealment against the sky." Walker Evans, "Underneath the Brooklyn Bridge, New York City," 1929. © Walker Evans Archive, The Metropolitan Museum of Art, 1994 (1994.251.245).

invested himself in this poem in a way that is perhaps difficult to understand nowadays. Yet his investment was not purely artistic. Crane saw himself as a modern Walt Whitman, and the bridge was his Lincoln: the key to America itself.[81]

Writing to Gorham Munson in 1923, Crane set out his hopes for the poem. Based on "History and fact, location etc. . . . it concerns a mystical synthesis of 'America.' . . . The initial impulses of 'our people' will have to be gathered up toward the climax of the bridge, symbol of our constructive future, our unique identity, in which is to be included also our scientific hopes and achievements of the future."[82] In this description we hear the language of Whitman, more specifically, the unrestrained optimism of Whitman's early years. Having set his task, however, Crane found no unique identity worth celebrating, and the history of the writing of *The Bridge* is really the history of Crane's disillusionment with America. By 1926, Crane was lamenting, "[I]f only America were half as worthy today to be spoken of as Whitman spoke of it fifty years ago there might be something for one to say . . . but that time has shown how increasingly lonely and ineffectual his confidence stands." The Brooklyn Bridge "as a symbol today has no significance beyond an economical approach to shorter hours, quicker lunches, behaviorism and toothpicks." Unable to place the bridge within an evolving historical tradition — "I am at a loss to explain my delusion that there exists any real links between that past and a future worthy of it"[83] — Crane began to retreat from "History and fact, location etc.," moving instead toward myth, archetype, and aesthetic idealism.[84]

Crane begins his poem on the bridge, with its backdrop of Lady Liberty, the harbor, and the river traffic. He then journeys into the heartland, surveying the cultural landscape of America: from "Far Rockaway to Golden Gate," through Ohio, Indiana, to Cheyenne, down the Ohio River to the Mississippi, under the Ozarks, from Memphis to Tallahassee, and on to Cape Hatteras and Virginia. We meet Pocahontas, Rip Van Winkle, Casey Jones, Walt Whitman, Herman Melville, and Edgar Allan Poe. Crane then returns to the bridge, having recognized little and having found no "mystical synthesis." As he treads the boards home, the city dissolves around him. In its stead, Crane wills into being a new Atlantis, a mythic Cathay. Unable to reconcile the ideal with the reality, Crane imagines a bridge that leads not to New York or Brooklyn, but to an imaginary celestial empire, a visionary ideal bathed in the hues of utopia. Shorn of its attachments to reality, the bridge is free to support Crane's original intent: a mystical celebration of a romantic wish. The Brooklyn Bridge, in effect, becomes the Hart Crane Bridge, a bridge of the mind and imagination, not one of commuters, Sunday strollers, and amateur photographers. As Trachtenberg observes, "to secure its link with eternity, Crane had to abolish the bridge's links with the opposite shores. . . . To serve as America's symbol it could no longer serve as Brooklyn's bridge."[85] Unable to reconcile the modern bridge with his Whitmanesque ideals, Crane fashioned a perfect, self-contained art object. The result is the decontextualized, purely aesthetic "frozen image" of New Critical thinking: the well-wrought urn.[86]

For some critics, Crane's poetic bridge connects with Roebling's physical bridge via Evans's photographs.[87] Its grounding within the granite-and-steel "reality" of Evans's images enables Crane's poem to escape cerebral abstraction. In the Black Sun edition of the epic, Gordon Grigsby argues, each of Evans's three photographs performs a dual function: to highlight Crane's perspective and tie it to the material structure. For example, Evans's first image — from beneath the bridge — echoes Crane's "Under thy shadow by the piers I waited," in addition to what Grigsby describes as "the ordinary, quotidian view — the view from below — of city men who are 'caught like pennies beneath soot and steam.'"[88] As noted, however, Evans's photographs from beneath the bridge are in fact devoid of the context that Grigsby ascribes to them. Evans's perspective may well correspond to the "quotidian view," but it ignores the "city men" whom Crane saw as "caught like pennies beneath soot and steam." Crane's "drunken stevedore"[89] makes no appearance in Evans's photographs, and there is nothing to suggest a life lived "beneath soot and steam." Instead, the image from beneath — all dynamism and thrusting energy — favors the splendors of the city's monumental façade.

Both Trachtenberg and Grigsby interpret Evans's second image — looking down from the bridge at a tugboat and barge passing beneath — as capturing literal experience or "modern reality."[90] The image serves to link Crane's historical imagination — he envisions a fleet of clipper ships sailing up the East River — with the river trade of his time. Even so, both critics seem more impressed by the photograph's style than its realism. For Trachtenberg, the "literal . . . experience" is "aesthetically transformed," and Grigsby states that "the picture engages reality but sees it with such artistic skill that modern fact acquires its own beauty."[91]

Yes, Evans is ostensibly interested in the "modern reality" of the river trade; but more significantly, and much like those photographers who made an art object out of New York's skyline, he is caught up in his own ability to transform that reality with his art. Unlike Paul Strand's "Overlooking Harbor, New York, 1916," for example, Evans's image is carefully framed and highly stylized. The river workers foregrounded in the illustrations that accompanied James B. Connolly's 1905 article on New York Harbor reside nowhere

39. Texture, shade, and form. Walker Evans, "Tug and Container Barge on the East River, from Brooklyn Bridge, New York City," 1930. © Walker Evans Archive, The Metropolitan Museum of Art, 1994 (1994.251.42).

within Evans's frame.[92] Instead, the "modern reality" of 1929 dissolves into an abstraction of texture, shade, and form.

Evans's last photograph in the Black Sun edition completes the process of decontextualized aestheticization. This final image—from the promenade, gazing up at the bridge towers—provides the perfect visual counterpart to Crane's final ecstatic walk across the bridge in "Atlantis." Where the original photograph includes a deserted section of the promenade, the published image is cropped to exclude the walkway. Also excluded is the bridge's urban milieu: empty space is all that surrounds the bridge tower. In essence, both context and function are absent. The bridge appears as if floating in space: the frozen image of a perfect art object, more the well-wrought urn of Crane's mystical imagination than the bridge between Brooklyn and Manhattan.

The Evans images used in the two Horace Liveright editions offer addi-

40. River workers. Anonymous illustration accompanying James B. Connolly, "New York Harbor," *Harper's New Monthly Magazine*, July 1905. Courtesy of the Department of Special Collections, Stanford University Libraries.

tional evidence for this reading. Both photographs employ a distinctly modernist aesthetic that further removes the bridge into abstraction. As one critic has noted, the photograph used in the first Liveright edition conceives "the bridge as launched into space . . . more sculpture than roadway."[93] In the various editions of *The Bridge*, Evans's photographs reinforce Crane's poem not by contextualizing the bridge within the life of modern New York and America, but by removing it. They meet only in the autotelic imagination, not in the passage between Brooklyn and Manhattan.

Lewis Mumford and the Ideology of the Skyline

The interplay between social context and aesthetic value troubled Lewis Mumford and exposed some essential tensions in his cultural criticism. Mumford frequently wrote of his adoration for the Brooklyn Bridge, and he took great pride in being the first architectural critic to appraise the structure since Montgomery Schuyler in 1883.[94] Yet his response to the bridge was problematic, especially when placed alongside the critical stance he assumed toward the new tall buildings that beguiled so many of his contemporaries.

Mumford spent much of the 1920s railing against the skyscraper and its influence.[95] He once described the Woolworth Building as "birthday cake Gothic," but his criticisms were not confined to aesthetic valuations.[96] Instead, he focused on the effects of the skyscraper on the urban dweller: "One

41. Depopulated and decontextualized, the bridge appears as if floating in space. Walker Evans, "Brooklyn Bridge, New York," 1929. © Walker Evans Archive, The Metropolitan Museum of Art, Gift of Arnold H. Crane, 1972 (1972.742.3).

42. "More sculpture than roadway." Walker Evans, "Brooklyn Bridge, New York," 1929. © Walker Evans Archive, The Metropolitan Museum of Art, Gift of Arnold H. Crane, 1972 (1972.742.2).

need not dwell upon the ways in which these obdurate overwhelming masses take away from the little people who walk in their shadows any semblance of dignity as human beings; it is perhaps inevitable that one of the greatest achievements in a thoroughly dehumanised civilization should, no doubt, unconsciously achieve this very purpose."[97] Mumford continued his assault in a short story, "The Intolerable City" (1926), in which he imagined the soulless life of a man who works in one skyscraper and lives in another. This disapproval was extended to the skyscraper in art. In a review of the "Titan City" exhibition held at the John Wanamaker Gallery in 1925, he bemoaned the fact that not one individual could be found in any of the images of the "ideal metropolis." For Mumford, "what our critics have learned to admire in our great buildings is their photographs."[98]

Having defined his opposition to the skyscraper along humane, social lines, Mumford adopted another set of criteria for the Brooklyn Bridge. If he considered the aesthetic potential of skyscrapers to be trivial in comparison with their stultifying effects on humanity, his writings on the Brooklyn Bridge rarely stray past its aesthetic achievement. In *The Brown Decades*

(1931), Mumford refers to the bridge as a "stunning act . . . necessary to demonstrate the aesthetic possibilities of the new materials." It "pointed to the logic and aesthetics of the machine"; it was "a work of art," "the first product of the age of coal and iron to achieve this completeness of expression." Equally, the Roeblings held the distinction of having made aesthetics visible in engineering.[99] As biographer Donald Miller notes, Mumford saw the bridge "as a poem in granite and steel," and this judgment is confirmed in *Brown Decades:* "The stone plays against the steel: the granite mass in compression, the spidery steel in tension. In this structure, the architecture of the past, massive and protective, meets the architecture of the future, light, aerial, open to sunlight, an architecture of voids rather than solids."[100] Mumford never relates the bridge to the lives of the city's inhabitants. Instead, he describes an art object, not a public utility. The criteria he applied so rigorously to the skyscraper evaporate before "such a powerful work of the imagination." When reflecting on the bridge, Mumford resembles Keats contemplating his urn, not the "vituperative interpreter of the skyscraper."[101]

Remarking on the bridge's construction workers, Mumford notes that "more than twenty were fatally hurt. Several succumbed to caisson disease. But the granite towers rose."[102] Apart from heroic portraits of John and Washington Roebling, this dramatic recitation is one of the few times Mumford refers to the human element in connection with the bridge. Yet he prioritizes the structure over the individual, and again the standards he applied to the skyscraper are abandoned. Perhaps fittingly, Mumford confines his interest in the individual to a small group, those for whom aesthetics were a ruling force: "beyond any other aspect of New York, I think, Brooklyn Bridge has been a source of joy and inspiration to the artist."[103]

One should not be surprised that Mumford singled out the artist, given his aesthetic concerns. More puzzling is the discrepancy between his damning review of the "ideal metropolis" presented at the "Titan City" exhibition and his approval of artistic representations of the bridge: whereas he chastised the lack of human presence in the former, he failed to note the same in a majority of the later. As an amateur painter, Mumford himself produced two views of the Brooklyn Bridge, both of which feature a traditional combination of bridge and skyline.[104] No human presence intrudes in either image, and their tone is reminiscent of the grand-style heroism of Sonntag or Feininger. If we return to the chastening remark, "what our critics have learned to admire in our great buildings is their photographs," we can detect a tension within Mumford's cultural criticism. Not only does this statement fail to correspond to Mumford's published appreciation of Stieglitz; it fails to jibe with his thoughts on the Brooklyn Bridge.[105] What Mumford "learned to admire" in the Brooklyn Bridge was the art and poetry it inspired.

Mumford's treatment of the skyscraper and the bridge are curiously resolved in his autobiography, published in 1982. Echoing the words he used fifty years before, he rhapsodizes on the aesthetic excellence of the bridge: "it was the Brooklyn Bridge that I loved best, partly because of its own somber perfection of form, with its spidery lacing of cables contrasting with the great stone piers." He also describes an epiphany. Significantly, it takes place on the bridge in "a twilight hour in early spring":

> As I reached the middle of Brooklyn Bridge, the sunlight spread across the sky, forming a halo around the jagged mountain of skyscrapers. . . . the towers topped by the golden pinnacles of the new Woolworth Building, still caught the light even as it began to ebb away. Three-quarters of the way across the Bridge I saw the skyscrapers in the deepening darkness become slowly honeycombed with lights until, before I reached the Manhattan end, these buildings piled up in a dazzling mass against the indigo sky.
>
> Here was my city, immense, overpowering, flooded with energy and light. . . . below me the bridge moved in a relentless tide to carry tens of thousands homeward. And there I was, breasting the March wind, drinking in the city and the sky, both vast, yet both contained in me. . . . In that sudden revelation of power and beauty all the confusions of adolescence dropped from me.[106]

His biographer notes that "for Mumford the skyscraper was a principal cause and symbol for everything that had gone wrong with Walt Whitman's 'Manahatta.'"[107] Yet the image remembered from his youth intimately connects both Whitman's "Manahatta"—"high growths of iron, slender, strong, light, splendidly uprising towards clear skies . . . / City of hurried and sparkling waters! city of spires and masts! / City nested in bays! my city!"[108]— and the skyline viewed from the bridge. By no means demonized, the city's skyscrapers are haloed and linked with the bridge in an onrush of "overpowering" energy. Mumford's description is the literary equivalent of Stieglitz's "The City of Ambition," where even the "relentless tide carry[ing] tens of thousands homeward" seems to flow from the power of the skyline. On the bridge, Mumford gazes with reverence toward the skyline, and then looks down at the undifferentiated mass of humanity below. In so doing, he succumbed to the forces he so vituperatively challenged.

Mumford's epiphany illustrates a spilt in his personality. At his desk and on the streets, Mumford was the committed cultural critic railing against the social ills inherent in the city's new tall buildings. On the bridge, he was beguiled by the very same structures. Perspective, as we have seen, is all-important. Following in a tradition that includes, among others, Don Marquis and Charles Carroll, Mumford, disappointed on the streets, was enchanted on the bridge.

Alfred Kazin's New York Street

Reviewing Trachtenberg's *Brooklyn Bridge: Fact and Symbol*, Alfred Kazin chided the author for ignoring the bridge's role as a street. Yet Kazin, who drew great inspiration from Mumford and acknowledged the critic's influence throughout his life, never addressed the oppositional relationship between the street and the bridge in Mumford's writing.[109] Like Mumford, Kazin was in thrall to Whitman's infectious idealism and projected it onto the city through the bridge. *The Open Street* (1948) is Kazin's homage to "Crossing Brooklyn Ferry," and within this slim volume we see much that reminds us of Mumford's youthful reminiscences. For Kazin, as for Mumford, the Brooklyn Bridge made "New York . . . my city."[110] Yet, however much the bridge facilitated this transition, "New York" became "my city" for each writer through entirely different means.

As youths, both Kazin and Mumford experienced an epiphany while traversing the Brooklyn Bridge. From the bridge, Mumford described a reverent vision rooted in the romance of the skyline. In comparison, Kazin mentions only "the electric sign of the *Jewish Daily Forward*, burning high over the tenements of the East Side."[111] The perceptual implications are important. When viewing from the bridge, what does one see? Where Mumford notices only the speculative and corporate towers, Kazin's gaze alights on a progressive immigrant newspaper and the homes of many of the city's poorer residents.[112] The two authors also acquire their sense of the city's powerful energy from differing sources. Mumford is stimulated by the sublime vision of the skyline. For Kazin, only one generation removed from the immigrant experience, the city's great dynamo is its rich humanity. Kazin places himself not above those traveling home, but among them. His bridge is noisy and bustling with life. It is a bridge of "rush hour above, on every side, below," of newsboys hawking the evening papers, the "clanging, clanging" of trolley cars, and "the smell of popcorn and frankfurters" and of "roasting coffee" on the streets below. In wide-eyed contrast to Mumford's reverential gaze, Kazin eagerly looks about him and sees myriad details of life on the bridge. He describes "the battered wooden planks of the promenade" and "a painter's scaffold" hanging "down one side of the tower over a splattered canvas." Mumford, in the tradition of Beal and Carroll, saw the grand-style city in its monumental "relations." Kazin, looking with the keen eye of "detail," saw past the ideology of the skyline to the people and places that constitute a less lustrous, but equally valid New York. Mumford's bridge was a place of aesthetic and social transcendence; Kazin's was a New York street.[113]

The Poverty of Waldo Frank's New York

An ideological compatriot and associate of Lewis Mumford, Waldo Frank was equally entranced and critical of modern New York. Like Henry James, he viewed the modern metropolis as a cultural battleground. He found the city full of Whitmanesque vitality, yet he also feared for its future. Confronting the all-embracing soul of Whitman was the national "pioneer spirit," which was by necessity "intolerant, materialistic, unaesthetic." In its modern incarnation, it represented the source and motivation of modern industrialism, a force that "had swept the American land and made it rich. Broke in on the American soul and made it poor."[114]

Frank illustrated the effects of this national malaise in a caustic assessment of New York: "The men and women who have made this city and whose place it is, are lowly, are driven, are drab. Their feet shuffle, their voices are shrill, their eyes do not shine . . . the millions of human sources are sucked void. . . . The New Yorker of today is stiff and slack: he has been fathered by steel and broken by it. . . . Pioneer and Puritan and Industrialist have made New York. And like the sky, Joy has been shadowed out."[115] For Frank, American cities were "not so much of men and women as of buildings . . . there is a chasm between the created thing and the creator."[116] Later, he would resolve this dichotomy and distill its implications into a single defining image: "The American gods of Power have a temple. It is the best we can show as formal articulation of what we are. . . . we call it the Skyscraper."[117]

Frank's social reading of the technological and financial forces at work in modern New York is comparable to Mumford's. Entrenched within the new tall buildings, a nefarious force presides over the city. In their criticisms, both Mumford and Frank recall Henry Adams's frenetic description of New York: "The outline of the city became frantic . . . power seemed to have outgrown its servitude and to have asserted its freedom. The cylinder had exploded, and thrown great masses of stone and steam against the sky. The city had the air and movement of hysteria, and the citizens were crying, in every accent of anger and alarm, that the new forces must at any cost be brought under control."[118] Mumford was able to sidestep Adams's conviction of social rupture through his belief in the aesthetic transcendence of the Brooklyn Bridge, and he could even describe a scene in which the forces of disarray are seemingly brought under control. Frank could not make such a leap of faith. In his novel *The Unwelcome Man* (1917), the dreadfully unhappy Quincy Burt—a thinly disguised Frank—takes himself to the Brooklyn Bridge to learn something of the nature of New York:

> Before him swept the bridge. He felt that every cable of the web-like maze was vibrant with stress and strain. . . . Beyond, through the network of steel, huddled Brooklyn. And below his very feet, tumbled together as if some giant had tipped the city eastward and sent all the houses pell-mell toward the down-tilted corner, lay the wharves and slums of Manhattan. It seemed to Quincy that he was being caught upon a monstrous swing and swept with its pulsed lilt above the grovelling life of the metropolis. Suddenly, the fancy flashed upon him that from his perch of shivering steel the power should indeed come to poised and judge the swarm above which he rocked. The bridge that reeled beyond him seemed an arbiter. It bound the city. It must know the city's soul since it was so close to the city's breath. In its throbbing cables there must be a message. In its lacings and filigrees of steel, there must be subtle words![119]

Finding the bridge's "message" is the key to understanding Burt's New York and, to a large degree, Frank's. Yet this passage is suffused with uncertainty. Burt's contemplation begins as a "fancy." The bridge's power "*should*"—rather than *does*—"come to . . . judge," and "*seemed*"—rather than *was*—"an arbiter" (my emphasis). Amid New York's industrial landscape, Burt's hopes start to collapse. He becomes one of Adams's hysterical New Yorkers, and his exhortations to the Brooklyn Bridge become desperate: "It *must* know the city's soul . . . there *must* be a message . . . there *must* be subtle words!" (my emphasis). Yet he receives no response, and the importance of the bridge's "message" is revealed: there is, in fact, no message at all. Where Mumford was seduced by the bridge's orderly aesthetic, Frank finds no such revelation. As beautiful as it is, the bridge has neither answer nor antidote to the problems of city life.

Disillusioned, Burt attempts to escape, but is accosted by the city: "The vaster buildings rose all white and impervious. . . . Monsters indeed, they seemed to have sucked the strength for rising from the nondescript ruck that they submerged. Ferocious, sapping prodigies they seemed . . . the sort to which men are sacrificed and that makes slaves of their creators."[120] With no possible escape, Burt returns to the bridge: "under the bridge itself he went—looming above him like a curse . . . he was frightened, horrified."[121] Where Burt had pleaded with the bridge for a message, he now runs from it in hatred. He understands that the bridge is not a key to the city's Whitmanesque soul but, like the skyscraper, merely a part of its "ferocious" anatomy. Frank's bridge represents the "curse" of industrial modernity as social vampire; its "millions of human sources" are "sucked void." The image also reminds us of the poetry of Lola Ridge, a contemporary of Frank's. Like James before her, and Lorca to come, Ridge imagined the bridge as a monstrous reptilian organism, a gigantic "Pythoness . . . arching / over the night. . . ." "I feel your coils tightening . . . / And the world's lessening breath."[122]

Unlike the ennobling image of achievement put forward by subscribers to the grand style, Frank's city squeezes its inhabitants, draining their humanity. The bridge stands as a place not to rediscover the city's Whitmanesque vitality, but to realize how much it has been crushed. Mumford was able to separate the bridge and the skyscraper. Frank could not: the skyscraper and the bridge—both "fathered by steel"—were aspects of the same cultural engine. Both reveal "the dire fate of the individual in an atmosphere made by the machine."[123]

In a much more lighthearted manner, Benjamin De Cassares helps us to understand both Frank and Crane. He concludes his extraordinary *Mirrors of New York* (1925) with the fictional "resignation of New York." Finding himself on Riverside Drive, De Cassares hears "a titanic footfall, like the march of Thor." "Looking down the drive," he sees "the Woolworth Tower, struck clean from the rest of the building from pillar to dome, coming up the Drive":

> The Tower led the most astonishing procession that ever mortal eye shall look upon. Behind the Tower tramped thunderously the Statue of Liberty. She held her torch extinguished, in her hand. Then came Diana, from the top of Madison Square Garden; the two Library Lions, the statue of Shakespeare from the Mall in Central Park, and the old City Hall Clocks, the Golden Lady from atop the Municipal Building, and last of all the Brooklyn Bridge, crawling along like a tired snake, its cables making a most unearthly racket, which nearly drowned the earth-quivering thuds of the Woolworth Tower and the Statue of Liberty.[124]

Each of the icons in turn explains the reason for its "resignation." From the Woolworth: "My soul is a series of pigeon-holes called rooms. I am Business. I am Profit and Loss. I am Beauty come into the hell of the Practical. Farewell! I am marching back to the deep-earth quarries whence I came." From the Golden Lady: "Justice is a dice-box. The rich always win, while the poor get the box. I'm going in yon icy river at a warm spot near Hastings." Bringing up the rear, "the Brooklyn Bridge was making such an uproar that I could not hear what it said."[125] Like all icons, the bridge speaks no known language. Amid the white noise of cultural history, De Cassares finds what Frank feared and Crane discovered: no single message, no unique, exemplary identity. In De Cassares, however, this insight is at least understood by the icons themselves. Sick of their own role in the rhetoric of progress, they march off to whence they came.

The Perspective of Mildred Stapley and Henri De Ville

Amid the grand-style corroborations of Le Gallienne and Coburn, Crane and Evans, words and images were occasionally used to present a different Brooklyn Bridge. In 1921, for example, Scribner's brought out *Four Years in the Underbrush: Adventures as a Working Woman in New York*. Published anonymously, the book featured a grand-style image of the Brooklyn Bridge both on the cover and as the frontispiece. Yet *Four Years in the Underbrush* was no glorious vision of New York as "a complete work of art" à la Marquis or Evans. As indicated by the title, the author "was interested" in a different kind of narrative, one that took place under the bridge. In attempting to gather material for her exposé, she enters "the greatest jungle of civilization . . . the world of the unskilled working woman in New York City." Her investigation places her in the midst of the massive influenza epidemic of 1918–1919, and she is forced to work as a nurse among the city's poor. Her only contact with the span is to visit "narrow tenements, jammed between others . . . dark and smelly, with crooked stone steps and slimy stone walls . . . below Brooklyn Bridge," where "a long line of coffins before a church . . . waiting for burial" are a daily sight.[126]

Six years earlier, a more systematic and comprehensive example of writing against the grand-style Brooklyn Bridge had appeared in the *Architectural Record*. Mildred Stapley's essay, "Six Etchings of Brooklyn Bridge," begins: "Wander for an hour along lower Broadway and you soon feel how conspicuously fantastic its tall buildings are. From the Pulitzer . . . to the new Woolworth, every business structure is an avowed effort to go higher."[127] Here, the economic business conducted within the skyscraper is allied with the competitive nature of skyline dominance. Furthermore, this correlation finds a home in the realm of the "fantastic," the spirit of which — not exemplary, but unreal — is highlighted soon after: "Yet after an hour's straining gaze up at these beautiful facades one begins to feel a certain monotony in their appeal. . . . This is the moment for turning due east along Frankfurt Street where the splendid masonry arches of Brooklyn Bridge give the lie to the merely stone draped steel monsters."[128]

Stapley begins to explore the regions below the bridge and around the waterfront. There she finds a life rich in flavor and activity yet "spurned of

43. Beneath the bridge. One of Henri De Ville's illustrations for Mildred Stapley, "Six Etchings of Brooklyn Bridge," *Architectural Record*, 1915. Courtesy of the Library of Congress.

Broadway." She describes the work, housing, manners, and customs of those for whom the bridge is a continual presence. She interviews stevedores, truck drivers, pie sellers, carters, and families. Revising the grand-style tradition, Stapley's "imagination is straightway invited . . . where Cliff Street passes under [the bridge], or William Street": "In summer such spots are the friend of tired carters and horses who spend the noon hour in their cool shade, but in winter they are the enemy of those who must face the icy eddies and the gusts that scutter through." By comparison, the view from the bridge walkway is a disappointment to Stapley: "But from up above on the monster bridge all small and separate pictures are lost."[129] For Stapley, the New York skyline is no substitute for the rich life she finds beneath the bridge.

The illustrations in "Six Etchings," by Henri De Ville, are equally important. They conform to Kevin Lynch's comprehensive approach to the city's image and provide a visual equivalent to poet William Meredith's thoughts on the bridge, expressed in 1958: "The growing need to be moving around to see it, / To prevent its freezing, as with sculpture and metaphor."[130] Although two of De Ville's six images concern the view from the bridge toward the skyline — one through the cables, one through the bridge arch —

they also complement Stapley's words. Two images depict the streets around the bridge—including, as the article's first illustration, the carters' Cliff Street lunch spot—and the others foreground the work carried on beneath the bridge's approach. Although perhaps less committed than Stapley's prose to the life beneath and around the bridge, De Ville's illustrations reach toward a more comprehensive depiction. By presenting six differing ways of seeing the bridge, Stapley and De Ville preclude the "freezing" process so desired by the grand style and so feared by Meredith. The bridge of "Six Etchings" is seen, as Lynch recommends, "in relation to its surroundings" and "in all lights and in all weathers."

"Six Etchings" represents a specific urban and cultural argument: through which criteria can the bridge, and by extension the city, be best evaluated? Challenging the grand-style tradition, Stapley and De Ville attempted to introduce a set of shifting perspectives. Certainly, the bridge is a unique engineering achievement; yet at what point does the bridge stop being an icon for American technological progress and start becoming a part of human interaction? Are the bridge and the skyline best evaluated through the lens of aesthetic criticism, or as aspects of the social life of the city? Such concerns occupied the young journalist Ernest Poole as he gathered inspiration to write his second novel.

Ernest Poole's *The Harbor*

Mumford categorized Poole's *The Harbor* (1915) as "a minor work that nevertheless took a special place in our imagination."[131] Neither literary criticism nor cultural history has been so kind, and the novel's reputation has languished. To the extent that it is read at all, *The Harbor* is regarded as a curious example of socialism's turn-of-the-century naïveté. Although Peter Conn calls it "a novel of singular ideological energy," he agrees that "its energy is eventually dissipated in a retreat from its own leading ideas."[132] This is perhaps a fair judgment if one accepts that Poole's "leading ideas" were essentially informed by socialism. Yet, as his subsequent novels show—especially *Beggar's Gold* (1921)—Poole was rarely so doctrinaire. His "leading ideas" were in fact more akin to Woodrow Wilson's "New Freedom" than to socialist dogma. And as applied in *The Harbor*, they point more to the complexities of perceiving the modern urban environment than to a coming socialist revolution.[133]

An American bildungsroman, *The Harbor* presents a journey through the prevailing ways in which citizens comprehend and define the modern environment. Although ostensibly concerned with New York Harbor, Poole's setting is a microcosm of the nation at large: "You could feel the pulse of a continent here. From the factories, the mines and mills, the prairies and the forests, the plantations and the vineyards, there flowed a mighty tide of things — endlessly both day and night — you could shut your eyes and see the long brown lines of cars crawl eastward from all over the land, you could feel the stuff converging here."[134] Divided into three distinct thematic phases, the novel follows its protagonist, Billy, from childhood into early manhood. Poole himself thought the book's major theme was "the challenge of change," and this "change" is measured by perception.[135] Each section is governed by a specific way of seeing. In essence, Poole traces a perceptual trajectory that conjugates the image of the harbor and its dominant symbol, the Brooklyn Bridge. It strives to develop a mental vocabulary through which to perceive change.

In childhood, Billy's relationship to the harbor is romantic. From his window, he stares down at the waterfront and imagines tales of adventure: "High over all" — equally framing and symbolizing the vision — "the Great Bridge swept across the sky . . . high as the clouds."[136] Entranced, Billy descends to the harbor and is shocked by what he finds. The drunks and prostitutes that patrol the region disgust him, and he flees the area after witnessing a suicide jump from the bridge. Under his mother's tutelage, Billy retreats into the haven of books and begins to envision the world in specifically aesthetic terms. He attends Princeton University and from there travels to Paris to become a writer. In the French capital, he scorns those who talk of "factories, wages, strikes, of railroads, peasant's taxes, of plows and wheat and corn and hay." He concludes that any revolution not based in art is intrinsically worthless. As Conn notes, Billy has "no interest in evaluating the social or economic conditions of others, only in registering those conditions elegantly."[137]

Billy returns to New York after the death of his mother, and there he meets and marries Eleanore Dillon. In the novel's second phase, Billy's loyalties pass to his father-in-law. Mr. Dillon is an engineer, bridge builder, and urban planner involved in restructuring the harbor. Backed by Wall Street, he desires a corporate consolidation to convert the harbor from a chaotic array of independent concerns into a sophisticated technological and commercial machine. Under Dillon's influence, Billy can imagine a new harbor. His vision of a world perfected through art is replaced by a new ideal of a world perfected through commerce, scientific management, and technology.

Prompted by Dillon, Billy begins to write "glory stories" for magazines. His twin subjects are the country's great capitalists — the "America They Know" — and the marvels being achieved in the harbor.[138] On his first visit to the massive tower overlooking the harbor where Dillon lives and works, Billy experiences a revelation. Gazing down at the scene below, he is dazzled by the "distant twinkling arch of the Bridge" and professes to have "the first social vision of his life":

> My view of the harbor was different now. I had seen it before as a vast machine molding the lives of all people around it. But now behind the machine itself I felt the minds of its molders. I saw its ponderous masses of freight, its multitudes of people, all pushed and shifted this way and that by these invisible powers. And by degrees I made for myself a new god, and its name was Efficiency.
>
> Here at last was a god that I felt I could stand! . . . For it was armed with Science, its feet stood firm on mechanical laws and in its head were all the brains of all the strong men at the top.
>
> And all the multitudes below seemed mere pigmies. . . . How small they seemed, how petty their thoughts compared to mine, how blind their views.[139]

This "social vision" is pointedly ideological. It is the vision expressed by Beal, Carroll, the magisterial gaze, and the urban grand style. While implying social progress, Billy's "new god . . . Efficiency" supports the unfettered commercial and technological juggernaut that benefits Dillon and his Wall Street cronies. The view from the tower illustrates Billy's new literary outlook; it is the view from above, looking down at the harbor's "relations," not its "detail." Seduced by the tower perspective, Billy and Eleanore soon move in with Dillon.

The third stage of Billy's development is achieved under the influence of his college friend Joe Kramer. Kramer, an avowed socialist, is appalled by Billy's attitude to those who work in the harbor: "you treat us all like a mass of dubs that need gods above to do everything *for* us because we can't do it all by ourselves!" Billy answers from his tower perspective: "I don't believe the people can . . . from what I've seen I honestly don't believe they count." "Your stokers and dock laborers," he says later, "are about as fit to build up a new world as they are to build a Brooklyn Bridge! When I compare them to Eleanore's father and his way of going to work— . . . Can't you see you're just floundering in a perfect swamp of ignorance?"[140]

Billy's passage toward a third perspective is completed when Kramer finally coaxes him down from the tower and into the harbor. Although he has been promoting Dillon's achievements, Billy "had hardly been near the harbor in years."[141] No longer high above the bridge in Dillon's tower, Billy's magisterial gaze is subverted as he is forced to confront the "detail" of harbor life.[142] Kramer leads Billy into a ship's hull, where, "out of sight," Billy witnesses a scene entirely removed from that of the tower, and it shocks him.

Forced to labor in intense heat, foul air, and darkness, the men in the hull regularly risk death or disablement.[143]

Unable to sustain the tower perspective of commercial and technological achievement, Billy begins to write from another. His next "America They Know" story features union leader Jim Marsh, and he struggles to report a long, bitter, and violent strike that grips the harbor. Although the novel ends with the strike broken and Billy on the verge of poverty, the tone is hopeful. Billy's education is complete, and its value is manifest. In critic John Hart's estimation, he has found a perspective from which to "rediscover a segment of the American story that had somehow got tangled in several decades of business consolidation and organized efficiency: the social and human rights of plain people."[144]

At the novel's conclusion, Billy gazes out at the harbor and notices "the Great Bridge of my childhood."[145] By evoking the novel's opening pages, Poole underscores Billy's journey. With its three distinct phases, *The Harbor* highlights the extent to which understanding and perspective are linked within the modern urban environment. Billy's search to know the harbor is a drive toward contextualization. Passing through a scornful rejection of circumstance and the ideology of civic boosterism, Billy's story is an education in the most literal sense: a process through which knowledge and understanding are acquired. Ultimately, Billy rejects the weighted view and confirms the whole.

As noted, *The Harbor* is an "American story," not a battle between international capitalism and international socialism. Poole does not advocate the overthrow of Dillon or the forces for which he works, just the rejection of a point of view that values aesthetics or commercial dominion over social, economic, and political context. As Billy states, the corporate oligarchy represented by Dillon will fail "because it's not democracy."[146] What Poole details in *The Harbor* is the importance of social context within social change, and the ways in which democracy can be subverted through perspective. Dynamic and beautiful, the view from Dillon's tower is nevertheless undemocratic. It is the grand-style magisterial gaze weighted by an ideological predisposition to exclude.

"Sympathy" and the Urban Observer

The events in *The Harbor* can be charted on both temporal and spatial lines. Billy's initial contact with the harbor, stimulated by his youthful desire for romantic adventure, is marked by revulsion and flight. Unable to connect his idealism with the reality of harbor life, Billy literally moves *away*. He retreats to his home and from there to Princeton, then on to Paris. The purely aesthetic yearning of his time in France represents Billy's furthest removal from the harbor, both physically and contextually. From Paris, Billy's spatial movement is back to the harbor. Dillon's tower represents identification with the financial and technological forces of modernity; it is a contextualization, but one weighted by a corporate ideology of economic absolutes. The last stage, from the tower above the bridge to life below the bridge, is the completion of Billy's spatial journey. In effect, Billy's educational path is a "ritual process," as defined by Victor Turner. Billy moves from a familiar to an unfamiliar place, then back to the familiar place with a more clearly understood sense of community, of "ethical standards . . . vis-à-vis others."[147] Billy's education provides him with the ingredient he lacked in youth: he returns to the familiar setting of the harbor with a capacity for human empathy.

This change results in what Adam Smith called "sympathy," a concept that forms the backbone of Richard Sennett's 1990 study *The Conscience of the Eye*.[148] For Sennett, "sympathy" is the outcome of human identification. It is an act of will and belief that results in a rejection of difference. By creating an atmosphere in which difference is understood as threatening, not energizing, the modern city, according to Sennett, is designed to deter sympathy. The ideological consequences of Sennett's "conscience of the eye" provide an important key to the question posed earlier: when looking around, what does one see? Furthermore, where does one place one's sympathy? In many of the literary and visual works noted above, difference is accounted through *absence*. Isolated individuals on the bridge, who see only the skyline and the bridge towers, are without sympathy. Consequently, they promote the modern urban environment that itself promotes difference. For Sennett, this viewpoint translates into the distinctly ideological "modern cult of the object": "The modern cult of the object is about what is left when the artist no longer strives to arouse that momentary sympathetic union between people and their environment. He or she seeks only for the sublime effect—the seizure, the shock in itself, for itself. At that moment anti-social art is born."[149]

Implicit here is the orientation and organization of vision, and the implications of this taxonomy are within the story it narrates. For numerous critics, the "modern" object both appealed to and supplied natural unity. Yet this natural unity was inherently devoid of sympathy. It failed to orientate individuals toward each other, instead directing their attention toward the trappings of technological modernity. In short, the modern cult of the object, like the opening of the Brooklyn Bridge, created spectators out of participants.

This isolating redefinition is the essence of *The Harbor*. While under Dillon's influence, Billy sees the urban environment as a stage upon which only certain actors are fit to play. His writing directs attention to individuals with influence and creates an audience out of the population. Unity is presented through progress, yet this unity is based upon on a polar spilt between speaker and listener. As was the case at the bridge's opening, the population exists to be directed and ameliorated. By removing himself from the tower, Billy divorces himself from Dillon and unites in sympathy with the harbor. Although Mumford admired Poole's novel, the ideology of *The Harbor* is far removed from the "sudden revelation of power" found in *Sketches from Life*.

Within representations of the Brooklyn Bridge, the idea of sympathy forms the basis of an important counternarrative. Sennett himself writes of the graffiti artists of the 1970s who slept in transit authority storage dens beneath the bridge. Believing graffiti to be intrinsically linked to crime, the city government barricaded the dens, forcing the homeless onto the streets. The reasoning was simple: graffiti was written by an underclass that represented a potentially threatening, no doubt criminal, "difference."[150] The issue of the marginalized in relation to the bridge has been a theme in literature: Lawrence Ferlinghetti referred to the homeless who sleep beneath the bridge, and Gregory Corso wrote of the humiliating, poverty-stricken life of a kindly Jew who "fell and died beneath the Brooklyn Bridge."[151]

The story of Bud Korpenning in John Dos Passos's *Manhattan Transfer* (1925) provides literature's most famous story of hopelessness on the bridge. Unprepared for the modern urban environment—which reads as a novel-length exposition of the hysteria detailed by Henry Adams—the young and provincial Bud seems to be one of the few characters to hold Dos Passos's sympathy. Constantly looking for "the center of things," he wanders the island in a pathetically futile search. In a scene reminiscent of Quincy Burt's search for the soul of New York, Bud finally ends up on the bridge. His arrival there has been inspired by a realization, not a question. Drawn into the city's cutthroat environment, consumed and rejected, Bud's educational journey is at an end: "Dont matter where I go; cant go nowhere now."[152]

The story of Bud represents an interesting commentary on Le Gallienne's "Brooklyn Bridge at Dawn." Where Le Gallienne finds a "center" on the bridge at dawn, Bud finds only the need to escape. Even his suicide is ignominious and pathetic: "Bud is sitting on the rail of the bridge. The sun has risen behind Brooklyn. The windows of Manhattan have caught fire. He jerks himself forward, slips, dangles by a hand with the sun in his eyes. The yell strangles in his throat as he drops."[153] Where Le Gallienne gazes with reverence at the skyline, the characters in *Manhattan Transfer* seem to be perpetually mocked by the city's skyscrapers. Like Ralph Ellison's "invisible man," they realize that there is no "center of things" on the streets of Manhattan.

The "center of things" exists only in the corporate and speculative towers that dominate the city high overhead. If there is a tragic element to the novel, it is that Dos Passos's characters never really notice one another: they are too busy gazing with envy, reverence, or hatred at the city's skyscrapers.[154]

One of the most strenuous attempts to codify the modern environment of New York can be found within the voluminous work of Thomas Wolfe. According to Wolfe biographer Louis Rubin, the novelist's relationship with New York consisted of five stages, each of which is marked by a distinct image of the city. The first stage is distinguished by a shining vision of the city, and the last "identifies the city with absolute negation and death."[155] In between we find a gradual disillusionment. Yet, although it is true that Wolfe's protagonists tend to exhibit great anger and frustration, hope is nevertheless a constant.[156] What is in process in Wolfe's treatment of New York is a gradual realignment of the essence of this hope.

In *The Web and the Rock* (1939), Wolfe's protagonist, George Webber, is enchanted by the idea of New York while growing up in North Carolina. Wolfe's descriptions echo with the rhetoric of civic boosterism: "The city flashed before him like a glorious jewel, blazing with countless rich and brilliant facets of life so good, so bountiful, so strangely and constantly beautiful and interesting, that it seemed intolerable that he should miss a moment of it." Webber conjures this image from "a thousand isolated sources," one of which includes "a picture of Brooklyn Bridge with its great, winglike sweep, the song and music of its cables."[157]

Webber's first visit to the city causes an immediate adjustment in his expectations: "in the hairbreath of that instant recognition a whole new city is composed." Opulent achievement and aesthetic transcendence coexist alongside an environment—"hideously ugly for the most part"—marked by high levels of hunger and poverty.[158] Nevertheless, wishing to preserve his exemplary image, Webber goes in search of "the center of things." For Wolfe's characters, "the center of things" rests on a shifting, ambiguous set of ideas concerning the nature of success. Although in search of literary fame and accomplishment, Webber is intoxicated by wealth and influence, and he is diverted away from his writing and into an affair with Esther Jack, the wife of a Wall Street tycoon.

Webber's disillusion occurs because of this relationship with Esther, and its place within the narrative is central, not concluding, as Rubin believes. Faced with a city of polar opposites, Webber resolves his confusion through a realization: the city of Esther and her circle, although it was "the city he had longed to know," was not "the city of the homeless wanderer . . . the stranger looking at a million lights, the terrible, lonely, empty city of no doors." Esther's city is not Webber's, nor that of a majority of its inhabitants. Her life is an illusion sustained by wealth and influence.[159] After Esther recounts the key moments in her life — including her attendance at the opening of the Brooklyn Bridge —Wolfe states: "The effect of these stories was to evoke a picture of the world that was at first fabulous and fascinating in its Baghdadlike enchantments, but that quickly took on a more sinister hue as [Webber] read the meaning of its social implications. . . . It was a world that seemed to have gone insane with its own excess, a world of criminal privilege that flouted itself with an inhuman arrogance in the very face of a great city where half the population lived in filth and squalor."[160]

Unable to reconcile Esther's New York with the reality he finds on the street, Webber takes to wandering the city at night. His travels are an education, akin to Billy's in *The Harbor*. Nightly, Webber delves deeper into the regions of "filth and squalor" so absent in his youthful imaginings. He is horrified by what he witnesses, yet his walks provide a pathway out of disillusion and back to hope: "Sometimes in such a place, the madness of the shapes of death would leave him . . . and he would come back in the morning, from death to morning, walking on the bridge."[161]

In *You Can't Go Home Again* (1940), Webber breaks with Esther's circle and moves to Brooklyn. From there, he continues his search to know the city: "he would walk to Brooklyn Bridge and cross it to Manhattan, and ferret out the secret heart of darkness in all the city's ways, and then at dawn come back across the Bridge once more." Through this process, Webber is able to realize an alternative social vision. Unlike the bright city glorified in the promotional material available to a young man in North Carolina, this city is based on nightly trips to such places as the "comfort station" at the foot of the Brooklyn Bridge. Passing through disillusion to hope, Webber finds a connection with New York: "my intense and passionate concern for the interests and designs of my own life were coming to seem petty, trifling, and unworthy, and I was coming more and more to feel an intense and passionate concern for the interests and designs of my fellow-men and of all humanity."[162]

Early in *The Web and the Rock*, Webber states his "overwhelming conviction . . . that there were 'good' places and 'bad' ones."[163] In his search to know New York, his conception of the city flows from one to the other and back again. It does not end with "negation and death." Instead, Webber passes out of darkness and into morning. The lie is given to Webber's youthful image of the city and the bridge, and as that falls away, hope is rediscovered. Webber's education is a rejection of the influence of wealth and an acceptance of hope through sympathy. At either end is the Brooklyn Bridge. The first view of it is a decontextualized and promoted grand-style visual image; the second is based in the lived experience of the city's rich humanity. As the poet Edwin Morgan succinctly notes, if Wolfe's bridge "has magic, the magic comes from use." [164]

Shortly after Wolfe died in 1938, Langston Hughes published *The Big Sea* (1940). Although entirely different in substance and style, this autobiography offers an interesting parallel to the New York experience Wolfe described for his protagonist. Like Webber, Hughes was a Southerner who dreamed of coming to New York. Unlike the young man from North Carolina, Hughes was black, and the importance of race would be played out in his experience of New York.

Arriving in the city for the first time in 1921, Hughes was dazzled by the image of downtown Manhattan: "But, boy! At last! New York was pretty, rising out of the bay in the sunset — the thrill of those towers of Manhattan with their million golden eyes, growing slowly taller and taller above the green water, until they looked as if they could almost touch the sky! Then Brooklyn Bridge, gigantic in the dusk! Then the necklaces of lights, glowing everywhere around us, as we docked on the Brooklyn side. All this made me feel it was better to come to New York than to any other city in the world." [165] Yet Manhattan's towers would not long stand for and define Hughes's New York. Almost immediately, he was on the subway to Harlem, and a lifetime's obsession with the black neighborhood was formed. Just as Wolfe described, "in the hairbreath of that instant recognition" when Hughes steps out of the subway at 135th Street, "a whole new city is composed." The center of Hughes's New York was redefined from the skyline and the bridge to the "low-down folk" of the neighborhood. Henceforth, the lived experience of Harlem would dominate Hughes's literature, and he never returned to the iconography of downtown New York.

Conclusions

Sujata Bhatt's poem "Walking across the Brooklyn Bridge, July 1990" (1991) illustrates and clarifies many of the points made throughout this chapter. Bhatt begins by contrasting the morning news with the experience of walking the bridge. In New York, she writes, "children are being shot" and a man has fed "his six-day old son / to a hungry German Shepherd." But on the bridge "one feels removed from everything / as if one were passing in a low flying plane." Like Max Weber, Bhatt has "two worlds" before her. Yet Weber's triumphant declaration — "I lived in both!" — is for Bhatt a misgiving. Her lament continues: "today I see work being done. / Repairs. Clean, clear-cut / adjustments. Renovation." The contrast implies that similar "repairs" are not being conducted within the world around the bridge. Explicitly, a question is raised by this contrast: "I pause, look around. / What is real in this symbol, / in that other one over there. . . ?" She continues: "The steel cables have become a cage, / a sanctuary. Whose cage? / Whose hope?"[166]

Ultimately, Bhatt answers her own questions. Hope is not the reality of the children being killed in New York. It is, however, the dream of those wishing to enter the United States:

> Looking across the water
> I think of those people from Vietnam
> The mothers, the fathers,
> what they wouldn't have given,
> what they would still give—
> their blood, their hair, their lives, their kidneys,
> their lungs, their fingers, their thumbs—
> to get their children
> past the Statue of Liberty.

Within the world of the poem, the idea of hope is entirely ironic. Death is as likely to visit the Vietnamese children in New York as in Vietnam.[167]

Bhatt's poem epitomizes the effort to examine and destabilize the ways national cultural icons are perceived. At the center of her image of the Brooklyn Bridge is a question asked by Stephen Mills: "does the urban landscape overtly include its people?"[168] What is the relation between symbols and context, between rhetoric and reality? From the time of settlement, the reality of the New World has been defined through the abstractions "unity" and "hope." At the opening of the Brooklyn Bridge, both were referred to repeatedly. The structure was itself an emblem of unity and hope, fulfillment and promise. Bhatt addresses this idea. Who defines these concepts? Where do they reside, and where can they be sought? Do we illustrate unity and hope through the attainment of a "more perfect" social body or through the icons of technological progress and financial accomplishment? In short, should hope and unity be sought through the internal workings of the body politic or through the external phenomena of the modern cult of the object?

The cultural history of "viewing" the Brooklyn Bridge tells two stories. Artists working in the grand-style urban tradition produced visual and literary proof of New York's vast "splendors" by employing a depopulated, decontextualized aesthetic. They fashioned an image of the city defined by its technological and financial icons. Under their gaze, the city became a perfect art object, an aestheticized showcase for industrial and commercial progress. Moreover, it was emptied of any internal contradictions. As Sam Warner notes in "The Management of Multiple Urban Images," the skyline and the slum "described the same place, the modern city, but they did so without mutual recognition of interaction." [169] The title of Warner's essay contains the key: urban images may be "multiple" but they are also "managed."

Arthur Miller understood this concept. In *A View from the Bridge* (1956)—significantly not *the* view but *a* view—Miller gazed toward Brooklyn, not Manhattan. In effect, he turned his back on the "splendors" of the now "vast metropolis" and focused on the struggles of poor American immigrants. Unlike the artists and writers working in the urban grand style, Miller chose to populate and contextualize his view. To borrow from Henry George, he saw poverty where others saw progress. With "sympathy," Miller wrote his message in his representation. While some people were staring at the skyline, others were communing on the streets.

4 American Memory
History, Fiction, and the Brooklyn Bridge

Time dissipates to shining ether the solid angularity of facts.
— Ralph Waldo Emerson, "History," 1841

History is selective memory, and in time, the crisp contours of immediate experience slowly dissolve into the misty regions of folklore. Although the State's memory is geared to organize perception of public monuments around the official ideology of a given era, the survivors and the opponents of the State may provide alternative historical interpretations that change the way people perceive both the forms and the original meanings.
— Albert Boime, *The Unveiling of the National Icons*, 1998

In the end, he who screens the history makes the history.
— Gore Vidal, *Screening History*, 1992

The grand-style urban tradition of defining New York's cityscape sought to posit an essential truth. First and foremost, the Brooklyn Bridge was a physical manifestation of the monumental, economic city, not the anthropomorphic city of social context. Although this formulation elides human agency, the history of personal interaction with the bridge is also problematic. As Stanley Hyman noted in 1952, "the two things Brooklyn Bridge is most noted for — that confidence men used to sell it to gullible outlanders, and that Steve Brodie jumped off it — have little basis in fact."[1] Hyman's observation is as valid today as it was five decades ago. The "selling" of the bridge and Brodie's jump remain entrenched in the popular consciousness as the two most notable "events" in the bridge's post-opening history. Yet both stories exist in the contested realm of popular folklore, and neither can be confirmed with any real certainty. Through almost a century and a quarter, the bridge's cultural history has been dominated by episodes that, in all probability, never happened. Consequently, the bridge's place in the national memory owes as much to invented tradition as to historical accuracy.[2]

The Case of Steve Brodie

Of the two events, Brodie's is the more instructive. No evidence exists that the bridge has ever been sold to a "gullible outlander," whereas the fact of Brodie's claim, if not the substance of its content, *is* historically accurate. On

44. The fear and fascination of falling from the bridge have long been threaded into the bridge's cultural fabric, beginning before the bridge was even finished. "A Young Girl Plunged Headlong from the Bridge," *Street and Smith's New York Weekly*, May 16, 1881. Courtesy of the Library of Congress.

July 23, 1886, witnesses saw what appeared to be a human figure plummeting from the Brooklyn Bridge into the East River. Several minutes later, Brodie was dragged from the water by a boatload of his associates. Loudly, he claimed to have just leapt from the bridge, and he repeated his assertion upon reaching the shore. After hearing the claim, the police promptly arrested Brodie and carted him off to the Tombs, where he was examined by a police physician.

A year earlier, Robert Odlum had made history by jumping from the bridge. Although the fear and fascination of falling from the bridge had long been threaded into the bridge's cultural fabric, Odlum's was the first recorded jump. And the outcome was fatal: his body was crushed by the impact, and he died a few hours later. By contrast, Brodie sustained only minor injuries. Physically, he appeared shaken, had a small bruise on his chest, and complained of a pain in his midriff. The examining doctor believed the bruise had likely been incurred by climbing into the boat, and Brodie's wife later testified that her husband often suffered from abdominal pain. As for his shaken state, it is easily explained by the copious amounts of whiskey he was reported to have drunk subsequent to his rescue. Concluding his examination, the police physician noted that Brodie was "in excellent condition."[3]

However suspicious the circumstances surrounding Brodie's leap, no one in the press seemed to care. The *Tribune* led with the banner, "From the

Bridge in Safety," and the *Times* with "A Leap from the Bridge, Steve Brodie's Plunge into the East River."[4] The *Tribune* and the *Times* offer paradigmatic examples of the press's response to the supposed feat. Both chronicled Brodie's "actions" in minute detail and with no doubts as to their validity. Yet these accounts, although written only a few hours after Brodie emerged from the river, belong to the imaginative life of the event, not to the historical evidence of the happening itself. In essence, they constitute the first retelling of an event that would ultimately be retold countless times.

As a media event, Brodie's leap shows remarkable similarities to the bridge's opening ceremonies. In both cases, "rhetoric" and "reportage" became inseparable: by July 24, 1886, Brodie's claims and the press reports were identical. Needless to say, such confluences cause profound historical tensions. Odlum's fatal leap of a year earlier initiated a minor craze for the "sport." This enthusiasm in turn led to greater police vigilance, and potential jumpers resorted to increasingly covert schemes to evade detection. In the coverage of Brodie's "leap," however, the abundance of details defies the level of secrecy needed to accomplish the feat. A majority of the press reports provided firsthand accounts of the entire day: from Brodie's efforts to elude the police, through the jump, landing, and rescue, and on into custody. Direct quotations punctuate the stories, and the action is detailed "blow-by-blow." With so much "on-the-spot" reporting, one imagines a large pack of forewarned and intrepid journalists following Brodie on every step of his adventure — a scenario that could not have been the case. Instead, the coverage reads like a press release, authored by a single vested interest rather than a variety of impartial sources.[5] Here the evidence verifying Brodie's jump takes on the contours of Boorstin's pseudo event: it was both "planned" and "planted."[6]

Why was Brodie's jump so swiftly and conclusively validated by the press? There are two main reasons, both of which remind us of the journalism found at the bridge's opening. First, like the bridge's trustees, Brodie had strong connections with the press. His brother ran a restaurant just off Printing House Square that was much frequented by newsmen, and his friend Tom Brennan, a principal figure in the day's events, was a printer with "numerous connections in the newspaper world."[7] In addition, most of the city's journalists were already familiar with Brodie. A minor celebrity in New York's Fourth Ward, Brodie was well known for his antics and showmanship.

The second reason for journalistic validation stems from Brodie's popularity and charisma. Odlum's jump had been derided in the press. The *Times* felt that "it was not too valuable a life to be used in demonstrating the folly of the performance," and the paper later editorialized on "Captain" Boyton, who had aided Odlum in his attempt: "Had he decided to jump from the bridge there is not a man in this city who would have been so heartless as to interfere with him. The very policemen would have forgotten their orders and would have turned their backs on *Boyton* as soon as he made his appearance on the bridge. Indeed, it would have been easy to raise by popular subscription a large sum of money to induce *Boyton* to jump."[8] In an editorial titled "Notoriety Hunting," the *Times* mocked Odlum's stunt as stupid and irresponsible.[9] A year later, however, its opinion of publicity seekers had changed. Under the headline "Brodie's Path to Wealth," the paper celebrated the Irishman's newfound celebrity and the financial rewards it might bring. Where Odlum's quest for notoriety was deemed idiotic, Brodie's was somehow commendable.

Behind the *Times*'s ethical shift lay the issues of personality and perceived outcome. Brodie was popular, attractive, and ostensibly a success. In addition, he played out his role with the skill of a seasoned actor. Appearing for his arraignment, "Brodie was not unmindful of the fame which he had achieved, and when he was escorted into the court room he entered it like a conquering hero."[10] In short, Brodie's claim was irresistible news, too good to question.

Several years later, the journalist Ernest Jarrold began to research Brodie's claims. Although he tracked down and interviewed everyone involved, he could find no one outside of Brodie's circle who could substantiate the episode.[11] Even the journalists who had provided "on-the-spot" coverage denied having witnessed the jump. Concurrent with Jarrold's inquiry, a rumor began to circulate that it was not the Irishman but a weighted dummy that had plunged from the bridge on July 23, 1886. Brodie, it was said, stationed himself under a nearby pier and swam out only after the dummy hit the water. This version of events quickly gained currency and today stands as the dominant historical interpretation.[12]

Paradoxically, this suspicion grew alongside the public's mounting fascination. Brodie's "famous saloon" quickly became a tourist hotspot, and the abundant publicity helped launch his successful stage career.[13] By all accounts a mediocre actor and singer, Brodie nevertheless commanded large audiences whenever he appeared. Although he mostly performed in theatrical standards and vaudeville, Brodie played himself in two popular plays, *On the Bowery* (1894) and *One Night in Brodie's Barroom* (1898). In the latter, references to the "leap" abound. In the former, the event was re-created in a suitably heroic manner: an innocent young lady has been ruthlessly thrown from the bridge; to save her, Brodie must again make the dive. "There's one chance in a thousand that you can save her," he is told. "Will you take it, Brodie?" "You bet your life I will!" he responds. Even for Victorian melo-

45. "Steve Brodie, Champion Bridge-Jumper of the World." Fly poster for *On the Bowery*, 1894. Courtesy of the Library of Congress.

drama, *On the Bowery* was hackneyed, but it was also a smash hit. It crystallized the leap within the public's imagination and added to Brodie's box-office appeal. "To say that the play was a success is an absurd understatement," reported Alvin Harlow, who attended the premiere. "[T]he day of the opening . . . was like Inauguration Day in Washington."[14]

Despite Brodie's own theatrical endeavors, the most remarkable re-creation of his leap occurred decades later in *The Bowery*, a film directed by Raoul Walsh and produced by Darryl Zanuck in 1933. Its narrative weaves together history and folklore in a vision that ultimately affirms Brodie's claim. Set in the 1890s, *The Bowery* concerns the rivalry between Brodie, played by George Raft, and the infamous (and also Irish) Chuck Connors, played by Wallace Beery. Each fronts a fire brigade; both desire the affections of Lucy Calhoun, played by Fay Wray. To resolve the rivalry, Brodie makes a wager with Connors: if Brodie survives a leap from the bridge, Connors's saloon, the neighborhood, and Lucy will be his; if not, his death will leave Connors in full control. Connors agrees, and Brodie begins to prepare for his big day.

Unbeknown to Connors, Brodie intends to throw a dummy from the bridge, swim out into the East River, and claim victory. Everything goes according to plan until, at the last minute, Brodie's prop goes missing. To save face, he makes the leap himself and survives.

In the end, *The Bowery* displays the power of cultural fiction to validate historical memory. Patently fabricated, the film nevertheless supports and sustains a historical position. In the world of film, Brodie wins his bet; in the world of American memory, George Raft sustains the Brodie myth. As Luc Sante notes, "the fact is that people very much wanted to believe the story, regardless of its improbability. It became legend very quickly, and thus joined that body of lore which nobody cares to upset, since, after all, the literal truth hardly matters."[15]

In *The Man Who Shot Liberty Valance* (1962), film director John Ford explored these questions of "literal truth" and the complexities of historical memory. In Shinbone, a lawless western town, Ransom Stoddard, played by Jimmy Stewart, is a dishwasher who rises to become a U.S. senator after he shoots and kills the notorious outlaw Liberty Valance. When Stoddard confides to the editor of the *Shinbone Star* that he did not in fact kill Valance, the journalist is unconcerned: "This is the West, sir. When the legend becomes fact, print the legend!" For the editor, as for those who promoted the legend of Steve Brodie, the truth is beside the point. Few contemporaries seemed to believe that Brodie actually leapt from the bridge, yet the tale persists. Even those investigators who deny Brodie's claim seem drawn to the romance of the affair: more column inches are always accorded to the claim than to the refutation. As a result, Brodie has become a central figure in the cultural history of the Brooklyn Bridge. His name is synonymous with the structure, second only to that of John Roebling.

With no definitive proof on either side, the events of July 23, 1886, exist in the shaded region between fact and fiction, truth and legend. This duality is precisely what makes the episode so distinctive. Although we may never know whether Brodie jumped or whether a stuffed dummy fell, we may be sure of the life of the story and its place within the wider sphere of American public memory. And it is this cultural space — between rhetoric and veracity, fiction and history, permanence and change — that has dominated the bridge's cultural history from the onset of the Great Depression to its centennial in 1983.

Reception, Representation, and Commemoration

American history is often defined by its "bent toward visual presentation," as David Lowenthal explains.[16] This emphasis provides an index to the life of the Brooklyn Bridge. Because of its striking visual prominence, the bridge has often served as a stage for public demonstrations. From the newsboy strike of 1899 to the pro-choice march of August 2004, protesters have taken to the bridge in order to increase the visibility of their campaigns. Yet social protest and American cultural memory rarely exist in a comfortable alliance. Clio is a discriminating muse, and as many critics have noted, "official" national memory tends to elide social dissent in favor of celebration and praise.[17] The history of the Brooklyn Bridge confirms this tendency, with official commemoration prioritized over protest's multiple voices.

Although the bridge's key historical moments seem to substantiate Lowenthal's observation, there is a crucial distinction: they are often less *visual* than *visualized*. Brodie's jump was not witnessed but imagined. Like bird's-eye representations of New York City in the nineteenth century, the event was a mental image, not an observed and recorded fact. The dichotomies between the visual and the visualized are aptly summarized by Christopher Isherwood: "I am a camera with its shutter open, quite passive, recording, not thinking. Recording the man shaving at the window opposite and the woman in the kimono washing her hair. Someday, all this will have to be developed, carefully printed, fixed."[18] Here Isherwood juxtaposes the accuracy of the "recording" with the as yet unfixed "reading." The process is paramount: the neutral visual evidence collected by Isherwood the observer awaits the interpretation of development, printing, and fixing by Isherwood the author. The trajectory is from *reception* to *representation*.

The interplay between reception and representation has troubled numerous critics of cultural memory. For several, the historical connection that links event to commemoration is often broken by the reconfiguration of history into idealized myth.[19] The effect produces a "consensual" American master narrative that is at once unchanging and abstracted. Lifted above the messy business of history, such narratives separate social values from social conditions. Likewise, the complexities of context are ignored. Although it is possible to agree with these critics in their conclusions, one must realize that the relation between event and commemoration is less a historical divorce than a thematic link. John R. Gillis notes that, in the twentieth century, "memory and identity" became "detached from their original meanings, they have the status of free-floating phenomena."[20] Certainly, Gillis's conclusions would seem accurate were it not for his reliance on "original meanings" and thus on a fixed set of standards and beliefs. Cultural critics, for example, have rarely agreed about the essence of America's original meanings. In fact, the attractiveness of such canonical figures as Thomas Jefferson and Abraham Lincoln, in addition to their pivotal roles in such events as the

American Revolution and the American Civil War, lies precisely within their "free-floating" malleability.[21] This idea is compounded when we recall the nature of the "original meanings" ascribed to the Brooklyn Bridge at its opening day. In the history of the bridge, commemorations have not perverted "original meanings" but sought to confirm them.

Unlike Isherwood's camera eye, official commemorations of the Brooklyn Bridge have rarely been "passive . . . not thinking." Instead they have actively reinforced the message — ideologically specific, yet historically abstract — promulgated at the bridge's opening. Commemorations have attempted to fix a mental image of the bridge that is both visual and rhetorical. They have inextricably linked the idea of progress and achievement to the bridge, while simultaneously denying the changing social climate. Periodic tributes to the bridge have continued the opening day's assignment by visualizing the structure as a prime, unchanging American symbol. This ritualized "assent" has marked the bridge's history, and at no time has this process been more overt than at the fiftieth anniversary of the bridge's opening.

The Fiftieth Anniversary

In August 1928, Herbert Hoover informed America that "today we are nearer to the final triumph over poverty than ever before in the history of any land. The poorhouse is vanishing from amongst us."[22] In three months Hoover would win the presidency; within fifteen months the U.S. economy would be in freefall. By the end of Hoover's four-year term, his administration and reputation were in tatters. America's Great Depression was the most severe and prolonged economic crisis in the nation's history, profoundly affecting the lives of millions of Americans. Just as the national psyche appeared to be "index-linked" to the bubbling national economy in the 1920s, so the economic hemorrhaging of the early 1930s traumatized the country. The election of Franklin Roosevelt in 1932 somewhat staunched the nation's anguish, yet the depression refused to lift. Despite Roosevelt's energetic and far-reaching legislation, the ailing economy would not be resuscitated. Paradoxically, it would take war in Europe to rouse the national psyche from its sickbed.

The last days of Hoover's presidency provided the backdrop to the bridge's fiftieth anniversary. In July 1932, the American industrial index had declined 87 percent from the highs of September 1929. The following winter was the depression's worst; as the year turned, unemployment reached 25 percent. By general consensus, the early months of 1933 were the decade's bleakest. Unemployment paralyzed many cities; farm incomes, already low in 1929, had declined still further by 60 percent; and the stolid leadership of the lame duck president only exacerbated the national mood.[23] In February, the nation's banking system began to collapse, and by March 4, the day of Roosevelt's inauguration, the panic had reached the financial powerhouses of Chicago and New York.

Roosevelt inspired optimism, but the nation needed results, not rhetoric. Certainly the new president's four-day "bank holiday," coupled with his fireside chats, helped Americans regain their confidence. Yet confidence alone could not offset mass unemployment and increasing poverty. Roosevelt's first one hundred days amounted to an ambiguous period. The National Industrial Recovery Act's promise of improved workers' rights hid what was effectively the suspension of antitrust laws, and to many observers the Agricultural Adjustment Act of May 1933 appeared an exercise in absolute lunacy. Although the act would ultimately revive the farming economy, its immediate effects proved shocking to poverty-stricken Americans. As New York geared up to celebrate the Brooklyn Bridge's fiftieth year, many hungry Americans were forced to witness the mass destruction of crops and livestock.[24]

By May 24, 1933, such important legislation and programs as the Glass-Steagall Act and the Civil Works Administration had yet to be drafted, and the Federal Emergency Relief Administration was awaiting adequate funds. The nation's sense of its own crisis was acute; the national errand was stalled. Yet it is in such times that American rituals of assent are most effective. They can project and confirm a set of abstract historical values, even when they stem from a troubled social climate. By focusing on carefully selected historical moments, standards, and achievements, the contemporary context can be undermined and the national mood reinvigorated. In this respect, the celebration of the Brooklyn Bridge's fiftieth anniversary represents an American ritual of assent *par excellence*.

On May 24, 1933, a "mythic concordance" between event and anniversary was achieved with precision.[25] In historical terms, the opening and the fiftieth anniversary were linked: both transpired during times of extensive economic depression, social turmoil, and political division. Consequently, both events should have been colored by serious national concern. Yet when invoking history, myth rarely reflects it accurately. Both celebrations practiced a studied avoidance of social context. No mention was made of the nation's current economic collapse at the fiftieth anniversary; in fact, the news reports of the day would lead readers to believe the celebration was occurring during the boom conditions of the 1920s. This contextual denial — perhaps best described as a flight from the present — pervaded the entire day. Observations on present conditions were subjugated to idealized memories of the past.

46. The visible presence of the Great Depression. No amount of rhetoric could explain away breadlines next to the Brooklyn Bridge. Anonymous, "Bread Line beside the Brooklyn Bridge Approach," ca. 1930–1935. Courtesy of the Farm Security Administration, Office of War Information Photograph Collection, Library of Congress.

The historian Mike Wallace has criticized public history programs for presenting the past as "a vision of a total social order." Wallace's quarrel is not with selection—which he rightly sees as a historical necessity—but with the way in which "selections and silences . . . generate ways of *not* seeing" and become "instruments of . . . dominance" (my emphasis).[26] As noted earlier, the opening celebrations generated "ways of *not* seeing" by rhetorically reconfiguring the social climate, and this blinkered approach to history was replicated at the fiftieth anniversary. The *New York Times* proclaimed "Brooklyn Bridge: Fifty Vivid Years," but the ceremonies belied the paper's view of a dynamic history.[27] There was almost no mention of the massive social, political, and economic changes wrought in the intervening years; to the extent that it was noticed at all, the historical path from 1883 to 1933 was a simple tale of continued progress, increasing prosperity, and social harmony.[28]

The *Eagle* evoked an almost mystical relationship between 1883 and 1933, yet also referred to the bridge "when it had no skyline" to frame its magnificence.[29] Despite the claim of historical kinship, the reference to New York's evolving skyline is revealing: no amount of rhetoric could deny that the physical, economic, and social landscape surrounding the bridge *had* altered, and radically. In effect, the anniversary mentioned little that was true to the life of the nation's people; only the bridge and its opening ceremonies stood in vivid relief.

This backward-looking flight from the present was confirmed when the office of Mayor Fiorello La Guardia declared that the fiftieth anniversary would constitute a "re-enactment of the celebrations of 1883."[30] For all intents and purposes, the jubilee was a historical pageant, and, as David Glassberg has shown, historical pageants of the 1930s characterized the past "as a stable refuge insulated from present crises, rather than also as a way to comprehend how those crises developed." They sought to place America on the firm ground of yesteryear, and the implications were clear. Despite the changing context, the country's foremost moral index was the past.[31] The massive social changes swirling around the bridge over the past fifty years were irrelevant: if the bridge had symbolized hope, progress, and achievement in 1883, so it did in 1933. As numerous commentators noted, the bridge embodied timeless traits fundamental to the American character.[32] The country's moral climate was fixed, not subject to social forces, nor ethnic, political, or economic change. The America that had built the bridge was the same America that was celebrating its first fifty years.

The fiftieth anniversary extended the social fiction of the opening day by relying heavily on its rhetoric. Not only did writers ignore the social realities of their own time, but their understanding of 1883 was taken entirely from the opening-day speeches. The orations of Abram Hewitt and Seth Low were cited to highlight American prosperity, social harmony, and economic equity. The Reverend Richard Storrs was quoted to demonstrate how deeply the city's general population had concurred with official opinion.[33] Commentators in 1933 granted Hewitt's speech priority just as those in 1883 had. In "The Story of the Brooklyn Bridge," Harvey Douglas updated Hewitt's fanciful claim that "the distribution of the fruits of labor is approaching from age to age to more equitable conditions, and must, at last, reach the plane of absolute justice between man and man." After reciting Hewitt's comparison between the wage scales on the pyramids and those on the Brooklyn Bridge, Douglas compared Hewitt's figures for 1883 with figures from 1933. For a nation wracked by depression, Douglas's findings were remarkably positive. Since 1883, average daily earnings had risen from $2.50 to $10.40. Douglas, however, based these figures on "prevailing union wage scales"—a fantasy to most workers—and made no mention of the nation's crippling unemployment rate or its effect on average wages. Douglas confidently reached the same conclusions as Hewitt: "with faith in existing systems of good government, sound business and scientific invention," America would continue on its path toward national equity.[34]

Douglas also noted the second major theme of Hewitt's opening-day speech, with some modification. Just as Hewitt deemed the bridge's "post-Tweed" history to have been honest and transparent, so in 1933 the press went to great lengths to stress the absolute integrity of the construction. Even where Hewitt was unable to claim unqualified honesty — Tweed still loomed large in the public consciousness — writers in 1933 overlooked the now distant memory. Tweed's $60,000 payoff received no mention during the fiftieth anniversary, and Hewitt's intimate connection to the infamous wire fraud had yet to become public knowledge. Douglas explained the transference of ownership — from a private to a public venture — by subjugating truth to a comforting falsehood. Ironically, as Hewitt noted, it was scandal, fraud, and public outrage that forced the New York and Brooklyn Bridge Company to become a public entity. Douglas, on the other hand, described the change as an economic necessity: when private investors failed to raise sufficient capital, the city's good citizens took on the burden for the public benefit. By muddying the historical record, Douglas was able to conclude "that the trustees . . . emerged from all this turmoil and detraction with clean hands and completely vindicated for their management."[35]

Paul Connerton's "mythic concordance" can be established only when history's detailed contours have been smoothed away. It is through this leveling that acts of commemorative retelling become pointedly ideological. The cultural process of selection and invention allows the past to be shorn of conflict. In describing the opening, the *Times* helped to dispel some of the contradictions and conflicts found in 1883. It noted, for example, that "the entire city took a holiday."[36] Although it might seem trivial to point out that only Brooklyn declared the opening a public holiday, the point is an important one. On the opening day the *Times* itself declared that, for the residents of Manhattan, "there could be no specific cause of congratulation, since not one in one thousand of them will be likely ever to have occasion to use the new structure."[37] Conversely, several Brooklyn newspapers expressed anger at the fact that Manhattan had failed to mark the day with a public holiday. By claiming that "the entire city took a holiday," the *Times* nullified a rift that had deeply divided the two then independent cities.

The *Times* was also responsible for redefining the significance of the opening date itself. As noted in chapter 1, the decision to open the bridge on Queen Victoria's birthday was met with agitation and outcry. This public disapproval was not mentioned in 1933. Instead, the *Times* found another important historical association: on May 24, 1883, it claimed, Americans had also celebrated the centenary of the British evacuation of Manhattan at the close of the American Revolution. Unfortunately, the year was correct, but the date was spurious: the British evacuation took place on November 25. Nevertheless, by inventing an important national lineage — even though no mention of the centenary had been made in May 1883 — the *Times* cast aside one of the most contentious aspects of the opening day.[38]

The flight from the present at the fiftieth anniversary was graphically illustrated in a nineteen-page commemorative supplement issued by the *Eagle*. Although it incorporated history, trivia, and apocrypha, its main focus, apparently, was public opinion. In the preceding weeks, *Eagle* reporters had interviewed numerous Brooklynites about the bridge, and their remarks were printed throughout the supplement. The outcome was far from comprehensive, however. The interviewees were selected and segregated into two distinct groups. The first group constituted "old *Eagle* readers," whose memories of the opening were mainly brief and somewhat nostalgic.[39] Several were members of prominent families who had walked over the bridge on the afternoon of the opening day.[40] Nevertheless, these wistful recollections were occasionally countered by less happy memories. The immigrant Peter Ciancimion told how he "Escaped Theater and Bridge Tragedy"; A. J. Leonhardt recounted how he was "Made Ill by Visit to Bridge Caisson"; and W. H. Hickerson described having been "Marooned 6 Hours in Bridge Crowd" (while sustaining "three broken ribs").[41] The Memorial Day panic featured heavily in the reminiscences: Lena McDicken remembered how she "Had Dress Torn Off in Bridge Tragedy"; Mrs. Christine Wagner "Recall[ed] the Shock of Bridge Tragedy"; Alfred E. Shipley described how he "Barely Escaped Bridge Tragedy"; and "H. J." from Islip narrated how he "Was Able to Save 2 from Death in Panic."[42] These recollections constitute a mixed response, yet they all concerned the past. Judgments about the state of contemporary Brooklyn, or the hopes for its future, were reserved for other commentators.

Larger headlines and more space were devoted to another of the supplement's sections: "Business and Civic Leaders of Borough Look into Future, Give Views on Progress Made in Half-Century and Tasks Remaining."[43] Unlike the remembrances of some older readers, the opinions recorded in this section sounded no negativity. Here, Brooklyn's progression from a small village to a bustling industrial center was an uncomplicated tale of great political leadership and heroic commercial achievement. In accord with the status of those interviewed — mostly company presidents — social history was overridden by economic history. In effect, social merit was linked to corporate profits, and the story presented was of universal prosperity. To borrow from Susan Davis, the *Eagle* helped ratify the corporate "privatization of public historical memory."[44]

Amid the "vigorous optimism,"[45] one might logically wonder what these business leaders made of the devastated contemporary economy. Quite simply, it was ignored. Despite the hardships suffered throughout Brooklyn and the nation, none of the interviewees mentioned the national depression; their opinions focused on exceptional economic achievement. For some, conditions in contemporary America were both buoyant and healthy: "Growth Substantial Says McLaughlin" (George V. McLaughlin, president of the Brooklyn Trust Company); "Namm Sees Growth in Every Field" (Benjamin H. Namm, president of the Namm Store); and "No Spot in America So Bright — Gorman" (Charles A. Gorman, president of Henry Baiterman Company). Others linked the past to the future without reference to the uncomfortable present: "Hesterberg Sees Future Unlimited" (Henry Hesterberg, borough president of Brooklyn); "Wills Sees No Limit to Possibilities" (Louis Charles Wills, president of the Brooklyn Chamber of Commerce); and "Anything Possible, Declares Hammitt" (Walter Hammitt, president of Frederick Loeser and Company).[46] Striking notes usually reserved for times of genuine prosperity, all of these prominent Brooklynites employed the rhetoric of the American ritual of assent. The commemoration's self-evident truth was that America, equally stalled and anxious in 1933, was actually soaring toward ever greater achievement. Wallace has written that, in the early years of the twentieth century, "the bourgeoisie buckled History around themselves like moral armor."[47] At the Brooklyn Bridge's fiftieth anniversary, this formulation was extended to include both the present and the future.

The demarcation between ordinary and influential Brooklynites illustrates an important aspect of commemoration, and replicates an ideological theme prevalent at the bridge's opening. Whereas average citizens were invited to remember, only business leaders were given the opportunity to project and define. At the fiftieth anniversary, those who spoke for contemporary and future America were all of a type. In this respect, there was little difference between Hewitt and the men to whom the *Eagle* turned for guidance about contemporary and future America. Additionally, the *Eagle*'s coverage raised a crucial question of citizenship. Through selection and precedence, a social canon was formed. What the *Eagle* supplement underscored was the differing status of Brooklyn's residents. Those able to "Give Views on Progress Made in Half Century and Tasks Remaining" were Brooklyn's political and commercial elite, those with their "finger on the pulse." In short, these opinions were important, whereas those of average citizens were not.

John Bodnar has written that "cultural leaders orchestrate commemorative events to calm anxiety about change or political events, eliminate citizen indifference toward official concerns, [and] promote exemplary patterns of citizen behavior. . . . They feel the need to do this because of the existence of social contradictions, alternative views, and the indifference that perpetuate fears of societal dissolution and unregulated political behavior."[48] This "calming" is distinctly ideological; it is expressed and enacted through crucial decisions of selection, denial, and invention. The narrative at the Brooklyn Bridge's fiftieth anniversary was an intriguing combination of both fact and fiction. Outstanding levels of achievement were evoked in the midst of an economic collapse; progress was hailed as the result of reactionary values. When the "legend" of the opening day became the "fact" of the 1930s, the legend found its way into print.

Conformity and Modernization

The Brooklyn Bridge emerged from 1933 as an unchanging, independent cultural icon. Not bound by New York's protean social realities, the bridge was free to support the rhetoric of the city's political and commercial elite of corporate growth and prosperity. Subsequent commemorations only furthered this trend.[49] Yet outside the realm of national symbolism, the bridge *was* changing. Increased automobile traffic had put an immense physical strain on the bridge, and remodeling was often discussed. In 1934, bridge engineer David Steinman submitted a proposal that called for replacing the entire roadway, the elevated walkway, and the bridge's distinctive diagonal stays—everything, in fact, that made the Brooklyn Bridge the Brooklyn Bridge. Not surprisingly, this plan was rejected. Fourteen years later, however, Steinman was asked to submit a less radical proposal, and in 1950 he was awarded the task of renovation.

By all accounts, Steinman loved the Roeblings' famous span. He "grew up in the shadows of the bridge," published an early biography of John and Washington Roebling, composed poetry that praised its "haunting beauty," and lost no occasion to trumpet its influence on his professional career.[50] He even included an image of the bridge on his Christmas cards. Steinman "took five years out of my professional life" to write his biography of the Roeblings, he explained, "to repay my debt of inspiration to the Brooklyn Bridge and its builders." And "when people expressed concern about the proposed reconstruction and modernization of the beautiful old span," he was "glad to reassure them that the appearance of the Bridge would not be changed. To me, Brooklyn Bridge is sacred."[51] Steinman's earnest professions are difficult to reconcile with his twenty-year campaign to remodel the bridge. On the

47. Before Steinman. New York City, Department of Public Works, "The Brooklyn Bridge, Outer Roadway," 1939. Courtesy New York City Municipal Archives.

48. After Steinman. Encasing the entire outer roadway in steel girders. The Brooklyn Bridge, outer roadway, 2004. From the author's collection.

one hand the bridge was "sacred"; on the other, it required fundamental change. When Steinman finally began the modernization, his declarations that "the appearance of the Bridge would not be changed" and that the "Brooklyn Bridge is sacred" were finally tested.

Steinman's renovation was controversial, if perhaps inevitable. To stiffen and strengthen the bridge's roadway so that it could accommodate increased vehicular traffic, Steinman effectively encased the entire outer roadway in steel girders. Several critics voiced dismay at what was to them no renovation but an all-out remodeling. At the reopening ceremony in 1954, Mayor Robert F. Wagner affirmed that "the original beauty has not been impaired" and that the bridge had not been altered in any fundamental way. Yet the title of the day's souvenir program—*New/Old Brooklyn Bridge*—contradicted his appraisal: where once there had been an "old" Brooklyn Bridge, now there was a "new" one.[52]

An acerbic reply to the renovation, "What Happened to Brooklyn Bridge," soon appeared in the *Architectural Forum*. The editors declared that Steinman's changes had destroyed "what was most appealing in it at first." The additional steel girders impaired the view from the walkway, all but blocked the view from the lower deck, produced a significantly heavier, more muscular span, and flattened its graceful, lilting curvature.[53] The journal's reaction centered on the criticism that modernization had destroyed the bridge's most vital attribute: its sight lines. By failing to retain a consulting architect or to confer with New York's Municipal Art Society, the city's Public Works Commission had subjugated all considerations to economic expediency. After modernization, the *Forum* complained, "everything was there — except the old soaring magic" that constituted John Roebling's "chief message" and the bridge's most vital aspect.[54] Neither Steinman nor the city had taken account of the elder Roebling's intentions: "the sightlines that are now destroyed *he put there.*"[55] Underlying this claim was the conviction that the bridge now spanning the East River was no longer the one designed, built, and dedicated in the nineteenth century. The Roeblings' bridge now belonged to the past; in its place stood Steinman's bridge.[56]

The bridge's remodeling explains an important moment in the bridge's cultural history: at midcentury, the "old soaring magic" of Roebling's bridge gave way to the pedestrian utility of Steinman's. This realignment seemed to consign the bridge's influence to the past. Yet even before Steinman's remodeling, several writers had questioned the bridge's timeless nature and contemporary significance. In 1915 James Huneker lamented that the bridge had become "too familiar," and in 1930 Carl Van Vechten wrote that "the 'sights' of New York change perpetually. . . . The Brooklyn Bridge is still to be observed, but the Hudson Tube is a more modern wonder."[57] At the bridge's fiftieth anniversary three years later, only a fraction of the anticipated crowd — about five thousand people — attended the commemorative re-creation of the opening day. Although the anniversary's rhetoric stressed the bridge's continued relevance, few New Yorkers were interested enough to attend. Neither Nikolaus Pevsner's *Pioneers of Modern Design* (1936) nor Sigfried Giedion's *Space, Time, and Architecture* (1941) — arguably the two most significant studies of modern architecture — assigned the bridge any real importance, despite devoting considerable attention to the design of bridges. In comparison with more modern marvels — the George Washington Bridge, the Golden Gate Bridge, and bridges designed by the Swiss engineer Robert Maillart — the Brooklyn Bridge seemed an antiquated relic.[58]

Contemporary with Pevsner and Giedion, the Swiss architect, critic, and apostle of the new modernism Le Courbusier clarified the issue while maintaining a certain generosity: "Brooklyn Bridge, which is old (elevateds, cars, trucks, pedestrians all have special lanes), is as strong and rugged as a gladiator, while George Washington Bridge, built yesterday, smiles like a young athlete." The George Washington Bridge "is the most beautiful bridge in the world," he continued, "it is blessed. It is the only seat of grace in the disordered city."[59] Seemingly, a new champion had emerged to greet a new era. The Brooklyn Bridge no longer dominated the New York skyline; the span's heavy form and Gothic aesthetic was no match for the sleek, raw-steeled modernism of the George Washington Bridge.[60]

For G.W.F. Hegel, the leading idea behind each historical era expresses itself in an appropriate physical form.[61] Roebling wrestled with Hegel's dictum when designing the bridge. His solutions, so fitting for the late nineteenth and early twentieth century, seemed to have outlived their relevance by the 1940s and 1950s. According to the Russian poet and architect Andrei Voznesenski, the bridge in 1961 was struggling to compete with the industrial aesthetic of Eero Saarinen's Trans World Airlines terminal building at the New York International Airport:

Airport—accredited embassy
Of Ozone and sun!

A hundred generations
have not dared what you have won—
The discarding of supports.

In place of great stone idols
A glass of cool blue
without the glass,
Beside the baroque fortresses of savings banks
As anti-material
as gas.

Brooklyn Bridge, rearing its idiot stone, cannot consort
With this monument of the era,
The airport.[62]

Clearly, for a number of cultural commentators, the bridge had become — in its formal and vernacular usage — history.

Henry Miller, Harvey Shapiro, and American History

The Brooklyn Bridge was an integral part of American history for the writers Henry Miller and Harvey Shapiro. Unlike the people responsible for official commemoration, however, Miller and Shapiro articulated complex, vernacular responses to the bridge. Alan Trachtenberg has argued that

"Miller stripped the bridge altogether of its ties with American life,"[63] and this opinion seems borne out by Miller himself: "instead of joining me to life, to men, to the activity of men, the bridge seemed to break all connections."[64] Yet these two statements contain different subjects. Certainly, the bridge was capable of breaking "all connections" between Miller and society; nevertheless, this individual experience does not refute *the bridge's* connections with "American life." As Miller wrote:

> In studying the air-conditioned quality of the American nightmare, I am enchanted by the prospect of re-arranging the debris which has accumulated. . . . I see among countless other things a faded flower from Death Valley, a piece of quartz from the Bad Lands, a Navajo bead, a rusty meat-axe from the slaughterhouse, a drop of serum from the Cancer Institute, a louse from a Jew's beard, a street called Myrtle Avenue, a city made entirely of celluloid, another of cellophane, a cereal like dried brains called Grape Nuts, and so on. In the dead center of the debris, thoroughly renovated and thoroughly ventilated, stands the Brooklyn Bridge.[65]

By no means "stripped . . . of its ties with American life," the bridge stands at the center. Both "renovated and thoroughly ventilated," it is refreshed and ready to synthesize the nation's historical detritus. In essence, Miller's evocation of the bridge "in the dead center" of American life is remarkably similar to Sacvan Bercovitch's description of the American ritual of assent: "Technology and religion, politics and art, individualism and social progress, spiritual and economic values—all the fragmented aspects of thought, belief, and behavior in this pluralistic society flowed into *America*."[66] Miller, however, surrounds the bridge with "debris," not symbols of achievement and progress. Rubbish and wreckage mark out Miller's "American life," and all of it "flowed into" the Brooklyn Bridge.

In *Tropic of Capricorn* (1939), Miller linked the bridge to more significant aspects of American history. While journeying over the bridge with his friend Hymie, Miller observes: "For him the skyscrapers had been built, the wilderness cleared, the Indians massacred, the buffaloes exterminated; for him the twin cities had been joined by the Brooklyn Bridge, the caissons sunk, the cables strung from tower to tower; . . . for him the anesthetic was invented."[67] Here, Miller revises the era's dominant ideas about progress and expansion. The values championed at the bridge's opening are converted into acts of brutality and ruthless imperialism. Furthermore, they all are linked to a tradition of historical anesthesia. The violent hostility that accompanied Manifest Destiny results not in historical insight but in a deadening desensitization.

Miller's fiction is steeped in aggressive thoughts and violent behavior, and these threats surface regularly when he journeys across the bridge. In *Tropic of Capricorn* he muses that "five more years, ten more years perhaps, and I will wipe these people out utterly." And in *Black Spring* (1936): "Ought to go back to the subway, grab a Jane and rape her in the street. . . . Ought to grab a revolver and fire point-blank into the crowd." In his essay "The Brooklyn Bridge," Miller regarded Roebling's span as "destructive of hope and longing," and — revising the harp image favored by Hart Crane, Lewis Mumford, and, at the 1954 reopening, by Meyer Berger — called the bridge "the harp of death."[68] Miller's view from the bridge was "unlike any other described in poetry or fiction, a macabre vista, a panorama of death," according to Ed Schilders.[69] It was also an image of America writ large. Miller wrote a form of anti-commemoration; what he produced was both a reminder of and a remedy for American anesthesia. In place of the deadening fiction of exemplary progress, Miller positioned the painful legacy of violent expansion.[70]

Harvey Shapiro's poem "National Cold Storage Company"—written in response to the death of President John F. Kennedy in 1963 — also links American historical violence to the bridge:

> The National Cold Storage Company contains
> More things than you can dream of.
> Hard by the Brooklyn Bridge it stands
> In a litter of freight cars,
> Tugs to one side; the other, the traffic
> Of the Long Island Expressway.
> I myself have dropped into it in seven years
> Midnight tossings, plans for escape, the shakes.
> Add to this the national total—
> Grant's tomb, the Civil War, Arlington,
> The Young President's dead.
> Above the warehouse and beneath the stars
> The poets creep on the harp of the Bridge.
> But see,
> They fall into the National Cold Storage Company
> One by one. The wind off the river is too cold,
> Or the times too rough, or the Bridge
> Is not a harp at all. Or maybe

A monstrous birth inside the warehouse
Must be fed by everything—ships, poems,
Stars, all the years of our lives.[71]

Shapiro's America resembles a cultural Frankenstein's monster. In line with Henry James's, H. G. Wells's, and Lola Ridge's depictions, the bridge is "monstrous"; and like Miller, Shapiro revises the familiar harp imagery used to glorify the bridge. Although Shapiro's bridge is not the center of the nation's debris, it is the conduit through which everything flows: it is a vital national artery.[72] "Hard by the Brooklyn Bridge," the National Cold Storage Company is also an American monument. Yet it is an explicitly secretive one. Situated incognito, it represents the national archive as covert culture, more Federal Bureau of Investigation than Smithsonian Institution. Additionally, Shapiro's "midnight tossings" add a hint of nightmare to the "monstrous birth." This sense of horror is reflected in "the national total": death, war, and murder—not progress and prosperity—connote America's achievement.

At once paradoxical and ironic, Shapiro's key images are derived from the American commemorative tradition. The company is equally a "Cold Storage" unit and a national furnace. The nation's symbols, artifacts, and debris are destroyed in order to fuel the larger, "frozen" image of America. Its poets—surely a reference to Hart Crane—are fooled into creeping on the bridge. It is a perilous activity, and their paeans to beauty energize only the nation's self-image while destroying the poet. Molded from the ashes of history, Shapiro's American ritual of assent begets "a monstrous birth"; important details become a vestige of the petrified, unchanging body of America.[73]

By situating the bridge within an alternative historical tradition, Miller and Shapiro provide a significant counternarrative to that offered at the opening and at subsequent commemorations. By doing so, they join an American literary tradition that is similarly imaginative yet more overtly historical. At the bridge's opening, *Harper's Weekly* stated: "it is not likely that the 'inauguration' of the bridge will ever attract a historical painter as a subject."[74] Although this forecast has proven accurate, several historical novelists and dramatists have taken the bridge's building and opening as their subject. Their contributions help to assess how cultural memory plays against national history.

The Romance of Building the Bridge

The building of the Brooklyn Bridge was a seminal event in the history of technology. The scope of its ambition, the heroic task of its construction, and the immensity of its achievement have assured the bridge a decisive place in our history books. Yet the central drama of the construction has not been the exclusive province of historians. Inspired by the sheer adventurism of the undertaking, a number of historical fiction writers have framed their stories around the building of the bridge. Some of these writings are now long forgotten; others are curios, footnotes to larger bodies of work. All allow us an illuminating glimpse into the ideological complexity of the bridge's cultural legacy. Moreover, the building of the bridge continues to fascinate writers today, as shown by William Marshall's *The New York Detective* (1988) and Richard Crabbe's *Suspension* (2000).[75]

History and fiction, of course, have a complex relationship. As C. Vann Woodward reminded us, they can interact in two distinct ways: as historical fiction and as fictional history. For Woodward, the latter is "the greater source of mischief, for it is here that fabrication and fact, fiction and nonfiction, are most likely to be mixed and confused."[76] Arthur Schlesinger Jr. acknowledges this danger while allowing for a more positive reading: strict veracity occasionally must be tempered by a sense of vitality:

> The literary imagination is more closely allied to myth than to history. But this is far from saying that it is of no use at all to the historian. . . . In breathing life into a historical figure, novelists and playwrights may well get things wrong and are not likely to alter professional verdicts. But the power of the imagination may force historians to look freshly at the frieze and to perceive historical figures not as abstractions but as human beings in all their idiosyncrasy and uniqueness. . . . The artistic vision may thus reinvigorate that fundamental historical exercise, the imaginative leap into the past. . . . In this manner the literary imagination may fertilize the historical mind and serve to stretch and enrich historical understanding.[77]

Fictional re-creations of the building of the Brooklyn Bridge lean on these historical assessments. With very few firsthand accounts left to us, especially by the men who performed the physical labor of construction, writers of historical fiction have sought to fill this void and expand our historical understanding. By dramatizing the lives of individuals who toiled day by day to create the bridge, they have tried to imagine silent historical actors "not as abstractions but as human beings in all their idiosyncrasy and uniqueness." Nevertheless, the dramas and fictions that share this goal have varied greatly in interpretation, in emphasis, and often in accuracy.

The first attempt to dramatize the bridge's construction was Dorothy Landers Beall's verse drama *The Bridge* (1913). Setting her story against the social and political conflicts that surrounded the building of the bridge,

Beall foregrounds the romantic relationship between Robert Cameron, the bridge's chief engineer, and Hilda, a settlement worker. Robert's mania to complete the bridge dominates not only the drama but also Hilda, who teaches the workers to "cry home their wrongs" and actively supports their demand for a trade union. Unfortunately, these activities threaten to delay Robert's bridge. "How *can* you put yourself so openly, / So absolutely . . . *against* me?" he cries before counseling Hilda: "Learn to relinquish your own puerile aim / To one vast arching love — one mighty truth / like mine!" In the great drama of bridge construction, *her* work is an offense against *his*. Worker safety and appropriate compensation cannot stand in the way of progress. Luckily for Robert, the play's dramatic thrust is romantic not social. As a strike approaches, one of the labor leaders is found to be dishonest, a discovery that prompts Hilda to recant: "Robert, my lover — I have borne a sin / Hideous as a little crooked life . . . I have taught dissention." The play ends with Hilda saluting the great bridge and the workers returning to work. Her and their unquestioning loyalty to Robert is confirmed, and his absolute authority is reestablished.[78]

Beall's drama is specific in its ideological message. Labor must silence its collective voice and unite in an obedient, homogenous mass under the will and direction of a single dominant leader. The promise of fair pay and working conditions is destroyed in the effort to erect Robert's bridge. Likewise, Hilda is transformed from activist worker to devoted fiancée. In the battle between social justice and technological progress, the former is trivialized and the latter glorified. In the play's denouement, social context dissipates before theatrical melodrama: fictional history's vitality becomes the "mischief" of historical romance.[79]

John Cawelti notes that "in the 'serious' novel public events tend to make us increasingly aware of the limitations and complexity of reality"; in melodrama, on the other hand, "historical events become a means by which morally appropriate fates are portioned out and thus both affirm the significance of individual events and the ultimate morality of the universe."[80] Although Beall hints at the disturbing complexities of reality, their importance is negated before the final act, and the play's moral universe reveals itself to be profoundly conservative. Nor is the "ultimate morality of the universe" questioned in Frances Browin's *Big Bridge to Brooklyn: The Roebling Story* (1956), Kathryn E. Harrod's *Master Bridge Builders: The Story of the Roeblings* (1958), and F. Wenderoth Saunders's *Building Brooklyn Bridge* (1965).[81] These Algeresque tales are devoid of even the most trifling social complexity. Presenting the bridge's construction as a seamless tale of uncomplicated heroism and adventure, the narratives offered by Browin, Harrod, and Saunders capture the essence of Cawelti's melodrama within the framework of cold war America.

Of the three, Browin's tale is the most instructive. *Big Bridge to Brooklyn* was one of the first books published by *American Heritage* magazine. With an overwhelmingly upper-middle-class subscription base, *American Heritage* enjoyed both popularity and influence in the 1950s. As a historical venture, the magazine promised "tales of adventure," "things to smile at," and "a good deal of nostalgia." Unsurprisingly, the type of history it favored was overtly celebratory and shorn of controversy or complexity. As Roy Rosenzweig explains, "The *American Heritage* version of the past almost always had a happy ending, and, by implication, so would the future . . . there was no reason to let . . . unpleasantness . . . disturb your faith in American society." Nevertheless, the magazine was an important cultural force. As Rosenzweig continues, "*American Heritage* has shaped the historical consciousness of a large and crucial segment of the American public; it has given the public its *definition* as well as its *interpretation* of history." [82]

Despite the promise of its subtitle, *Big Bridge to Brooklyn* treats the Roeblings sparingly. The principal protagonists are two young Brooklynites, Pete Schimdt and Jim Carter. Neither starts as far down the social ladder as Alger's Ragged Dick, yet their stories are similar. Both meet Washington Roebling accidentally, join a bridge construction crew at a young age, work hard, and prosper. Willingness, honesty, amiability, and good fortune mark their ascent. By contrast, in the few instances when misfortune surfaces, Pete and Jim are entirely unaffected.[83] Befitting *American Heritage*'s historical approach, controversy and conflict are elided or modified to seem absurd. The voices of individuals struck down by caisson disease or blighted by urban renewal are dismissed; the fears expressed by the ferry companies are phrased to seem illogical. When the residents of the Old Ferry community complain about forced relocation, Jim is exasperated: "what beats me is the way they refuse to see that a bridge simply has to come." [84] For Browin, as well as Beall, Harrod, and Saunders, the need to build the bridge is never questioned; as an aspect of national progress, it is, to them, a self-evident blessing. At one point, Pete and Jim gaze out at the nearly finished bridge: "Now they saw it for the first time. . . . And it was good." [85] Browin's phrasing—echoing God's creation of the natural world in Genesis—invokes an aura of celestial providence. Here, technological progress is sovereign: a divine, national triumph unencumbered by social cost.

According to Edward Countryman, fictional history "can work to undermine rather than strengthen historical consciousness. It can substitute for an awareness of the *social* character of historical development a general ahistorical sense that whatever exists is natural and unchallengeable."[86] In Browin, Harrod, and Saunders, the complexities of "historical consciousness" are hidden behind an Algeresque moral universe where social class is meaningless, opposition is foolish, and hard work *always* brings reward. Fittingly, Browin's tale ends with the realization of Pete's American dream. On the opening day, he strolls along the bridge as a prosperous and fully qualified engineer—a "chief civilizer of our century," in the words of Richard Harding Davies.[87] On his arm is Lucy Roberts, the daughter of a wealthy and influential New York family.

Richard King has stated that, "while the new conventional wisdom maintains that we should neither regard history or fiction as natural kinds or privilege one over the other, the effect of eliding the distinction between history and fiction has been generally to elevate the literary and fictional . . . over the factual and historical. When the emphasis falls upon making not finding, upon 'proposal' not 'discovery' . . . upon internal coherence . . . rather than correspondence with reality, then we have the 'aestheticization' of reality."[88] Within this framework, the fictional history of Beall, Browin, Harrod, and Saunders joins the poetry of Marquis and Le Gallienne, the photography of Struss and Evans, the etchings of Lozowick and Pennell, and the paintings of Sonntag and Redfield. Rather than "fertilize the historical mind," as Schlesinger hopes, they leave it bereft. By joining together to aestheticize the bridge experience, they engage in the historical "mischief" of printing legend, not fact.

Fables of Change

In 1927 Lewis Mumford took time out from writing his biography of Herman Melville to compose a play about the building of the Brooklyn Bridge. The completed drama languished in his files for nearly fifty years before being published in 1975. Both Mumford and his biographer offer the same reason for the delay between composition and publication: the play was terrible.[89] Yet, in spite of its literary failings, *The Builders of the Bridge* is an intriguing cultural artifact, especially when measured alongside Mumford's more considered architectural criticism.

Ostensibly, the structure of the play is familiar in that it follows chief engineer Jefferson Baumgarten through the long process of bridge construction. Unlike the fiction of Beall, Browin, Harrod, and Saunders, however, *The Builders of the Bridge* does not portray the construction as a triumphant step in the march of American technological progress. Rather, the effort involves a complex social burden that brings about a profound change in

Baumgarten, who begins the drama firmly on the side of the capitalists. His view of laborers is disparaging and callous. Like Beall's Robert Cameron and Browin's Pete Schmidt, Baumgarten regards all opposing concerns as peripheral to the ultimate realization: "after all, the Bridge must be built!"[90] The ways and means by which the bridge is built are secondary to its final concrete existence. Social principles must bend to technological achievement; the bridge is fundamentally a great deed, an end in itself.

Yet Baumgarten's shining ideal is challenged by experience. Unlike Cameron or Schimdt, his perspective *does* change as the social and political dimensions of the bridge's construction begin to take precedence over its technological and iconic ones. As the work progresses, he comes to know many of the bridge workers, and their experiences affect him deeply. By the end, Baumgarten has grown unsure and cynical. When asked, "Don't you believe that the Bridge is an epoch-making stride in the march of humanity towards the peaks of progress?" he replies: "The Bridge hasn't altered the proportion of rogues and honest men in the world. . . . I don't know whether the Bridge is good or bad: I don't know whether it will help a single human being to be better or wiser or saner or sounder."[91] After the bridge has been officially dedicated, Baumgarten is angered by the same rhetoric of technological progress he himself espoused at the onset: "Did you ever listen to such gas and wind before! (*Imitating*) This greaaaat peepul—this greaaat city—these greeeat financiers and far-sighted business men!! . . . the way those windjammers talked you'd think that stock certificates wound the cable and greenbacks hammered in the rivets."[92] Although admitting the bridge's engineering greatness, Baumgarten ends the drama in dejection: "I almost killed myself working on this Bridge — and what for? So that property values might go up around Borough Hall? So that Baxter [a local politician] and Co. might graft more extensively?"[93] A friend of Baumgarten's clarifies the repercussions of working on the bridge: "it's moralized you: you've worked with a great company of men and you know your place with them."[94] In effect, the work has reversed Baumgarten's earlier creed: technological achievement must now bend to social principles. Where Pete Schmidt's involvement with the bridge leads to his rise in social *status*, Baumgarten's leads to his awareness of social *values*.

Mumford himself was unhappy with the play's ending: "it lacked the inherent dynamism, the resonate, affirmative quality I had found in . . . the great Bridge itself."[95] In certain respects, this judgment is misleading. *The Builders of the Bridge* is concerned with a process of labor, not with its product. Through the lens of architectural criticism, Mumford saw a perfect art object, an aesthetic triumph; through fictional drama, he was able to realize the bridge's complex social context.

Albert Idell's best-selling historical novel *Bridge to Brooklyn* (1944) — the second in a trilogy devoted to Gilded Age America — mirrors the trajectory of Baumgarten's character development. In the book's depiction of the life of the Rogers family from 1877 to 1883, the bridge and its construction provide the central drama. Directly or indirectly, it changes the mindset of each of the characters, most notably the patriarch, Jesse Rogers.[96]

Bridge to Brooklyn opens on the eve of the railroad strikes that would dominate the year 1877. As an official of the Philadelphia and Reading Railroad, Rogers finds himself embroiled in the coming turmoil.[97] Described as "completely the railroad man," Rogers vehemently opposes the strikes:

> It is nothing more or less than revolution, that's what it is. . . . Only a year ago we celebrated the anniversary of this country's hundredth milestone and now you plan to overthrow the Constitution and everything else with it. . . . I'll say to you what I say up at the yards. Go on with your strike. Stop the trains from moving! Barricade the tracks! Do you know what will happen? The President will call out the army, that's what. He'll have you shot down. The rights of property must be upheld.[98]

Notwithstanding this profound belief — "capital has to be protected, otherwise what would become of society?" he reiterates[99] — Rogers fears for his job. Grimly appraising the Philadelphia and Reading's precarious financial position and the mounting labor tension, he accepts a position as a supervisor on the construction of the Brooklyn Bridge.[100]

Rogers views the bridge project as "an ill-starred, impractical, visionary attempt, foredoomed to failure." Yet he gradually begins to identify with both the work and the workers. His misgivings dissipate before the unfolding achievement, and his distant superiority vanishes after he witnesses a worker's death. Within a few weeks, Rogers, the engineers, and the on-site laborers are all "confederate[s] in the task." Thus, he is appalled when the city is presented with a petition — signed by John Jacob Astor, Hamilton Fish, and J. P. Morgan — calling for a halt to the construction, and he looks from a new perspective on the men whose interests and influence he previously glorified: "this is part of a deep-dyed plot. The bridge doesn't belong to Mr. Morgan and his ilk. There is no profit in it for them, that is the root of their dissatisfaction."[101]

Rogers's opinions have changed radically by the time President Rutherford B. Hayes is up for renomination in 1880:

There stood one very black mark against Mr. Hayes. As an ex-railroad man, Mr. Rogers could never forget the fact that the President had used the Federal troops against Mr. Rogers' co-workers. For the first time in the history of the United States the army had been called out in a wage dispute. Although Mr. Rogers had never identified himself with laboring men, he was coming more and more to sympathize with their problems and he knew it had been no small shock for them to discover that the army their taxes supported had become a weapon against them.[102]

Rogers's ideological transformation is now complete. In 1877, his co-workers consisted of the railroad management, which presided over the use of troops against the strikers, an outcome Rogers had confidently predicted. Now an "ex-railroad man," Rogers identifies "with laboring men," not with the interests of management. His ideological realignment is confirmed two years later, when he reflects on a statement made by William H. Vanderbilt on October 9, 1882: "The public be damned."

The words echoed and re-echoed throughout the nation and nowhere more loudly than at the Rogers' breakfast table. In those four words the class to which Mr. Vanderbilt belonged convicted itself. The public should have been aware of the situation. Mr. Rogers had known it all long! The men who talked about performing a service for the people, expanding the borders of a nation, pioneering courageously with their capital—why, they were only using specious words to cover their greed![103]

Of course, Rogers had *not* "known it all along." "The class to which Mr. Vanderbilt belonged" had given Rogers *its* patronage and, consequently, *his* values. Vanderbilt's strong identification with the railroads signals Rogers's final estrangement from the influence and rhetoric of management. As a railroad man, Rogers firmly believed that "capital has to be protected, otherwise what would become of society?" As a bridge man, he rewrites the equation: capital has to be restrained, "otherwise what would become of society?"

Rogers's estrangement is dramatized through two main issues. The first concerns the interests of capital and property. Although "most people felt that a free bridge would be an unsafe experiment in socialism," Rogers vehemently opposes the imposition of tolls: "The benefits from the bridge will accrue to the merchant in New York and the employer in Brooklyn who never sets foot on it. The poor devil who crosses it daily by shank's mare ought not to bear the cost."[104] As capital and property accrue their interest, the individual must be compensated. The second key issue concerns the bridge's opening. Although Rogers and his family could expect to receive reserved-seat tickets for the celebration, he vows to "refuse them, to show where we stand." [105] Where he stands is in solidarity with those laboring men angered by the decision to open the bridge on Queen Victoria's birthday. The members of the Rogers family join the workers in their boycott of the opening and celebrate instead on Memorial Day, the "Bridge Opening Day for good Americans." [106]

For Michael Kammen, historical fiction has traditionally flourished during periods of "cultural indirection." One such period, he believes, can be identified between 1933 and 1948. At this time, "neither literary nationalism, nor nostalgia is any longer the key element. They have not disappeared entirely, but both become far less important than a new rationale: the assessment of our national character." [107] Written in the latter half of this period, Idell's trilogy charts the path that national character must take in order to realize the promise of American life. As the novel's title suggests, *Bridge to Brooklyn* is literal and symbolic. For his protagonist, Jesse Rogers, it represents both a bridge built and a route taken. It maps the course of his transformation: from aristocratic Philadelphia to democratic Brooklyn, from proponent of capital and property to labor sympathizer, from haughty disdain to personal identification.

The Brooklyn Bridge at the Crossroads, 1953–1979

In the thirty years that followed the onset of the Great Depression, the Brooklyn Bridge was commemorated and reevaluated, championed as a perfect, unchanging American icon and substantially remodeled. Its history became the stuff of fiction as the span was used to support differing ideological positions, and its supremacy in the American technological pantheon was on the one hand confirmed and on the other superseded. In 1939 Berenice Abbott published her photographic portrait *Changing New York*. Her title was inaccurate — despite such large-scale developments as Rockefeller Center (1932–1940), the physical changes wrought in 1930s New York were minimal — yet strikingly prophetic. New York's profound metamorphosis would begin after World War II. As the city's real estate market boomed, corporate America, in partnership with a group of ultra-modernist architects, remade the New York landscape with a revolutionary zeal. As "glass boxes" arose all over Manhattan, the bridge's late-nineteenth-century eclecticism looked increasingly old-fashioned.

In 1883 John Roebling prefigured Ezra Pound's modernist battle cry, "Make it New," but by the 1950s, others had made architecture significantly newer. Positioned alongside contemporary New York icons—Emery Roth's Look Building (1950), Skidmore, Owings, and Merrill's Lever House (1952), or Mies van der Rohe and Philip Johnson's Seagram Building (1958)—the bridge could no longer claim a place in the vanguard of architectural modernism. Where it had once seemed a precursor of the coming century—the most twentieth-century structure of the nineteenth century—it now seemed left behind. Amid the city's onward march into architectural high modernism, the bridge was marginalized to its beginnings in the nineteenth century. Its revolutionary aesthetic, it seems, had faded into fond nostalgia.

During the 1950s, the bridge seemed at a cultural crossroads, if not on a downward path of influence. Yet the structure still spoke to those artists, film-makers, writers, and historians who cared to listen,[108] and between the mid-1950s and the late 1970s the bridge's cultural standing underwent a transformation as profound as that in the 1920s. If artists and writers in the 1920s reconfigured the bridge into a somewhat unlikely modernist icon, later intellectuals remade the bridge into a dynamic cultural barometer. No longer so visually modern, the bridge was nevertheless as pertinent to social understanding as it had ever been.

In 1953, for example, Swiss immigrant and filmmaker Rudy Burckhardt shot his compelling documentary, *Under the Brooklyn Bridge*. This short, improvised, and highly personal film refused the stately elegance and striking iconography of, for example, Walker Evans's photographs of the bridge's underside. Instead, Burckhardt focused on the hidden history of life at the feet and in the shadows of the bridge: decrepit warehouses, laborers at demolition work and on their lunch break, young boys diving gleefully into the East River, women traipsing home beneath the bridge's arches, and, finally, the deserted region beneath the bridge at the end of the day.

Around the same time, Beat writers Jack Kerouac and Allen Ginsberg would often walk the bridge together, discussing Hart Crane, New York, and the state of cold war America. For Kerouac and Ginsberg, the bridge was a place to meet and escape from contemporary, corporate America, not to glorify it.[109] Their walks were the first step in their poetic mission to rediscover and acknowledge the "lost battalion of platonic conversationalists . . . listening to the crack of doom on the hydrogen jukebox." They sought out those "who sat [beneath the span] in boxes breathing in the darkness" and "who jumped off the Brooklyn Bridge . . . and walked / away unknown and forgotten into the ghostly daze of Chinatown / soup alley ways & firetrucks, not even one free beer."[110]

As Burckhardt's documentary illustrates, and the New York Beat writers confirmed, the thirty-year period leading up to the bridge's centennial in

1983 was marked by a new cultural understanding, a drive to realize a more accurate portrait of the nineteenth century's most famous and beloved span.

William Gedney's Photographic Narrative

Personal identification is the key to the remarkable photographic project, "Brooklyn Bridge," by William Gedney. Shot during the late 1950s, Gedney's photographs were taken at a time when the bridge's visual history had stalled. On a trajectory that led from documentary depictions of the bridge's construction and opening to the decontextualized, aestheticized grand-style images of the 1920s, the visual representation of the bridge reached a logical end point in the late 1940s and 1950s. In 1949, Howard Cook's lithograph *Brooklyn Bridge* visualized the bridge on an aesthetic plane that bordered on abstraction. That same year Georgia O'Keeffe's *Brooklyn Bridge*, a work intimately connected to Walker Evans's more conceptual images of the bridge, took the process further toward aesthetic generalization. The trend continued through Franz Kline's *The Bridge* (1955) and reached its zenith in Ellsworth Kelly's series of minimalist paintings, *Brooklyn Bridge* (1958–1962), which reduced the bridge still further to the purely geometric.[111] In Kelly's monochrome canvases, the bridge is no longer an object in space and context, but simply a figurative idea.

Against this backdrop, Gedney's photographs return the bridge to the context of the city. His Brooklyn Bridge project comprises twenty-five images of the span, which he intended to collect into a single, bound volume. The extant handmade photo-book, held at Duke University, contains no textual accompaniment, although Gedney planned the project as a visual complement to Hart Crane's *The Bridge*. He eventually rejected that poem in favor of Walt Whitman's "Crossing Brooklyn Ferry," perhaps because Crane's mythic epic did not fit the tone and mood of the photographs. Instead, Gedney wrote, "the bridge pictures would be best paired with Whitman's Brooklyn Ferry poem under the overall title 'Brooklyn Crossing.'"[112]

The connection is apt. No doubt aware that Whitman makes no reference to the bridge, Gedney nevertheless chose a poem that informs his photographs. "Crossing Brooklyn Ferry" is intimately concerned with the relationship of the individual to the city. It is a record of passage and encounter, of tangible movement and physical participation. That Gedney's photographs and Whitman's poem refer to different modes of transport is ultimately of no account. Both are Brooklyn crossings, and both share a concern with the personal exploration of immediate urban experience.

Gedney's photographic series demands to be read as a narrative. Just as Whitman re-creates the ferry journey from Brooklyn to Manhattan, so

49. The bridge bordering on abstraction. Howard Cook, *Brooklyn Bridge*, 1949. Lithograph. Smithsonian American Art Museum, Gift of Barbara Latham.

50. The bridge as aesthetic generalization. Georgia O'Keeffe, *Brooklyn Bridge*, 1949. Oil on masonite, 121.8 × 91.0 cm (47¹⁵/₁₆ × 35⅞ in.). Brooklyn Museum of Art, Bequest of Mary Childs Draper. © The Georgia O'Keeffe Foundation / Artists Rights Society (ARS), New York.

51. The bridge as figurative idea. Ellsworth Kelly, *Brooklyn Bridge VII,* 1962. Oil on canvas, 92 × 37½ in. (233.7 × 95.3 cm). Collection Museum of Modern Art © Ellsworth Kelly.

Gedney brings to life the same journey by bridge. He begins on Water Street in front of the Empire Stores Warehouse. He dallies around the base before stepping up onto the roadway, where he begins to cross. Nineteen of the twenty-five images are taken on the roadway, beginning with approach and following a trajectory from contact through exploration. The cumulative effect is an extraordinary approximation of walking the bridge for the first time. Gedney prioritized no specific viewpoint, and he championed the experience on a personalized scale. Like photographers working in the grand-style tradition, Gedney certainly views the bridge as an aesthetic experience; furthermore, it is ostensibly depopulated. Yet his images are presented on a human scale. In effect, Gedney places the viewer at the heart of his aesthetic. The traditional distance between viewing audience and viewed object collapses; the grand-style gaze is rejected in favor of immediate personal identification. In Gedney's photographs we recognize ourselves.

The interaction between proximity and perspective are the key to Gedney's re-creation of our experience of traversing the span. In the images he numbered "16" and "20," we ascend the approach and glimpse for the first time the great stone towers. Gazing up at the towers, we stop to linger and lean on the massive support cables; attracted by their size and longevity, we pause to examine at close range the details of their condition. In image "21" we are again in motion, treading the boards on our way toward the towers. In images "17," "18," and "19" we advance on the towers and pass through the bridge's unique system of suspender cables and diagonal stays, pausing again to glance from side to side and experience the indomitable matrix for the first time. But soon we are again within reach of the bridge's steelwork. Images "10" and "13" initiate us into a Brooklyn Bridge ritual. They invite us to reach out and touch the bridge's cables, to feel their strength as they vibrate to the rhythm of the bridge's traffic.

In images "7," "8," and "9," we arrive at the great Gothic arches, where once again personal proximity is stressed. The images replicate our first moments at the towers. We are encouraged to press ourselves against the granite, consider its texture and gaze upward. Here, Gedney's sense of perspective is distinctive. Overarching a legacy of literally thousands of tower photographs, Gedney manages to capture new angles. The effect is at once unique and familiar. We recognize the images not from art history but from personal experience.

Like Mildred Stapley's "Six Etchings," Gedney's photographic narrative refuses the static, single interpretation. The photographer and the camera are in motion, enacting the journey across the Brooklyn Bridge. From the

179

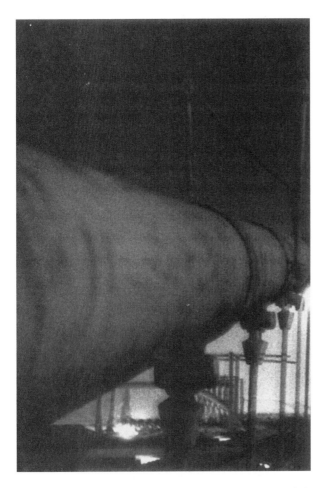

52. We stop to linger and lean on the massive support cables. William Gedney, "Brooklyn Bridge, Image 20," 1958–1959. William Gedney Collection © 2000 Rare Book, Manuscript, and Special Collections Library, Duke University.

53. We are in motion, treading the boards on our way toward the towers. William Gedney, "Brooklyn Bridge, Image 21," 1958–1959. William Gedney Collection © 2000 Rare Book, Manuscript, and Special Collections Library, Duke University.

54. We reach out and feel the bridge's cables as they vibrate to the rhythm of the bridge's traffic. William Gedney, "Brooklyn Bridge, Image 10," 1958–1959. William Gedney Collection © 2000 Rare Book, Manuscript, and Special Collections Library, Duke University.

55. We are encouraged to press ourselves against the granite, consider its texture and gaze upward. William Gedney, "Brooklyn Bridge, Image 7," 1958–1959. William Gedney Collection © 2000 Rare Book, Manuscript, and Special Collections Library, Duke University.

Brooklyn waterfront up onto the bridge, through the network of cables to the towers, and on, Gedney's journey is our own. Each photograph is a new step in the experience of crossing; with each image we relive our first moments of acquaintance and come to a deeper understanding of the structure.

Gedney also integrates some more traditional views into his ongoing narrative. Image "25," for example, reminds us of O'Keeffe's aesthetic, image "24" of Andreas Feininger's photograph "Walking on Brooklyn Bridge, Going towards Manhattan" (1940), and images "11" and "12" of Walker Evans. Yet by placing these familiar perspectives in an unfamiliar context, Gedney transforms the stale into the sprightly. The effect is dialectic: the familiar plays against the surprising, thereby reinventing and recharging the classic view. Just as the bridge synthesized the old with the new—the conservative with the revolutionary—so does Gedney's photographic narrative. And in consequence, Gedney's "Brooklyn Bridge" project points the way forward. It

56. We find new angles. William Gedney, "Brooklyn Bridge, Image 8," 1958–1959. William Gedney Collection © 2000 Rare Book, Manuscript, and Special Collections Library, Duke University.

represents an extraordinarily apt replication of the immediate experience of contact and provides a visual blueprint for how to elucidate an intimate relationship to a national monument. To borrow from Lawrence Weschler: in Gedney "your eyes go for a walk." [113]

Alan Trachtenberg's Cultural History

In 1958, around the same time Gedney began his photographic portrait, New York poet William Meredith wrote "A View of the Brooklyn Bridge," in which he expressed "the growing need to be moving around to see it, / To prevent its freezing, as with sculpture and metaphor." [114] We do not know whether Gedney was familiar with Meredith's poem, but we can certainly detect an affinity between the two artists.

Gedney, through photography, and Meredith, through poetry, found new ways to understand the physical presence of the Brooklyn Bridge. Soon after, a young academic at the University of Minnesota would usher in a new way of exploring the bridge's history. As Gedney began to photograph the bridge,

57. We find the familiar. William Gedney, "Brooklyn Bridge Towers and Cables at Night," 1960. William Gedney Collection © 2000 Rare Book, Manuscript, and Special Collections Library, Duke University.

and Voznesenski was mocking its "idiot stone," Alan Trachtenberg began researching the bridge's cultural history. The results—published in 1965 as *Brooklyn Bridge: Fact and Symbol*—would revolutionize conceptions of the Brooklyn Bridge.

The implications of Trachtenberg's pioneering study have been wide and substantial. Hailed as a major text in the "myth and symbol" school of American studies, Trachtenberg's work, along with those of Henry Nash Smith, John William Ward, and Leo Marx, significantly expanded the study of the U.S. past. And within this context, his study holds a further, unique distinction. Unlike Nash's *Virgin Land*, Ward's *Andrew Jackson*, and Marx's *The Machine in the Garden*, Trachtenberg's book has suffered no major criticism. In fact, according to at least one young academic, *Brooklyn Bridge: Fact and Symbol* should be "valued . . . as a work of contemporary, critical cultural studies . . . *a full decade in advance* of the critical developments signaled by [Roland] Barthes."[115]

Trachtenberg's work stands in stark contrast to that of his predecessors. Certainly, the history of the bridge's construction had been told time and again. Yet few authors had bothered to look anew at the sources and facts of conception, construction, and reception. A survey of the majority of works by popular historians, historians of technology, and journalists before — and in some cases after — Trachtenberg reveals a fundamental similarity. Each account seems based upon the last, with the ur-text revealing itself as the opinions and interpretations offered on the opening day. The effect is a history painted in broad assenting strokes; the result is a grand-style history.

One of Trachtenberg's major achievements was to work from and draw attention to the large collection of source materials to be found in the Archibald S. Alexander Library at Rutgers University and the Folsom Library at Rensselaer Polytechnic Institute. Mining the rich resources of these archives and ignoring the repetition of established dogma, Trachtenberg brought a fresh approach to the bridge. He understood the structure as a reflection of the United States, New York, and the mind of its designer. The bridge, for example, illustrated the paradox of the wilderness: technological industrialism was not antithetic to, but entirely consistent with the promise of rural America. "The lack of a market," he noted, "mocks the great fertility of the land." To reap the harvest of the American continent, the nation required industrial development, a massive infrastructure of roads, factories, and warehouses.[116]

New York's constructed environment added a further dimension to this paradox. The bridge exemplified the tension between "alternative ways of creating the future," between the "acquisitive" and the "aesthetic." Against the commercial appeal of the grid system, Trachtenberg wrote, the bridge represented the visionary allure of Thomas Pope's "Rainbow Bridge," conceived in 1811 at the same time as New York's grid. Pope's arc-shaped "rainbow" design stood in direct contrast to the city's emerging framework of streets and avenues. Opposed to what Whitman would later call the rigid "abomination" of the grid, Pope sought to represent the unchained, "freeborn soul" of America itself.[117]

At the bridge's opening, Brooklyn Mayor Seth Low declared: "it is distinctly an American triumph. American genius designed it, American skill built it, and American workshops made it." Yet nothing could have been further from the truth, as Trachtenberg shows. Roebling's European roots proved essential to his last great bridge project. His training at Berlin's Royal Polytechnic Institute introduced him to the philosophy of Hegel, the practical design of suspension bridges, and the emerging tradition of European liberalism. Equally, it began a literary journey that would amount to more than three thousand pages of manuscript, and an intellectual journey that would lead directly to the United States.[118]

Roebling was a frenetic, and often disorganized, amateur philosopher. At times maddeningly convoluted, at others tortuously abstract, Roebling's un-published writings nevertheless provide important clues to the design of the bridge. Under Trachtenberg's judicious (not to mention tolerant) eye, these writings reveal the backbone of the bridge's design. They explain Roebling's drive toward what Hegel termed "actuality": "the unity of essence and expe-rience of the inner world of life and outer world of its appearance"—a con-cept that, with hindsight, seems born in the application of European thought to the physical conditions of America. Indebted as much to Hegel and Emanuel Swedenborg as to Jefferson and Emerson, the bridge can be un-derstood as a landmark of the trans-Atlantic idea so prevalent in current his-torical and literary scholarship. As Roebling intended, leaning heavily on Hegel, the bridge is less an American creation than a world-historical icon. By placing the bridge within the context of its design, Trachtenberg lifted it above the rhetoric of American exceptionalism.[119]

Trachtenberg redefined our conception of the Brooklyn Bridge in a man-ner reminiscent of the writers he himself admired: Montgomery Schuyler, Mumford, Crane, and Kazin. Amid the swirl of fictional histories, imagina-tive assessments, and tired cant, he offered studious examination, definitive research, and discerning historical evidence. By revealing the extent of Abram Hewitt's involvement in the infamous wire-rope scandal, he cor-rected the historical record; by contextualizing the bridge within the life of the mind of the nation and designer, he understood the bridge as a definitive and prime American symbol. For Trachtenberg, the bridge deserved a place in the vanguard of American historical scholarship. It reflected the historical complexities and interpretational tensions of the American project itself. The measure of Trachtenberg's achievement can be found in the way in which he revolutionized the study of a major American icon. And within this framework, Trachtenberg himself is by now a major part of the bridge's cul-tural history. For the contemporary enthusiast, he is our modern Mumford, as committed as Crane, as compassionate as Kazin, and more generous than Schuyler.

After Steinman's controversial remodeling, Trachtenberg's study helped to raise the bridge back to its former glory. Shortly afterward, David McCul-lough further added to our understanding of the structure with *The Great Bridge: The Epic Story of the Building of the Brooklyn Bridge* (1972), his grand account of the span's construction. Despite, perhaps, a downturn in cultural representations of the bridge, these two books ensured that our ap-preciation of the bridge, as both a cultural object and a historical event, rested on the most complete research possible. The fact that neither book has been out of print in more than thirty years attests to both their importance and the bridge's popularity.

Nancy Veglahn's Historical Novel for Children

While recognizing that Trachtenberg and McCullough are the bridge's most influential historians, we should not overlook the importance of a small, popular young adult book, *The Spider of Brooklyn Heights* (1967). Whereas Gedney offered new ways of looking at the bridge and Trachtenberg provided a new framework within which to explore its cultural history, Nancy Veglahn offered a new approach to the people who designed and built it. In stark contrast to all other attempts to convey the bridge's history to young people, *The Spider of Brooklyn Heights* refuses the social simplicity of the Algeresque moral universe. In its place we find complex personal history and palpable social tension. Veglahn's story, however, is not a challenge to the venture's essential heroism, but a credible reflection of the struggle to understand that heroism.

The unique nature of Veglahn's historical re-creation stems from her research. Although much of the narrative is presented in dialogue (and is thus fabricated) and, by her own admission, elements "have been invented for dramatic effect," the narrative is "based on material in Washington Roebling's letters and journals, and on other contemporary writings."[120] What may sound like an escape clause — suggesting Woodward's historical "mischief" — introduces an extremely well-balanced book. The bridge's major historical characters are presented as human beings, not abstractions, as Schlesinger would hope. Great emphasis is placed on the era's virulent racism, the hardships suffered by many of the workers, and the presence of municipal corruption. The importance of Emily Roebling in the construction is clearly shown, as are the troubles and doubts that affected Washington Roebling after his paralysis. Conversely, the bridge trustees are presented in a surprisingly unflattering light. Hewitt's strained relationship with the younger Roebling — who fully understood Hewitt's involvement in the wire-rope fraud — is brought to the fore, as are Roebling's battles with the trustees.

Veglahn's reliance on primary sources allows her to illuminate the intimate and private as well as the public dimensions of the project. It also enables her book to act as a bridge between the divergent work of Trachtenberg and McCullough. Where Trachtenberg was interested in the mind behind the bridge's design — the philosophical blueprint for the sources and shape of the bridge — McCullough was concerned with the historical facts of construction. Crucially, Veglahn's portrait mediates between Trachtenberg's primary interest in John A. Roebling and McCullough's in Washington A. Roebling, clarifying both.

Veglahn's account of the construction mirrors that of Washington Roebling, as does her portrayal of John Roebling. Often regarded as a visionary genius, the elder Roebling is unmasked by Veglahn for his single-minded brutality, particularly the callous disregard with which he treated his wife, Johanna, and his many children. In presenting these rarely broached flaws in the character of the elder Roebling, Veglahn brings Washington Roebling's highly critical, unpublished, and seldom read biography of his father before the public eye. As the younger Roebling recounts, John was hardly a model of civic virtue and temperance: "his domestic life can be summed up in a few words, domineering tyranny only varied by outbursts of uncontrolled anger. His wife and children stood in constant fear of him and trembled in his presence. . . . There was something of the tiger in him, the sight of blood following the strokes of the raw hide, brought on fits of ungovernable fury." John Roebling's temper and iron discipline plainly terrified his son: "my good old grandmother once saved my life by knocking him down with a fence rail as I lay writhing on the floor in my last agonies. . . . Any man with more spunk than I had would have killed him." [121] Veglahn's John Roebling is not the received myth — neither the heroic bridge builder of popular history nor the New World philosopher of Trachtenberg — but the terrifying father described by his son. Equally, Veglahn's Washington Roebling is not the dutiful son, but the emotionally complex product of "strict German discipline . . . angry scoldings and birch rods." [122]

The Spider of Brooklyn Heights concludes in a manner similar to Mumford's *The Builders of the Bridge*. For Veglahn, the end of the great bridge project brings not triumphal celebration but a troubling question:

> "Was it worth it?" Washington asked the question more of himself than of Emily. "Fourteen years, twenty lives lost . . . and fifteen million dollars. And here I am, nearly useless because of it. I know I'll never build another bridge. Was this one worth all that?"
> "What do you think?" asked Emily.
> "I don't know . . . I don't know." [123]

After a lengthy pause, Roebling quietly answers Emily's question again, this time in the affirmative. But his response is no emphatic endorsement. The tone of the conclusion is reserved and unsure. Yes, the bridge is an incredible accomplishment, but at what cost? By ending on a note of genuine complexity, Veglahn's account reflects the experience of working on a troubled

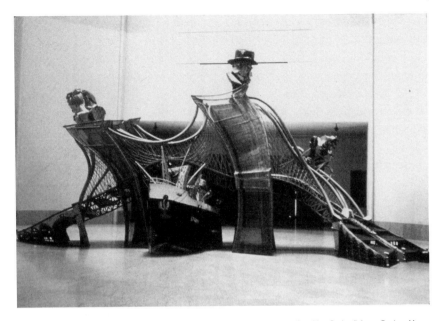

58. Lovingly re-imagined, the bridge as madcap installation. Red Grooms, "The Brooklyn Bridge," from *Ruckus Manhattan*, 1976. © 2004 Red Grooms/Artists Rights Society (ARS), New York. Photo courtesy of Marlborough Gallery, New York.

and dangerous, although ultimately grand, municipal project. And in so doing, the author lends vitality and animation to the historical narrative.

Gedney, Meredith, Trachtenberg, Veglahn, and McCullough all brought a more active engagement to the cultural history of the Brooklyn Bridge. They assumed a questioning stance, a willingness to inquire rather than repeat established dogma. Their work refused the idealized, uncritical image of the bridge. They bookmarked the ambiguous and ambivalent, noting conflicts, contradictions, and misrepresentations. Yet these works were also celebrations, enriching our understanding with a full and frank approach.[124] And in their wake, the bridge enjoyed something of a renaissance in the 1970s.

Throughout the decade, the structure was subject to remarkable commemoration. In 1971, the city held a three-day celebration to mark the bridge's eighty-eighth birthday, which led the *New York Times* to wonder "why an 88th anniversary should have touched off so heavy a municipal extravagance?" The following year, Daniela Gioseffi inaugurated the Brooklyn Bridge Poetry Walk, an event now curated annually by the New York–based Poet's House. In 1973, the *Municipal Engineers Journal* devoted an entire issue to the bridge. The structure was lovingly re-imagined in 1976 by the artist Red Grooms in his madcap installation *Ruckus Manhattan*. The following year, the bridge played an integral part in the box-office phenomenon *Saturday Night Fever*. Juxtaposed with the darkly menacing Verrazano Bridge, the Brooklyn Bridge represented an avenue of escape from gritty, working-class Brooklyn to the Promised Land of Manhattan. By 1978, the bridge's revival reached something of an apotheosis. In Sidney Lumet's *The Wiz*, the bridge became a section of L. Frank Baum's yellow brick road.[125]

Conclusions

America's historical imagination has consistently revisited the significance of the building of the Brooklyn Bridge. Commemorative events, journalism, and certain historical fictions have enacted a collective ritual of assent. They have adopted the consensus interpretation of technological progress and confirmed the essential soundness of the national venture. Through the theme of bridge building, these cultural artifacts have fashioned a unified vision of historical order while eliding the complexities of social context. Discussing the nature of national traditions, M. J. Bowen could equally be describing Brodie's leap or the building of the Brooklyn Bridge: "The people of regions and the nation itself tended to congratulate and glorify themselves, adopting ennobling self-images and embarking upon legend-building campaigns. The dearth of eyewitnesses to the real past often produced an increasingly sharp curve of erasure of memory of the original actual . . . conditions, giving rise to an . . . invented tradition . . . so deeply internalized by a nation/group that [it] is practically impervious to scholarship that shows it to be largely factitious."[126]

Against the ritualized rhetoric of legend building stands an equally vital tradition. The authors of these counternarratives have followed the advice offered by Alfred North Whitehead in 1927: "The art of free society consists first in the maintenance of the symbolic code; and secondly in fearlessness of revision. . . . Those societies which can not combine reverence to their symbols with freedom of revision, must ultimately decay either from anarchy, or from the slow atrophy of a life stifled by useless shadows."[127] Revisionist authors have measured American progress by social values and historical complexity, not technological accomplishment. Through the lens of historical rigor and personal identification, they have stated that, like Brodie's jump and the selling of the bridge, the unified vision of technological progress had little basis in fact.[128]

The essence of this criticism is found in the national propensity to elide the conflicts of context. Authors working in the consensus tradition have constructed their histories around such assertions as Kenneth Clark's "all modern New York, heroic New York, started with Brooklyn Bridge." On the other side, the era's nefarious alliance of politics, finance, and industry is the bridge's prehistory; staggering levels of public corruption and the rise of the economic titan defined the Gilded Age. For these revisionist authors, the building of the bridge brought into vivid relief the gulf between historical memory and historical fact, and dispelled the opening day's claims of unity and brotherhood. They have taken the unified vision of historical order, the exemplary image of American progress, and, by restating its complexities, have shown it for the historical mischief it is. Dissatisfied with printing the legend, a number of writers, artists, and critics have sought "to enrich historical understanding" by imagining, researching, and then interpreting the facts.

Revision and Dissent

5

The Brooklyn Bridge from Its Centennial until the Present

A self contradiction is matter, it is and is not:
An ever-changing form, whose truth is hid within
A form, that blooms today,
Exhibits fruit tomorrow,
And next death and decay.

—John A. Roebling, "A Treatise on Metaphysics," 1860

It is in the nature of journalism that no day is like any other; your life's work is shaped by events. One result is that you come to cherish those things that do not change. They provide stability of place in a world that insists upon altering its look, its cast, and its rules. The Bridge never changed.

—Pete Hamill, "Bridge of Dreams," 1983

The American dialectic assumes argument not only as normal but as the necessary condition of its continued existence. The structure of the idea resembles a suspension bridge rather than a pyramid or a mosque. Its strength depends on the balance struck between countervailing forces, and the idea collapses unless the stresses oppose one another with equal weight.

—Lewis Lapham, "Democracy in America?" 1990

After the renaissance, came the reverence. On May 24, 1983, one story dominated the headlines in U.S. newspapers. The Brooklyn Bridge was one hundred years old, and New York was determined to celebrate its birthday in style. The predominant emotion may perhaps have shifted from sublime awe to fond devotion, but the centennial festivities were no less lavish, enthusiastic, or proud than those of the opening. By all accounts, the anniversary was an exuberant outpouring of love. After the fiscal crises of the 1970s, the anniversary allowed New Yorkers en masse a rare opportunity to express their veneration for their city and its public structures.

Exhibitions on the art and history of the bridge were mounted at the Brooklyn Museum of Art, the New-York Historical Society, the Museum of the City of New York, the Municipal Archives, the Pelham Arts Center, inside the bridge's Brooklyn anchorage, and further afield at the Smithsonian Institution and the Library of Congress in the nation's capital. New York's

Findlay Gallery assembled a show inspired by the bridge, and the Pratt Institute organized a series of outdoor sculpture exhibitions along similar lines. Concerts celebrating the music of the 1880s were held at historic sites in the city, and composer Tobias Picker was commissioned to create a bridge salute: "Between Two Worlds."

Souvenirs, both official and unofficial, proliferated; Tiffany's produced a special line of commemorative merchandise, and Macy's of Manhattan and Abraham and Strauss of Brooklyn teamed up to produce a catalog offering what they termed "Bridge-a-Brac." Andy Warhol designed the event's official poster, the U.S. Postal Service issued a commemorative stamp, a large-scale light show illuminated the bridge at night throughout the summer, and the New York Academy of Sciences sponsored a two-day colloquium.

On the anniversary itself, crowds headed to the East River in unprecedented numbers. Speeches were given, a parade was staged, and Brooklyn's famous sons and daughters lined up to offer commendation and praise. In the evening, a massive fireworks display culminated the day's events, and the Public Broadcasting System presented Ken Burns's Oscar-nominated documentary *Brooklyn Bridge*. As one source observed, "the bridge seemed to be literally everywhere."[1]

As the bridge's opening had inspired a mass of written material, so did the centennial. Reports of the event appeared in the vast majority of newspapers throughout Europe, Asia, and South and Central America. At home, America's fourth estate devoted considerable attention to the bridge, leading with such headlines as "Ode to Girders and Greatness," "A Radiant 100-Year-Old," "Brooklyn's Glory Road Marks a Century," "Span-Tastic," "City Alight with Joy," "Dazzling Centennial for a Heroic Span," and "100 Candles Blaze in Birthday Glory of B'klyn Bridge."[2] Additionally, no periodical seemed complete without a specially commissioned article, and many devoted entire issues to the centennial.

Amid this torrent of prose and the public's genuine passion, most of the articles produced at the centennial were standard heroic accounts of the bridge's construction, mixed with personal evocations of the joy found in walking the span. George Will used the occasion to lambaste those critics who pointed to financial exploitation in the bridge's construction: "Persons uneasy with any but banal explanations can say that the motivation for the building of the bridge was economic: the raising of property values in Brooklyn. But from the first conception, the bridge was an expression of the intangible beneath the tangible in America, the heroism of what has been called America's heroic materialism."[3] Unfortunately of course, the raising of property values certainly *was* a major issue during the construction.[4] Equally,

59. A centennial pennant: the official logo, 1983. From the author's collection.

Will's explanation of the bridge as "an expression of the intangible beneath the tangible in America" is itself an abstract, if not banal, explanation.

Yet the essence of Will's comments—pointing to the easy alliance between aspiration, heroism, materialism, and integrity—was articulated throughout the United States. Some writers went to great lengths to stress the bridge's positive immigrant symbolism; others employed the familiar trope of the perfect art object. For Pete Hamill, the bridge "was New York's supreme example of the Well-Made Thing." It was "beautiful without history, the way a master's painting of some forgotten duke or king is beautiful quite apart from the facts."[5] In an article that sought to relate the bridge to the city, Paul Goldberger rarely strayed past the bridge's aesthetic beauty: "The cables offer a gentle counterpoint, so delicate that they look like harp strings, and though they are, in fact, made of heavy strands of steel bound together, they make us feel that if we plucked them they would respond with beautiful music. And the roadway lifts in a gentle curve, animating the entire composition."[6]

The official centennial logo also promoted the bridge as a purely aesthetic achievement, as a decontextualized, depopulated "well-wrought urn." In the style of a contemporary corporate trademark, it pictured the bridge in an abstracted, modernist style combining a frontal view of one of the bridge towers with a sidelong view of the intricate cable structure. This "official" bridge was not the bridge between Manhattan and Brooklyn, but a free-floating insignia shorn of its urban context. It elided social function in favor of aesthetic, commercial appeal. Trademarked by the centennial commission, the image was used to sell the bridge, the centennial, and a vast array of official merchandise: posters, kitchenware, paperweights, commemorative medals and spoons, bags, hats, badges, T-shirts, coasters, beach towels, mugs, glassware, banners, umbrellas, patches, and key chains. A similar treatment was found on the commemorative postage stamp, which again pictured the bridge shorn of context against a white background.

For the centennial poster, Joel Greenberg's *Brooklyn Bridge I* was offered

60. The working bridge. Andy Warhol, *Brooklyn Bridge*, 1983. Screenprint printed on Lenox museum board, 39¼ × 39¼ in. © 2004 The Andy Warhol Foundation for the Visual Arts/Artists Rights Society (ARS), New York. Photo: The Andy Warhol Foundation, Inc./Art Resource, New York.

alongside Warhol's bridge. The latter image, which, significantly, looks toward Brooklyn, not toward the Manhattan skyline, made "good sense as a centennial poster," according to Colleen Sheehy. It "expresses the working bridge that is part of the urban landscape." Conversely, Sheehy found Greenberg's effort to be counteractive. It proposed "a romanticized 'Dream Bridge' . . . an isolated and deserted structure, unconnected to a larger urban landscape. In his images the sounds of the city are absent. Unlike Warhol, Greenberg's angles make the most of the Bridge's 'photogenic qualities,' capturing its well-known profiles. His photographs interpret the Bridge as a timeless work of art, a structure to revere."[7]

Greenberg produced a total of twenty-one photographs of the bridge for

195

the anniversary, and a number of these images remain fashionable as post-cards and posters. All employed the classic grand-style aesthetic: his bridge is monumental and entirely depopulated, even on the walkway. In direct contrast to Warhol—arguably America's most famous living fine artist at this time—Greenberg was (and still is) a commercial photographer.[8] Yet Greenberg's aestheticized, mythic, and overtly romantic work seemed to capture the mood, not to mention the intent, of the centennial commission. Like the official logo, his bridge was an object without a past or a context. Perhaps not surprisingly, his poster outsold Warhol's "unsentimental . . . working bridge"[9] by a large margin. Yet, even as the commercial photographer captured the "official" vision, he also exposed a basic tension in the centennial celebration itself: designed to mark the bridge's place in the history of the city, it was happy to picture the bridge without the presence or support of either history or the city.

Theory, Practice, and the Individual

Grand-style history and aesthetic beauty were not the only interpretations offered at the bridge's one-hundredth anniversary. Officially labeled "Rededication Day," the event was a contemporary ritual: a time to restate and reemphasize national achievement and identity. It was also, however, a time to *reconsider* those issues. Bill Reed, a journalist writing for a West Coast audience, took as his subject the bridge's relationship with Brooklyn. He contrasted the outpouring of nostalgic affection for the bridge and the borough with the names of thirty-two famous Brooklynites who "got out as soon as possible." "We hear a lot these days about how great Brooklyn was," he wrote, "but if Brooklyn was so great, why did people who love it leave it?" Repeatedly, Reed's question met with the same response from the people he interviewed: "Brooklyn changed" sometime in the 1950s and 1960s. Left unsaid was the problem of American race relations. Brooklyn changed after World War II because African Americans became a significant, visible presence in the borough.[10]

The *Boston Sunday Globe* also broached the subject of national character. Although many observers felt that the bridge reflected fundamental American traits—heroism, integrity, ambition, and accomplishment—the *Globe* writers offered a somewhat profane reading of national origins: "For while this country uniquely owes its history to ideas and concepts—life, liberty and the pursuit of happiness and so many others—they reveal exceedingly little about the nation that propagated them. They are slippery, treacherous, *abstract*, not the sort of thing a man could hitch his wagon to. All things being equal — or at least 'created' equal — your average American will take the wagon any day." [11] The *Globe* placed the rhetoric of the American errand under inspection. The history of the bridge's construction showed that the facts of American life and its conceptual ideal are only rarely conjoined.[12] Instead, their relationship is frequently oppositional. The bridge "embodies the visionary *and* the pecuniary: those simultaneous urges in our national character to build a city on a hill — and then subdivide it for a quick profit." [13]

The *Globe*'s "American Bridge" was not the span promoted by the ritual of assent. Rather, it exposed a nation of irreconcilable differences. Architectural critic Martin Filler, writing in *Art in America*, also noted this ambiguity. In its ability to display and highlight the "monstrous two-headed nature" of "Victorian schizophrenia . . . the dichotomy between romanticism and materialism," the bridge, for Filler, was *the* prime symbol of the Gilded Age.[14] Against the centennial's numerous evocations of democratic, exemplary progress, Filler and the *Globe* took a different position: theory and practice have only rarely shared common ground in America's evolving errand.

The separation between theory and practice, the visionary and the pecuniary, played a vital role in the centennial. Jimmy Breslin believed that, "now, in 1983, the bridge reflects a city that has so confused glory with making money that it allows a priceless monument to rot." The opportunity for rampant commercialism was also a concern. As Deirdre Carmody observed, "at no time . . . has the selling of the Brooklyn Bridge been raised to such an art as it has for its centennial." [15] Melvin Maddocks broadened the assault to include the media's complicity. No sooner had the nation's journalists finished "selling the Brooklyn Bridge" than they "turned their hyper-attention to *Return of the Jedi*." For Maddocks, Rededication Day prioritized profit over commemoration; once the celebrations were concluded, the nation's "psychedelic blink" was fixed on other commercial possibilities: "off with the old souvenir T-shirts and on with the new." [16]

Richard Eder also attacked America's pecuniary bent. At the opening, the city's moneyed citizens had walked across the bridge in comfort and seclusion, untroubled by the lower and middling classes. One hundred years later, only dignitaries and official paraders were allowed on the bridge for the celebrations, but the affluent retained a privileged viewing position.[17] Grandstands were erected at prime sites along the East River shore, and admission was granted, not by favor or influence, but by wealth alone. For those wishing to avoid contact with the common crowd, bleacher seats were available for $500. The fee included a street fair, champagne, smoked salmon, and parking permits. By contrast, members of the general public were forced to negotiate the numerous limousines and find space where they could. As Eder noted:

> Other symbolisms were not so widely remarked. One of them, somewhat below the occasion, had to do with the popular festivities. Two street fairs were announced, conjuring up an image of New Yorkers turning out to stroll, mingle, buy sausages, listening to street musicians and the like. There was quite a bit of that, in fact, but not at these fairs. These were by admission only . . . and included cocktails.
>
> Cocktails at a street fair. Shades of Marie Antoinette and her Trianon milkmaids. Was that what the Brooklyn Bridge had come to: a span joining two tiny islets of gentrification?[18]

Clearly, the *Globe's* outlook was both reflective and predictive. All the rhetoric of equality, freedom, and mutual progress could not disguise the fact that democratic access did not define the bridge's anniversary. At the centennial celebrations, America's classless ideals had indeed become "slippery, treacherous, *abstract*," revealing "exceedingly little about the nation that propagated them." Even as the visionary was lauded, the pecuniary triumphed.

Privileged viewing does not always correspond to Susan Davis's "privatization of public historical memory."[19] A number of centennial commentators actively shunned the "corporate" history found at, for example, the bridge's fiftieth anniversary, focusing instead on the bridge's relation to ordinary individuals. In a review of the centennial exhibitions mounted by the Smithsonian Institution and the Brooklyn Museum of Art, Donald Jackson derided most official commentators for succumbing to the "lure of the superlative." In addition, he faulted both exhibitions for failing to address the bridge's "economic and social impact" on the lives of the city's residents. In particular, the Smithsonian exhibition, although titled "Building Brooklyn Bridge," failed to take note of the "men who, though they played no role in designing the bridge, actually built it":

> We learn almost nothing about the workers who risked their lives deep in the caissons or high on the towers, and, in the light of the attention given to the technical minutiae, this was most unfortunate. For example, the exhibit catalog lists "vital statistics," such as the length of the main span, the grade of the roadway, the volume of timber in the caissons, the length of the wrapping wire in each cable, the total number of diagonal stays, and the depth of the floor

beams. It makes no mention of the number of men who worked, and in some cases died, on the bridge.

Although the Brooklyn Museum's exhibition featured some "eye-catching engravings" of "men high in the air working on the cables or the towers," Jackson lamented that it did "not exploit—and explain—the human element more fully."[20]

Filler also believed the bridge's defining element lay in its relationship to the individual. In direct opposition to such critics as Goldberger, he wrote: "the general public . . . has little interest in how well a work of art evokes the spirit of the period that produced it. Of much greater concern . . . is how well a work of architecture relates to one's own life." By positioning "the human figure as the ultimate focus of the structural system," the bridge was an American place in the broadest and most democratic sense. It represented a neutral area where the city's diverse populace could interact on equal terms. Filler described it as a "human cynosure . . . the world's one great anthropocentric bridge."[21] As an urban icon, it marked the potential for urban sympathy, not the march of technological progress: "Thus the great bridge was never a remote prodigy of incomprehensible science, but a vital fact of everyday life, an adjunct of livelihood, a trysting place, a source of recreation—proof of the continuing validity of the social contract in an age of unprecedented social and technological upheaval."[22]

Jimmy Breslin's essay "The Bridge" synthesized and crystallized much of the revisionist flavor of the anniversary. Published at the height of the centennial, it encapsulated the bridge's positive elements alongside its darker complexities. By declaring that "it is not a bridge with a clean history or new clean lines," Breslin revised the many evocations of the bridge's laudable past. Furthermore, his judgment on what Goldberger described as "New York's great and heroic age"[23] was equally recalcitrant: "it is only right that [Alfred E.] Smith's should be the one political name used in mentioning the bridge at this time, for the rest of them, even the President of the United States, who was present at the opening, don't deserve to be remembered." For Breslin, the bridge is an exemplary achievement only in context. Neither its epic construction nor its structural aesthetics are as important as its relation to its users: it is "the only large span in the world that really belongs to the people . . . that has anything to do with people." Concomitantly, Breslin shunned the grand-style aesthetic favored by, among others, Joel Greenberg: the bridge is "most beautiful when you see people walking across it."[24]

Within the framework of the centennial, Breslin's treatment of the bridge was unique. "The Bridge" is a frank piece of journalism concerning Emer-

gency Serviceman Richard Seaberg's attempt to talk down a potential suicide. Seaberg "has climbed the bridge a dozen times to pull people off"; although the practice is dangerous, he "always comes back, climbing the
cable, trying to save a life." In this instance, however, Seaberg's attempts are
unsuccessful. Taking a defiant swig of his beer, a young man jumps to his
death. Although the episode's conclusion is bleak, Breslin's bridge is characterized by both failure *and* hope. Two weeks later, Seaberg is back on the
bridge. This time he is successful: "then Seaberg's large hands went out and
he had the guy. He yanked him back into life. And he will do this again,
Seaberg will, for his beat is a bridge traveled by people who are all so flawed."
Breslin's bridge is typified by the realities of its daily life: by troubled, anonymous New Yorkers and those who risk their lives to aid them. By focusing on
the mundane, Breslin eschewed the centennial's two dominant themes: the
bridge's triumphant construction and the anniversary's celebratory zeal. For
Breslin, neither aspect reflects the contemporary bridge. The lives and
deaths of the ordinary and the nameless present a more accurate picture.
Against the centennial's glorious rhetoric, Breslin posits an alternative symbolism; against tradition, he conceives of new standards and a new canon. In
place of the celebrated, the illustrious, and the iconic, "up high, Seaberg
stands for all the years of the Brooklyn Bridge." [25]

Structural Disquiet

In a review of the Brooklyn Museum of Art's centennial exhibition,
Daralice Boles declared that "the show's most poignant images are not the
naïve celebrations of its beginning but the apocalyptic painting of its destruction by O. Louis Guglielmi, whose work explodes the myth of the
bridge's immortality." [26] Questions pertaining to the bridge's "immortality"
have shadowed the structure throughout its history. In 1873, *Appletons' Journal* prefigured Montgomery Schuyler's seminal "The Bridge as a Monument" when it looked to the future of New York: "If New York were to fall
into ruins to-day, Macaulay's 'New Zealand' would search in vain five hundred years hence for any trace of its present magnificence. There might be
enough of the piers of the Brooklyn bridge left for him to sit upon amid the
desolation, but it is doubtful whether his eye would be gratified with the sight
of a standing column or a wall." [27]

Ten years later Schuyler cast his eye upon a similar, imagined future,
when the bridge and New York might lay in ruin: "The web of woven steel
that now hangs between the stark masses of the towers may have disappeared,
its slender filaments rusted into nothingness under the slow corrosion of the
centuries. Its builders and the generation for which they wrought may have

61. "The two monuments in the river": "in the smaller river on the right stood two colossal structures, rising high in the air, and standing like twin brothers, as if to guard thedeserted streets below." J. A. Mitchell, *The Last American,* 1889. From the author's collection.

been as long forgotten as are now the builders of the Pyramids." "It is not unimaginable," continued Schuyler, "that our future archeologist, looking from one of these towers upon the solitude of a mastless river and a dispeopled land, may have no other means of reconstructing our civilization than that which is furnished him by the tower on which he stands."[28]

Schuyler's question — "What will his judgment of us be?" — was answered in J. A. Mitchell's utopian novel *The Last American* (1889). Set in the very distant future, the story follows the Persian navy as it sails into New York Harbor. The invaders find a city that is derelict, its most prominent "relics" being two great towers that stand on either shore of the city's eastern river: "in the smaller river on the right stood two colossal structures, rising high in the air, and standing like twin brothers, as if to guard the deserted streets below." Journeying up the East River, the Persians sail "close under one of the great monuments in the river" and, in what seems a direct reference to Schuyler, admit that "we . . . are at a loss to divine its meaning."[29]

In the same year that Mitchell published his apocryphal novel, the

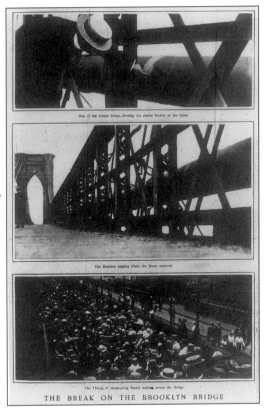

62. "The Break on the Brooklyn Bridge," *Harper's Weekly*, August 3, 1901. Courtesy of the Library of Congress.

THE BREAK ON THE BROOKLYN BRIDGE

bridge's first major structural problem occurred. Early in the year, a cable girder broke, and the bridge had to be closed for two days. Further problems were encountered nine years later. On July 26, 1898, in the midst of the evening rush hour, the span's roadway suddenly dropped several feet when several trusses under the roadbed buckled. No one was hurt, and the investigating engineers judged the incident "harmless." Three years later, on July 24, 1901, a similar incident occurred. A number of suspender rods near the bridge's center snapped, and the bridge again visibly sagged. This time the debate over safety was more extensive. The city appointed bridge engineers Edwin Duryea and Joseph Mayer to investigate, and their subsequent report censured both the bridge's design and its upkeep. To counter such claims, Wilhelm Hildenbrand, a civil engineer and author of *Cable Making for Suspension Bridges, With Special Reference to the Cables of the East River Bridge* (1877), issued a prompt response. He charged Duryea and Mayer with "unjust and unscientific" analysis, attributed the damage to heat expansion, and concluded that "the bridge must in every respect be declared to be as safe as it ever was." Ironically, Hildenbrand also stated that he had "not examined the bridge" himself.[30]

On July 3, 1922, the bridge was again in trouble. The steel saddles that supported the two most northern cables slipped their rollers and inched toward the span's center. Again the public was alarmed, and this time official opinion was divided. Grover Whalen, commissioner of plants and structures, called for the bridge to be rebuilt. Ernest Cuozzo, ex-secretary of the department of bridges, recommended that the bridge be shut down "before a calamity occurs." Conversely, Gustav Lindenthal, then America's foremost authority on bridge construction, stated publicly that neither the bridge nor the public was in any danger. Eighty-five-year-old Washington Roebling joined the debate and concurred with Lindenthal: the saddles had been *designed* to slip. Nevertheless, for the next three years, automobile traffic was barred from the bridge, and strict guidelines were put into effect for the passage of light rail trains and trolleys.[31]

Throughout the bridge's history, strenuous claims for its longevity have existed alongside structural anxiety. On May 17, 1933, City Finance Commissioner Albert Goldman warned that municipal support was falling seriously short of escalating maintenance costs. Should the funding shortfall continue, he concluded, the bridge would be in serious danger of deterioration and even collapse. Just one week later, on the bridge's fiftieth anniversary, the *Eagle* interviewed the city's chief engineer, Austin Byrne. "[A]ll the talk of its deterioration which has been heard from time to time in recent years is groundless," he declared. "[T]he splendid structure is as good today as it ever was." Emphasizing the point, the *Eagle* predicted the bridge would last at least another "1,000 years."[32]

Such assertions were a mainstay of reporting on the bridge's centennial. In a banner headline, the *New York Post* proclaimed that the bridge "May Outlive the City Itself." McCullough believed that "it could last forever," and the *Daily News* felt it would "outlast us all."[33] Despite these claims, the myth of the bridge's immortality has come under increasing scrutiny. Very real problems have severely tested the bridge's serviceability and provided one of the most disquieting elements of the bridge's contemporary history.

On October 22, 1980, only two days after a press conference announcing the creation of the centennial commission, George Zaimes, director of engineering in the Office of New York Affairs in the New York State Transportation Department, declared that "the bridge may barely survive its centennial." According to his evaluation, 50 percent of the wires in many of the cables were either heavily rusted or completely eroded by salt and water leakage. Brooklyn Borough President Howard Golden countered that the department was trying to ransom the city into imposing tolls on a free bridge. Six months after some minor repairs were carried out, City Council President Carol Bellamy charged that the city had no comprehensive or coherent plan to halt the mass deterioration of the city's bridges, highways, and sewers. She also criticized the city's plan to spend 42 percent less on bridge rehabilitation during the coming year.[34]

Barely fifty-eight days after Bellamy's report, one of the bridge's main support cables snapped, fatally striking Japanese tourist Akira Aimi. Although the city immediately announced a $115 million renovation program, fears over the bridge's structural integrity only increased. Replacement cables, attached to the bridge immediately after the tragedy, began to sag only days into use. The incident prompted historian Donald Jackson to publish a damning article on the state of American bridge preservation. Declaring that "the recent tragedy on the Brooklyn Bridge underscores the threat faced by thousands of historic bridges," Jackson cited a recent study by the Federal Highway Administration: the Brooklyn Bridge was only one of a staggering two hundred thousand American bridges that were "functionally obsolete" or "structurally deficient."[35]

Engineer John Wiedeman continued the attack in an address to the Newcomen Society. He detailed the appalling state of bridge maintenance and then proclaimed: "for too long, we have been managing our multi-billion dollar infrastructure — one of the nation's most vital assets — in a disorganized, stopgap fashion. . . . we can no longer afford to leave such a vast national resource to the whims of pork-barrel politics."[36] Breslin also highlighted the bridge's structural frailties in his centennial essay: "Seaberg wore a safety belt that was hooked to one of the guide cables, but he reminded himself to be wary of the cable and to put no faith at all in the decorative rails. Now 100 years old, the Brooklyn Bridge is in such disrepair that any part can snap off."[37]

Public disquiet heightened a month after the centennial, when the Connecticut Turnpike Bridge collapsed. Amid an intense debate over bridge safety in the New York–New Jersey–Connecticut area, the Pequonnock River Bridge in Bridgeport and a bridge in Old Saybrook were found to be near collapse. On September 2, barely three months after the centennial, a fourth scare occurred when a bridge collapsed in Hartford. Two months later, New Jersey State Senator Laurence Weiss complained of the many "potential killer bridges" in his state.[38]

Toward the end of 1983, Governor Mario Cuomo finally succeeded in his struggle for a $1.25 billion bond issue to finance the repair of New York's highways and bridges. Nevertheless, the Brooklyn Bridge continued to be associated with tense and unnerving events. Violent crime on the span increased so markedly that surveillance cameras were installed. In 1984, the bridge was sealed off and a manhunt conducted after a police detective was injured by gunfire; in 1986, an unidentified gunman positioned on the bridge took aim at a passing cruise boat, injuring a female passenger; and in 1988, city employee Dutch Payton was shot at while he worked on the bridge. In both 1986 and 1992, freighters struck the bridge while passing beneath the span.

The most infamous event of recent years occurred in 1994, when the bridge was the scene of a terrifying car chase as Lebanese-American Rashid Baz opened fire at a van containing four Lubavitcher students, killing fifteen-year-old Aaron Halberstam.[39] Violence came to the fore again on the morning of October 28, 1995, when a motorcyclist and a car driver got into a traffic dispute. Swearing to get revenge, the motorcyclist followed the car off the bridge and then fired several shots through the car's rear window, hitting the driver in the shoulder. Presiding Judge Jack Weinstein called the incident a "strange and troubling case of a faceless violent" man.[40] Less than three months later, on January 15, 1996, racial tensions were front-page news when Mayor Rudolph Giuliani ordered the city's police department to stop the sixth annual Martin Luther King Day march from crossing the Brooklyn Bridge. The denial of their democratic right to march incensed the city's black population, and the event led to widespread charges of institutional racism.

In 1998, as New York City celebrated the centennial of its consolidation, the bridge again stood in the midst of a municipal quarrel. The opening of the span in 1883 had forced the issue of civic consolidation: now physically connected, should not New York and Brooklyn join in metropolitan union? For city planner and prime lobbyist Andrew Haswell Green, the answer was more than obvious, and the issue was widely popular in four of the region's five independent districts. In Brooklyn, however, the matter was highly controversial—the consolidation measure passed by only 277 votes out of a total ballot of 129,211—and in retrospect much lamented. With unification, Brooklyn lost its separateness, its individuality, and, for many, its authenticity. Its fate was subjugated to decisions made on the Manhattan side of the bridge, not at home in Brooklyn Borough Hall. According to John Tierney, author of the most provocative reevaluation of unification, the incorporation of the five boroughs cost Brooklyn "the nimbleness that helped it adapt before consolidation."[41] The borough's stagnation through much of the twentieth century, and especially from midcentury to the 1990s, Tierney felt, could be traced directly to the autonomy ceded in 1898. Certainly, the bridge was a magnificent achievement that helped introduce Brooklyn to the world, but in due course it also made a sibling of the former city.

No event so dramatically illustrates the fortunes of the borough after consolidation than the fate of its most famous newspaper. The *Brooklyn Daily Eagle* lobbied hard for the Brooklyn Bridge, yet its support and idealism blinded it to a crucial reality. With the bridge came substantial new competition. As New York papers flooded east over the bridge, the *Eagle's* primacy as the voice of the city came under challenge. And with consolidation, those Manhattan papers took on a new significance. Literally across the road from City Hall in Printing House Square, they seemed closer to the heart of the new metropolis. By contrast, Brooklyn's newspapers were relegated to the periphery. The incorporation of New York City in 1898 forced the *Eagle* and the borough to confront a new historical reality: their fate was no longer in their own hands. Successively, the *Eagle's* influence withered: first with the bridge, then with consolidation. It would never again be the power broker it once had been before the bridge. It limped on through the first half of the twentieth century, not with the strong voice of an independent city, but with the quiet murmurings of a subordinate province. On January 28, 1955, the voice of Brooklyn halted its presses and ceased publication.

Tierney's skeptical interpretation of consolidation was arresting, yet ultimately overshadowed by the city's obvious desire to celebrate, not question, its own centennial. To accompany the anniversary, the Museum of the City of New York staged an exhibition titled "Bridging New York." The show was popular, and its intention was easily gauged from the catalog—*Stone and Steel: Paintings and Writings Celebrating the Bridges of New York*—which excerpted many literary depictions of New York's bridges.[42] To fit the theme of the catalog, however, those excerpts required a certain amount of editing; Dos Passos's description of Bud Korpenning's final moments, for example, stops short of his suicide. The exhibition also showcased the artist Bascove's many playful, Georgia O'Keeffe–inspired paintings of the bridges of New York. Also exhibited at New York University, the Uptown Gallery, the Hudson River Museum, and the National Arts Club, these loving tributes presented the city's spans as ageless, almost pastoral works of unblemished art.

Not long after the celebrations, the bridge was pictured in ruins in two major summer blockbusters, and its structural integrity was again questioned. Repairs to the roadway were conducted—"quietly" according to the *New York Times*—in both the summer and the fall, and by the end of the year bright red stanchions appeared under the bridge's New York approach. The city denied any new problems, but the need for such immediate and substantial supports was another unsettling reminder of the bridge's vulnerability.[43]

In 1999 another visual text took the bridge as its subject. Where Bascove's spans seem forged for eternity, Burhan Dogançay's *Bridge of Dreams: The Rebirth of the Brooklyn Bridge* took on the subject of impermanence and managed to make a virtue of poor maintenance. The context of neglect—the political failure that directly led to the repair work Dogançay documents—is ignored as structural decline is transformed into "rebirth."[44]

No new beginnings seemed imminent for the bridge early in 1999, however, as fresh news of structural problems emerged. On February 4, a full-page picture of the bridge appeared on the front page of the *Daily News*, accompanied by the headline: "Bridge Needs a Fix: City Orders Emergency Work as Pieces Fall from Brooklyn Span." Large chunks of the concrete roadway were falling into the East River, and experts blamed the quick-fix repaving work done the previous summer. The city, however, claimed that the problems were the result of ordinary wear and tear, and the New York transport commissioner stated that "the bridge is not in jeopardy."[45] Despite these assertions, the bridge continued to attract negative publicity.[46] Early in 2001, Al Groh surprised the sports world by resigning as head coach of the New York Jets football team. It was the third such resignation in a year, yet cornerback Ray Mickens was philosophical: "this is New York, nothing should surprise you in New York. The only thing that would be a surprise is if they fixed the construction on the Brooklyn Bridge."[47]

Just as the bridge has often played a supporting role to the Statue of Liberty in the celebration of American immigration, so it has in the apocalyptic imagination. In the years between the imagined futures of *Appletons' Journal* in 1873 and Montgomery Schuyler in 1883, *Life* magazine twice envisioned the destruction of New York, first by some "hostile fleet." As the sun rises "the next morning," Liberty has been decapitated and the Brooklyn Bridge lies fallen amid the East River. Shortly after the bridge was opened, *Life* was at it again, this time casting a satiric eye on the long-running issue of who should pay for Liberty's pedestal. Imagining the statue "as it will appear by the time the pedestal is finished," *Life* depicted a hunched over, wizened old hag before an equally decrepit Brooklyn Bridge, its cables rusted through and its roadway collapsed.[48] The *Life* conceit was replicated by Joseph Pennell in his famous World War I–era poster for Liberty Bonds: "That Liberty Shall Not Perish from the Earth."

The most famous image of the destruction of Liberty occurred in 1968 in Franklin J. Schaffner's film *Planet of the Apes*. Its final sequence is an iconic moment of profound influence, reverberating throughout culture. The implications—that humankind will bring about its own destruction and that a return to pre-nuclear innocence is impossible—have been analyzed by

63. Post-apocalypse: the Brooklyn waterfront as it might appear in 5004. Alexis Rockman, *Manifest Destiny*, 2003–2004. © Alexis Rockman, 2003–2004. Courtesy Gorney Bravin + Lee, New York.

numerous critics and satirized in countless films and television shows. Most recently, the film has served as an inspiration for eco-artist Alexis Rockman and his enormous mural *Manifest Destiny* (2003–2004), a post-apocalyptic rendering of the Brooklyn waterfront as it might appear in 5004. In formulating his vision, Rockman did not stumble upon Brooklyn as his subject; he was led by Schaffner's film: "I felt that I needed something iconic, like the Statue of Liberty in *Planet of the Apes* . . . and I decided that the Brooklyn Bridge was it."[49]

For the cold war America of *Planet of the Apes*, the fear was martial; for Rockman it is ecological. Nevertheless, the end results are the same. *Manifest Destiny* anticipates the destruction of New York and Brooklyn through biohazards, genetic disease, and global warming. The waters of the East River have risen eighty-two feet, species have mutated into abominable new creatures, and cells representing modern plagues float freely beneath the water's surface.[50] As Schuyler predicted, "the web of woven steel that now hangs between the stark masses of the towers [has] disappeared, its slender filaments rusted into nothingness under the slow corrosion of the centuries." No New Zealander surveys this landscape: humans are nowhere to be found in

64. The rising waters of the East River. Chesley Bonestell's cover for *Astounding Science Fiction*, November 1951. From the author's collection.

Rockman's vision. Although they created this scene, they are no longer around to bear witness to the consequences of their actions. The Brooklyn Bridge stands forlornly as one of the few visible records of human achievement, although the once mighty span is pock-marked, decrepit, and covered in thick tropical greenery.

The painting's title distinguishes it from *Planet of the Apes* while marking it as an equally political work. Rockman's mural is no mere fantasy: "I see this as a very traditional history painting," he told the *New York Times*. "And as far as I can tell, it is also the most credible version of our history."[51] Clearly, Rockman envisions the logical end point of Manifest Destiny, the natural culmination of unfettered technological progress. Manifest Destiny was an attitude toward the North American landscape — a dream of domination and order — cast as an obligation, not as a choice, and offered as an excuse for arrogant misuse. It found its clearest cultural expression in nineteenth-century American landscape painting.

Rockman has cited the Hudson River School, along with Albert Bierstadt's *Storm in the Rocky Mountains* (1866), as an influence on his mural. Yet this impact is Janus-faced. On the one hand, Rockman incorporates many formal aspects of nineteenth-century American landscape painting. Equally, he seems to detect in Bierstadt a lost Eden of ecological innocence. On the other hand, many of the Hudson River artists were intimately connected with the ideology of Manifest Destiny, with promoting and plotting the same course of American empire that Rockman attacks. The most obvious point of reference between Rockman and the Hudson River School is Thomas Cole's series of five paintings, *The Course of Empire* (1836). Both artists share an obsession with ruin and dissolution; yet there is nothing cyclical in Rockman, no return to nature, no possibility of renewal. More applicable, although slightly less obvious, is Frederic Church's *Cotopaxi* (1862), the painter's dramatic treatment of the Ecuadorian volcano.

Like *Manifest Destiny*, *Cotopaxi* is intimately concerned with evolution and destruction, albeit on a cosmic rather than a local level. Church's canvas depicts a battleground of contending forces — the creative impulse of nature and the devastation of catastrophe — indicating a world at war with itself. Visually, the paintings share the same otherworldly orange glow, but they are separated by a divergent sense of futurity. Painted in the midst of the American Civil War, *Cotopaxi*'s deep ambivalence is tempered by hope. As the dawn begins to penetrate the thick, massed ash of the erupting volcano, the scene promises renewal. The transience of the volcano's dense smoke will dissipate, we sense, before the stability of the morning sun.

Manifest Destiny is also an image of morning, but here the rising sun speaks more to global warming than to ecological renewal. And it is in these implications that Rockman inverts Church's message. Rockman's mural represents an updated version of *Cotopaxi*—with one important addition: the hand of humanity. Church's natural history is primordial; it speaks to humanity's coexistence with a bountiful nature. By contrast, Rockman deals with the consequences of ecological devastation. Gross mutations transmogrify animal and aquatic life in reaction to man's intrusion into the natural world — to biological pollution, artificial climate change, and genetic modification — and with it, order and harmony are transformed into chaos and discord. In *Cotopaxi*, the creation belongs to nature; in *Manifest Destiny*, the destruction belongs to man.

Manifest Destiny was a mission and a myth. It projected the nation into a millennial future. For Rockman, the apocalypse is coming, and it promises no new Eden. Instead, America's destiny is made manifest through its utter disregard for the environmental basis of its dream. In comparison to *Planet of the Apes*, the implications of *Manifest Destiny* are *not* that progress will give humankind the weapons to destroy itself, but that progress *itself* will destroy humankind. The irony implicit in *Manifest Destiny* is that the dream of order — celebrated by nineteenth-century American painting—will ultimately lead to chaos and destruction. Amid the future devastation, the bridge towers will still stand, but the civilization that built the span will have been banished by its own internal logical. In *Planet of the Apes*, the Statue of Liberty stands as a stark reminder of human aggression; in Rockman's mural, the Brooklyn Bridge stands as a silent witness to an ecological holocaust. Were Henry James or Federico Lorca inclined to think three millennia ahead, they might well have dreamed up something similar to Rockman's *Manifest Destiny*.

Rites of Separation

Retold from the opening to the centennial, the story of the bridge's construction has served as an American rite of passage. Illustrating the transition from innocence to maturity, the narrative describes the resolution of social conflict and the realization of a new, superior cultural landscape. The American Revolution was just such an event, and to it we can add the Civil War, as well as countless major technological "events": the Atlantic cable, the transcontinental railroad, the Hoover Dam, and the Apollo space program. Where, for example, the Revolutionary War has been employed to underline America's coming of age as a people, the building of the bridge stands as one

of the foremost evocations of America's coming of age as a modern, industrial nation.[52]

With their emphasis on recollection and repetition, commemorative occasions have sustained the bridge as a symbol of the national rite. The trope
is also present in the fictional history discussed above. Whether "fables of
change" or "reactionary romances," these narratives conform to the traditions of the rite of passage: from separation (or social detachment) to margin
(or liminal phase), and finally to reaggregation within the communal body.[53]
In essence, they differ only in the ideological implications of the reaggregation each author presents. The main protagonists in the fiction of Dorothy
Beall, Frances Browin, Lewis Mumford, and Albert Idell are "reincorporated" into society with "rights and obligations vis-à-vis others of a clearly
defined and 'structural' type."[54] In Beall and Browin, Robert Cameron and
Pete Schmidt are reincorporated into society as the agents of technological
progress.[55] By contrast, Jefferson Baumgarten (in Mumford) and Jesse Rogers
(in Idell) rejoin society with the sort of "rights and obligations" that, as Herbert Gutman has pointed out, defined the American tradition of working-
class republicanism.[56] Yet, however different the circumstances, the passage
from separation to reaggregation *is* achieved.

Charles Dickinson revised the national rite of passage in his short story
"Colonel Roebling's Friend" (1995). In common with the fictional histories
already discussed, Dickinson's story focuses on a central protagonist and his
place within the bridge's construction. Howard Alston's social separation occurs before the bridge project, when he is sent over a thousand miles to fight
in the American Civil War. "Shot through the leg at Vicksburg," he journeys
two years to return home to his wife and child in New York. He arrives in the
city without a war pension, partially disabled, and unable to find work. In a
liminal state, Alston is forced to take the only job he can get: digging the
bridge's caissons. Among the bridge workers, however, Alston fails to achieve
reaggregation. Within a few weeks, he is struck down by caisson's disease and
paralyzed.[57]

Throughout the story, Dickinson is careful to contrast Alston's fate with
that of Washington Roebling. Both are Civil War veterans, and both are
left physically incapacitated after an attack of the bends. Roebling's status,
however, is never liminal. His fame increases with his disability, and he
continues to orchestrate the building of the bridge. By contrast, Alston is
abandoned and forgotten by the bridge company. From disabled war veteran
to underground sandhog, he falls into redundancy; his immobile body, restricted to a wheelchair, symbolizes his liminality.

Angered by her husband's fate, Alston's wife, Eva, visits the bridge office to demand compensation.[58] Alston believes Roebling to be his friend, and the latter's cheery manner, coupled with their shared history, seems to confirm their bond. Yet the title of Dickinson's short story is ironic: when Eva gives her husband's name to an assistant, Roebling does not even "look up from his work." The claim is met with bureaucratic harshness, and Alston receives a mere $100, an amount equal to forty days' pay. The amount shocks Eva — "that's all? He may never walk again" — and is juxtaposed with Roebling's financial status. While Eva is applying for reparation, Roebling signs a check for $77,500.[59]

Roebling's failure to respond to Alston's name initiates a new form of marginalization. Increasingly, Alston's liminality comes to encompass silence and anonymity, in addition to immobility. Just before the bridge opening, Alston's son William meets the wealthy Dreamina Trobst in Brooklyn Heights. In an attempt to impress Dreamina, William declares: "my father built the bridge.... He's a close friend of Colonel Roebling." Dreamina responds positively, "I'd love to meet him someday," but her afterthought is revealing: "and your father too." Within this brief exchange, Alston's position is clarified: from focus to afterthought, from subject to margin.[60]

Alston's anonymity is further compounded at the bridge's opening. Although a rumor circulates that every man who worked on the bridge "would be invited to the opening ceremonies," Alston receives no invitation. He is no longer even a footnote to the construction. Unable to negotiate the crowds at the East River, Alston waits outside Roebling's house, hoping to catch a glimpse of his friend. All day, "the front door of the Roebling house never quite closed entirely," as visitors, florists, and caterers flowed in and out. Late in the afternoon, President Chester A. Arthur and New York Governor Grover Cleveland appear to pay their respects. Their actions only confirm Alston's liminality. Although "passing within an arm's length," the president declines to shake Alston's outstretched hand. Alston fares little better with the governor: "Cleveland ... paused in his arrival to take Howard's hand in a sweaty, fleeting grip. But he heard nothing that Howard said."[61] Alston's descent into anonymity is completed a week later on Memorial Day. Confined to his wheelchair, he is pushed across the bridge by his wife and son. As they promenade, Alston recounts his experiences in the New York caisson — "his one story" — yet "Eva's attention was elsewhere," and "William did not even pretend to listen."[62] "Colonel Roebling's Friend" ends with Alston embroiled in the Memorial Day panic. His immobility is compounded as the crowds close in around him; concerned for their own safety, the frightened sightseers pay Alston no heed.

Focusing on the bridge's relation to the anonymous individual, "Colonel

Roebling's Friend" answers the concerns that Donald Jackson and Martin Filler expressed at the bridge's centennial. Dickinson narrates a rite of separation, not a rite of passage.[63] Like Ralph Ellison's indiscernible protagonist, Alston takes on a mantle of invisibility; like Herman Melville's Israel Potter, Alston cannot escape liminality as a permanent state.[64] Regarded as the pinnacle of late-nineteenth-century American achievement, the building of the Brooklyn Bridge hid the tragedy of broken lives and shattered families. Its construction furthered the nation's sense of its own advancement while leaving numerous workers bereft. Dickinson's short story also challenges William James's thesis that the "disciplinary function" of industrial progress—"the immemorial human warfare against nature"—is a social benefit: the "moral equivalent of war."[65] There is no essential heroism in "Colonel Roebling's Friend." Where Roebling and the bridge are exalted, Alston is broken and then forgotten. For Dickinson, national progress hides individual dissolution.

Rites of Dissent

America's historical continuity has dominated cultural arguments—and cultural wars—for the past twenty years. The debate clarifies the questions raised in Chapter 4: what relationship, if any, can be said to exist between nineteenth-century America and its twentieth-century incarnation? Is the passage from one to the other a seamless, linear tale of continued national progress, or a complex tale of rupture and entropy?[66] In the case of the Brooklyn Bridge, its centennial, not surprisingly, stressed the former view, as have a number of recent critics. In *American Visions* (1997), Robert Hughes asserted that "the bridge summed up the whole burgeoning imagery of benign industrial capitalism shedding its benefits on society."[67] Such claims correspond to a specific American self-image. In the nineteenth century, according to Leo Marx, "Canals, steamboats, mechanized power machinery, locomotives, and the telegraph were repeatedly cited as evidence that the human mind could penetrate the surface of nature, unlock its secrets, and therefore put more and more natural processes to use for human purposes."[68]

In *Underworld*, released the same year as Hughes's *American Visions*, novelist Don DeLillo disagreed. Discussing the Fresh Kills landfill site on Staten Island, the largest base-to-summit rubbish dump in the world, and the highest point on the U.S. Eastern Seaboard, DeLillo proclaimed that New York's various "bridges, tunnels, scows, tugs, graving docks, container ships, all the great works of transport, trade and linkage were directed in the end to this great culminating structure."[69] Here, the "benefits" of "benign industrial capitalism" are literally garbage. Where nineteenth-century America put the engineer at the forefront of America's quest for political and social liberation, DeLillo places him at the rear, responsible not as a social leader, but as its garbage man, charged with overseeing society's waste. Furthermore, just as "all the great works of [American] transport, trade and linkage" led to the conquest of the West in the nineteenth century, in DeLillo's twentieth century they lead back to the East Coast's largest trash pile. In the nineteenth century, the engineer represented the harbinger of history; for DeLillo, the engineer trails behind Walter Benjamin's "angel of history," a slave to the litter produced by contemporary consumer society.[70] Predating Alexis Rockman, DeLillo signals a break in the continuity of the American ritual of assent: the logical result of Manifest Destiny is a landfill, not a garden.

In *Americana* (1971)—signifying the very stuff of American culture—DeLillo began his inquiry into the linear version of American historical continuity. His subject was the changes wrought in the post–World War II American landscape:

> We wish to blast all the fine old things to oblivion and replace them with taste-less identical structures. . . . We want to be totally engulfed by all the so-called worst elements of our national life and culture. . . . We want to come to terms with the false anger we so often display at the increasing signs of sterility and violence in our culture. Kill the old brownstones and ornate railroad terminals. Kill the rotten stinking smalltown courthouses. Blow up the Brooklyn Bridge.[71]

As a New Yorker, DeLillo had witnessed entire rows of nineteenth-century brownstones torn down to make way for new commercial development and often poorly planned public housing. The process reached its nadir with the destruction of Pennsylvania Station in 1963, described by both Lewis Mumford and Daniel Moynihan as "the greatest act of civic vandalism" in New York's history.[72] Such events were clearly on DeLillo's mind when he began to write his first novel. In *Americana*, history's advance brings depreciation, not improvement, and progress is defined by destruction. The observation is aptly summarized in Ada Louise Huxtable's observation of New York's "civic vandalism": "Pennsylvania Station succumbed to progress at the age of fifty-six, after a lingering decline."[73] If "progress" could seal the fate of McKim, Mead and White's great railroad terminal, would the Brooklyn Bridge be next? And, more important, would anyone care?

Certainly, Daniela Gioseffi and Harvey Shapiro would. To these poets, the bridge is one of New York's greatest treasures—precisely because of the contemporary U.S. cultural scene. Writing a year after *Americana* was published, Gioseffi used the bridge to contrast the nineteenth and the twentieth centuries:

> you beautiful monster of the harbor,
> now a cultural symbol
> bridging Whitman's age of hope
> to our age of anxiety and despair . . .
> I walk over you and couch out the thick air
> that muffles your "choiring strings"–
> the smoke that hazes the beauty Crane knew . . .
> I walk suspended by the ghost of all that could have been
> since you were christened by the city
> and a country
> where Lorca's worst nightmares
>   have come true.[74]

In 1978, Shapiro cast his eye on the history of "Whitman's crummy fish-shaped island":

> opening the Bridge!
> Fireworks and exultation! Crowds moving
> In a mighty congress back and forth.
> While we, unmoving on the starry grid of America,
> Stare failure in the face, our blazing star.[75]

Gioseffi and Shapiro celebrate the bridge as an icon of nostalgia.[76] As they gaze upon it, they honor the memory of what the United States once was and mourn what it has become. Both authors explicitly contrast the era of the bridge's creation and 1970s America; equally, they find no similarities. History is the source of their lament. From "hope" to "anxiety," "exultation" to "failure," the course of American history is defined as entropy not improvement.

Written during the bridge's centennial, Paul Auster's *Ghosts* furthers the debate surrounding American continuity. Forming the middle section of *The New York Trilogy* (1985–1986), the story has been subject to much critical comment. For Dennis Barone, Auster's principal character, Blue, is "haunted by the ever-present, unceasingly real"; according to John Zilcosky, the novella "precludes any sense of the past"; Tim Woods has argued that the story is "bound up with a meditation on the American ideology of progress and expansion, especially as it was figured and represented in the settlement of the American wilderness."[77] These statements are both insightful and misleading. They reveal Auster's theme while denying its basic polarity. *Ghosts* is distinguished by an overriding concern with *both* the real and the unreal, the past and the present. Representing the unreal, and present, are the narrative's principal characters: Blue, White, Black, Green, Brown, and the (ex) future Mrs. Blue. On the side of the real are characters emblematic of nineteenth-century America: Nathaniel Hawthorne, Henry David Thoreau, John and Washington Roebling, Walt Whitman, Abraham Lincoln, and Henry Ward Beecher. Consonant with both sets of characters is the current and historical location of New York City. Mediating between these opposing forces are confusion and uncertainty, the intention of which is an inquiry into identity.

The key to Auster's inquiry lies within the real past/unreal present dichotomy, which is introduced in a conversation between Blue and Black. Discussing Henry Ward Beecher's Plymouth Church, Black tells Blue that "many great men have gone there . . . Abraham Lincoln, Charles Dickens — they all walked down the street, and went into the church." Blue responds with a single word: "ghosts." In a discussion shortly thereafter, Blue responds to the mention of Hawthorne with "another ghost."[78] These references to nineteenth-century America are furthered through literary influence. At heart, *Ghosts* is a modern retelling of Hawthorne's short story "Wakefield" (1837). Nevertheless, the events in Hawthorne's story neither help nor guide Blue: unlike Wakefield, Blue is unable to return home after his long absence. Another important writer who appears in the story is Thoreau. After reading *Walden* (1854), Blue imagines himself living a similar life: "walking through the woods and swinging an axe over his shoulder. Alone and free, his own man at last . . . a pioneer, a pilgrim in a new world." Equally, however, the example of Thoreau is of no help: Blue perpetually imagines Black "sneaking up on him and slitting his throat."[79]

Auster solidifies his view of America's past by associating historical figures with specific locations. Beecher and Whitman are linked with the neighborhood of Brooklyn Heights, yet they too prove to be irrelevant "ghosts." The most important emblem of this device is the Brooklyn Bridge. Blue's knowledge of the bridge is encyclopedic. He knows more about its genesis, its construction, and the fate of both Roeblings — all of which he recounts while traversing the span — than he does, it seems, about his own life.[80] The recitation presents the story's most comprehensive historical data. Once again, however, Blue is unable to extract any truth that is germane to his current situation. He is lost before the machinations of White and Black, and helpless in his relationships with his ex-partner Brown and the (ex) future Mrs. Blue.

Auster's Blue fails to understand what Gioseffi and Shapiro set out so clearly: the "mythic concordance" between the nineteenth century and the twentieth has been broken. Its great personalities and deeds are just "ghosts," haunting memories of the past, inadequate and immaterial—and of no account. Thoreau's pioneer existence haunts America's cultural memory, as does Whitman's democratic optimism, but in *Ghosts* they are no guide to the modern urban environment. Blue's is a life of anxiety and failure, and he foolishly searches for solutions in the hope and exultation of the past. As Blue's life collapses around him, he cheerfully recounts the details of the building of the Brooklyn Bridge. Like America itself, perhaps, Blue is not "haunted by the ever-present, unceasingly real"; he is haunted by a history that cannot help him.

In Cynthia Hogue's poem "Crossing Brooklyn Bridge" (1994), the idea of help and history are intertwined. Walking home across the bridge, Hogue happens upon a young homeless man intent on ending his life. In many popular histories, the act of leaping from the bridge is treated as folly and remembered as trivia. This distancing from individual despair is not the case in Hogue's poem. Like Bud Korpenning in Dos Passos's *Manhattan Transfer*, her young man seems to have been consumed by the city's cutthroat environment, and his condition—"I saw how thin he was / and young, and helpless"[81]—is essentially tragic, not trivial. Hogue describes a profound human moment, and her immediate response is sympathy. Accounting no difference between herself and the young man, the narrator invites him home, and progress is made. Yet their accord is shattered:

> Then the police got me out of the way
> and crawled toward him.
> He said *Leave me alone,*
> and, *You make another move*
> *I'll Jump.* They came on
> because they'd heard those words
> a thousand times and never
> when they were meant.[82]

With a final, defiant gesture, the young man jumps. Hogue's story is of identification, of sympathy sought and realized. Yet it is also about ascribing difference, and the devastating impact it can have. Hogue's act of sympathy and identification are thwarted by those meant to protect and serve.

The title of Hogue's poem is a direct reference to Whitman's "Crossing Brooklyn Ferry." Hogue's narrator and the young man can, in this light, be seen as the embodiment of the future envisioned in Whitman's poem: "you that shall cross from shore to shore hence. . . . The others that are to follow me."[83] Unfortunately, so can the police. In "Crossing Brooklyn Bridge," Hogue takes on Whitman's role as adviser, counselor, friend, and helpmate; yet she is overrun by the bureaucratic steel of official policing. Where Hogue offers sympathy and identification, the police offer disregard and uninterest. They have the advantage, and the valuable lessons of Whitman's "metropolitan pantheism" are lost in the modern environment.[84] Within this framework, "Crossing Brooklyn Bridge" is bleak indeed, and it highlights the extent to which Whitman's nineteenth-century idealism has been debased in the late-twentieth-century urban landscape. Equally, Hogue's question is the same as Gioseffi's: how could "Whitman's age of hope" lead to "our age of anxiety and despair"?[85]

Steven Millhauser proposed one answer in his Pulitzer Prize–winning novel *Martin Dressler: The Tale of an American Dreamer* (1996). Many critics have pointed out that our fond nostalgia obscures the historical realities of the Gilded Age, that contemporary America is the product of the society that flowed out of the Civil War.[86] Set in late-nineteenth-century New York, *Martin Dressler* follows the life and career of its eponymous hero, from his humble origins as a bellhop to the heights of fame as a great builder of hotels, and on to his financial ruin. The Brooklyn Bridge appears throughout the novel. It functions, initially, as the inspiration for Dressler's drive toward greatness and, subsequently, as the motivation behind his gargantuan ambition. From his youthful awe as he watches the bridge rise, to his desire to build ever higher and bigger, Dressler keeps the image of the bridge before him.[87]

Although his novel is specific in character, location, and era, Millhauser is committed to examining the national character in its broadest sense. In his career as a hotelier, Dressler reminds us of Henry James's observation that "the hotel-spirit may . . . *be* the American spirit most seeking and most finding itself."[88] Furthermore, the novel's "American spirit" is highlighted in its subtitle. As Janet Burroway notes, Millhauser's theme is the twentieth century's obsession with unregulated ambition: "*Martin Dressler* coolly explores this American Dream: as aim, vision, intention, nightmare, hallucination, delusion, death."[89] Central to Millhauser's critique is the degree to which ambition has become wholly equated with the pursuit of influence and wealth. Dressler himself is an amalgam of such real-life figures as John D. Rockefeller Sr., J. P. Morgan, Robert Moses, and Donald Trump. As Burroway observes, "he is the apogee of all that Willy Loman would admire."[90]

Dressler's downfall comes as he attempts to realize his final project, the Grand Cosmo Hotel. An enormous phantasmagoria, the Cosmo is the ultimate expression of Dressler's American Dream and the ultimate debasement of individual liberty. The Cosmo is an exercise in absolute monopoly, not just in terms of accommodation, but also over the city and experience in general: "The Grand Cosmo . . . rendered the city unnecessary. For whether the Grand Cosmo was the city itself, or whether it was the place to which one longed to travel, it was a complete and self-sufficient world, in comparison with which the actual city was not simply inferior, but superfluous."[91] Conceived through Dressler's almost limitless ambition to control, the Cosmo represents an attempt to make direct experience obsolete. Its myriad floors replicate the world around it as a simulacrum. The Cosmo is a synthetic environment under the monopoly control of a single individual.[92] Ultimately, Dressler's dream collapses when the Cosmo fails to attract even a minimal clientele. Paradoxically, the Cosmo's artificiality reflects the excesses of the Gilded Age too well: it "was an act of disobedience" whose "extravagance and flamboyance and hunger had been carried to such heights of excess as to turn into the grotesque."[93]

For Millhauser, the Cosmo illustrates the very ambiguities and doubts that underlie the concept of American progress. Equally, he points to their genesis: the forces that have defined the twentieth century were first encapsulated in Roebling's Great East River Bridge. Millhauser's "modern New York," like that of Kenneth Clark, "started with Brooklyn Bridge." Yet there is no heroism in *Martin Dressler,* only the folly of outsized ambition. The American Dream is debased when the pursuit of happiness is interpreted as the pursuit of wealth, power, and monopoly.

Millhauser's cautionary tale reminds us of DeLillo's *Americana.* Both novels attack the reconfiguration of culture in the twentieth century; both deride the subjugation of historical authenticity to "hyperreality."[94] Strikingly, both also find the origins of this process in the nineteenth century's great acts of nation building. Long thought to sustain the heroic, consensus interpretation of U.S. history, these projects instead led to outsized, reckless ambition and its derivatives: gluttony and refuse. For Millhauser and DeLillo, the past *is* a guide to contemporary society. The same entrepreneurial zeal that created the Waldorf-Astoria Hotel, Standard Oil, and the Brooklyn Bridge, for example, also led to the destruction of Pennsylvania Station. Once unleashed, "the universal will to move — to move, move, move, as an end in it-self, an appetite at any price," as Henry James put it, could not be stopped. New York's "salient characteristic" has always been "*the* feature that speaks loudest for the economic idea."[95] Conversely, for Auster, Hogue, Gioseffi, and Shapiro the past is *no* guide to the present. The continuity of the American enterprise has been broken. The nation is no longer capable of sustaining Whitman's "age of hope."[96]

The revisionist impulse has been strong in the years since the Brooklyn Bridge's centennial. Such authors as Sujata Bhatt, Lawrence Ferlinghetti, and Yusef Komunyakaa, along with Julia Kasdorf, Jack Agüeros, Geoffrey Godbert, William Marshall, and Richard Crabbe, have reworked the image of the bridge, extrapolating interpretations vastly at odds with those found in more official forms of cultural expression.[97] Nevertheless, these oppositional interpretations — the vernacular and the official — highlight an essential similarity. As Sacvan Bercovitch notes, the American ritual of assent attained its primacy by "diffus[ing] all issues in debate by restricting the debate itself, symbolically *and substantively,* to the meaning of America."[98] As exemplified by Bhatt's "Walking across the Brooklyn Bridge, July 1990," for example, these contemporary authors have contributed to "the symbolic construction of America" to the same extent as those who spoke for the bridge at its opening. Yet recent authors have used the bridge to criticize the meaning of contemporary America, not to celebrate it. These "debates" have been marked by dissent, not assent.

The issue of historical interpretation mirrors the bridge's structural problems. Splits, cracks, and fissures have emerged in recent years, testing the bridge's physical and symbolic infrastructure. No longer sound, stable, permanent, it has come under increasing scrutiny and stress, its load-bearing capacity reevaluated and revised. If the spirit of revision has dominated the discourse surrounding the Brooklyn Bridge since its centennial, no author has used the bridge as darkly as Leslie Kaplan.

For generations, the Brooklyn Bridge has served as a lovers' lane. On pleasant days, couples of all descriptions flock to the bridge to enjoy the view and each other. This charming and somewhat innocent tradition informs Kaplan's disturbing novel *Brooklyn Bridge* (1987). Her protagonist is Julien, a successful, twenty-eight-year-old New Yorker. Julien has two obsessions: the Brooklyn Bridge and Natalie, the eight-year-old daughter of his friend Mary. As the narrative progresses, Julien's obsessions intensify. He states repeatedly that he will take Natalie to the bridge; when the opportunity finally arises, the novel's theme is revealed:

221

From a distance, Julien points out the framework, the arches, he makes comments. When they get out of the taxi, they take the foot and bicycle path above the cars.

Julien and Natalie. Julien, tall, his felt hat and wide pants with a trim waist. Natalie, short, her ponytails. They hold hands. . . .

They walk forward. They see the first arch. Julien, it's true, had said cathedral.

From both sides, the steel net, hitched up.

They walk inside the net. . . .

Julien has begun to tell her about the things they see. The Gothic towers, peaks and lacework, the newer towers, of plastic cubes, so light. The old green ferry, the island of the immigrants. The hacked-up neighborhoods. . . .

Natalie looks at the water. Then she says she's tired of being here, she wants to go home.

Julien starts caressing Natalie's hand. Small, sweet and cunning hand.

He kisses her hair.

Natalie says nothing and looks at the water.

Julien feels his dick become hard between his thighs.[99]

Kaplan's novel illustrates the degree to which the image of the Brooklyn Bridge has been revised in recent years. Midway through the novel, Julien "pictures to himself the Bridge's grand, flat progression, he needs it, he wants those precarious boards thrown between a beginning and an end."[100] The phrase is aptly suited to the bridge. Beginning in celebration and praise, its history has been "precarious." Imagined in the contemporary era, the boundaries of assent have been transformed into those of dissent. Here, the bridge is not the lovers' lane of tradition, but a site of predatory sexual deviance.

Although an extreme example, Kaplan's *Brooklyn Bridge* is nevertheless part of a wider cultural phenomenon. From the centennial until the present, imaginative representations of the Brooklyn Bridge have shunned the tradition of unequivocal greatness so characteristic of the bridge's official history. Instead, they have illustrated an uncertainty that more accurately mirrors the bridge's recent structural history. Where it would be foolish to believe that the city would knowingly allow the structure to crumble, what is undeniable is that the bridge, as an exemplary symbol of American promise and achievement, has altered. The history of the bridge, from its centennial until the present, despite its continued use as a prime subject for advertisements, postcards, and tourism, plainly tells a very complex story: its place in the American imagination is marked by apprehension, revision, and dissent, not just celebration and praise. At the opening of the Brooklyn Bridge, assent tri-umphed over dissent. In the years since the bridge's centennial, these posi-tions have been reversed. In the representational history of the Brooklyn Bridge, manufactured assent has been superseded; individual expressions of revision and dissent are in the ascendancy.

Conclusions

The cultural history of the Brooklyn Bridge is the product of two some-what disorganized yet equally distinct communities. Drawing upon the cul-tural work performed at the span's official dedication in 1883 — a wildly suc-cessful attempt to define as well as control the image of the bridge for subsequent generations, to fix and freeze its immutable authority into a last-ing petrified form [101] — one community has kept its eyes on the bridge and been awestruck. Like those transfixed by the beauty of Aphrodite, these observers have been captivated by the bridge's majestic elegance and held spellbound by its sheer sublimity. Their interpretations and representations fashioned and sustained an exemplary image of the bridge at once decon-textualized and aestheticized. Sometimes unwittingly, sometimes not, such responses have elided both dissent and revision. Unable to look below or around, these authors and artists presented a cohesive story, stripped of discordant detail. Bolstered by ritualized repetition, their narrative has ulti-mately busied itself with fueling the larger self-image of America. Mani-fested in tourist guidebooks, the visual arts, journalism, personal essays, fictional literature, historical writing, and commemorative practice, this trend has seen national unity eclipse social plurality, while New York's "vast" technological "splendors" have been championed at the cost of social con-text. Like the formalist New Critics, beguiled by poetic symmetry, this as-senting culture has proved itself blind to all but artistic perfection, by the bridge's relationship to itself.

By contrast, another community has sought to look beyond the rapture of the sublime effect and relate the bridge to the city's vast humanity. Theirs is not the picture-perfect bridge of our inherited common understanding. In-stead, this vernacular approach — always present yet rarely recognized — has stressed anthropocentrism, a need for human understanding and sympathy in the urban environment. These commentators have not kept their eyes solely on the bridge, but instead allowed their gaze to sweep around and be-low the span's triumphant, compelling anatomy. By contextualizing the bridge, this tradition has fully engaged with Alfred North Whitehead's cau-tionary advice: "The art of free society consists first in the maintenance of the symbolic code; and secondly in fearlessness of revision. . . . Those societies which can not combine reverence to their symbols with freedom of revision, must ultimately decay either from anarchy, or from the slow atrophy of a life stifled by useless shadows." [102] As technological advancement altered the landscape of American social relations, as habitual assent became the tired cant of perfunctory repetition, the bridge was enlivened by these myriad voices of revision. Their subject, as Whitehead understood, was distinctly national. The history of any important monument is also the history of the people who produced, sustained, questioned, and venerated it. Icons are *tabula rasae*, communal notice boards upon which individuals and groups inscribe their thoughts and feelings. In this regard, the Brooklyn Bridge has proved itself a powerful cultural barometer. As an American icon, it has served official as well as vernacular concerns. Over the past 120 years, the Brooklyn Bridge has told the story of America's cultural history as well as any other national artifact.

Epilogue

Crisis and Change: *The Brooklyn Bridge in the Wake of Terror*

In the last two years borough dwellers working in Manhattan have twice been forced to evacuate, and both times the bridges have played a pivotal role in the exodus.

—Robert Julavits, *The Village Voice*, August 27, 2003

The happiest day of the bridge's life came in 1983, when the city threw a mammoth party for the span's 100th birthday. The saddest? Sept. 11, 2001, when the bridge carried downtown workers fleeing the World Trade Center catastrophe to safe harbor on the shores of Brooklyn.

—Rod Dreher, *New York Post*, November 16, 2001

Most Brooklynites caught in Manhattan during Thursday's blackout had three choices. . . . Most chose the Brooklyn Bridge, using the walkway and both roadbeds.

In some ways, it resembled the trek home on Sept. 11, 2001. But unlike that awful day, these foot-powered commuters were neither panicked nor in shock and bore no signs of terror. . . . In fact, most people who chose to brave the Brooklyn Bridge seemed to be having a good time. As tens of thousands streamed across the bridge, the mood was nearly festive. Standing at the Brooklyn side of the footpath, Borough President Marty Markowitz used a police bullhorn to welcome the sweaty throng home. . . . "Let's have the biggest barbecue Brooklyn ever saw — tonight — all over Brooklyn!" he shouted as crowds clapped and cheered.

—Amy Sara Clark, *The Brooklyn Paper*, August 21, 2003

The Brooklyn Bridge entered 2001 in relatively good shape and with much to look forward to. With repairs to the nearby Manhattan Bridge completed, the traffic overspill that had congested the bridge seemed certain to decrease, reducing wear and tear. This last issue — the almost constant need for maintenance — seemed sure to be resolved by funds from the proposed East River tolls. In addition to improved upkeep, the bridge could also anticipate some interesting new neighbors. Through much of the twentieth century, the bridge's majestic elegance had presided over neglect and poverty; tenement slums run to seed, abundant garbage, and rampant crime defined the area around its bases and in its shadows. More recently, the bridge's surroundings had been enriched by the creation of Empire–Fulton Ferry State Park (1979) and through the redevelopment of Brooklyn's Old Ferry Slip (1977) and Manhattan's South Street Seaport (1983–1985). In 2001, further improvements seemed assured.

Preparations for the Brooklyn Bridge Park—a lavish eighty-acre riverfront recreational area championed as "the Central Park of the new century"[1] and stretching 1.3 miles from the Manhattan Bridge, past the Brooklyn Bridge, to Atlantic Avenue—were at an advanced stage. In addition, the Guggenheim Museum's proposal for a Frank Gehry–designed affiliate site had recently received a $68 million financing pledge from the city. Encouraged by the exceptional success of the museum's outpost in Bilbao, Spain, the Guggenheim's board had already decided upon a location: a four-pier site fronting the East River, just a few hundred feet south of the Brooklyn Bridge. The bridge, it seemed, finally would be granted the spectacular surroundings its admirers had long craved. Consequently, a new optimism seemed to envelop the span. As the summer arrived, the bridge swarmed with fascinated sightseers and happy New Yorkers: "on nice days [the bridge] has become a little like Times Square without the buildings," reported the *New York Times*.[2] All of these propitious signs would be subverted on September 11, 2001. The public would again swarm over the bridge, but not since the Memorial Day panic of 1883 would calamity become so intrinsically linked to the Brooklyn Bridge.

It is difficult to evaluate the implications of September 11, 2001, and, in late 2004, perhaps even too soon to do so. Nevertheless, the events of 9/11 changed the image of the Brooklyn Bridge, and continue to affect it. On the day itself, the span was a vital artery of escape and the scene of heartrending grief. No one who watched, heard, or read about that day can forget the sheer terror of individual recollections or the haunting images of dust-covered New Yorkers fleeing Manhattan over the bridge.[3] During those same hours, the traditional landscape view of the bridge and the skyline was reconfigured to include the horror of explosion and mass murder. In the work of Magnum Agency photographers Alex Webb and Thomas Hoepker, for example, great anguish, intense sorrow, and apocalyptic destruction were woven into the fabric of the bridge's visual history. Outside of Ground Zero itself, the bridge, along with the Brooklyn Heights Promenade, has been the most visually arresting point from which to contemplate the city's loss. Nowhere are the Twin Towers more *absent* than in the view *from* the bridge.[4]

Equally, nowhere have the implications of 9/11 been more obvious than *on* the bridge. Since that terrible day, the bridge has been widely regarded as one of the next logical targets, if for no other reason than its continued use.[5] Unlike the Statue of Liberty, Ellis Island, or the viewing deck of the Empire

State Building, the bridge could not be closed. Instead, checkpoints were set up and warnings given on a regular basis. Public consternation was palpable in Lucy Blakstad's documentary film *The Brooklyn Bridge* (2001), in which a number of city residents were interviewed about their post-9/11 fears. Several admitted to panic attacks while crossing the bridge; others confessed to staying away entirely. What had been an exemplary tourist site and a consummate lovers' lane — even a place for confronting personal demons — had become a target, a place of worry and alarm.

Blakstad's documentary graphically illustrates the bridge's fate in the wake of 9/11. Filming had begun a year before the attack, but the project was completed afterward and finally released in November 2001. The film was conceived as the middle section of a trilogy charting the "cycles of life" through the history of three distinct bridges. Blakstad intended London's new Millennium Bridge to represent birth and the Mostar Bridge in Bosnia to represent death. In between, the Brooklyn Bridge would represent life. But the events of 9/11 ruptured the bridge's image: "when the Twin Towers went . . . it almost reversed the whole of the film." For Blakstad, the bridge could no longer stand so innocently for life, for "the rainbow" that led to "the crock of gold" in downtown Manhattan. Death now clung to the Brooklyn Bridge.[6]

Fear and threat continued to haunt the bridge throughout the winter months, but the city began to move on. Early in May 2002, Governor George Pataki and Mayor Michael Bloomberg attended a ceremony formalizing the creation of Brooklyn Bridge Park. With the city guaranteeing $65 million and the state $85 million, Brooklyn was about to gain its first sizable new green space since Prospect Park was opened in 1868. Some observers derided such a large commitment of public money when the city was in fiscal chaos, yet most New Yorkers seemed pleased.[7] The gesture signaled the city's desire to invest in itself; it was a rebuilding decision that looked to the future, not the recent past.

Outside of New York, however, the future seemed anything but bright. Later that month, dire warnings began to emerge from Washington. On May 21, 2002, just three days before the bridge was due to celebrate its 119th anniversary, the Federal Bureau of Investigation (FBI) issued a major new terrorist warning. In response to the possible targeting of the Brooklyn Bridge, "the city imposed security measures not seen since the first months after the Sept. 11 terrorist attacks." Just a day later, alarm intensified when an unidentified package was found on the span. Quickly, the news spread across the city, the nation, and the world; the scare found its way onto the front pages of newspapers from London to Melbourne. For an uncertain few

227

hours, the bridge was closed and evacuated. Anxiety again gripped New York, but for a different reason: in the midst of a host of conflicting messages, no one appeared to know exactly what was happening.[8]

As the new warnings came in, Cable News Network (CNN) reported on its *Newsnight* program that "both the FBI and New York City police downplay any possible attacks." By the next morning, however, "police officers were everywhere" around the Brooklyn Bridge, stopping cars and pedestrians. According to a high-ranking law enforcement official, who spoke anonymously with the *New York Daily News*, a tip expressly mentioning the bridge had come from Abu Zubaydah, a recently captured al Qaeda operative. Further confirmation proved illusive. As the *Newsnight* reporters told their viewers, "the warning comes with plenty of disclaimers."[9]

Public anxiety prompted Mayor Bloomberg and Governor Pataki to speak up. Both downplayed the new warnings and urged tourists and New Yorkers alike to get out and enjoy the city. The Fleet Week celebrations were in full swing, the weather was perfect, and the bridge's birthday was just around the corner. Equally, they noted, these new threats were no different from the ones that had stalked the city for the past eight months. Based on "vague and uncorroborated" evidence, they were no reason for New Yorkers to hide from the everyday business of life.[10]

Unfortunately, this local message was hamstrung by the national government. While regional politicians tried to assuage the city's unease, the administration of President George W. Bush continued to issue ominous warnings. On May 22, Homeland Security Director Tom Ridge told the public that further terrorist strikes were "not a question of if, but a question of when." Ridge was backed up by Vice President Dick Cheney (further attacks were "almost certain"), FBI Director Robert Mueller (they were "inevitable"), and Defense Secretary Donald Rumsfeld ("not if, but when, where and how"). The commander-in-chief even felt compelled to add his assessment to the scare-mongering: "al Qaeda," Bush warned, "is poised to strike again."[11] Clearly, the public had a right to feel alarmed, but also more than a little confused. On the one hand, citizens should get out and enjoy Fleet Week; on the other, a repeat of 9/11 was not only "inevitable" but seemingly imminent.

Amid the doomsaying, mixed messages, and general confusion, the bridge's slow rebirth began in May 2002. A young woman interviewed on the bridge could still "wonder just how long I can live like this. . . . I'm starting to think there are a lot safer places for my family than New York."[12] But hers was not a typical response. Instead, defiance was found on the bridge, aimed as much at those who would scare the public as those who would do it harm.

In a report headlined "In NY, 'Not If, but When' Wears Thin; Residents of a City on Edge Question Value of Vague but Unsettling Warnings," *Washington Post* staff writer Michael Powell interviewed New Yorkers on the Brooklyn Bridge about the latest round of terrorist warnings. "You really want to know what I really think?" a young man asked Powell. "Mr. Bush and his FBI-CIA-intelligence boys got to stop putting ideas in people's minds." Another man added, "You feel that they're playing you. . . . Well, I have this to say: Don't scare me. Fix the problem." As Powell noted, "there's a nagging sense, shared by New Yorkers of all political stripes, that maybe the recent federal warnings are for political effect." A developmental psychologist who had studied the effects of 9/11 on children further complained that the "vague" warnings would "only exacerbate" the problems of the many young children he had worked with recently.[13]

Powell began with an implicit contrast: "On one of those cloudless May days when river, city and sun seem in spin, thousands of New Yorkers strolled, biked, rollerbladed, and unicycled across the Brooklyn Bridge. Which is otherwise known as national terror target 1A or 1B, if one listens to the vague but unsettling warnings emanating from Washington."[14] Despite the checkpoints, the warnings, and the bridge's brief closure, "thousands" of people were still out on the span. Reporters for the *Daily News* and the *Christian Science Monitor* also noted the volume of human traffic. For the *Daily News*, "it was more than a bridge yesterday, it was a span of hope. On a brilliant day in May, New Yorkers and tourists refused to let terrorist threats take away the exhilaration of crossing the bridge." The reporter interviewed a family visiting from Wales, a writer from Brooklyn Heights, a Holocaust survivor who lived in Queens, and a jogger who would be "damned" if he was going to give up his daily run.[15]

The *Christian Science Monitor* led with "Brooklyn Bridge Still Draws Visitors, Despite Terror Alert." Again, none of the many New Yorkers who were interviewed seemed especially worried. A bridge tour guide asked his party, "Is anyone afraid of being on the bridge?" No one answered. "Business is booming," he concluded. Another man declared that "driving in New York is more dangerous than walking across the bridge"; others insisted that no amount of hearsay was going to keep them from their favorite New York pursuits. "It is part New York defiance about nonspecific threats, and part patriotism," wrote the reporter, "but there's also a lot of love of the span itself."[16]

The same distinction that made the bridge "terror target 1A or 1B" was the same reason people took to its boards. It was a place where New Yorkers could show their commitment to their city, their lives, and their public spaces. In the pages of the *Post*, the *Daily News*, and the *Monitor*, among others, the bridge was not a target but an essential environment of human interaction — neither a strategic objective nor an abstract symbol, but an indispensable public space. In the ongoing and so-called "war on terror," citizens claimed the bridge as a route *back* to their pre-9/11 lives. The span had, it seems, begun to renew its promise as New York's most anthropocentric location. For Alfred Kazin, as for Lewis Mumford and a host of others, the bridge existed as a force of profound connectedness. It bound individuals to the city they loved and supplied a deep reservoir of optimism and affection. As thousands rushed over the bridge on 9/11, such interpretations seemed altogether untenable, perhaps banished forever. Yet, seven months later, the structure was once again a palpable, affirmative presence in the lives of New Yorkers.

Unfortunately, Brooklyn Borough President Marty Markowitz could not feel that optimism. Even as Mayor Bloomberg counseled against a rash retreat in the face of the new threats, Markowitz canceled the "Brooklyn Bridge to the World" celebrations marking the span's 119th anniversary, just two days away. The decision angered the mayor. "[I]f there was ever a time to hold a ceremony on the Brooklyn Bridge it is when terrorists threaten that structure, not the reverse," Bloomberg curtly told the audience listening to his weekly radio address. "[W]e have to stand up to terrorists and say we aren't going to let you destroy everything we hold dear." As the *Post* noted, "Mayor Bloomberg all but accused Brooklyn Borough President Marty Markowitz of cowardice." Markowitz himself said he was acting on the advice of the New York Police Department, which denied the statement.[17]

Many New Yorkers were angered by the decision to cancel the 2002 celebrations and they took to the span anyway. With or without the sanction of an official commemoration, enthusiasts were determined to mark the bridge's birthday. All day, they poured over the structure, happy in the opportunity to rejoice after eight months of grieving. A further year later, in 2003, the festivities to mark the bridge's 120th anniversary would be hailed as New York's first public celebration since 9/11. Grandiloquently, reporter Jeffrey Page called it "a decision in the gritty spirit of Bensonhurst, Bath Beach, Coney Island, and Canarsie: a fist to the miserable jaw of anyone who would rain terror on Brooklyn on Saturday."[18] But if May 2003 marked the first *official* celebration, the occasion was certainly not the first post-9/11 commemoration undertaken by New Yorkers themselves. For that honor we must look to the slightly disorganized, but nevertheless passionate group that took to the bridge in 2002 for the 119th anniversary.

Clearly, the Brooklyn Bridge stood at the heart of the debate about how New Yorkers would ultimately respond to 9/11. Under the headline, "The Home of the Brave, or the Timid," *New York Times* columnist Joyce Purnick wondered whether "New York's future will be [conducted] on its own terms[?]" Her answer derived from the actions of ordinary New Yorkers:

> New York glimpsed two versions of its future last week. We present them for your consideration, with no pretense of objectivity. One is the future of Robin Lister, Synge Maher, Kevin Smith and hundreds of other people who ventured onto the pedestrian walkway of the Brooklyn Bridge on May 22 despite those vague warnings the day before of a possible terrorist attack on city landmarks. . . . The other is a future narrowed and pinched by fear, reflected in the decision of the Brooklyn borough president, Marty Markowitz, to cancel a celebration of the bridge's 119th birthday.[19]

In 1906, Henry James asked the city, "what are you going to make your future *of*, for all your airs, we want to know?"[20] In the post-9/11 world, this question was again relevant, and a new answer was forthcoming: New Yorkers began to make their future on the Brooklyn Bridge.

As one might expect, the mood of the city was somber in September 2002, the first anniversary of the fall of the Twin Towers. *New York Times* reporter Somini Sengupta took to the bridge to gather accounts from those who had crossed one year earlier. An office worker had spent the last year just trying to forget. A man sweeping a local courtyard clarified the point: the mind can try to forget, he said, but the nose cannot. Some people had not been on the bridge since fleeing over it, but they came back on the anniversary as "a sort of offering to the dead." Others could not bring themselves to return. "I don't want to remember all that," said one man.[21] Associated Press journalist Richard Pyle also returned to the bridge he had fled over on 9/11. There he met a former New York City schoolteacher who refused to see the span as merely "an escape route from calamity. 'It's a place where our family gathers when we all come together,' she said, 'It is very grounding and healing, just being here.'"[22]

Such sentiments dominated the first anniversary of 9/11. People gathered on the bridge, as they had since the creation of the "Tribute in Light" earlier in March, to participate in a larger narrative of remembrance, to share stories and experiences. In this regard, the first anniversary of 9/11 made a monument of the bridge in the fullest sense of the word: not just an outstanding achievement venerated for its enduring historical significance, it was also a memory trigger (from the Latin *monumentum*: "a thing that reminds").

Removed from the official commemoration at Ground Zero, the bridge on September 11, 2002, emerged as a "real environment of memory," a "hybrid place" where "multiple voices" held common weight and found com-

65. People gather on the bridge to view the "Tribute in Light" and to participate in a larger narrative of remembrance, to share stories and experiences. "Tribute in Light Memorial in New York." © REUTERS/Chip East, 2002.

mon ground.[23] On the bridge, history and memory were conjoined in a spontaneous act of remembrance. The span functioned as a fluid and flexible arena — neither constructed nor planned, not yet fixed in meaning — containing many different experiences, truths, and interpretations. Amid the strenuous attempts to codify and calcify the meanings of 9/11 and its aftermath — the failures of American foreign policy, the unprovoked acts of "evildoers" — the bridge gave New Yorkers and others an unmediated environment in which to share the immediacy of the attacks, the complexities of emotion, and the weight of memory. It was a place of tolerance and difference: a place for people, not politics.

On a national and municipal scale, September 11, 2002, continued the work begun earlier in the year at the bridge's 119th birthday. After a year's formal mourning, it was a time to make peace with the past and begin the process of civic renewal. To accomplish this rite, thousands of New Yorkers took themselves to the Brooklyn Bridge to remember, to talk, and to listen.

The span's role in the city's rebirth was also noted by city planners and architects. In October 2002, Peter Burgener, a senior partner at BKDI Architects, visited New York to participate in an urban design conference organized to debate the idea of a "successful public place." To prepare himself, Burgener walked across the Brooklyn Bridge. For this architect, as for most of the conference participants, the bridge was "more than a structure"; it was an "amazing public space . . . a great example of how a simple, functional structure . . . can be significantly more than a single-purpose element." Despite the strides made in engineering science since its completion in 1883, the bridge still "adds immeasurably to the life of the city" and supplies countless relevant lessons for urban designers and city planners. Unsurprisingly, Burgener singled out the bridge's central boardwalk. Its significance encapsulated the entire debate: it made the bridge "into something that represents larger community values." [24]

The idea of a "successful public place" encompassing "larger community values" has also driven the debate surrounding the plans for the former World Trade Center site. On December 18, 2002, nine proposals for development of the site were put on public display at the Winter Gardens, just yards away from Ground Zero. Most of the visual technology used to envision the finished structures included images of the Brooklyn Bridge. One plan imagined the new skyline as seen from the bridge's walkway; others presented lower Manhattan panoramas with the bridge in the foreground. In these proposals, New Yorkers were provided images of the bridge within a healed and restored skyline. Although both provisional and visionary, the exhibition was an integral part of the renewal process. For the first time in more than a year, Americans could begin to imagine a new skyline, a new city space, and a new backdrop for the bridge. During the previous fifteen months, the topic of conversation most often overheard on the bridge concerned the Twin Towers. Many visitors paused at the Manhattan tower and tried to recollect where exactly the Twin Towers had stood. Still more clustered around the itemized diagrams of the New York skyline that run around the Manhattan tower railings. The Winter Garden exhibition offered the first opportunity to imagine not just what *had* been there, but what *might* arise in the future. [25]

Celebrations returned to the bridge in May 2003 as the city marked the span's 120th birthday. Reviving the previous year's theme — "Brooklyn Bridge to the World" — Markowitz promised "a big, old-fashioned celebration in every part of the borough." The events included guided tours, poetry readings, an amateur photography contest, open-air history classes, and a performance by the Brooklyn Philharmonic Orchestra. The main event involved a series of crossings conducted in the morning. After Markowitz, Mayor Bloomberg, Senator Charles Schumer, and Manhattan Borough President C. Virginia Fields, there came groups of bikers, joggers, and walkers, respectively. [26]

Unfortunately, neither time nor tide was accommodating. Because the event was scheduled for the long Memorial Day weekend — when residents traditionally flee the city — turnout was low. Equally, the weather was rainy and unseasonably cold, further reducing attendance. At the morning's ceremonial crossings, only a handful of people braved the wretched weather to traverse the bridge to Brooklyn. Coverage of the event was mixed. The *New York Times* gave it a mere paragraph at the rear of the paper, accompanied by a photograph of a lone walker clutching an umbrella and marching through the rain across the bridge.[27] By contrast, the *Post* made no mention of the poor attendance or the driving rain. Leading with "120th B'day Is Cakewalk for B'klyn Bridge," the paper focused on Mayor Bloomberg's admiring remarks and the tributes offered by Markowitz. The reporter also interviewed a few bridge crossers, as did *Newsday*. Unwittingly, the two papers revealed the extent of the poor turnout: despite appearing under different bylines, the stories in both the *Post* and *Newsday* featured interviews with the same people.[28]

In a stark turnaround only a month after the 120th anniversary, a new visual image entered the bridge's lexicon, an image that had nothing to do with commemoration and everything to do with its role as a target. Developed to accompany the lead story, "Al Qaeda in America: The Enemy Within," *Newsweek*'s cover imposed a set of crosshairs upon a standard photograph of the bridge from its walkway. The image was a frightening reconfiguration of the grand-style vision. The same monumentality, the same glorious network of cables, the same enchanted walkway were now firmly placed in the crossfire of international terrorism.

The article itself was concerned with the arrest, trial, and sentencing of Iyman Faris, a thirty-four-year-old truck driver from Columbus, Ohio, who had cased the Brooklyn Bridge for the al Qaeda terrorist network. Apparently Faris, a naturalized U.S. citizen born in Kashmir as Mohammed Rauf, had been instructed to study "the bridge in the *Godzilla* movie" as a possible terrorist target. His objective was to evaluate the feasibility of using an acetylene torch to sever the bridge's main suspension cables, although the plan never got past the idea stage. Officials credited increased security for preventing the attack, although structural engineer Matthys Levy put the matter more persuasively: the plan itself was more than a little ridiculous. It would take about two days to cut the bridge's main suspension cables with an acetylene torch, and even then the bridge's load-bearing capacity would be transferred to the cable stays. For terrorists to bring down "the bridge in the *Godzilla* movie" swiftly, they would need to find their very own Godzilla.[29]

For some officials, Faris's arrest and trial represented a moment of vindication; for other commentators, the episode was filled with national shame. Writing in *Newsday*, Jimmy Breslin attacked the events surrounding the arrest, trial, and sentencing. While purportedly "protecting the bridge, the government was doing frightening damage to the life of the country." Government officials effectively kidnapped an American citizen and subjected him to a secret trial. Their attitude was a throwback to the thinking that led to the Japanese American internment camps of World War II and the practices of the secret police in the "Old Soviet Union": "This government's kidnapping of Faris/Rauf violated the laws handed down by Madison, Jefferson, Marshall. A small religious zealot, John Ashcroft, takes their great laws and bravery and using our new Patriot Act, turns it into Fascism."[30] With Faris's incarceration, the terrorist threat seemed thwarted. Yet the bridge remained in the crosshairs of a polarizing national argument.

The attacks of September 11, 2001, altered the cultural history of the Brooklyn Bridge. Once idealized as the urban roadway of constitutionals and fresh air, the bridge has since become identified with the ongoing debate over global terrorism. The events of the past three years have also revised all previous narratives. The rhetoric that surrounded the bridge's opening established the span as "an ambassador for the city"[31] and a prime icon of American progress. Sadly, in the current geopolitical climate, "prime icon" often translates into "potential target." The images sent around the world on September 11 fundamentally altered the bridge's visual history, and subsequent events have only added to the convoluted history of foreign responses to both the bridge and the United States. Moreover, the bridge's historical relevance has also been reinterpreted to suit a new historical outlook. In spite of its age, it has proved itself the most significant of New York's many structural icons. It has been dragged from the nineteenth century through the twentieth, and now into the twenty-first. One of the oldest structures in the city, it is still, as Katherine Hobson recently noted, "one of the most visible symbols in a town that doesn't lack for them."[32]

Yet New York has always proved itself a resilient city. Slowly, the crowds have returned to the bridge, and anxiety about the structure seems to have dissipated. Although the new Guggenheim Museum project is officially dead, plans for the Brooklyn Bridge Park are proceeding. On the bridge itself, the crowds seem as large as they ever were. Although the lingering threat of terrorism has altered the bridge since 9/11, it has also, I think, brought us back full circle to its beginnings. On a much larger scale, 9/11 reminds us not only of the fear and panic that accompanied the Memorial Day tragedy one week after the bridge's opening, but also of the hope that accompanied its completion. If we remember Sarah Bernhardt's response from 1883 — "Oh, that bridge! It is insane, admirable, imposing, and it makes one feel proud. . . . I returned to the hotel reconciled with this great nation"[33] — we can see that in some small way, the bridge might now be emerging as a force of reconciliation: a place to understand the loss of 9/11 and go forward. I imagine that no one walking the bridge today can ignore the absence of the Twin Towers; nevertheless, and despite the worry of further attacks, people are there, getting on with their lives, enjoying the bridge, and, perhaps, forging a new bond with the city.

Since 9/11, the bridge's role as a public highway—not a "well-wrought urn"—has dominated its cultural history. In the face of traumatic events and the renewed focus on civic culture, the propensity to decontextualize and depopulate the bridge has been shunned. Seldom now do we hear paeans to New York's "perfect art object." Instead, the bridge's contributions to the life of the city's residents—both in flight and in leisure—have been heralded. Interviews with bridge walkers, for example, have supplanted aesthetic contemplation and glorification. As New York's foremost, not to mention unique, civic space, the bridge has been returned to the people who tread its boards.

We can see this development most clearly, along with the many complexities that constitute the bridge experience, in Colson Whitehead's *The Colossus of New York* (2003), a contemporary take on E. B. White's famous "Here Is New York" (1949). For Whitehead, the bridge is a profoundly public place. His mini-narrative follows a woman—an "immigrant" from an "unfashionable area code"—as she walks from Brooklyn to Manhattan. The description of her journey is a literary descendant of William Gedney's photographic project: an internal monologue that delightfully replicates the experience of walking the bridge. Revising the grand-style tradition, Whitehead describes Manhattan as "a pack mule and palimpsest," its skyline composed of "so many arrogant edifices, it's like walking into a jerk festival." Far more important are the idiosyncratic inner thoughts that occupy the solo walker: random memories, the hopes and fears of daily life, casual daydreams riffing on arbitrary subjects, observations on tourists and photographers—"Why they pick their particular spots is a mystery. They just look and stop and declare, I want this forever"—and the distinctive caprice of personal observation. On the bridge, "bronze plaques here and there maintain history. But [there is] nothing to commemorate the magic spots of people": people like our immigrant women, people like Whitehead himself, and people like ourselves.[34]

Arriving in Manhattan at the end of her journey, Whitehead's bridge walker finds that "everything is where it should be. No miracle. The key to the city fell out of her pocket somewhere along the way and she's level again." The woman is disappointed, but we sense that she is okay. The bridge epiphany described by Mumford and others is an illusion sponsored by the bridge's unique location; we should not confuse a wonderful view with a social reality. Exiting the bridge in Manhattan, we find no single entrance, just "multiple choices into this labyrinth": "Today she picks a new route into it, learning from mistakes. Who knows where she will end up this time. Disappear into a crowd. It's right there in the city charter: we have the right to disappear. The city rushes to hide all trace. It's the law."[35] There are no answers to the city, just people, places, and moments. We are always admitted but only very rarely honored.

In *City of God* (2000), novelist E. L. Doctorow wrote, "What kind of word is *infrastructure?* It is a word that proves we have lost our city. Our streets are for transit. Our stories are disassembled, the skyscrapers crowding us scoff at the idea of a credible culture. Christ, how wrong to point out the Brooklyn Bridge or SoHo or the row houses of Harlem as examples of our continuity. Something dire has happened." Images of old New York, he continues, seem "to prophesy hauntingly our forfeiture of their worlds."[36] Doctorow's point? Do not look to the bridge as an example of U.S. culture. Contemporary America is no longer able to claim kinship with the society that dreamed, and then built, such a marvelous city. Our city is not their city, and we have no right to claim that it is.

Doctorow's line of reasoning, I think, has some validity. Yet he seems to miss something essential. The Brooklyn Bridge is of great value to us precisely because it has survived. It is one of the few great nineteenth-century structures that this kinetic, restless city has left us. It reminds us of how the city once coupled great ambition with public utility. It provides us with a cultural archive, an index to the state of the city. Also, of course, it is the city's great boulevard. And despite concerns over the direction of social continuity, one thing is certain: people love to walk the Brooklyn Bridge and no more eagerly than in the past three years. In the wake of terror, amid the chaos of change, the bridge has survived unscathed. And for this we can thank myriad ordinary New Yorkers and their sightseeing kin who have reclaimed the bridge as their own. It is still the people's bridge, the city's most anthropocentric landmark. In the 120 years since the span's opening, the city and the nation may have changed, but the Brooklyn Bridge still belongs, as Kazin always claimed it did, to the walker. And that, perhaps, is how it was always meant to be.

"Like a Giant Block Party": Darkness and Good Humor

On September 11, 2001, the Brooklyn Bridge was the road out of Manhattan, and the throngs fleeing the city amid dust and ash are not likely to be forgotten. But alongside the images of that tragic day are those from another, more recent day.

At 4:11 p.m. on Thursday, August 14, 2003, the lights went out in New York City. Although thousands believed terrorism had returned to the metropolis, news began to spread through the darkness: this was no act of violence but a simple power failure, albeit the largest one in American history.

The city and its residents handled the first major power outage since 1977 with great civility and genuine good humor. Several helpful New Yorkers directed traffic; thousands waited patiently for passage home. Others found festivity in the breakdown by congregating in candle-lit bars and cafés or staging impromptu block parties. Needless to say, many thousands more decided to hoof it home across the city's various bridges.

Once again, the Brooklyn Bridge was a route home for many New York-

66. Young walkers helped older New Yorkers; people joked and handed around bottles of water. "People Cross the Brooklyn Bridge after Power Outage."
© REUTERS/Shannon Stapleton, 2003.

ers. For hours they trudged over the span. The weather was muggy, and most had already walked many miles from midtown or farther. We probably will never know how many of the thousands making their way home across the Brooklyn Bridge on that sweltering day thought of the span in the crosshairs of international terrorism. But if any did, their thoughts were not voiced. Instead, the atmosphere was good humored and friendly: "like a giant block party," according to one pedestrian.[37] Young walkers helped older New Yorkers; people joked and shared bottles of water. The following day, the news media — in New York, Washington, DC, and around the globe — brought a fresh image of the city to itself and the world. Several front-page pictures showed the Brooklyn Bridge full of weary but affable New Yorkers on their way home. In contrast to the chaos and looting of 1977, and the panic of 9/11, the world saw a different New York. In place of fear, the world saw

camaraderie; in place of desperate flight, it saw genial residents smiling in the darkness with strangers.

In 1867, John A. Roebling set out his hopes for the new East River bridge project. He envisioned the finished structure as a new "Broadway," a great urban "avenue" between New York and Brooklyn. Specifically, he championed the bridge's *elevated promenade.* "I need not state that in a crowded commercial city, such a promenade will be of incalculable value," he noted. Certainly, the bridge would serve the interests of commerce and communication; but it would promote "the interests of the community as well." [38] On the afternoon and in the evening of August 14, 2003, Roebling's hopes were realized once again. A city plunged into darkness did not panic. Instead, its citizens emitted a collective sigh of relief. The blackout of 2003 helped to reconcile the city with its tragic past. New Yorkers' worst fears were, for the moment, forgotten, and the bridge was once again a grand thoroughfare teeming with human traffic. On 9/11 New Yorkers fled over the bridge in fear; on 8/14 they happily sauntered. As one pedestrian discovered, walking the bridge in the blackout "causes New Yorkers to slow down and get to know each other. . . . They don't realize how much they have in common." [39] Roebling, we imagine, would have approved.

Notes

Introduction
Culture, History, and the Brooklyn Bridge

1. Arthur Miller, quoted in *New York Times Magazine*, March 27, 1983, 80.

2. See, for example, Merrill D. Peterson, *The Jefferson Image in the American Mind* (New York: Oxford University Press, 1960), and Peterson, *Lincoln in American Memory* (New York: Oxford University Press, 1994); Albert Boime, *The Unveiling of the National Icons: A Plea for Patriotic Iconoclasm in a Nationalist Era* (New York: Cambridge University Press, 1998); Elizabeth McKinsey, *Niagara Falls: Icon of the American Sublime* (New York: Cambridge University Press, 1985); Neil Harris, Wim de Wit, James Gilbert, and Robert W. Rydell, *Grand Illusions: Chicago's World's Fair of 1893* (Chicago: Chicago Historical Society, 1993); and Wilton S. Dillon and Neil G. Kotler, eds., *The Statue of Liberty Revisited* (Washington, DC: Smithsonian Institution Press, 1994).

3. A dominant feature of the scholarship that has focused on the bridge is exemplified by the major essay in the Brooklyn Museum's centennial exhibition catalog: Deborah Nevins, "1869–1883–1983," in *The Great East River Bridge, 1883–1983* (New York: Harry Abrams, 1983), 10–106. Nevins's title is somewhat misleading. Her essay focuses on the history of the bridge from its inception to its opening, and all but ignores the bridge from its opening to its centennial. The "1883–1983" section of her essay appears in the final few pages, and only the last paragraphs address the years between 1904 and 1983. Similarly, both David McCullough, *The Great Bridge: The Epic Story of the Building of the Brooklyn Bridge* (New York: Simon and Schuster, 1972), and Marilyn E. Weigold, *Silent Builder: Emily Warren Roebling and the Brooklyn Bridge* (New York: Associated Faculty Press, 1984), are concerned exclusively with the bridge's construction, and even Alan Trachtenberg's exemplary *Brooklyn Bridge: Fact and Symbol*, 2nd ed. (Chicago: University of Chicago Press, 1979) is dominated by the bridge's inception, design, and construction; he devotes only a quarter of his text to the post-opening history and primarily discusses only two figures, Hart Crane and Walker Evans. The essays in Margaret Latimer, Brooke Hindle, and Melvin Kranzberg, eds., *Bridge to the Future: A Centennial Celebration of the Brooklyn Bridge* (New York: New York Academy of Sciences, 1984), are equally vague on this subject: many take the era of the bridge's construction, not the bridge itself, as their topic. One essay that does look at the post-opening cultural history of the bridge is Bernice Braid, "The Brooklyn Bridge in Literary and Popular Imagination," *Long Island Historical Journal* 2 (1989), 90–103. Unfortunately, Braid's overview is compromised and unhelpful. Essentially, she uses the same cultural materials as Trachtenberg to come to the same conclusions. Also see the following essays by Trachtenberg: "Brooklyn Bridge and the Mastery of Nature," *Massachusetts Review* 5 (1963), 731–41; "The Rainbow and the Grid," *American Quarterly* 16 (1964), 3–19; "Cultural Revisions in the Twenties: Brooklyn Bridge as 'Usable Past,'" in *The American Self: Myth, Ideology, and Popular Culture*, ed. Sam Girgus (Albuquerque: University of New Mexico Press, 1981), 58–75; and "Brooklyn Bridge as a Cultural Text," in *Bridge to the Future*, ed. Latimer, Hindle, and Kranzberg, 213–24. As well, see Edwin Morgan's suggestive "Three Views of Brooklyn Bridge," in *Essays* (Cheadle, UK: Carcanet, 1974), 43–57. Regarding the bridge in popular culture, the *Brooklyn Bridge Bulletin* provides many interesting examples of the bridge's use in cartoon art and on book covers. On the bridge in music, see Nancy Groce, *New York: Songs of the City* (New York: Watson-Guptill, 1999), 40–46. The use of the bridge in film has yet to receive serious analysis; useful introductions are Joseph Gelms, "Brooklyn in the Movies," *Brooklyn Bridge* 4 (1999), 58–63, and John B.

Manbeck and Robert Singer, eds., *The Brooklyn Film: Essays in the History of Filmmaking* (Jefferson, NC: McFarland, 2003).

4. Christopher Morley, "'City of Glory and Despair,' For the World's Fair," in *As I Pass, O Manhattan: An Anthology of Life in New York*, ed. Ester Morgan McCullough (New York: Coley Taylor, 1956), 1202–3; Allen Keller, "The Great Brooklyn Bridge," *American History Illustrated* 8 (1973), 5; Kenneth Clark, *Civilization: A Personal View* (New York: Harper and Row, 1969), 228.

5. Lucy Kennedy, *The Sunlit Field* (New York: Crown, 1950), 274.

6. Lucille Fletcher, *The Daughters of Jasper Clay* (New York: Henry Holt, 1958), 313.

7. On the links made between Whitman and the bridge at its 1983 centennial, see Arthur Geffen, "Silence and Denial: Walt Whitman and the Brooklyn Bridge," *Walt Whitman Quarterly Review* 1 (1984), 1–11.

8. *Time Out: New York* 399 (2003), 76; Ellen Fletcher, "Brooklyn Bridge," in *The Encyclopedia of New York City*, ed. Kenneth T. Jackson (New Haven: Yale University Press, 1995), 155; Hendrik Hertzberg, "Gorgeous George," *New Yorker*, March 23, 2001, 76; Gloria Deák, *Picturing New York: The City from Its Beginnings to the Year 2000* (New York: Columbia University Press, 2000), 294. In reply to Fletcher, one might more reasonably assert that for Whitman the transcontinental railroad, and not the Brooklyn Bridge, was "the work of engineering that completed Columbus's mission."

9. Jim Collins, "How It Works: Bridges Are Architectural and Engineering Wonders," *Attaché* (April 2002), 26.

10. http://www.newyork.com/attraction/at/bio.html. Unfortunately, the quotation does not concern the bridge and is taken from a prose piece written in 1878, five years before anyone would tread upon the bridge's completed roadway. See Walt Whitman, "Human and Heroic New York," in *Specimen Days & Collect* (1883; facs. repr., New York: Dover, 1995), 118. Also see http://gonyc.about.com/cs/attractions/brooklynbridge.htm.

11. http://www.nyc.gov/html/dot/html/motorist/bridges.html#brooklyn. Since I last accessed its Website in June 2003, the New-York Historical Society has removed a statement there that claimed Walt Whitman wrote poetry in honor of the Brooklyn Bridge.

12. Walt Whitman, "The Future of Brooklyn," *Brooklyn Daily Times*, July 14, 1858, reprinted in *I Sit and Look Out: Editorials from the Brooklyn Daily Times by Walt Whitman*, ed. Emory Holloway and Vernolian Schwarz (New York: AMS Press, 1966), 146.

13. Walt Whitman, "Brooklyniana: No. 17," *Brooklyn Standard*, April 5, 1862, reprinted in *Walt Whitman's New York: From Manhattan to Montauk*, ed. Henry M. Christman (New York: New Amsterdam, 1963), 137.

14. For the history and development of Brooklyn, see Henry R. Stiles, *A History of the City of Brooklyn, Including the Old Town and Village of Brooklyn, the Town of Bushwick, and the Village and City of Williamsburg*, 3 vols. (1867–1870; Bowie, MD: Heritage Books, 1993); Harold Coffin Syrett, *The City of Brooklyn, 1865–1898* (New York: Columbia University Press, 1944); and Ralph Foster Weld, *Brooklyn Is America* (New York: Columbia University Press, 1950).

15. See Stanley Edgar Hyman, "This Alluring Roadway," *New Yorker*, May 17, 1952, 53–54.

16. See the souvenir program, *Brooklyn Bridge Re-Unveiling Celebration, 3:00 P.M. Sunday, December 2, 1945, Manhattan Bridge Plaza* (New York: The Association, 1945), Roebling Collection, Archibald S. Alexander Library, Rutgers University, no pagination.

17. Edgar Kaufman Jr., "The Brooklyn Bridge and the Artist," *Art in America* 46 (1958), 56, also noted this fact: "among poets not Walt Whitman but Hart Crane and Garcia Lorca celebrated the bridge."

18. "Song of the Exposition" was revised from an earlier poem, "After All, Not to Create Only" (1871), which was read by Whitman at the Fortieth National Industrial Exposition in New York on September 7, 1871. Originally, no mention was made of the Brooklyn Bridge; the reference to the structure was added during rewriting and first published in 1876. For "Song of the Exposition," see *Walt Whitman: Poetry and Prose*, ed. Justin

Kaplan (New York: Library of America, 1996), 341–50. For "Manhattan from the Bay," see *Specimen Days*, 116–17.

19. It is possible that Whitman was preoccupied with other concerns around this time. The eve of the bridge's opening marked the ten-year anniversary of the death of the poet's mother, an event that caused him immeasurable sadness. As he wrote shortly after her death: "I feel that the blank in life and heart left by the death of my mother is what will never to me be filled." See Walt Whitman, *The Correspondence*, ed. Edwin Haviland Miller, 3 vols. (New York: New York University Press, 1964), 2:225.

20. Ibid., 2:123.

21. For a more comprehensive assessment of Whitman's relationship to the Brooklyn Bridge, see Richard Haw, "American History/American Memory: Reevaluating Walt Whitman's Relationship to the Brooklyn Bridge," *Journal of American Studies* 39 (2004), 1–22.

22. John Bodnar, *Remaking America: Memory, Commemoration, and Patriotism in the Twentieth Century* (Princeton: Princeton University Press, 1992), 13–14.

23. Martin Filler, "The Brooklyn Bridge at 100," *Art in America* 71 (1983), 142.

24. See Bodnar, *Remaking America*, 13–14.

Chapter 1
Manufacturing Consensus, Practicing Exclusion:
Ideology and the Opening of the Brooklyn Bridge

1. See Hamilton Schuyler, *The Roeblings: A Century of Engineers, Bridgebuilders, and Industrialists* (Princeton: Princeton University Press, 1931), 250–56; David Steinman, *The Builders of the Bridge: The Story of John Roebling and His Son* (New York: Harcourt, Brace, 1945), 409–19; McCullough, *The Great Bridge*; David McCullough, "The Great Bridge and the American Imagination," *New York Times Magazine*, March 27, 1983, 28–38; Trachtenberg, *Brooklyn Bridge*, 75; Trachtenberg, "Brooklyn Bridge as a Cultural Text," 213–24; Braid, "Brooklyn Bridge in Literary and Popular Imagination," 90–103. In addition, among the numerous journalistic accounts, see Harvey Douglas, "The Story of Brooklyn Bridge," *Brooklyn Daily Eagle*, May 24, 1933, 15; Harry Gilroy, "It's Art, Poetry–And a Way to Brooklyn," *New York Times Magazine*, May 24, 1953, 26–28; Alan Keller, "The Great Brooklyn Bridge," 4–11; Paul Goldberger, "Brooklyn Bridge, at 100, Embodies the Spirit of the Age," *New York Times*, May 24, 1983, A1 and B2; and Dan Falk, "New York's Bridges Stand as Monuments to Great City's Past," *Toronto Star*, July 4, 1998, 10.

2. My understanding of ideology leans heavily on Sacvan Bercovitch's definition: ideology represents "the web of ideas, practices, beliefs, and myths through which a society, any society, coheres and perpetuates itself." It "arises out of historical circumstances, and then represents these, rhetorically and conceptually, as though they were natural, universal, inevitable and right; as though the ideals promulgated, by a certain group or class . . . were not the product of history but the expression of self-evident truth." Sacvan Bercovitch, *The Rites of Assent: Transformations in the Symbolic Language of America* (New York: Routledge, 1993), 13 and 356.

3. Master mechanic E. F. Farrington succinctly captured the working conditions: "on a work of this description, running through so many years, many changes and casualties must occur. In the morning you greet your old friend and fellow workman, at night his mangled remains are all that is left to you." It is likely that Farrington was referring to Harry Supple. A young foreman on the bridge, Supple was one of only a handful of laborers to receive individual attention in the press, first for a serious injury, and then for repeating Farrington's historic ride between the two bridge towers in a boatswain's chair in 1876. His final appearance in the press came with his death in June 1878. A cable wire snapped and knocked Supple off the New York anchorage. He survived the eighty-foot fall, but died a few hours later. As Jim Rasenberger has remarked, laborers on the bridge usually got their names in the press only "by dying in a manner the papers deemed news-

worthy." Rasenberger, *High Steel: The Daring Men Who Built the World's Greatest Sky-line* (New York: HarperCollins, 2004), 47, 49. For deaths on the bridge project, see E. F. Farrington, *Concise Description of the East River Bridge, with Full Details of the Con-struction, Being the Substance of Two Lectures Delivered at the Cooper Union, March 6 and 13, 1880* (New York: C. D. Wynkoop, 1881), 62. Given the lax records kept at the time, it is likely that the number of deaths was much higher.

4. A sampling of this criticism is available from the following sources. Eight months before the opening, the *New York World* began a long series of articles under the heading "The Bridge Ring, Overwhelming Proofs of Systematic Jobbery and Official Corruption." *New York World*, September 18, 1882, 1. As a date for the opening was confirmed, *Iron Age* wondered whether the trustees had finally realized that they would be unable to loot anymore money from the project. The report concluded that "fraud and dishonesty" were built into the bridge's "dark towers and cables," and that "scandal and dishonor have been faithful companions" throughout construction. Equally, the *New York Star* declared that the names of those who had promoted the bridge were "synonymous with dishonesty and fraud." The methods "by which the work was done are censurable in the extreme . . . this bridge is a monument of what every American should be ashamed to confess and anxious to forget." And, under the headline "Will It Be Disappointing?" the *New York Evening Telegram* wondered if "the game was worth the candle" and decided that it was not. In ad-dition, a number of people were angered by the imposition of tolls on a bridge that had been constructed with public funds. As John Tuel satirically noted: "The act to make the Brooklyn Bridge free to foot passengers is at present the most talked about among the mys-terious disappearances of the session. . . . Before it vanished there were reports in circu-lation that the ferry companies had a hatful of money to defeat it. It may be that the money and bill went in the same direction." See *Iron Age*, May 3, 1883, 2; *New York Eve-ning Telegram*, May 24, 1883, 2; *New York Star*, May 24, 1883, 1; and John Tuel, *Facts for the People: A Report of the Anti-Monopoly League of the State of New York* (New York: Anti-Monopoly League of New York State, 1883), 36–37. The classic statement of aes-thetic hostility was Montgomery Schuyler's "The Bridge as a Monument," *Harper's Weekly*, May 26, 1883, 326. Schuyler's article has been evaluated by a number of critics, and I do not wish to add to the debate here. Instead, my focus in this chapter will be on assent, not dissent. See William H. Jordy and Ralph Coe, introduction to *American Ar-chitecture, and Other Writings*, by Montgomery Shuyler, 2 vols., ed. Jordy and Coe (Cam-bridge, MA: Belknap Press, 1961), 47–53; David P. Billington and Robert Mark, "The Cathedral and the Bridge: Structure and Symbol," *Technology and Culture* 25 (1984), 37–52; and Trachtenberg, "Brooklyn Bridge as a Cultural Text," 213–24.

5. The turnaround is exemplified in a report by the *Brooklyn Daily Times*, May 24, 1883, 4: "In the bright and shining light of the opening ceremonies of to-day these criti-cisms and jealousies are wholly lost sight of, and the very men upon whom suspicion may be said to have rested for years, are the foremost heroes of the hour."

6. Alan Trachtenberg, *The Incorporation of America: Culture and Society in the Gilded Age* (New York: Hill and Wang, 1982), 8.

7. James Gilbert, *Perfect Cities: Chicago's Utopias of 1893* (Chicago: University of Chicago Press, 1991), 83.

8. As Henry Nash Smith notes, the Columbian Exposition "was embarrassingly un-related to American experience." Smith, ed., *Popular Culture and Industrialism* (New York: New York University Press, 1967), xvi. The literature on the 1893 Chicago exposi-tion is voluminous. Important for my conception of the fair are Gilbert, *Perfect Cities*, 75–130; David F. Burg, *Chicago's White City of 1893* (Lexington: University Press of Ken-tucky, 1976); R. Reid Badger, *The Great American Fair: The World's Columbian Exposi-tion and American Culture* (Chicago: Nelson Hall, 1979); and Robert W. Rydell, *All the World's a Fair: Visions of Empire at American International Expositions, 1876–1916* (Chi-cago: University of Chicago Press, 1984), 38–71.

9. Trachtenberg, *Incorporation of America*, 111.

10. Charles Mackay, quoted in Douglas T. Miller, *Jacksonian Aristocracy: Class and Democracy in New York, 1830–1860* (New York: Oxford University Press, 1962), 162; Whitman, "A Fine Afternoon, 4 to 6," in *Specimen Days*, 135; Walt Whitman, *Daybooks and Notebooks*, ed. William White, 3 vols. (New York: New York University Press, 1978), 1:144. On the park as a playground for the wealthy, see Richard Sennett, *The Conscience of the Eye: The Design and Social Life of Cities* (London: Faber, 1990), 95, and David Schuyler, *The New Urban Landscape: The Redefinition of City Form in Nineteenth-Century America* (Baltimore: Johns Hopkins University Press, 1986), 126. Although he describes Olmsted as somewhat "manipulative," Thomas Bender offers a more positive judgment of the designer. See Bender, *Toward an Urban Vision: Ideas and Institutions in Nineteenth-Century America* (Baltimore: Johns Hopkins University Press, 1975), 159–88. Olmsted's essay "Public Parks and the Enlargement of Towns" can be found in Frederick Law Olmsted, *Civilizing American Cities: Writings on City Landscapes*, ed. S. B. Sutton (New York: Da Capo, 1997), 52–99. Olmsted's vision for remodeling Niagara Falls should also be considered here: Frederick Law Olmsted and Calvert Vaux, *General Plan for the Improvement of the Niagara Reservation* (Niagara Falls, N.Y.: Gazette Book and Job Office, 1887), 1–11. Olmsted's proposal to convert the falls from a sublime, popular tourist attraction to a picturesque, "genteel" resort strengthens the case for his "practical pedagogy."

11. Robert H. Bremner, *From the Depths: The Discovery of Poverty in the United States* (New York: New York University Press, 1956).

12. *Opening Ceremonies of the New York and Brooklyn Bridge* (Brooklyn: Eagle Book and Job Printing, 1883), 89.

13. Ibid., 7–8.

14. *New York Herald*, May 25, 1883, 1.

15. *New York World*, May 22, 1883, 3.

16. *Opening Ceremonies*, 91. On the links between technology and American republicanism, see John F. Kasson, *Civilizing the Machine: Technology and Republican Values in America, 1776–1900* (Harmondsworth, UK: Penguin, 1976).

17. *Report of the Special Committee of the Common Council of the City of Brooklyn upon the Celebration of the Opening of the New York and Brooklyn Bridge* (Brooklyn: Eagle Book and Job Printing, 1883), 4.

18. Although the bridge had been converted from a private into a public venture after the exposé of Tammany Hall in 1873, the new ownership made no changes to ensure public accountability. From start to finish, the board of trustees directed the bridge's construction in private. Likewise, elections to the board of trustees saw no public involvement and were handled by the trustees themselves.

19. *Puck*, May 23, 1883, 183.

20. *New York Star*, May 21, 1883, 1. For a continuation of this barrage, see *Irish Nation*, May 26, 1883, 4. The "Alabamas" referred to by Gallagher were steam-powered sloops-of-war—the most famous of which was the CSS *Alabama*—built in British shipyards during the Civil War and used by the Confederate states to terrorize the Union's North Atlantic shipping. Clearly, Gallagher's remarks were designed to reopen the wounds of the Civil War, most notable British sympathy for the Confederacy.

21. One reason the trustees may have wished to avoid a Memorial Day opening concerned the lingering rifts of the Civil War. As David Blight explains, Memorial Day "shaped Civil War memory as much as any other cultural ritual," reflecting the deep divides of Reconstruction and emancipation. Founded by "black South Carolinians and their Northern abolitionist allies" in the aftermath of the conflict, the holiday took root in the North as a "victory cult"; in the South it was an annual reminder of defeat. To hold the bridge opening on such a partisan occasion—or worse, to schedule it for that day through the influence of a Union army veteran—would have been politically and economically divisive. The relationship between the South and New York City has always been complex. On the eve of the Civil War, the city's business elite, led by Mayor Fernando Wood, had considered seceding from the Union as an independent state. It was

thought that New York's trading interests with the South outweighed ideological ties with the North, and the city joined the Union cause only after the Confederacy announced its prohibitive tariff policy of 1861. With the end of Reconstruction, the South was again foremost in New York's economic mind. Hosting a national event on Memorial Day would hardly have furthered the interests of the business elite. And in New York, the pre-eminence of business has rarely been challenged. See Blight, *Race and Reunion: The Civil War in American Memory* (Cambridge, MA: Belknap Press, 2001), 64–97, and Edwin G. Burrows and Mike Wallace, *Gotham: A History of New York City to 1898* (New York: Oxford University Press, 1999), 867–68. Also see W. Lloyd Warner, "An American Sacred Ceremony," in Warner, *American Life: Dream and Reality*, rev. ed. (Chicago: University of Chicago Press, 1962), 5–34.

22. See *Brooklyn Daily Times*, May 15, 1883, 2; *New York World*, May 4, 1883, 4, and May 21, 1883, 2. Snubbed by the trustees, some Irish Americans vandalized houses displaying the British flag. In addition, New York's leading Irish American newspaper virtually ignored the event. See the *Daily Graphic*, May 25, 1883, 596, and the *Irish-American*, May 24, 1883, 5. The situation was only inflamed by a group called the Brooklyn Britannia Benefit Society. Just days before the opening, the society wrote an open letter to the trustees, thanking them for honoring Queen Victoria by their choice of opening date. See *New York Sun*, May 21, 1883, 1.

23. Craig Steven Wilder, quoted in *New York: A Documentary Film*, episode 3, *Sunshine and Shadow*, directed by Ric Burns (New York: PBS Home Video, 1999).

24. *New York Star*, May 21, 1883, 1.

25. Quoted in Sean Wilentz, "American Republican Festivals and the Rise of Class Conflict in New York City, 1788–1837," in *Working-Class America: Essays on Labor, Community, and American Society*, ed. Michael H. Frisch and Daniel J. Walkowitz (Urbana: University of Illinois Press, 1983), 50.

26. See Thomas Bender, *New York Intellect: A History of Intellectual Life in New York City, from 1750 to the Beginnings of Our Own Time* (Baltimore: Johns Hopkins University Press, 1987), 171.

27. *New York Herald*, May 22, 1883, 3.

28. *Report of the Special Committee of the Common Council of the City of Brooklyn*, 11. In a related incident, the American Society of Civil Engineers complained about the treatment of its members, who had received ornate invitations to the opening. Nevertheless, they were unable to gain access to the bridge or the various events: "The card of invitation was simply an empty honor, entitling the bearer to elbow his way as best he could through the dense mob of 'outsiders.'" *Engineering News and American Contract Journal*, May 26, 1883, 247. Conditions for would-be attendees were difficult. The parade route was heavily barricaded and policed: "one poor fellow who had innocently got outside of the lines was clubbed by one policeman and in endeavoring, in a dazed state, to find his hat, was clubbed from behind by another. Then the two worthies shook hands over their sport." *New York Sun*, May 25, 1883, 1.

29. See Washington Roebling, *Report of the Chief Engineer on the Strength of the Cables and Suspended Superstructure of the Bridge, Made to the Board of Trustees, January 9, 1882* (Brooklyn: Eagle Book and Job Printing, 1882), 1–9.

30. *Brooklyn Daily Eagle*, May 24, 1883, morning edition, 1.

31. See Daniel J. Boorstin, *The Image: A Guide to Pseudo-Events in America*, 25th anniversary ed. (New York: Atheneum, 1987), esp. 7–44.

32. *Report of the Special Committee of the Common Council of the City of Brooklyn*, 8 and 14.

33. *Brooklyn Daily Eagle*, May 24, 1883, morning edition, 8. By comparison, it was reported that the shops of Manhattan were just as busy as on any other day. See *New York Times*, May 25, 1883, 3.

34. Not only were the ferries understandably overrun on the opening day, but they

were also forced to maneuver around a variety of warships, as well as private and official vessels.

35. The best descriptions of the parades attending the Federal Procession, the Erie Canal, and the Croton Aqueduct can be found in Brooks McNamara, *Day of Jubilee: The Great Age of Public Celebrations in New York, 1788–1909* (New Brunswick: Rutgers University Press, 1997), 17–24 and 84–91.

36. Gilbert, *Perfect Cities*, 117.

37. John Kouwenhoven, "Eads Bridge: The Celebration," *Bulletin of the Missouri Historical Society* 30 (1974), 166–68.

38. Susan G. Davis, *Parades and Power: Street Theatre in Nineteenth-Century Philadelphia* (Berkeley: University of California Press, 1986), 1–22. Also see Wilentz, "American Republican Festivals," 37–77.

39. See Davis, *Parades and Power,* 167–68; McNamara, *Day of Jubilee,* 126–29; and David Glassberg, *American Historical Pageantry: The Uses of Tradition in the Early Twentieth Century* (Chapel Hill: University of North Carolina Press, 1990), 21–22.

40. T. J. Jackson Lears, "The Concept of Cultural Hegemony: Problems and Possibilities," *American Historical Review* 90 (1985), 583. When discussing the restricted participation of the lower classes at this time, it is worth remembering the influence that the Tilden Commission had on urban politics. Created in the 1870s and named after Samuel J. Tilden, an early sponsor of the bridge, the commission advocated making suffrage wholly dependent upon the payment of property tax. Although ultimately defeated, the commission's recommendations had lasting influence and offered a popular, unifying issue for the city's elite citizens. See David Quigley, *Second Founding: New York City, Reconstruction, and the Making of American Democracy* (New York: Hill and Wang, 2004).

41. *New York Herald,* May 25, 1883, 2. In addition to the official exclusion, an attempt was made to dissuade the general public from lingering and enjoying the bridge's physical beauty. In a circular put out just days before the opening, first assistant engineer C. C. Martin stated that "the bridge was constructed for the purpose of providing sure and rapid communication between the two cities and not as a place where leisure hours are to be spent . . . it is earnestly urged upon all citizens and visitors to remember that the bridge is a great business thoroughfare, and when necessary everything else must be sacrificed to the demands of business." *Brooklyn Daily Eagle,* May 21, 1883, 2.

42. For the most substantial treatment of the experience of the "technological sublime" in America, see David E. Nye, *American Technological Sublime* (Cambridge, MA: MIT Press, 1994), esp. 17–44 and 77–87.

43. *Brooklyn Daily Eagle,* May 24, 1933, A3.

44. *New York Herald,* May 26, 1883, 3.

45. See *New York Sun,* May 26, 1883, 3; *New York Commercial Advertiser,* May 27, 1883, 4; Reginald Fairfax Harrison, Diary, May 12, 1883, p. 27, Museum of the City of New York; and *Puck,* July 4, 1883, 285. Crushes on the Brooklyn Bridge were a dominant feature for many years. More than twenty years after the opening, *Harper's Weekly* was proclaiming "greatest crush yet seen on the bridge"; *Harper's Weekly,* February 23, 1895, 174. The *New York Times Index* contained a subsection on Brooklyn Bridge crushes well into the twentieth century.

46. *New York Herald,* May 28, 1883, 5.

47. *Daily Graphic,* May 31, 1883, 630.

48. See Immanuel Kant, *The Critique of Judgment,* trans. James Creed Meredith (1790; New York: Oxford University Press, 1952), 110–11.

49. Nye, *American Technological Sublime,* 27.

50. *Opening Ceremonies,* 32 and 36.

51. Abram S. Hewitt, *Address Delivered by Abram S. Hewitt on the Occasion of the Opening of the New York and Brooklyn Bridge* (New York: John Polhemus, 1883), 3–9. For Perry Miller, the rhetoric of the American errand projected a society where "the fact

could be made one with the ideal." Unsurprisingly, this type of rhetoric saturated the speeches at the opening. See Miller, *The New England Mind: The Seventeenth Century* (1939; Boston: Beacon Press, 1961), 462.

52. *Opening Ceremonies*, 24–28 and 84–122.

53. Trachtenberg, "Brooklyn Bridge as a Cultural Text," 218–19; Sacvan Bercovitch, *The American Jeremiad* (Madison: University of Wisconsin Press, 1978), 168. Also see Sacvan Bercovitch, "The Rites of Assent: Rhetoric, Ritual, and the Ideology of American Consensus," in *American Self*, ed. Girgus, 5–42.

54. William C. Conant, "Will New York Be the Final World Metropolis?" *Century* 26 (1883), 687. Conant was also responsible for one of the most exhaustive articles concerning the bridge at its opening: "The Brooklyn Bridge," *Harper's New Monthly Magazine* 66 (1883), 925–46.

55. Conant, "Will New York Be the Final World Metropolis?" 691.

56. In 1948, Conant's trope was (perhaps unwittingly) revived by New York City's planning commissioner, Cleveland Rodgers, in an extravagantly celebratory tribute to the city. Rodgers begins his triumphant narrative: "A bench on Brooklyn Bridge is a good place to study the history not only of New York but of modern civilization as well. . . . It brings one closer than any street or building to the heart of the metropolis." See Cleveland Rodgers and Rebecca B. Rankin, *New York: The World's Capital City, Its Development and Contributions to Progress* (New York: Harper and Bros., 1948), 3.

57. For examples of the overwhelming endorsement accorded Hewitt, see *New York Herald*, May 25, 1883, 1; *Brooklyn Union*, May 24, 1883, evening edition, 1; and *New York Commercial Advertiser*, May 24, 1883, 1.

58. Trachtenberg, *Brooklyn Bridge*, 120.

59. Hewitt, *Address*, 16. Despite Henry Adams's claim that Hewitt was "the most industrious . . . the most useful public man," recent scholarship has proved Hewitt complicit in the bridge's infamous wire fraud. Hewitt lobbied intensely to divert the wire contract to one J. Lloyd Haigh. Hewitt owned the mortgage on Haigh's business and received 10 percent of his income as a result. Haigh contrived to supply cheap wire below specification and very quickly amassed profits over $300,000. Even though the board of trustees was well aware of the links between Haigh and Hewitt, no action was taken against Hewitt. See Henry Adams, *The Education of Henry Adams* (1918; Harmondsworth, UK: Penguin, 1995), 355; Trachtenberg, *Brooklyn Bridge*, 99–113; McCullough, *The Great Bridge*, 389–96; and Raymond A. Schroth, *The Eagle and Brooklyn: A Community Newspaper, 1841–1955* (Westport, CT: Greenwood Press, 1974), 77–79.

60. The era's paradoxical relationship to honesty was best summed up in the *New York Tribune*, which stated that "it is an era of honest building, and the Bridge is its greatest fruit," but strangely included in its definition of honest building the "necessary condition . . . that somebody must profit unlawfully" (May 24, 1883, 2). Just three weeks prior to the opening of the bridge, the *New York Commercial Advertiser* ran a story under the headline "Democratic Jobbery Thriving, Disgraceful Conditions, the Factions United for the Spoils." Political corruption was now more rampant, it declared, than in the days of "old Tweed and Tammany Hall" (May 1, 1883, 1). Also see Margaret Latimer, *Two Cities: New York and Brooklyn the Year the Great Bridge Opened* (Brooklyn: Brooklyn Educational and Cultural Alliance, 1983), 14 and 58.

61. *New York Times*, May 25, 1883, 2.

62. Hewitt, *Address*, 9. It is interesting to compare Hewitt's comments with those of the banker in William Dean Howells's novel *A Traveler from Altruria* (1894): "The economic status of the workingman among us is essentially the same as that of the workingman all over the civilized world. . . . I suppose most Americans honestly believe because we have a republican form of government, and manhood-suffrage, and so on, that our economic conditions are peculiar, and that our workingman has a status higher and better than that of the workingman anywhere else. But he has nothing of the kind. His circumstances are better, and provisionally his wages are higher, but it is only a question of

years or decades when his circumstances will be the same and his wages the same as the European workingman's." One is left to wonder whether Howells was familiar with Hewitt's speech. See Howells, *A Traveler from Altruria*, ed. David W. Levy (Boston: Bedford Books, 1996), 54–55.

63. As John Bodnar observes, the guardians of "official public memory . . . share a common interest in social unity, the continuity of existing institutions, and loyalty to the status quo. They attempt to advance these concerns by promoting interpretations of past and present reality that reduce the power of competing interests that threaten the attainment of their goals." See Bodnar, *Remaking America*, 13–14.

64. Robert Wiebe notes that the spectacle of the violent railroad strikes of 1877 and their brutal suppression was "quickly classified an exception and, once categorized, it became no more than a bad memory, an incident rather than an index to fear or failure." By the opening of the Brooklyn Bridge, that battle between labor and capital was no longer seen as an exception; it was no longer seen at all. Banished from cultural memory, both the strikes and their wider significance were lost. See Wiebe, *The Search for Order, 1877–1920* (New York: Hill and Wang, 1967), 10.

65. Trachtenberg, "Brooklyn Bridge as a Cultural Text," 220.

66. *New York Tribune*, May 24, 1883, 1. On public indifference to the speech giving, see *Daily Graphic*, May 25, 1883, 596; *New York Herald*, May 25, 1883, 2; and *New York Star*, May 25, 1883, 1.

67. *New York Herald*, May 25, 1883, 2.

68. See Boorstin, *The Image*, 3 and 11.

69. Ibid., 12; David Waldstreicher, "Rites of Rebellion, Rites of Assent: Celebrations, Print Culture, and the Origins of American Nationalism," *Journal of American History* 82 (1995), 54.

70. For example, Pete Coutros stated that "May 24, 1883, dawned with a brilliance which suggested an extra supply of sunlight had been ordered for the occasion," and McCullough begins his re-creation of the opening day with: "the weather was perfect." See Coutros, "Suspended Animation: Brooklyn Bridge Will Be 75 Years Old on Saturday . . . ," *Sunday News*, May 18, 1958, 10; McCullough, *The Great Bridge*, 525. Episode 3 of Ric Burns's *New York: A Documentary Film* contains the following narration: "the [opening] day dawned fair and mild, without a cloud in the sky." Also see Steinman, *Builders of the Bridge*, 409–18, and Schuyler, *The Roeblings*, 250–56.

71. *Daily Graphic*, May 24, 1883, second edition extra, 592.

72. *Brooklyn Daily Eagle*, May 24, 1883, 4 p.m. edition, 2, and May 24, 1883, evening edition, 2.

73. *New York Herald*, May 25, 1883, 2. The descriptions in both the *Herald* and the *Eagle* conform to Peter Shaw's observations on the American revolutionary *rite de passage*. As Shaw notes, the symbolism of the passage of nature — most often the emergence of spring, or the revolution of the sun — translated well into the idea of national rebirth and was often employed. See Shaw, *American Patriots and the Rituals of Revolution* (Cambridge, MA: Harvard University Press, 1981), 208.

74. *New York Sun*, May 25, 1883, 2.

75. This sentiment is confirmed in the official report: "The heavens were radiant with the celestial blue of approaching summer; silver fragments of cloud sailed gracefully across the firmament like winged messengers, bearing greeting of work well done." See *Opening Ceremonies*, 8.

76. See E. P. Thompson, *Customs in Common* (Harmondsworth, UK: Penguin, 1991), 92, and Robert A. Ferguson, "'We Hold These Truths': Strategies of Control in Literature of the Founders," in *Reconstructing American Literary History*, ed. Sacvan Bercovitch (Cambridge, MA: Harvard University Press, 1986), 1–28.

77. David Waldsteicher, *In the Midst of Perpetual Fêtes: The Making of American Nationalism, 1776–1820* (Chapel Hill: University of North Carolina Press, 1997), 228. The impact of the written word on public opinion was especially significant during the Revo-

lutionary period. The image of George III was fatally altered through public consumption of Thomas Paine's *Common Sense* and the Declaration of Independence. As Peter Shaw notes in *American Patriots*, 8–47, "Americans turned on George III with a fury as remarkable as the loyalty that preceded it." A similar fate visited the reputation of Massachusetts Governor Thomas Hutchinson, whose letters opposing the Stamp Act were edited, doctored, and published under the title "Threatened Total Destruction to the Liberties of All America." The etching of political opinion in the stone of the written word provided its own authority: it was believed because it was written.

78. Latimer, *Two Cities*, 81.

79. Simon Newman, *Parades and the Politics of the Street: Festive Culture in the Early American Republic* (Philadelphia: University of Pennsylvania Press, 1997), 3. On the eve of the opening, the *Brooklyn Daily Eagle* urged its readers to secure copies early and created a subscription service for the day's paper. Emphasizing the "permanent value" of the day's copy, the *Eagle* also offered to ship anywhere in the world. *Brooklyn Daily Eagle*, May 23, 1883, 2.

80. Whether President Arthur even wished to make contact with guests at the exclusive receptions is debatable. With derision, the *Daily Graphic* noted: "Mayor Low urges upon the citizens at the reception not to shake hands with the President. The power of the right arm of the Chief Executive is limited, and he desires to return to Washington whole and sound with all his members intact." *Daily Graphic*, May 23, 1883, 580.

81. Schroth, *The Eagle and Brooklyn*, 87. These tropes and strategies appeared in a majority of the papers, but for reasons of brevity I will focus on the *Brooklyn Daily Eagle*, which held the record for the day's highest circulation. Although the *New York Herald* had the largest circulation of any New York paper in 1883 at 60,000 copies, the circulation of the *Eagle* on opening day was 250,000. These statistics only further the importance of the press in evaluating the event. See Schroth, 83, and Latimer, *Two Cities*, 81.

82. Hewitt, *Address*, 3.

83. *Brooklyn Daily Eagle*, May 23, 1883, 2. The *Brooklyn Union* also emphasized America's progress from the seventeenth century to the nineteenth century. *Brooklyn Union*, May 24, 1883, evening edition, 2. Also see S. W. Green, *A Complete History of the New York and Brooklyn Bridge from Its Conception in 1866 to Its Completion in 1883* (New York: S. W. Green's and Sons, 1883), 3–10.

84. Hewitt, *Address*, 9.

85. *Brooklyn Daily Eagle*, May 23, 1883, 2. For similar sentiments, see *New York Evening Telegram*, May 24, 1883, 3rd edition, 2; *Brooklyn Daily Times*, May 24, 1883, 3; *New York World*, May 21, 1883, 4; and *Harper's Weekly*, June 2, 1883, 439. Also see Charles Barnard, "The Brooklyn Bridge," *St. Nicholas* 10 (July 1883), 689–700, and A. C. Barnes, *The New York and Brooklyn Bridge* (Brooklyn: Eagle Book and Print Job, 1883), 5.

86. See *The W.P.A. Guide to New York City: The Federal Writers' Project Guide to 1930s New York* (1939; New York: Pantheon Books, 1982), 441. For a comparable record of the economic blight suffered by the South Street area of Manhattan as a direct result of the building of the bridge, see Joseph Mitchell, "Up in the Old Hotel," in *The Bottom of the Harbor* (London: Jonathan Cape, 2000), 31–34.

87. See *Frank Leslie's Boys' and Girls' Weekly*, January 27, 1883, front cover. Just six years later, *Frank Leslie's Illustrated Newspaper* used its front cover to draw attention to the destitute people who made their homes beneath the Brooklyn Bridge. In the middle of the night beneath the bridge's great arch, a policeman makes his rounds amid a variety of poor New Yorkers. See *Frank Leslie's Illustrated Newspaper*, July 13, 1889, front cover.

88. *Brooklyn Daily Eagle*, May 24, 1883, evening edition, 2.

89. Nye, *American Technological Sublime*, xiv; Edmund Burke, *A Philosophical Enquiry into the Origin of our Ideas of the Sublime and Beautiful*, ed. Adam Phillips (1757; New York: Oxford University Press, 1990), 53.

90. *Brooklyn Daily Eagle*, May 24, 1883, morning edition, 1.

91. Comparisons were an integral aspect of late-nineteenth-century nationalism, and

especially with regard to world's fairs. As Robert Rydell notes, "world's fairs put the nations and people of the world on display for comparative purposes. Americans . . . often measured their achievements against those of different nations." See Rydell, *All the World's a Fair*, 5.

92. See Olga Peters Hasty and Susanne Fuso's introduction to their *America Through Russian Eyes, 1874–1926* (New Haven: Yale University Press, 1988), 6.

93. See McNamara, *Day of Jubilee*, 82–83, and James Gill, *Lords of Misrule: Mardi Gras and the Politics of Race in New Orleans* (Jackson: University Press of Mississippi, 1997), 93–97.

94. *Opening Ceremonies*, 90.

95. *Brooklyn Daily Eagle*, May 24, 1883, 4 p.m. edition, 2. For similarly charged assessments of the two events, see *New York Tribune*, May 24, 1883, 1, and *Brooklyn Daily Times*, May 24, 1883, 2.

96. *Brooklyn Daily Eagle*, May 24, 1883, 4 p.m. edition, 2. It is interesting to compare this statement with the *Brooklyn Union's* hostile characterization of Russian society. Little would seem to differentiate between the *Eagle's* "if they start any demonstration they will be quickly silenced in a forcible manner" and the *Union's* condemnation of how the tsar meets "protest with ruthless suppression." See *Brooklyn Union*, May 24, 1883, evening edition, 2.

97. See *Brooklyn Daily Eagle*, May 21, 1883, 5; *New York Truth*, May 19, 1883, 3; and *Brooklyn Daily Times*, May 11, 1883, 2.

98. Mary P. Ryan, *Civic Wars: Democracy and Public Life in the American City during the Nineteenth Century* (Berkeley: University of California Press, 1997), 123.

99. *Daily Graphic*, May 24, 1883, front cover.

100. Boime, *Unveiling of the National Icons*, 8.

Chapter 2
"The Eyes of All People Are upon Us":
Tourists, Immigrants, and the Brooklyn Bridge

1. Andrew Delbanco, *The Puritan Ideal* (Cambridge, MA: Harvard University Press, 1989), 72.

2. John Winthrop, "A Model of Christian Charity," in *The Journal of John Winthrop 1630–1649*, ed. Richard S. Dunn and Laetitia Yeandle (Cambridge, MA: Belknap Press, 1996), 1–12.

3. See James L. Machor, *Pastoral Cities: Urban Ideals and the Symbolic Landscape of America* (Madison: University of Wisconsin Press, 1987), 47–52, and Daryl Sasser, "Retaking the Hill: John Winthrop's Nineteenth-Century Influence," paper delivered at the Roosevelt Study Center, Middelburg, The Netherlands, June 14, 2000. The sole extant copy of the address was donated to the New-York Historical Society in 1809 and first published in *Massachusetts Historical Society Collections* in 1838. Recognition of Winthrop's importance was furthered in 1853 with the publication of his *History of New England from 1630 to 1649*, and again in 1864 with Robert Winthrop's widely read *Life and Letters of John Winthrop, Governor of the Massachusetts-Bay Company at Their Emigration to New England, 1630*.

4. See Hugh J. Dawson, "John Winthrop's Rite of Passage: The Origins of the 'Christian Charitie' Discourse," *Early American Literature* 26 (1991), 219–31.

5. All of the Roanoke colonists vanished without trace, and within eight months disease and starvation struck down 67 of the original 105 Jamestown colonists. See Lee Miller, *Roanoke: Solving the Mystery of England's Lost Colony* (London: Jonathan Cape, 2000).

6. *Brooklyn Daily Eagle*, May 24, 1883, 3; *Scientific American*, July 14, 1883, 265.

7. *New York Tribune*, May 25, 1883, 1.

8. Kenneth M. Roemer, *The Obsolete Necessity: America in Utopian Writings, 1888–1900* (Kent, OH: Kent State University Press, 1976), 7.

9. *Daily Graphic*, May 24, 1883, 588; Conant, "Will New York Be the Final World Metropolis?" 687–96.

10. *Brooklyn Daily Times*, May 5, 1883, 3; *Brooklyn Daily Eagle*, May 24, 1883, evening edition, 2.

11. Schuyler, "The Bridge as a Monument," 326–39. The New Zealander first appeared in 1840, when Macaulay predicted that London "may still exist in undiminished vigour when some traveller from New Zealand shall, in the midst of a vast solitude, take his stand on a broken arch of London Bridge to sketch the ruins of St. Paul's." The image of a foreign traveler surveying the future ruins of London became such an overused trope in mid-nineteenth-century England that *Punch* magazine labeled it the most "used up, exhausted, threadbare, stale and hackneyed" of literary devices. See T. B. Macaulay, "Ranke's *History of the Popes*," *Edinburgh Review* 72 (1840), 258, and "A Proclamation," *Punch*, January 7, 1865, 9.

12. In evaluating how new arrivals have responded to the Brooklyn Bridge, I make no differentiation among genres: all types of materials are treated as historical representations.

13. See John F. Sears, *Sacred Places: American Tourist Attractions in the Nineteenth Century* (1989; Amherst: University of Massachusetts Press, 1998), 4–10, and Dean MacCannell, *The Tourist: A New Theory of the Leisure Class* (1976; Berkeley: University of California Press, 1999), 111–12.

14. See Max Berger, *The British Traveller in America, 1836–1860* (New York: P. S. King and Staples, 1943), 26; Allan Nevins, *America Through British Eyes* (New York: Oxford University Press, 1948), 90; and Richard L. Rapson, *Britons View America: Travel Commentary, 1860–1935* (Seattle: University of Washington Press, 1971), 13.

15. Sir Henry Lepel Griffin, *The Great Republic* (New York: Scribner and Welford, 1884); W. T. Stead, *Satan's Invisible World Displayed; or, Despairing Democracy, a Study of Greater New York* (London: Review of Reviews, 1898). Griffin is especially important here. He hated America. In the Brooklyn Bridge and Tammany's new City Hall he saw the symbols of the age: municipal structures through which to siphon public money into private hands. Although often dismissed, his opinions on this matter were similar to those of Henry George.

16. See William Cobbett, *A Year's Residence in the United States of America* (1818; Carbondale: University of Southern Illinois Press, 1964); D. P. Crook, "The U.S. in Bentham's Thought," *Australian Journal of Politics and History* 10 (1964), 196–204; and Alexis de Tocqueville, *Democracy in America*, ed. J. P. Mayer, trans. George Lawrence (London: Fontana, 1975).

17. See Eric Foner, *The Story of American Freedom* (London: Macmillan, 1998), esp. 69–114; Samuel Johnson, quoted in Edward Countryman, *The American Revolution*, rev. ed. (New York: Hill and Wang, 2003), 120.

18. Eric Hobsbawm, *The Age of Capital, 1848–1875* (1975; London: Abacus, 1997), 15.

19. See Alexander Graham Bell to Mabel Hubbard Bell, November 29, 1885, Family Correspondence, folder: Mabel Hubbard Bell, Alexander Graham Bell Family Papers, Library of Congress; Charles Lord Russell, *Diary of a Visit to the United States of America in the Year 1883* (New York: United States Catholic Historical Society, 1910), 31; Edward Aveling, *An American Journey* (New York: John W. Lowek, 1887), 26; José Martí, "The Brooklyn Bridge," in *Selected Writings* (New York: Penguin, 2002), 140–44; and Sigmund Skard, "Bjørnstjerne Bjørnson, 1832–1910 and Halvdan Koht, 1873–1965," in *Abroad in America: Visitors to the New Nation, 1776–1914*, ed. Marc Pachter and Frances Stevenson Wein (London: Addison-Wesley, 1976), 195–201.

20. See R. David Arkush and Leo O. Lee, eds. and trans., *Land without Ghosts: Chinese Impressions of America from the Mid-Nineteenth Century to the Present* (Berkeley: University of California Press, 1989), 123, and Nicolaus Mohr, *Excursion Through Amer-*

ica, ed. Ray Allen Billington, trans. Lavern J. Rippley (1883; Chicago: Lakeside Press, 1973), 35.

21. See "Iron Mirgorod—Esenin's Impressions of America 1923," in *Esenin: A Biography in Memoirs, Letters, and Documents with Previously Untranslated Prose Works and Correspondence by Esenin,* ed. and trans. J. Davis (Ann Arbor, MI: Ardis, 1982), 70.

22. See Vladimir Mayakovsky, "The Brooklyn Bridge," in *Poems* (Moscow: Progress Press, 1972), 81–87, and Edward J. Brown, *Mayakovsky: A Poet in the Revolution* (Princeton: Princeton University Press, 1973), 280–85. For further background on Mayakovsky's impressions of America, see two fine essays by Charles A. Moser: "Mayakovsky's Unsentimental Journeys," *American Slavic and East European Review* 19 (1960), 85–100, and "Mayakovsky and America," *Russian Review* 25 (1966), 242–56.

23. Brown, *Mayakovsky,* 284.

24. See Peter Conrad, *The Art of the City: Views and Versions of New York* (New York: Oxford University Press, 1984), 223–25.

25. See Arthur C. Paulson, "Bjørnson and the Norwegian-Americans," *Norwegian-American Studies and Records* 5 (1930), 84–109; Harold Larson and Einar Haugen, "Bjørnson and America: A Critical Review," *Scandinavian Studies and Notes* 13 (1933–35), 1–12; and Skard, "Bjørnson and Koht," 195–201.

26. Those invited represent a contemporary "'Who's Who' of the world of government and finance." For example, the British contingent included Chief Justice Charles Russell (who also wrote a memoir of the trip), Lord Carrington, Lord James Bryce, and representatives of the Bank of England, the Royal Treasury, and Parliament. See Ray Allen Billington, "Historical Introduction" in *Excursion Through America,* by Mohr, xxxiii–xxxv. Also see Alexandra Villard de Borchgrave and John Cullen, *Villard: The Life and Times of an American Titan* (New York: Nan A. Talese, 2001).

27. Lord Russell wrote that "in space and lightness of appearance (elegance one might say) [the Brooklyn Bridge] greatly exceeds anything of the kind I ever saw . . . it is a thing of beauty." See Russell, *Diary of a Visit,* 31.

28. Klaus Lanzinger, "Nicolaus Mohr as a Foreign Observer of the United States," in *Excursion Through America,* by Mohr, 358.

29. Ibid., 365.

30. Ibid., 362.

31. Boorstin, *The Image,* 84–110. Also see Marguerite S. Shaffer, *See America First: Tourism and National Identity, 1880–1940* (Washington, DC: Smithsonian Institution Press, 2001), 4, 309. For Edward Relph, *Place and Placelessness* (London: Pion, 1976), 83, tourism is "an inauthentic attitude to place." Wai-Teng Leong, "Culture and the State: Manufacturing Traditions for Tourism," *Critical Studies in Mass Communication* 6 (1989), 361, puts the matter more bluntly: "the intrinsic nature of tourism is contrivance."

32. Rapson, *Britons View America,* 26, 27, 201.

33. See Shaffer, *See America First,* 1–6, and Sears, *Sacred Places,* 4–10.

34. MacCannell, *The Tourist,* 111. In its March 25, 2001, edition, *U.S.A. Weekend* attempted to review and rank "The American Experience": "With the boldness that has always been part of our character, *U.S.A. Weekend* takes on an awesome task: Rank the 10 sites that best help you understand our great country." The Brooklyn Bridge placed sixth on the list. For articles that summarize and rank New York specifically through the lens of its bridges, see J. D. Warner, "City of Bridges: New York," *Municipal Affairs* 3 (1899), 651–63; "Bridges Proclaim Might of New York," *New York Times Magazine,* December 26, 1926, 6–7; and Dan Falk, "New York's Bridges Stand as Monuments to Great City's Past," *Toronto Star,* July 4, 1998, 10–11. A similar propensity to rank the American nation by the quality and achievement of its bridges can be found in F. W. Skinner, "Nation of Great Bridges," *Harper's Weekly,* January 1, 1910, 10–11, and K. Waule, "Bridges as a Test of Civilization," *Scientific American Monthly* 3 (1921), 201–4.

35. This narrow vision is reflected not only in guidebooks and travelogues, but also in

fiction. For the Brooklyn Bridge as New York's preeminent tourist site, see, for example, Upton Sinclair, *The Moneychangers* (1908; New York: Prometheus Books, 2001), 10; Sinclair Lewis, *Dodsworth* (1929; New York: Modern Library, 1947), 278; and Charles Reznikoff, *By the Waters of Manhattan* (1930; New York: Markus Wiener, 1986), 216–19. Of course, American cities were often redefined through literature. Just as tourists flocked to Chicago to witness the furious wheat trading depicted by Frank Norris in *The Pit* (1903), they also came to see the reality behind Upton Sinclair's meatpacking exposé, *The Jungle* (1906). Although each presented a different side of the city, both books drew visitors to Chicago. On the relationship between literature and tourism, see Peter T. Newby, "Literature and the Fashioning of Tourist Taste," in *Humanistic Geography and Literature*, ed. Douglas C. D. Pocock (London: Croom Helm, 1981), 130–41.

36. Boorstin, *The Image*, 91.

37. Rapson, *Britons View America*, 27; Abraham Cahan, *The Rise of David Levinsky* (1917; Harmondsworth, UK: Penguin, 1993), 284. John Jakle makes the point more broadly to include all tourists. See John A. Jakle, *The Tourist: Travel in Twentieth-Century North America* (Lincoln: University of Nebraska Press, 1985), 254.

38. *A Visitor's Guide to the City of New York: Some of the Sights in and about the Metropolis Worth Seeing, Excursions and Trolley Rides* (Brooklyn: Eagle Book and Job Printing, 1901), 11. The analysis of guidebooks provided here represents a distillation, not a comprehensive survey. It is meant to illustrate the relentlessness of the dominant tropes.

39. *New York (Illustrated): Visitor's Guide and Tourist's Directory of Leading Hotels in New York and Principal Cities*, pamphlet issued by the *New York Journal* System of Information Bureaus, 1901, 3. Wai-Teng Leong, "Culture and the State," 355–75, notes that it is important to consider the role of the state in tourism. Through monuments, commemorative plaques, and designated historical sites, the state can influence tourist itineraries. Frank B. Kelly's *Historical Guide to the City of New York* (New York: Stokes, 1913), for example, relies entirely on commemorative plaques for a tour of the city. In such guides, tourists are directed by official cultural opinion, not independent inquiry. As a result, municipal culture is presented as monolithic, not plural.

40. *Rand, McNally & Co.'s Handy Guide to New York City, Brooklyn, Staten Island and Other Suburbs*, 4th ed. (New York: Rand, McNally and Co., 1896), 7. James Gilbert, *Perfect Cities*, 63, makes a similar point with regard to visitors to Chicago's 1893 exposition. The guidebooks to this event were intended to aid the visitor in getting out of, and past, the gritty reality of working-class Chicago and to the idealized exposition as speedily as possible, with the least amount of fuss, and, presumably, without noticing the intervening neighborhoods.

41. Introduced at the turn of the century, bus and boat tours exemplified this narrow approach. Literally whisking their passengers between symbolic markers, they directed the tourist experience absolutely and insulated visitors from the world in which they traveled. See advertisements for Royal Blue Line bus tours ("seeing New York—Uptown, Downtown, and over the great bridges to Brooklyn") and the Halcyon and Tourist boat tours ("Around New York Harbor and Manhattan . . . under all bridges") both in *New York Standard Guide* (New York: Foster and Reynolds, 1917), 145–47.

42. See *Visitor's Guide to the City of New York*, 39, and *New York (Illustrated)*, 12. According to Laura Hapke, nineteenth-century guidebooks "reassured a still-rural audience that one stays respectable by restricting one's experience. . . . They offered, in effect, a spurious way of making the city real. For they implied that if one is only armed with enough facts—or seeming facts—about which places to avoid and which to visit, one might pass unscathed through Babylon." See Hapke, "Down There on a Visit: Late-Nineteenth-Century Guidebooks to the City," *Journal of Popular Culture* 20 (1986), 52–53.

43. *McCoy's Centennial Illustrated, How to See New York and Its Environs: A Complete Guide and Handbook* (New York: Robert McCoy's, 1876).

44. Fremont Rider, *Rider's New York City: A Guide Book for Travellers*, 2nd ed. (New York: Henry Holt, 1923), 143; Karl Baedeker, ed., *The United States, with an Excursion*

into Mexico (1893; New York: Da Capo, 1971), 30. Similar sentiments can be found in Gustav Kobbé, *New York and Its Environs* (New York: Harper and Bros., 1891), 138; *A Visitor's Guide to the City of New York*, 43; and *What to See in New York* (New York: John Wanamaker, 1911), 36–37.

45. Robert Curtis Ogden, *New York City, and How to See It: A Complete Pocket Guide* (New York: Hurd and Houghton, 1876). Also see *McCoy's Centennial Illustrated*.

46. See Rydell, *All the World's a Fair*, esp. 2–8.

47. M. F. Sweetser, *How to Know New York: A Serviceable and Trustworthy Guide*, 11th ed. (New York: J. J. Little, 1895), 7.

48. *Rand, McNally & Co.'s Handy Guide*, 135; *Rider's New York City*, xiv.

49. *Rider's New York City*, 200.

50. See Nye, *American Technological Sublime*.

51. See Barbara Novak, *Nature and Culture: American Landscape Painting, 1825–1875*, rev. ed. (New York: Oxford University Press, 1995), 3–18, 54; Sears, *Sacred Places*; and Patrick McGreevy, "Niagara as Jerusalem," *Landscape* 28 (1984), 27.

52. William Irwin, *The New Niagara: Tourism, Technology and the Landscape of Niagara Falls, 1776–1917* (University Park: Pennsylvania State University Press, 1996), 130. Thomas Hughes makes a similar point when he writes that "foreigners have made the second discovery of America, not nature's nation but technology's nation." See Hughes, *American Genesis: A Century of Invention and Technological Enthusiasm, 1870–1970* (New York: Viking, 1989), 2.

53. Sarah Bernhardt, *Memories of My Life; Being My Personal, Professional, and Social Recollections as Woman and Artist* (1908; New York: Benjamin Blom, 1968), 389.

54. Paul Bourget, *Outre-mer: Impressions of America* (New York: Scribner's, 1895), 29–30.

55. Rapson, *Britons View America*, 39.

56. John Kirkwood, *An Autumn Holiday in the United States and Canada* (Edinburgh: Andrew Elliott, 1886), 63; Joel Cook, *An Eastern Tour at Home* (Philadelphia: David McKay, 1889), 62; and William Glazer, *The Peculiarities of American Cities* (Philadelphia: Hubbard Bros., 1886), 314. For a sampling of the many descriptions of the bridge as an exemplary and wholly positive tourist site, see John Leng, *America in 1876: Pencillings during a Tour in the Centennial Year, With a Chapter on the Aspects of American Life* (Dundee, UK: Dundee Advertiser Office, 1877), 20; W. G. Marshall, *Through America; or, Nine Months in the United States* (London: Sampson, Low, Marston, Searle and Rivington, 1882), 5; and G. W. Steevens, *The Land of the Dollar* (New York: Dodd, Mead and Co., 1897), 13.

57. Donald Pease, "Sublime Politics," in *The American Sublime*, ed. Mary Arensberg (Albany: State University of New York Press, 1986), 47.

58. Steevens, *Land of the Dollar*, 9–13.

59. Hana Wirth-Nesher describes the "totalizing impulse" as an act "whereby a landmark becomes a metonym for an entire civilization and is reduced to one 'meaning.'" Wirth-Nesher, *City Codes: Reading the Modern Urban Novel* (New York: Cambridge University Press, 1996), 116. Marguerite Shaffer, *See America First*, 128, makes a similar point: tourism's "totalizing process could mask the social, political, and cultural conflict with a universal ideal of a cohesive nation."

60. Eliza Margaret Humphreys, *America—Through British Eyes* (London: S. Paul and Co., 1910), 138. The Statue of Liberty was a familiar target. Another visitor, Philip Gibbs, noted that many people felt the statue to be "a figure of mockery" behind which lay an "autocratic oligarchy." See Gibbs, *People of Destiny: Americans as I Saw Them at Home and Abroad* (New York: Harper and Bros., 1920), 139.

61. Douglas Woodruff, *Plato's American Republic* (London: Paul, Trench, Trubner, 1926), 42.

62. James Bryce, *The American Commonwealth* (1883; New York: Anchor, 1956), 354; James Muirhead, *America, the Land of Contrasts* (London: Bodley Head, 1898).

63. Elijah Brown, *The Real America* (London: F. Palmer, 1913), 263; Alexander Francis, *Americans: An Impression* (London: A. Melrose, 1909), 16.

64. Philip Bourne-Jones, *Dollars and Democracy* (New York: Appleton and Co., 1904), 99, 108.

65. "The Spectator," *Outlook* 76 (1904), 306.

66. For an overview of Wells's increasingly complex relationship with the United States, and his ultimate frustration, see Sylvia Strauss, "The American Myth in Britain," *South Atlantic Quarterly* 72 (1973), 66–81. The paradoxical nature of the relationship can be sampled by comparing Wells's political writings with his fiction. Although, as Peter Conrad notes, "the schemes [Wells] devised for global recovery always depended on America," Wells often fictionalized the destruction of important American cities. In *The World Set Free: A Story of Mankind* (1914), Chicago is reduced to a radioactive wasteland, and in *The War in the Air* (1908) and *The Shape of Things to Come* (1933), New York is destroyed entirely. See Peter Conrad, *Imagining America* (New York: Oxford University Press, 1980), 131.

67. H. G. Wells, *The Future in America: A Search after Realities* (1906; London: Granville Press, 1987), 23, 37, 48.

68. Ibid., 29. Although Wells's impressions of America shifted during the course of his journey — for example, he was appalled by the condition and treatment of African Americans — his travelogue ends by stating that, for him, it is this first image, from the bay approaching New York, "which still . . . stands so largely for America." Ibid., 193.

69. Coburn, quoted in Mike Weaver, *Alvin Langdon Coburn, Symbolist Photographer, 1882–1966: Beyond the Craft* (New York: Aperture Foundation, 1986), 37. On Coburn and New York, see Alvin Langdon Coburn, *New York*, foreword by H. G. Wells (London: Duckworth, 1910); Coburn, "The Relationship of Time to Art," *Camera Work* 36 (1911), 73; and Weaver, *Alvin Langdon Coburn*, 37–42.

70. As Alfred Kazin notes, "Wells' sympathies naturally went to the exceptional men, not to the masses." See Kazin, "H. G. Wells, America and 'The Future,'" *American Scholar* 37 (1968), 139. In 1909, Amber Reeves, Coburn's cousin and Wells's mistress, noticed how Coburn's New York photography diminished the ordinary individual and exalted the epic manmade landscape: "All through the London pictures there are implied the men who made and use the things, but in the pictures of New York the sheer brute thing has become so untrammeled and so triumphant that it dwarfs its creator." Reeves, "The Finding of Pictures," *The Lady's Realm* 25 (1909), quoted in Weaver, *Alvin Langdon Coburn*, 42.

71. Wells, *The Future in America*, 29–30.

72. See Nye, *American Technological Sublime*, xiv, and Burke, *Philosophical Enquiry*, 53.

73. Wells, *The Future in America*, 35, 78. These observations confirm R. Lawrence Moore's claim that "European socialist views of the United States . . . were often perversely ill-informed." Moore, *European Socialists and the American Promised Land* (New York: Oxford University Press, 1970), 190.

74. As Gerd Hurm notes, a central theme of Stephen Crane's *Maggie* (1893) is the issue of trolley cars: "Modern commodities, teasingly present in the vicinity of working-class quarters, simply could not be afforded. The ride on a streetcar, for instance, was largely restricted to middle-class employees. . . . The frequent references to streetcars in *Maggie* thus acquire significance beyond their function as motifs of modernity. They also imply upper and middle-class privilege. They represent an unattainable New York." Hurm, *Fragmented Urban Images: The American City in Modern Fiction from Stephen Crane to Thomas Pynchon* (Frankfurt am Main: Peter Lang, 1991), 113.

75. Rapson, *Britons View America*, 46.

76. Wells, *The Future in America*, 187. Less than ten years later, Wells could detect little change in the American economic and social system, and he found himself not predicting but calling for a move to socialism. The disillusionment with the United States

that Wells began to feel increasingly in the 1920s became palpable by the 1930s. Wells saw Franklin Roosevelt as both an exemplary human being and a national anachronism. By the 1940s, Wells's faith in America had evaporated: Americans "have as a mass no philosophy whatever; their education is limited and dismally inadequate, their knowledge of history, if one may call it knowledge, is a training in patriotic bragging and lying. Their religion so far as America goes is a sincere worship of the dollar as a source of power." See the following by Wells: *Social Forces in England and America* (London: Harper and Bros., 1914), 321–82; "An Appeal to the American People," in *The War That Will End War* (New York: Duffield, 1914), 80–88; "The New American People: What Is Wrong with It?" and "Outrages in Defense of Order: The Proposed Murder of Two American Radicals," in *The Way the World Is Going: Guesses and Forecasts of the Years Ahead* (Garden City, NY: Doubleday, Doran, 1929), 248–69; *The New America: The New World* (London: Cresset Press, 1935); and *'42 to '44: A Contemporary Memoir upon Human Behaviour during the Crisis of the World Revolution* (London: Secker and Warburg, 1944), 81.

77. Wells, *The Future in America*, 16.

78. Harold Beaver, "In the Land of Acquisition," *Times Literary Supplement*, September 18, 1987, 1020.

79. Lorca had intended to title the volume "Introduction to Death." See Federico García Lorca, *Poet in New York*, ed. Christopher Mauer, trans. Greg Simon and Steven F. White (1940; Harmondsworth, UK: Penguin, 1990), xvi.

80. Conrad, *Art of the City*, 143; Morgan, "Three Views of Brooklyn Bridge," 57; Betty Jean Craige, *Lorca's Poet in New York: The Fall into Consciousness* (Lexington: University Press of Kentucky, 1977), 3.

81. Federico García Lorca, "Sleepless City (Brooklyn Bridge Nocturne)," in *Poet in New York*, 67–71.

82. Correspondents at the time, Wells and James visited America within a year of each other. Their travelogues were published simultaneously in Britain by Chatman and Hall, and in an identical format. Granville Press employed this same treatment when it reissued the two travelogues in 1987. The two men defended and disputed their views of America. James thought Wells too simple; Wells thought James not simple enough. James also thought that Wells was "too *loud*," but conceded that America was a "yelling country." See *Henry James and H. G. Wells: A Record of Their Friendship, Their Debate on the Art of Fiction, and Their Quarrel*, ed. Leon Edel and Gordon N. Ray (London: Rupert Hart-Davis, 1958), 113–17. Coburn admired James as greatly as he did Wells, photographed him numerous times, and illustrated all twenty-four volumes of the New York edition of James's complete works. Like James, Coburn was also an American expatriate who settled in England. See *Alvin Langdon Coburn, Photographer: An Autobiography*, ed. Helmut and Alison Gernsheim (1966; New York: Dover, 1978), 52–60.

83. Henry James to H. G. Wells, November 8, 1906, in Henry James, *Letters*, vol. 4, *1895–1916*, ed. Leon Edel (Cambridge, MA: Belknap Press, 1984), 421.

84. Henry James, *The American Scene*, ed. John F. Sears (1907; New York: Penguin, 1994), 72.

85. Ibid., 59.

86. Clark, *Civilization*, 334.

87. Ken Burns, interview by Brian Lehrer, *The Brian Lehrer Show*, WNYC-FM, June 16, 2003.

88. The issue of visiting versus staying is exemplified in the literary career of Cuban revolutionary José Martí. Martí was deported from Cuba in 1879 for conspiring against Spanish rule and spent the next three years in Europe, New York, and Venezuela. His early impressions of the United States were extremely positive. He felt the country to be a bastion of freedom and equality, and regarded the Brooklyn Bridge as the living embodiment of liberty. Unable to return to Cuba, Martí settled in New York and worked as a foreign correspondent, an experience that exposed him to the realities of daily life as a foreigner. His formerly admiring opinion of the United States changed to open criticism

by the early 1890s. See José Martí, "Impressions of America (by a very fresh Spaniard)" (1880), "The Brooklyn Bridge" (1883), "Our America" (1891), and "The Truth about the United States" (1894), in *Selected Writings*, 32–36, 140–44, 288–96, and 329–33.

89. Bill Prochnaw, "New Yorkers Throw a Bridge Party," *Washington Post*, May 25, 1983, A2.

90. See http://www.brooklyn-usa.org/poetry19.htm.

91. *Brooklyn Daily Eagle*, May 24, 1883, evening edition, 2.

92. See Lozowick's *New York* (1925), *Brooklyn Bridge* (1930), and *Through Brooklyn Bridge Cables* (1938) in Janet Flint, *The Prints of Louis Lozowick: A Catalogue Raisonné* (New York: Hudson Hills Press, 1982).

93. See McCullough, *The Great Bridge*, 547; Eric Rolfe Greenberg, *The Celebrant* (1983; Lincoln: University of Nebraska Press, 1993), 11; Pete Hamill, "Bridge of Dreams," *New York* 16 (1983), 30–32; Norman Rosten, *Neighborhood Tales* (New York: George Braziller, 1986), 87–90, 117–21; Grace Shulman, "Brooklyn Bridge," *Prairie Schooner* 71 (1997), 76–77; and *Night on Earth*, directed by Jim Jarmusch (Los Angeles: New Line Cinema, 1991).

94. Boime, *Unveiling of the National Icons*, 126. On the ambivalent nature of immigrant responses to the Statue of Liberty, see Rudolph J. Vecoli's important essay, "The Lady and the Huddled Masses: The Statue of Liberty as a Symbol of Immigration," in *Statue of Liberty Revisited*, ed. Dillon and Kotler, 39–70.

95. See Weld, *Brooklyn Is America*, 92–94, and Cecyle S. Neidle, *Great Immigrants* (New York: Twayne, 1973), 23–43.

96. Bercovitch, *American Jeremiad*, 157. On the Jacksonian hero, see John William Ward, *Andrew Jackson: Symbol for an Age* (New York: Oxford University Press, 1953). Neil Harris, *Humbug: The Art of P. T. Barnum* (Boston: Little, Brown, 1973), delineates much about the nature and effects of Jacksonian democracy on the individual success myth. On the self-made man in industrial America, see John G. Cawelti, *Apostles of the Self-Made Man* (1965; Chicago: University of Chicago Press, 1988), 125–65.

97. Alan M. Kraut, *The Huddled Masses: The Immigrant in American Society, 1880–1921* (Wheeling, IL: Harlan Davidson, 1982), 3. The concepts of "new" and "old" immigration have had their revisionists. They were prominently challenged by Maldwyn Allen Jones in *American Immigration* (Chicago: University of Chicago Press, 1960). Jones viewed American immigration as a continuous process wherein only country of origin can be seen to alter. On the other hand, one is forced to wonder how American nativism would have developed if the bulk of American immigrants had not slowly shifted from northern European to southern and eastern European. The religious element is important also. Responses to Catholic immigrants had always been hostile, and the rise in their numbers, along with the surge of Jewish newcomers, brought problems not seen earlier in the century. Jones also fails to account for the increased volume of immigration and the major social and economic changes — especially the rise of the urban environment — that accompanied the period.

98. Oscar Handlin, *The Uprooted: The Epic Story of the Great Migration That Made the American People*, 2nd ed. (Boston: Little, Brown, 1973), 241.

99. See ibid. The separation between old and new immigration has a further dimension. Herbert Gutman reminds us that America itself during the nineteenth century is often described as "old" (implying preindustrial) and "new" (signifying industrial). For Gutman, it is imperative to account for the preindustrial mentality of many working-class Americans when assessing American labor history. Be they native or immigrant, many saw the combination of capital and technology as culturally destructive. For native-born Americans, industrialism threatened the nation's republican values; for those arriving from Europe, it menaced their long-held customs of religion and culture. In addition, both groups feared that the forces of industrialism would make over America into a European country, with autocracy replacing democracy. To transpose the values of "new" America into the mindset of those whose orientation lay in a preindustrial past, warns

Gutman, is to pervert the truths that history may furnish. See Gutman, *Work, Culture, and Society in Industrializing America: Essays in American Working-Class and Social History* (New York: Knopf, 1976), 49–54, 67–73, 79–86.

100. For a precise description of Roebling's passage, see John Roebling, *Diary of My Journey from Muehlhausen in Thuringia via Bremen to the United States of North America in the Year 1831*, trans. Edward Underwood (Trenton: Roebling Press, 1931).

101. Mario Maffi, *Gateway to the Promised Land: Ethnic Cultures on New York's Lower East Side* (Amsterdam: Rodopi, 1994), 15.

102. Jacob Riis, *How the Other Half Lives: Studies among the Tenements of New York*, ed. David Leviathin (1890; Boston: St. Martin's Press, 1996), 114.

103. Ibid., 179–80. This general point is succinctly made by Lloyd Morris: "Many dwellers in the area below Fourteenth Street passed their lives without ever once crossing that barrier, or seeing the wonderful modern city that lay north of it. New York had become a metropolis virtually invisible . . . to millions of its own residents." Morris, *Incredible New York: High Life and Low Life from 1850–1950* (1951; Syracuse: Syracuse University Press, 1996), 276.

104. For organizational purposes, the following analyses of immigrant responses to the Brooklyn Bridge are arranged by theme rather than by chronology.

105. McCullough, "The Great Bridge and the American Imagination," 69.

106. Bourget, *Outre-mer: Impressions of America*, 29–30.

107. Edward King, *Joseph Zalmonah* (1893; Ridgewood, NJ: Gregg Press, 1968), 10.

108. Roth highlights the universality of the experience in the novel's second paragraph: "It was May of the year 1907, the year was destined to bring the greatest number of immigrants to the shores of the United States." Henry Roth, *Call It Sleep* (1934; Harmondsworth, UK: Penguin, 1963), 9.

109. Ibid., 10.

110. Ibid., 10–12.

111. Wirth-Nesher, *City Codes*, 144.

112. Roth, *Call It Sleep*, 409.

113. Ibid., 272. For Emma Lazarus, see "The New Colossus," in *The Faber Book of America*, ed. Christopher Ricks and William L. Vance (London: Faber and Faber, 1992), 43.

114. See, for example, Paul Goldberger, *The City Observed: New York, a Guide to the Architecture of Manhattan* (New York: Vintage Books, 1979), 28.

115. Harold Gorde, "Bridge Is Art for Every Generation," *The Villager*, May 19, 1983, 33; Cleveland Rodgers, *New York Plans for the Future* (New York: Harpers and Bros., 1943), 5. An important question of accuracy is involved here. As Ralph Foster Weld notes, it was the opening of the Williamsburg Bridge (1903)—commonly known as the Jew's Bridge—not the Brooklyn Bridge that signaled the great Jewish and Italian migration to Brooklyn. Consequently, Weld regards this bridge as the more appropriate symbol of exodus. See Weld, *Brooklyn Is America*, 111–13. This point was also noted by folklorist Kay Turner of the Brooklyn Arts Council upon the centennial of the Williamsburg Bridge: "The stately Brooklyn Bridge . . . was not exactly an immigrant pathway because it connected Wall Street and City Hall with the somewhat elite Brooklyn Heights." Quoted in *New York Times*, June 22, 2003, 25.

116. Harry Roskolenko, *The Time That Was Then: The Lower East Side 1900–1924, an Intimate Chronicle* (New York: Dial Press, 1971), 14; Rose Cohen, *Out of the Shadow: A Russian Girlhood on the Lower East Side* (1918; Ithaca: Cornell University Press, 1995), 298; Alfred Kazin, *A Walker in the City* (1951; New York: Harcourt Brace Jovanovich, 1979), 52–53, 105–8, 172; and Boris Todrin, *Out of These Roots: A Novel of Growing Up in America* (1944; New York: Popular Books, 1972), 67, 232, 345.

117. Sidney H. Bremer, *Urban Intersections: Meetings of Life and Literature in United States Cities* (Urbana: University of Illinois Press, 1992), 1–18. See also Eugene Arden, "The Evil City in American Fiction," *New York History* 35 (1954), 259–79.

118. As Luc Sante and John Higham note, the East River shore beneath the Brooklyn Bridge was a particularly hostile environment, patrolled by competing Irish and German gangs. See Sante, *Low Life: Lures and Snares of Old New York* (New York: Farrar, Straus, Giroux, 1991), 207, 221; Higham, *Send These to Me: Immigrants in Urban America*, rev. ed. (Baltimore: Johns Hopkins University Press, 1984), 114. Memorably, in Roth's *Call It Sleep*, 244–49, an Irish gang at the East River shore attacks David Schearl.

119. See Irwin, *New Niagara*, 36–37.

120. Thomas W. Knox, *Underground; or, Life Below the Surface* (Hartford, CT: J. B. Burr Publishing, 1875), 416–25.

121. *Scientific American*, July 9, 1870, 342.

122. Farrington, *Concise Description of the East River Bridge*, 27–28.

123. McCullough, "The Great Bridge and the American Imagination," 80. Al Smith, an Irish immigrant who became governor of New York, grew up in the shadows of the bridge. In adulthood he would often boast that "the bridge and I grew up together." Yet the bridge's construction was a source of some discomfort for his family. Smith's mother lamented that many Irish immigrants were disabled or killed during construction, and often wondered if this human cost was worth the construction: "perhaps if they had known . . . they never would have built it." Smith himself was traumatized by the Memorial Day panic, when twelve people were trampled to death: "That was my first view of a great calamity. I did not sleep for nights." See Mathew and Hannah Josephson, *Al Smith: Hero of the Cities* (London: Thames and Hudson, 1969), 20–25.

124. The relationship between Harris's novel and the events of his own life are interesting, yet ultimately clouded. Harris maintained that he worked in the caissons, and the claim recurs in his autobiography, *My Life and Loves* (1922). Unfortunately, Harris was an inveterate liar. We do know that he arrived in New York as a penniless immigrant during the period when the caissons were sunk, and his descriptions of the work are relatively accurate. John Dos Passos and, more recently, James Simmons have concluded that Harris's descriptions of the experience are genuine. See John Dos Passos, "Frank Harris' *The Bomb*: An Introduction," in *The Bomb*, by Frank Harris (1909; Chicago: University of Chicago Press, 1963), v–xx, and James C. Simmons, *Star-Spangled Eden: Nineteenth Century America Through the Eyes of Dickens, Wilde, Frances Trollope, Frank Harris, and Other British Travelers* (New York: Carroll and Graf, 2000), 259–88.

125. Although the novel has failed to achieve any lasting critical attention, *The Bomb* was warmly received by such contemporary literary and political figures as Arnold Bennett, Emma Goldman, and George Bernard Shaw. See David M. Fine, *The City, the Immigrant and American Fiction, 1880–1920* (Metuchen, NJ: Scarecrow Press, 1977), 91. Rudolph Schnaubelt was a real-life figure in the Haymarket affair and was named as the bomb thrower in the indictments brought afterward. He fled the country before capture, and mystery has surrounded his fate ever since. See Carl Smith, *Urban Disorder and the Shape of Belief: The Great Chicago Fire, the Haymarket Bomb, and the Model Town of Pullman* (Chicago: University of Chicago Press, 1995), 121–22.

126. As Nelson Graburn notes, "a major characteristic of our conception of tourism is that it is *not* work." See Graburn, "Tourism: The Sacred Journey," in *Hosts and Guests: The Anthropology of Tourism*, ed. Valene L. Smith, 2nd ed. (Philadelphia: University of Pennsylvania Press, 1989), 22. For Jakle, *The Tourist*, 30–31, tourist encounters with work can promote understanding and the appreciation of social and economic difference, yet the significance of the encounter ultimately depends on the depth of the desire to identify. Knox's observations are compromised by his reluctance to see past the differences between himself and manual workers.

127. Harris, *The Bomb*, 32–35.

128. There is some accuracy in this opinion. Similar problems occurred during the construction of the Eads Bridge at St. Louis (completed 1874). The supervising engineers, though, were feuding, and information on the problems of working in compressed

air was not shared. Casualties could have been greatly reduced if worker safety had been prioritized over professional rivalry. See Henry Petroski, *Engineers of Dreams: Great Bridge Builders and the Spanning of America* (New York: Vintage, 1995), 50–51.

129. John Higham, *Strangers in the Land: Patterns of American Nativism, 1860–1925*, 2nd ed. (New Brunswick: Rutgers University Press, 1988), 54.

130. Although neither Sacco nor Vanzetti is mentioned by name, Romagna is clearly meant to function as a composite. The events surrounding Romagna's trial mirror those of the real-life trial.

131. Maxwell Anderson, *Winterset* (New York: Dramatists Play Service, 1935), 20. Mio's derogatory reference to the Lost Generation provides an interesting commentary on the culture of 1920s America. For Mio, it is not the disaffected American writer/intellectual but the immigrant who is lost, both through internal prejudice and a restrictive immigration policy. A similar judgment is found in Reznikoff's *By the Waters of Manhattan*, when Russian-Jewish immigrant Sarah Yetta declares that "we are a lost generation" (p. 146).

132. *Winterset*, 5, 20. As Christopher Bigsby notes, "the set [of Anderson's drama] is plainly offered as a correlative to the action rather than simply its context." See Bigsby, *A Critical Introduction to Twentieth-Century Drama*, vol. 1, *1900–1940* (New York: Cambridge University Press, 1982), 150. Visiting New York in 1893, Giuseppe Giacosa, a compatriot of Sacco and Vanzetti and now chiefly remembered as the co-writer of the librettos for Giacomo Puccini's *La Bohème, Tosca,* and *Madame Butterfly,* noted the dichotomy between the riverside neighborhoods and the city as seen from the bridge. Overlooking the harbor, the city seemed "so full of life" and "so strongly strikes the imagination and mind." Yet "all the neighborhoods by the sea seem in incurable decay . . . dark, filthy." Quoted in Pachter and Stevenson Wein, eds., *Abroad in America*, 250.

133. *Winterset*, 5.

134. Ibid., 86–87.

135. Ibid., 9.

136. Ibid., 21–22.

137. Ibid., 49.

138. Ibid., 55.

139. Ibid.

140. Ibid., 68.

141. Susan A. Seim, quoted in *The Villager*, May 19, 1983, Brooklyn Bridge Birthday Special, 23.

142. See Roberta Strauss Feuerlicht, *Justice Crucified: The Story of Sacco and Vanzetti* (New York: McGraw-Hill, 1977).

143. Barbara Haskell, *Joseph Stella* (New York: Harry Abrams, 1994), 97. This opinion is also found in Helen Cooper, "Stella's *Miners*," *Yale University Art Gallery Bulletin* 35 (1975), 8; Wanda M. Corn, "In Detail: Joseph Stella and *New York Interpreted*," *Portfolio* 4 (1982), 40–45; Grace Glueck, *New York: The Painted City* (Salt Lake City: Gibbs-Smith Books, 1992), 82; Stephen May, "Joseph Stella's Pittsburgh," *Carnegie Magazine* 9 (1991), 33; Wieland Schmied, "Precisionist View and American Scene: The 1920s," in *American Art in the Twentieth Century: Painting and Sculpture, 1913–1993*, ed. Christos M. Joachimides and Norman Rosenthal (London: Prestel/Royal Academy of Arts, 1993), 50–52; and Ellen M. Snyder-Grenier, "Joseph Stella, *The Brooklyn Bridge* (1939)," in *Frames of Reference: Looking at American Art, 1900–1950*, ed. Beth Venn and Adam D. Weinberg (Berkeley: University of California Press/Whitney Museum of American Art, 1999), 114–18. Haskell's catalog reproduces all of the Stella paintings referred to here.

144. Thomas J. Ferraro, "'My Way' in 'Our America': Art, Ethnicity, Profession," *American Literary History* 12 (Fall 2000), 503.

145. Both the skull and the traffic light motifs are significantly more prominent in Stella's later *Old Brooklyn Bridge* (1940).

146. See Joseph Stella, "Americans in the Rough: Character Studies at Ellis Island," *Outlook* 81 (1905), 967–73, and Ernest Poole, *The Voice of the Street* (New York: A. S. Barnes, 1906), 24, 56, 92, 180, 264.

147. Paul Kellogg, "Monongah," *Charities and the Commons* 19 (1908), 1314.

148. See Antonio Stella, *Some Aspects of Italian Immigration to the United States* (New York: G. P. Putnam's Sons, 1924).

149. See Lincoln Steffens, *The Shame of the Cities* (1904; New York: Hill and Wang, 1957), 101. Steffens revised this popular phrase for the city's political machine; more accurately, Pittsburgh was "hell with the lid on." Stella's autobiographical essay, "Notes on Stella," is quoted in Irma B. Jaffe, *Joseph Stella* (1970; New York: Fordham University Press, 1988), 20.

150. "Notes on Stella," quoted in Jaffe, *Joseph Stella*, 20.

151. Joseph Stella, "Interview with Bruno Barilli" (1929), in Haskell, *Joseph Stella*, 208.

152. Joseph Stella, "New York" (n.d.), reprinted in Haskell, *Joseph Stella*, 219.

153. The essay is reprinted in Haskell, *Joseph Stella*, 206–7.

154. Although written and published in 1928, "Brooklyn Bridge (a page of my life)" is set during the late 1910s.

155. Where Stella's prose evocations of America often express a profound disappointment, his writings about his homeland are universally positive. See the undated essays "Autobiography: Muro Lucano," "My Birthplace," "Homeland," and "My Birthplace, IV," reprinted in Haskell, *Joseph Stella*, 216–18.

156. Joseph Stella, "Pittsburgh Notes" (ca. 1921–1925), reprinted in Haskell, *Joseph Stella*, 204.

157. Ferraro, "'My Way' in 'Our America,'" 502.

158. Stella would paint the bridge three more times in his later career: *Bridge* (1936), *Brooklyn Bridge: Variation on an Old Theme* (1939), and *Old Brooklyn Bridge* (1940). As their titles indicate, these painting represented nothing new. In effect, they are unabashed copies of his earlier popular work, perhaps undertaken with financial considerations in mind. His later folk classicism was by no means as popular with collectors as his previous vanguard modernism. Stella's recently discovered collages are also important in tracing his opinions about the city. In *Macchina Naturale #4* (1923) and *Macchina Naturale #18* (1938), Stella literally defaced his own New York works, pasting random newsprint and advertising copy over reproductions of his famous paintings. In *Macchina Naturale #28* (1938), he produced the same effect with an anonymous image of the Brooklyn Bridge.

159. The bridge as a prison is also a feature of Stella's more popular and — on the surface — more visually celebratory *The Bridge (Brooklyn Bridge)* (1922). See Robert J. Saunders and Ernest Goldstein, *Joseph Stella: The Brooklyn Bridge* (Champaign, IL: Garrard Publishing, 1984), 36–38.

160. Anthony W. Lee, introduction to *Yun Gee: Poetry, Writings, Art, Memories*, ed. Anthony W. Lee (Seattle: University of Washington Press, 2003), 6. The facts of Gee's life have long been shrouded in myth and clouded by error, a problem not helped by Gee's own — often deliberately inaccurate — self-promotion. Particularly questionable are two early studies: Diana Cochrane, "Yun Gee: Forgotten Synchronist Painter," *American Artist* 38 (1974), 46–51, 89–91, and Judith Tannenbaum, "Yun Gee: A Rediscovery," *Arts Magazine* 54 (1980), 164–67. My understanding of Yun Gee's life owes a great deal to the generosity and knowledge of Li-lan and Tunghsiao Chou.

161. Higham, *Strangers in the Land*, 316–24.

162. See Anthony W. Lee, "Another View of Chinatown: Yun Gee and the Chinese Revolutionary Artists' Club," in *Reclaiming San Francisco: History, Politics, Culture*, ed. James Brook, Chris Carlsson, and Nancy J. Peters (San Francisco: City Lights Books, 1998), 169.

163. Gee, quoted in Li Lundin, David Teh-Yu Wang, and Jane C. Ju, *The Art of Yun*

Gee (Taipei: Taipei Fine Art Museum, 1992), 24. Also see Anthony W. Lee, "Revolution in Art and Life," in *Yun Gee*, ed. Lee, 133.

164. See Yun Gee, "Sensation" (1935), in *Yun Gee*, ed. Lee, 65.

165. Yun Gee, "Yun Gee Speaks His Mind" (1954) and "Letter to Paul Bird" (1951), in ibid., 184, 187–88.

166. Gee, "Yun Gee Speaks His Mind," 188.

167. Lewis Kachur, "The Bridge as Icon," in *Great East River Bridge*, 165.

168. See Allen Guttmann, *From Ritual to Record: The Nature of Modern Sports* (New York: Columbia University Press, 1978), esp. 15–56.

169. In *Here's New York* (1943), painted eleven years later, Gee returned to the format of *Wheels*. This later canvas is almost identical to *Wheels*: the depiction of the bridge is more literal, but the skyline, perspective, and composition are the same. There is a crucial difference, however. Instead of menacing polo players, the foreground is inhabited by a blond Caucasian woman, her well-dressed husband, and the family dog. As they glance over their shoulders toward the artist, they wave, smile, and prepare to enter the city, leaving the artist behind. Compared with *Wheels*, the racial symbolism is obvious: New York belongs to these people, not Gee's. See Lundin, Wang, and Ju, *Art of Yun Gee*, 123.

170. Lee, "Introduction," in *Yun Gee*, ed. Lee, 8.

171. Tannenbaum, "Yun Gee," 166.

172. Neither Joyce Brodsky nor David Teh-yu Wang reads this figure as a suicide, although neither finds the painting menacing. Yet if one grants that the milieu of *Wheels* is sinister and foreboding, and that the polo players are menacing, one must also accept that the figure is jumping, not flying. See Joyce Brodsky, *The Paintings of Yun Gee* (Hartford, CT: William Benton Museum of Art, 1979), 29, and David Teh-yu Wang, "The Art of Yun Gee before 1936," in Lundin, Wang, and Ju, *Art of Yun Gee*, 28.

173. John Baker, *O. Louis Guglielmi: A Retrospective Exhibition* (New Brunswick: Rutgers University Art Gallery, 1980), 11–13. Baker's catalog reproduces all of Guglielmi's works referred to here. Closely related to *Wedding in South Street*, Guglielmi's *The Widow* (1938) pictures a disconsolate mourner — all in black — standing in front of the Brooklyn Bridge.

174. Quoted in ibid., 20.

175. Ibid.

176. Guglielmi lived until 1956. His thoughts on the military assistance agreement extended by the United States to the Spanish dictator Franco in 1953 have unfortunately gone unrecorded.

177. Baker, *Guglielmi*, 20.

178. Joyce Carol Oates, "The Calendar's New Clothes," *New York Times*, December 30, 1999, A27.

179. Max Weber, "On the Brooklyn Bridge," in *Max Weber: The Cubist Decade, 1910–1920* (Atlanta: High Museum of Art, 1991), 96.

180. Waldo Frank, *Our America* (New York: Boni and Liveright, 1919), 10.

Chapter 3
The View of the Bridge: Perspective, Context, and the Urban Observer

1. Quoted in Djuna Barnes, "Veterans in Harness," in *Djuna Barnes's New York*, ed. Alyce Barry (London: Virago, 1990), 78.

2. See Max Page, *The Creative Destruction of Manhattan, 1900–1940* (Chicago: University of Chicago Press, 1999). Also see David M. Scobey, *Empire City: The Making and Meaning of the New York City Landscape* (Philadelphia: Temple University Press, 2002), which describes a similar phenomenon in the nineteenth century.

3. See Mona Domosh, *Invented Cities: The Creation of Landscape in Nineteenth-Century New York and Boston* (New Haven: Yale University Press, 1996), 76; Jackson, ed., *Encyclopedia of New York City*, 216–18, 660, 923; and Moses Rischin, *The Promised City:*

New York's Jews, 1870–1914 (1962; Cambridge, MA: Harvard University Press, 1977), 258, 271.

4. The extent to which photographers documented New York City in the late nineteenth century can be sampled in Frederick S. Lightfoot, ed., *Nineteenth-Century New York in Rare Photographic Views* (New York: Dover, 1981); Mary Black, *Old New York in Early Photographs, 1853–1901,* 2nd rev. ed. (New York: Dover, 1976); and Roger Whitehouse, *New York: Sunshine and Shadow, a Photographic Record of the City and Its People from 1850–1915* (New York: Harper and Row, 1974). Strangely, given the extent to which New York was photographed in the nineteenth century, no daguerreotypes of city scenes are known to exist.

5. See Eric Sandweiss, "Claiming the Urban Landscape: The Improbable Rise of an Inevitable City," in *Eadweard Muybridge and the Photographic Panorama of San Francisco, 1850–1880,* by David Harris and Eric Sandweiss (Cambridge, MA: MIT Press, 1993), 16. On the relationship between new urban literature and the physical transformation of the city in the mid- to late nineteenth century, see Gunther Barth, *City People: The Rise of Modern City Culture in Nineteenth-Century America* (New York: Oxford University Press, 1980), 7–27, 58–109; Hans Bergmann, *God in the Street: New York Writing from the Penny Press to Melville* (Philadelphia: Temple University Press, 1995); and Trachtenberg, *Incorporation of America,* 101–39.

6. See Green, *Complete History of the New York and Brooklyn Bridge,* 4–5; Farrington, *Concise Description of the East River Bridge,* 36; and *New York Herald,* August 26, 1876, 1.

7. *Brooklyn Union,* January 18, 1877, 2.

8. E. F. Farrington, quoted in McCullough, *The Great Bridge,* 451.

9. For Beal, see John G. Morris, "A Century Old, the Wonderful Brooklyn Bridge," *National Geographic* 163 (1983), 567–68.

10. See John W. Reps, *Views and Viewmakers of Urban America* (Columbia: University of Missouri Press, 1984).

11. For an excellent source of photographs documenting the bridge construction, see Mary J. Shapiro, *A Picture History of the Brooklyn Bridge, with 167 Prints and Photographs* (New York: Dover, 1983).

12. Peter B. Hales, *Silver Cities: The Photography of American Urbanization, 1839–1915* (Philadelphia: Temple University Press, 1984), 3. Photography's innate ability to present "empirical truth" was championed from its inception. In his first public lecture on the daguerreotype in 1840, Samuel Morse claimed that daguerreotypes were not "copies" of nature but "portions." See Robert A. Sobieszek and Odette M. Appel, *The Daguerreotypes of Southworth and Hawes* (1976; New York: Dover, 1980), ix. The Reverend H. J. Morton stated the matter more directly a generation later: "[The camera] has an eye that cannot be deceived, and a fidelity that cannot be corrupted." Morton, "Photography as Authority," *Philadelphia Photographer* 1 (1864), 180–81.

13. Hales, *Silver Cities,* 64–65, 67–130. The origins of "grand style" as an artistic term — specifically in painting — can be traced to Sir Joshua Reynolds, who made it a central tenet of his *Seven Discourses on Art* (1797). For Reynolds, the grand style was a rhetorical visual strategy. It was a means through which to idealize the imperfect; it lent greatness and nobility — "elevation and dignity" — to its subjects, whether they possessed these traits or not. See Joshua Reynolds, *Discourses,* ed. Pat Rogers (Harmondsworth, UK: Penguin, 1992), 40–56. Also see Ann Uhry Abrams, *The Valiant Hero: Benjamin West and Grand-Style History Painting* (Washington, DC: Smithsonian Institution Press, 1985), for a discussion of the grand style in an American context.

14. Hales, *Silver Cities,* 83.

15. See, for example, the aquatint engraving by J. W. Hill and Henry Papprill, *New York from the Steeple of St. Paul's Church, Looking East, South, and West* (1849), and Charles Bachman's lithograph *New York* (1849). David Harris notes a similar propensity

to prioritize the "business end" of San Francisco in mid- to late-nineteenth-century panoramas of San Francisco. See David Harris, "Eadweard Muybridge and the Photographic Panorama of San Francisco, 1850–1880," in *Eadweard Muybridge*, by Harris and Sandweiss, 64.

16. See *Panoramic Maps of Cities in the United States and Canada*, 2nd ed. (Washington, DC: Library of Congress, 1984).

17. John Kouwenhoven, *The Columbia Historical Portrait of New York: An Essay in Graphic History in Honor of the Tricentennial of New York City and the Bicentennial of Columbia University* (New York: Doubleday, 1953), 332. The phrase is important in considering the development of bird's-eye panoramas. Used to promote real estate development, the "expansive optimism" of bird's-eye views occasionally led to charges of "lithographic fiction" and "lithographed mendacity." See John W. Reps, *Cities on Stone: Nineteenth Century Lithograph Images of the Urban West* (Fort Worth, TX: Amon Carter Musuem, 1976), 14, and Reps, *Views and Viewmakers*, 69. Whereas Reps believes bird's-eye views to be an accurate reflection of urban space, Peter C. Marzio and Milton Kaplan find these images to contain "idealized settings and gross exaggerations." See Marzio and Kaplan, "Lithographs as Historical Documents," *Antiques* 102 (1972), 674. On the ideological and cultural work of New York panoramas, especially their use as evidence of "the success of the mercantile economy," see Hans Bergmann, "Panoramas of New York, 1845–1960," *Prospects* 10 (1985), 119–37.

18. See James D. McCabe Jr., *Lights and Shadows of New York Life; or, The Sights and Sensations of the Great City* (1872; New York: Farrar, Straus and Giroux, 1970); *McCoy's Centennial Illustrated*; L. P. Brockett, *Handbook of the United States, and Guide to Emigration* (New York: Gaylord Watson, 1879); and Gale Research, *Currier and Ives: A Catalogue Raisonné*, with introduction by Bernard F. Reilly (Detroit: Gale Research, 1983).

19. Merritt Roe Smith, "Technological Determinism in American Culture," in *Does Technology Drive History? The Dilemma of Technological Determinism*, ed. Merritt Roe Smith and Leo Marx (Cambridge, MA: MIT Press, 1994), 10.

20. At the time of the commission, Gast's offices were on Fulton Street in Brooklyn, and Crofutt's were on Nassau in Manhattan. Crofutt would have passed the bridge construction site when visiting Gast, and Gast himself would have been able to see it from his office. In short, the creation of the Brooklyn Bridge would have seemed the most obvious aspect of American progress for both patron and painter. See J. Valerie Fifer, *American Progress: The Growth of the Transport, Tourist, and Information Industries in the Nineteenth-Century West, Seen Through the Life and Times of George A. Crofutt, Pioneer and Publicist of the Transcontinental Age* (Chester, CT: Globe Pequot Press, 1988), 202.

21. This idea is also found in paintings by Emile Renouf, *View of the Brooklyn Bridge* (1889), William Sonntag, *Brooklyn Bridge* (1895), and Charles Graham, *The Skyline of New York* (1896), among others. Kachur, "The Bridge as Icon," 155, notes in regard to Sonntag: "although Manhattan was hardly frontier America, the grandeur of the image suggests that [he] saw the Bridge as the apotheosis of America's westward march." It must be added that the bridge seems to lead straight over Manhattan and into a brilliant horizon in the West. In literature, Benjamin R. C. Low has also used the bridge in conjunction with westward expansion: "That blue . . . track-way to the West. / In steel and stone and windows of desire, / Is manifest." See Low, *Brooklyn Bridge* (New York: Harbor Press, 1933), 4.

22. See Hales, *Silver Cities*, 92, and William R. Taylor, *In Pursuit of Gotham: Culture and Commerce in New York* (New York: Oxford University Press, 1992), 9.

23. The state of the photographic technology available to Beal must be borne in mind. At this time, both film and shutter speeds were insufficiently developed to capture motion. Yet these limitations fail to account for the continuation of the static image of the city. As I will later stress, Walker Evans's photographs of the Brooklyn Bridge, for example, are as depopulated, silent, and still as Beal's.

24. John H. Wiedeman, *Why We Need Our Brooklyn Bridges: Address Delivered at the National Meeting of the Newcomen Society of the United States* (New York: Newcomen Society, 1983), 13.

25. Albert Boime, *The Magisterial Gaze: Manifest Destiny and American Landscape Painting c. 1830–1865* (Washington, DC: Smithsonian Institution Press, 1991), 1–23. The elevated viewpoint Boime describes is reconfigured and projected onto the bridge in a number of poems. For example, Charles D. Roberts, "Brooklyn Bridge," *Atlantic Monthly* 83 (1899), 839, saw the bridge as "kin to the cataract." For Edna Dean Proctor, it represented a "granite cliff on either shore." Proctor, "Brooklyn Bridge (May 24, 1883)," in *Poems of American History*, ed. Burton Egbert Stevenson (New York: Houghton, 1922), 593.

26. Charles Carroll, "Up Among the Spiders; or, How the Great Bridge Is Built," *Appletons' Journal* 4 (1878), 1–2. Ironically, in light of the subsequent wire scandal, Carroll goes on to describe the wire used on the bridge in terms more redolent of social class than engineering quality. Having inspected the wire, he pronounces it not "plebeian," but entirely "aristocratic."

27. Ibid., 7–8.

28. Ibid., 11. At the opening, the bridge's capacity to remove the city's ugly "details" was much commented upon. The *New York Sun*, May 24, 1883, 3, found that the city, viewed from the bridge, became wonderfully "orderly." For the *New York Commercial Advertiser*, May 24, 1883, 2, the view from the bridge made New York's "beauties apparent"; at the same time, the "squalor and dirt are thankfully hidden."

29. See *Great East River Bridge*, 91.

30. This image is reprinted in Paul Goldberger, *The Skyscraper* (New York: Knopf, 1981), 15.

31. See *New York Journal*, May 3, 1896, and Montgomery Schuyler, "The Sky-line of New York, 1881–1897," *Harper's Weekly*, March 20, 1897, 295.

32. See *King's Views of New York, 1915*, in *King's Views of New York, 1896–1915 and Brooklyn 1905*, ed. Moses King (New York: Arno, 1980), 4.

33. Quoted in Merrill Schleier, *The Skyscraper in American Art, 1890–1931* (New York: Da Capo, 1986), 104.

34. Domosh, *Invented Cities*, 2.

35. Schuyler, "Sky-line of New York," 295.

36. Carol Willis, *Form Follows Finance: Skyscrapers and Skylines in New York and Chicago* (Princeton: Princeton Architectural Press, 1995), 24, 153. Thomas van Leeuwen makes a similar point in *The Skyward Trend of Thought: The Metaphysics of the American Skyscraper* (Cambridge, MA: MIT Press, 1986), 9: "skywardness is not *caused* by business and traffic, but it *is* business and traffic."

37. Sheldon Cheney, *The New World Architecture* (New York: Tudor, 1930), 10.

38. Sam Bass Warner Jr., "The Management of Multiple Urban Images," in *The Pursuit of Urban History*, ed. Derek Frasler and Anthony Sutcliffe (London: Edward Arnold, 1983), 393.

39. The propensity to prioritize aesthetics over context is found in John Kouwenhoven's writing. The skyline, he says, "is the product of insane politics, greed, competitive ostentation, megalomania, the worship of false gods. Its by-products, in turn, are traffic jams, bad ventilation, noise, and all the other ills that metropolitan flesh is heir to." Yet when analyzing the skyline, he states that "it may be helpful to consider the skyline as we might consider a lyric poem." See Kouwenhoven, "What's 'American' about America?" in *The Beer Can by the Highway: Essays on What's American about America* (1961; Baltimore: Johns Hopkins University Press, 1988), 43. On the aestheticization of the urban cityscape, see Warner, "Management of Multiple Urban Images," 383–94; Alan Trachtenberg, "Image and Ideology: New York in the Photographer's Eye," *Journal of Urban History* 10 (1984), 453–64; and Taylor, *In Pursuit of Gotham*, 23–34. Of course, not

all of the city's visual artists were complicit in this process. For opposition to the tall building and the skyline, see Schleier, *Skyscraper in American Art*, 1–13.

40. Edward Abrahams, *The Lyrical Left: Randolph Bourne, Alfred Stieglitz, and the Origins of Cultural Radicalism in America* (Charlottesville: University Press of Virginia, 1986), 93–204.

41. See Taylor, *In Pursuit of Gotham*, 9; Maren Stange, *Symbols of Ideal Life: Social Documentary Photography in America, 1890–1950* (New York: Cambridge University Press, 1989); and Alan Trachtenberg, *Reading American Photographs: Images as History, Mathew Brady to Walker Evans* (New York: Hill and Wang, 1989), 164–230.

42. As regards the bridge, the same reading can be applied to Leon Kroll's painting *The Bridge* (1910–1911). See Schleier, *Skyscraper in American Art*, 141.

43. See Hewitt, *Address*, 3–9.

44. Trachtenberg, "Image and Ideology," 454.

45. Boime, *Magisterial Gaze*, 20–22.

46. Lincoln Steffens, "The Modern Business Building," *Scribner's Magazine* 22 (1897), 37.

47. See Cadman's speech in Edwin A. Cochran, ed., *The Cathedral of Commerce* (New York: Woolworth Building, 1916), no pagination.

48. Hales, *Silver Cities*, 100–101.

49. For examples, see Shapiro, *Picture History of Brooklyn Bridge*, 108–19, and *Great East River Bridge*, 66–71.

50. See *Great East River Bridge*, 68.

51. See ibid., 159. Louis Lozowick's lithograph *Brooklyn Bridge* (1930) continues this theme.

52. For Bonnie Yochelson, Struss's "awe-inspiring" view through the cables of the bridge and toward the Singer Building is directly related to Stieglitz's viewpoint in "The City of Ambition." See Yochelson, "Karl Struss' New York," in *New York to Hollywood: The Photography of Karl Struss*, by Barbara McCandless, Bonnie Yochelson and Richard Koszarski (Albuquerque: University of New Mexico Press, 1995), 104. Perhaps equally important thematically and stylistically is Struss's "Brooklyn Bridge from Ferry Slip, Late Afternoon" (1912). For Hoppé, see *Hundred Thousand Exposures: The Success of a Photographer* (New York: Focal Press, 1945), 135; for Reiner, Blumenschein, and a selection of anonymous prints, see *Shared Perspectives: The Printmaker and Photographer in New York, 1900–1950* (New York: Museum of the City of New York, 1993), 48–49; for Feininger, see *New York in the Forties* (New York: Dover, 1978), 16–17; for Nevinson, see John Sweetman, *The Artist and the Bridge, 1700–1920* (Aldershot, UK: Ashgate, 1999), 104. Rudolph Simmon's photographs of the bridge are held by the Museum of the City of New York.

53. On the conventions employed by Hassam in *Rainy Day, Boston* (1885) and *Une Averse, Rue Bonaparte* (1887), and on his links to the Ashcan School, see Elizabeth Broun, "Childe Hassam's America," *American Art* 133 (1999), 34–38. For Hassam's paintings of the bridge and of New York generally, see Ilene Susan Fort, *Childe Hassam's New York* (San Francisco: Pomegranate, 1993).

54. Childe Hassam, "New York the Beauty City," *New York Sun*, February 23, 1913, 16.

55. Until his move to East Hampton in 1919 and his subsequent retreat into "a mythologized postcard America," Hassam remained assiduously devoted to street culture. Broun, "Childe Hassam's America," 55.

56. For Strauss, see *Great East River Bridge*, 108; for Weegee, see *Naked City* (1945; New York: Da Capo, 1973), 2–3; for Feininger, see *New York in the Forties*, 28–30. Also see the many such images published by Moses King in his popular handbooks, e.g., King, ed., *King's Views of New York*.

57. Warner, "Management of Multiple Urban Images," 393. Trachtenberg, "Image

and Ideology," 463, makes the same point when he notes that the task of New York photography in the early twentieth century was "to transform the formless city, with its implied social and political threats, into aesthetic experience, into pictures that can then be consumed as signs of a reality from which threat has been utterly removed."

58. In his 1925 lithograph *New York*, Louis Lozowick presents skyscrapers, "el" tracks, and the Brooklyn Bridge in an effort to capture the city's totality. This image of the city as technology, transportation, and business is entirely depopulated. Even the windows of the many "el" trains are empty. For similar examples, see Edward Redfield's painting *Brooklyn Bridge at Night* (1909), in William H. Gerdts, *Impressionist New York* (New York: Abbeville Press, 1994), 172; Rudolph Ruzicka's engraving *Brooklyn Bridge* (1915) and Glenn O. Coleman's painting *Bridge Tower* (1929), in *Great East River Bridge*, 111, 155.

59. *Brooklyn Daily Eagle*, May 21, 1883, 2.

60. This painting is part of the Robert R. Preato Collection of the Museum of the City of New York. See http://www.mcny.org/Collections/paint/Painting/pttcat66.htm.

61. Jakle, *The Tourist*, 266.

62. Hales, *Silver Cities*, 124.

63. See Jesse Lynch Williams, *New York Sketches* (New York: Scribner's, 1902), 12; Helen Henderson, *A Loiterer in New York: Discoveries Made by a Rambler Through Obvious Yet Unsought Highways and Byways* (New York: George H. Doran, 1917), 15–19; Robert Shackleton, *The Book of New York* (Philadelphia: Penn Publishing, 1917), 67–69; and Peter Marcus, *New York: The Nation's Metropolis* (New York: Brentano's, 1921), 22, 28, 43.

64. Marcel Duchamp, "A Complete Reversal of Art Opinions," *Arts and Decoration* 5 (1915), 428.

65. Wells, *The Future in America*, 29–30; "Iron Mirgorod—Esenin's Impressions of America," 70.

66. Charles Reznikoff, *Rhythms* (New York: Charles Reznikoff, 1918), 15.

67. Marrion Wilcox, "North and South from the Brooklyn Bridge," *Harper's New Monthly Magazine* 89 (1894), 463.

68. Don Marquis, "The Almost Perfect State," in *Great Essays of All Nations: Two Hundred and Twenty-Nine Essays from all Periods and Countries*, ed. F. H. Pritchard (London: George G. Harrap, 1929), 986–87. Geoffrey Moorhouse's *Imperial City* illustrates the longevity of this trope. Moorhouse begins his book with an exuberant sixteen-page description of the walk across the bridge. Although he reacts with great aversion to the area surrounding the bridge, his mood becomes increasingly rapturous as he begins to tread the boards of the central promenade and comes in sight of the skyline. See Moorhouse, *Imperial City: The Rise and Rise of New York* (London: Hodder and Stoughton, 1988), 1–16.

69. Don Marquis, "From the Bridge," in *Dreams and Dust* (New York: Harpers and Bros., 1915), 134–35.

70. Don Marquis, "The Towers of Manhattan," in *The Book of New York Verse*, ed. Hamilton Fish Armstrong (New York: Putnam, 1917), 260–63. Marquis's desire to decontextualize, aestheticize, and romanticize the bridge is brought into sharp relief if we recall Joseph Zalmonah's mid-bridge lament: "a welcome to slavery and sorrow! A welcome to the living death." See King, *Joseph Zalmonah*, 10.

71. Richard Le Gallienne, "Brooklyn Bridge at Dawn," with photographs by Alvin Langdon Coburn, *Metropolitan Magazine* 23 (1905), 526–27.

72. Kevin Lynch, *The Image of the City* (Cambridge, MA: MIT Press, 1960), 1.

73. Trachtenberg, *Brooklyn Bridge*, 192.

74. See ibid., 181, 183–84, and Judith Keller, *Walker Evans: The Getty Museum Collection* (London: Thames and Hudson, 1995), 16–19.

75. Nye, *American Technological Sublime*, 87.

76. The relationship between the bridge and the commercial life of the city forms an important part of Evans's views from beneath the bridge. As Mick Gidley points out,

Evans's depiction of the bridge from below "transform[s] a structure that was actually horizontal into a near-vertical one." Although Gidley is discussing photography's propensity for abstraction, it should be noted that this vertical perspective places the bridge in a symbolic relationship with the city's tall buildings. Visually, the bridge is more skyscraper than public utility. See Gidley, "Hoppé's Romantic America," *Studies in Visual Communication* 11 (1985), 29.

77. It is useful to compare Evans's photographs from beneath the bridge with Berenice Abbott's "Brooklyn Bridge, with Pier 21" (1937). Although her perspective is somewhat different, Abbott's foregrounding of working tools provides a counterpoint to the absence of local culture in Evans. See Abbott, *New York in the Thirties* (1939; New York: Dover, 1967), image 17.

78. *W.P.A. Guide to New York City*, 441.

79. *Brooklyn Daily Eagle*, May 24, 1883, evening edition, 2.

80. Evans's photographs accompanied three different printings of *The Bridge*. Most famous is the Black Sun edition, published in Paris in March 1930, which included three images. Different Evans photographs served as the frontispieces to Horace Liveright's two trade editions, published in New York the same year (April and July). The discussion that follows is primarily concerned with the images from the Black Sun edition.

81. Crane's original plans for *The Bridge* included a large section—roughly one-sixth—devoted to Whitman. See *O My Land, My Friends: The Selected Letters of Hart Crane*, ed. Langdon Hammer and Brom Weber (New York: Four Walls Eight Windows, 1997), 236.

82. Ibid., 131.

83. Ibid., 259.

84. Crane's retreat into myth was noted early by many of his critic friends, as was his inability to formulate any meaningful connection between the Brooklyn Bridge and American experience in the 1920s. See R. P. Blackmur, "New Thresholds, New Anatomies: Notes on a Text of Hart Crane," in *Form and Value in Modern Poetry* (New York: Anchor, 1946), 269–85; Malcolm Cowley, "A Preface to Hart Crane," *New Republic* 62 (1930), 276–77; Allen Tate, "Hart Crane," in *Essays of Four Decades* (Chicago: Swallow Press, 1968), 310–323; and Yvor Winters, "The Significance of *The Bridge*, by Hart Crane; or, What Are We to Think of Professor X?" in *In Defense of Reason* (New York: Swallow Press and William Morrow, 1947), 575–603. On the history of the writing of *The Bridge*, see Edward J. Brunner, *Splendid Failure: Hart Crane and the Making of The Bridge* (Urbana and Chicago: University of Illinois Press, 1985).

85. Trachtenberg, *Brooklyn Bridge*, 168. As Trachtenberg elsewhere states, "the poem is hardly 'about' Brooklyn Bridge or a literal America in any sense." Instead, it concerns "the hope . . . for a purely aesthetic transformation of a world already transformed by industrial and corporate capitalism." See Trachtenberg's introduction to *Hart Crane: A Collection of Critical Essays*, ed. Alan Trachtenberg (Englewood Cliffs, NJ: Prentice-Hall, 1982), 11–12.

86. My understanding of the New Criticism is informed by Cleanth Brooks and Robert Penn Warren, *Understanding Poetry: An Anthology for College Students*, rev. ed. (New York: Henry Holt, 1950); John Crowe Ransom, *The New Criticism* (New York: New Directions, 1941); and Cleanth Brooks, *The Well-Wrought Urn: Studies in the Structure of Poetry* (New York: Harcourt, Brace, 1947). Perhaps unsurprisingly, those critics who have most effectively argued for the poem's essential success have employed the theoretical criteria of the New Criticism. See, for example, Stanley K. Coffman, "Symbolism in *The Bridge*," *PMLA* 66 (1951), 65–77, and John Unterecker, "The Architecture of *The Bridge*," *Wisconsin Studies in Contemporary Literature* 3 (1962), 5–20.

87. See Trachtenberg, *Brooklyn Bridge*, 185–93; Trachtenberg, "Cultural Revisions in the Twenties," 58–75; and Gordon K. Grigsby, "The Photographs in the First Edition of *The Bridge*," *Texas Studies in Language and Literature* 4 (1962), 4–11.

88. Hart Crane, *The Bridge*, in *The Complete Poems and Selected Letters and Prose of*

Hart Crane, ed. Brom Weber (New York: Anchor Books, 1966), 46; Grigsby, "Photographs in the First Edition," 7.

89. Crane, *The Bridge*, 54.

90. Trachtenberg, "Cultural Revisions in the Twenties," 72; Grigsby, "Photographs in the First Edition," 9.

91. Trachtenberg, "Cultural Revisions in the Twenties," 72; Grigsby, "Photographs in the First Edition," 9.

92. See Maria Morris Hambourg, *Paul Strand, Circa 1916* (New York: Harry Abrams, 1998), plate 9, and James B. Connolly, "New York Harbor," *Harper's New Monthly Magazine* 111 (1905), 228–36.

93. Evans furthered this approach in his "Brooklyn Bridge Composition" (1930). Here the bridge is aestheticized and abstracted by mirroring the image along a diagonal line that runs from the bottom left-hand corner to the top right-hand corner. See Edward Brunner, "Hart Crane: Illustrated Editions of *The Bridge*," at http://www.english.uiuc.edu/maps/poets/a_f/crane/bridge_ill.htm; this site also shows the photographs used in both Liveright editions. See also *Walker Evans: Simple Secrets, Photographs from the Collection of Marian and Benjamin A. Hill* (New York: Harry Abrams, 1998), 33.

94. See the following works by Lewis Mumford: *Sticks and Stones: A Study of American Architecture and Civilization* (1924; New York: Dover, 1955), 51–52; "The Buried Renaissance," in *Findings and Keepings: Analects for an Autobiography* (New York: Harcourt Brace Jovanovich, 1975), 188–91; "The Brooklyn Bridge," *American Mercury* 23 (1931), 447–50; *The Brown Decades: A Study of the Arts in America, 1865–1895* (1931; New York: Dover, 1971), 44–48; and *Sketches from Life: The Autobiography of Lewis Mumford, the Early Years* (New York: Dial Press, 1982), 127–30.

95. See the following Mumford articles: "Architecture and the Machine," *American Mercury* 3 (1924), 77–80; "High Buildings—An American View," *American Architect* 126 (1924), 423–24; "The Intolerable City," *Harper's Monthly* 152 (1926), 283–93; "Is the Skyscraper Tolerable?" *Architecture* 55 (1927), 67–69; and "Botched Cities," *American Mercury* 18 (1929), 143–50. Schleier, *Skyscraper in American Art*, 93, describes Mumford as the "most vituperative interpreter of the skyscraper" in the 1920s. Yet this characterization is tempered by Mumford's attitude toward such architects as John Welborn Root, Dankmar Adler, and Louis Sullivan.

96. Lewis Mumford, *Architecture: Reading with a Purpose* (Chicago: American Library Association, 1926), 12–13.

97. Mumford, *Sticks and Stones*, 81. The essence of Mumford's criticism is best understood with reference to the visual arts. In Childe Hassam's *Lower Manhattan* (formerly *Broad and Wall Streets*) (1907), for example, we find the familiar visual trope of the "canyons of New York": bright sunlight falls on the tall buildings, but not on the people who walk in their shadows.

98. See Mumford, "Intolerable City," 283–93, and *Sticks and Stones*, 81.

99. Mumford, *Brown Decades*, 44–48.

100. Donald L. Miller, *Lewis Mumford: A Life* (Pittsburgh: University of Pittsburgh Press, 1989), 174; Mumford, *Brown Decades*, 47.

101. See Mumford, "Buried Renaissance," 189. As Casey Nelson Blake explains, a major failing of the "Young American" critics was the advocacy of "purely aesthetic solutions to political problems." See Blake, *Beloved Community: The Cultural Criticism of Randolph Bourne, Van Wyck Brooks, Waldo Frank, and Lewis Mumford* (Chapel Hill: University of North Carolina Press, 1990), 6.

102. Mumford, *Brown Decades*, 46.

103. Mumford, *Sticks and Stones*, 52.

104. These are reprinted in Miller, *Lewis Mumford*, 304–5, and can be viewed at http://library.monmouth.edu/spcol/mumford/gallery.html.

105. See Lewis Mumford, "The Metropolitan Milieu," in *America and Alfred*

Stieglitz: A Collective Portrait, ed. Waldo Frank et al. (Garden City, NY: Doubleday, 1934), 33–58.

106. Mumford, *Sketches from Life*, 127, 129–30.

107. Miller, *Lewis Mumford*, 176.

108. Walt Whitman, "Manahatta," in *Walt Whitman*, ed. Kaplan, 585–86.

109. Alfred Kazin, review of *Brooklyn Bridge: Fact and Symbol*, by Alan Trachtenberg, *New York Review of Books*, 4 (1965), 7. The young Kazin was greatly impressed by Mumford's *Brown Decades* and stated in one of his last published essays: "Of all the father figures that guided New York's taste from the twenties on, Lewis Mumford was my favorite. He was the American Ruskin." See Kazin, *A Walker in the City*, 172, and "The Art City Our Fathers Built," *American Scholar* 67 (1998), 20.

110. See Paul John Eakin, "Alfred Kazin's Bridge to America," *South Atlantic Quarterly* 77 (1978), 45, and Alfred Kazin, *The Open Street* (New York: Reynal and Hitchcock, 1948), 11.

111. Kazin, *A Walker in the City*, 107.

112. This question—when looking from the bridge, what does one see?—was also relevant in a piece Kazin wrote about the bridge for *Harper's Bazaar*. Here he extends his gaze to take in Governor's Island, the other East River bridges, City Hall, the Municipal Building, Wall Street, and the Battery. Yet he again returns to the city's poorer neighborhoods: "on the right the tenements of the East Side and Chinatown . . . where the steerage still remains . . . from whose nightmare the children of the poor have not escaped." The value of the record is in its denial of priority. As an image, it is inclusive, not selective: "these are the extremes of New York, as the extremes make in their bizarre neighborliness the city itself." Kazin's article is also important as a photo-text. The piece is accompanied by ten photographs by Henri Cartier-Bresson, all of which foreground human interaction on or near the bridge. See Alfred Kazin and Henri Cartier-Bresson, "The Brooklyn Bridge," *Harper's Bazaar* 79 (1946), 397.

113. See Kazin, *A Walker in the City*, 106–7. These sentiments are also found in *Our New York* (1989), Kazin's collaboration with photographer David Finn. Like Cartier-Bresson, Finn emphasized human interaction in his photographs of the city. See Kazin and Finn, *Our New York: A Personal Vision in Words and Pictures* (New York: Harper and Row, 1989), 58–65.

114. Frank, *Our America*, 19, 45, 202–21.

115. Ibid., 171–75.

116. Waldo Frank, "Vicarious Fiction," *Seven Arts* 1 (1917), 294.

117. Waldo Frank, *The Re-discovery of America: An Introduction to a Philosophy of American Life* (New York: Scribner's, 1929), 90.

118. Adams, *Education of Henry Adams*, 471.

119. Waldo Frank, *The Unwelcome Man* (Boston: Little, Brown, 1917), 168–69.

120. Ibid., 170.

121. Ibid., 174.

122. Ridge also used the bridge/snake analogy in her poetry: "Over the black bridge . . . like a monstrous serpent." See Lola Ridge, "Frank Little at Calvary" and "Brooklyn Bridge" in *The Ghetto and Other Poems* (New York: B. W. Huebsch, 1918), 56, 87. Earlier, José Martí used the image for his assessment of the bridge at its opening: "those four colossal boa constrictors, those four parallel cables, thick and white, which uncoil like ravening serpents, lifting their sibilant bodies from one side of the river, rising to heroic heights, stretching out over the water upon sovereign pillars, and falling back to earth on the opposite side." Martí, "Brooklyn Bridge," 143.

123. *The Memoirs of Waldo Frank*, ed. Alan Trachtenberg, introduction by Lewis Mumford (Amherst: University of Massachusetts Press, 1973), 239.

124. Benjamin De Casseres, *Mirrors of New York* (New York: Joseph Lawren, 1925), 218–19.

125. Ibid., 220–21.

126. *Four Years in the Underbrush: Adventures as a Working Woman in New York* (New York: Scribner's, 1921), 1, 231–32. A similar depiction of the tenements beneath the bridge can be found in Helen Campbell, *Darkness and Daylight; or, Lights and Shadows of New York Life* (Hartford, CT: A. D. Worthington, 1892), quoted in Phillip Lopate, *Waterfront: A Journey Around Manhattan* (New York: Crown, 2004), 261–62.

127. Mildred Stapley, "Six Etchings of Brooklyn Bridge," illustrated by Henri De Ville, *Architectural Record* 38 (1915), 583.

128. Ibid.

129. Ibid., 583–91.

130. William Meredith, "A View of the Brooklyn Bridge," in *Earth Walk: New and Selected Poems* (New York: Knopf, 1970), 53.

131. Lewis Mumford, *The Golden Day: A Study in American Literature and Culture* (1926; New York: Dover 1957), ix. The influence of *The Harbor* is reiterated in Mumford, *Sketches from Life*, 128.

132. Peter Conn, *The Divided Mind: Ideology and Imagination in America, 1898–1917* (New York: Cambridge University Press, 1983), 110.

133. In *Beggar's Gold*, Peter Wells, a liberal schoolteacher, speaks at a rally to protest a police raid on a socialist school, but his message of tolerance, freedom of speech, and humane social treatment is dismissed by both sides. The socialist crowd drifts off, accusing Wells of reactionary bourgeois values, and the Board of Education afterward fires him for advocating socialism. See Ernest Poole, *Beggar's Gold* (New York: Macmillan, 1921), 209–15. For Poole's relation to Wilson's Committee on Public Information, see Robert Cuff, "Ernest Poole: Novelist as Propagandist, 1917–1918: A Note," *Canadian Review of American Studies* 19 (1988), 183–94.

134. Ernest Poole, *The Harbor* (New York: Thomas Nelson, 1915), 164.

135. Ernest Poole, *The Bridge: My Own Story* (New York: Macmillan, 1940), 259.

136. Poole, *The Harbor*, 13, 17.

137. Ibid., 89; Conn, *Divided Mind*, 111.

138. Poole, *The Harbor*, 208.

139. Ibid., 183–89.

140. Ibid., 195, 259.

141. Ibid., 236.

142. The shocking social conditions of life below the bridge are illustrated by Poole: beneath "the great arch of the Bridge," Billy discovers "a heavy paper bag with what would have been a baby inside." Ibid., 132.

143. Ibid., 241–48. The conditions in the ship's hull are conspicuously similar to those in the bridge's caissons.

144. John E. Hart, "Heroism Through Social Awareness: Ernest Poole's *The Harbor*," *Critique* 9 (1967), 84.

145. Poole, *The Harbor*, 358.

146. Ibid., 363.

147. Victor Turner, *The Ritual Process: Structure and Anti-Structure* (1969; Ithaca: Cornell University Press, 1977), 94–95.

148. See Adam Smith, *The Theory of Moral Sentiments* (1759; New York: Cambridge University Press, 2002), 1–17, and Sennett, *Conscience of the Eye*, esp. 97–117.

149. Sennett, *Conscience of the Eye*, 102–3.

150. Ibid., 205–7.

151. See Lawrence Ferlinghetti, "#89," in *A Far Rockaway of the Heart* (New York: New Directions, 1997), 107, and Gregory Corso, "The Last Warmth of Arnold," in *Gasoline* (San Francisco: City Lights, 1958), 20–21.

152. John Dos Passos, *Manhattan Transfer* (1925; Harmondsworth, UK: Penguin, 1986), 117.

153. Ibid.; Le Gallienne and Coburn, "Brooklyn Bridge at Dawn," 526–27.

154. Dos Passos also used the Brooklyn Bridge as a site of futility and hopelessness in the story of Dutch Robertson (*Manhattan Transfer*, 266–67) and for Joe Williams in *U.S.A.* See John Dos Passos, *Nineteen Nineteen*, in *U.S.A.* (1932; Harmondsworth, UK: Penguin, 1966), 383–84. It is interesting to compare Bud's final moments on the bridge with Holliwell's walk across it in Robert Stone's *A Flag for Sunrise* (London: Picador, 1981), 24: "It was not until he was halfway across the Brooklyn Bridge that . . . a chill touched his inward loneliness. He was, he knew at that moment, really without beliefs, without hope — either for himself or the world."

155. Louis D. Rubin Jr., *Thomas Wolfe: The Weather of His Youth* (Baton Rouge: Louisiana State University Press, 1955), 108.

156. Wolfe's final novel ends with the assertion, "I believe that we are lost here in America, but I believe we shall be found." Thomas Wolfe, *You Can't Go Home Again* (1940; Harmondsworth, UK: Penguin, 1970), 678. In the interest of brevity, the following discussion focuses mainly on Wolfe's character George Webber as portrayed in *The Web and the Rock* and *You Can't Go Home Again*.

157. Webber's image illustrates the relation between promotion and aesthetics in the modern city. As William Taylor notes, "by 1900, the camera . . . had become the single most important agent in extending the sensory experience of the people beyond their immediate surroundings. . . . Thus cosmeticized, it was this [mythologized] perception of urban society . . . that was invoked to sell every imaginable product, not least of which was urban life itself." See Taylor, *In Pursuit of Gotham*, 30–33, and Thomas Wolfe, *The Web and the Rock* (1939; Harmondsworth, UK: Penguin, 1970), 114–16. Interestingly, none of Wolfe's critics has noted the centrality of the bridge in Wolfe's conception of New York, especially in *The Web and the Rock*, which codifies the bridge in its very title.

158. Wolfe, *The Web and the Rock*, 259–66.

159. Ibid., 441. The illusory nature of New York's exemplary image is a recurrent theme throughout Wolfe's fiction. See Thomas Wolfe, *Of Time and the River* (New York: Scribner's, 1935), esp. 532–37, and "No Door," in *The Complete Short Stories of Thomas Wolfe*, ed. Francis E. Skipp (New York: Collier, 1987), 68–105. In *You Can't Go Home Again*, the sequel to *The Web and the Rock*, Esther's husband states his relationship to the physical and economic nature of the city: "Every cloud-lost spire of masonry was a talisman of power, a monument to the everlasting empire of American business. It made him feel good. For that empire was his faith, his fortune, and his life. He had a fixed place in it. . . . 'My city,' he thought, 'Mine'" (144–45). Again, the ruination of Whitman's democratic idealism can be read into this quotation.

160. Wolfe, *The Web and the Rock*, 454.

161. Ibid., 619.

162. Wolfe, *You Can't Go Home Again*, 366, 380, 396, 663. Wolfe's experiences in interwar Germany may well have had some influence here. Having greatly enjoyed his time there in 1930, Wolfe returned in 1935. After realizing the belligerent intentions of the National Socialists, he left the country in a hurry. On the train to Paris, Wolfe watched "with a murderous and incomprehensible anger" as a Jew with whom he had been conversing was arrested and hauled off the train. See David Herbert Donald, *Look Homeward: A Life of Thomas Wolfe* (London: Bloomsbury, 1987), 389–90.

163. Wolfe, *The Web and the Rock*, 24.

164. Morgan, "Three Views of Brooklyn Bridge," 44. A similar motif incorporating the Brooklyn Bridge can be found in Edmund Wilson's autobiographical *The Princess with the Golden Hair*, in *Memoirs of Hecate County* (1946; London: Hogarth Press, 1986), 224–34.

165. Langston Hughes, *The Big Sea* (1940; New York: Hill and Wang, 1964), 80. In an intriguing little speech delivered at the Tremont Temple in Boston in 1891, T. McCants Stewart linked the building of the bridge with the struggle for racial equality. Both the bridge and "the doctrine of human rights," he believed, arose from "popular discon-

tent": "All the great inventions that have blessed mankind grew out of a chafing discontent at oppressive conditions. We gaze with wonder at the greatest triumph of engineering skill to be seen anywhere in the world . . . the New York and Brooklyn Bridge. . . . This mighty bridge grew out of the discontent of men and women [who] did not expend [themselves] in muttering against the God of nature . . . but in agitating for a remedy in the form of increased facilities of transportation." See Stewart, "Popular Discontent," *African Methodist Episcopal Church Review* 7 (1891), 357–72.

166. Sujata Bhatt, "Walking across the Brooklyn Bridge, July 1990," in *Monkey Shadows* (Manchester, UK: Carcanet, 1991), 84–86.

167. Ibid. Bhatt's political reading of the bridge is reminiscent of Mickey Lovett's ideological awakening while on the Brooklyn Bridge in Norman Mailer's *Barbary Shore* (1951; London: Abacus, 1998), 119–26.

168. Stephen F. Mills, *The American Landscape* (Edinburgh: Keele University Press, 1997), 86.

169. Warner, "Management of Multiple Urban Images," 391.

Chapter 4
American Memory: History, Fiction, and the Brooklyn Bridge

1. Hyman, "This Alluring Roadway," 55.

2. In using the term "post-opening history," I have deliberately excluded the Memorial Day panic that occurred a week after opening. The panic is intrinsically tied to the opening day and, for many contemporaries, represented the bridge's unofficial opening. As such, I have treated the events of Memorial Day as part of the opening history, not its post-opening history. See Eric Hobsbawm and Terrance Ranger, eds., *The Invention of Tradition* (New York: Cambridge University Press, 1983), esp. 1–15.

3. See *New York Tribune*, July 24, 1886, 1; *New York Herald*, July 24, 1886, 1; *New York Sun*, July 24, 1886, 2; and *New York Star*, July 24, 1886, 1.

4. *New York Star*, July 24, 1886, 1; *New York Times*, July 24, 1886, 1.

5. Although the day's events are set out in great detail in the *Tribune*, the paper later admitted that its reporter caught up with Brodie only "in the late afternoon." See *New York Tribune*, July 24, 1886, 1.

6. See Boorstin, *The Image*, 3, 11.

7. *New York Tribune*, July 24, 1886, 1; Sante, *Low Life*, 122.

8. *New York Times*, May 20, 1885, 4, and May 22, 1885, 4.

9. *New York Times*, May 24, 1885, 8.

10. *New York Times*, July 25, 1886, 3. Alvin Harlow notes that even before his supposed jump, Brodie "was a clever and tireless seeker of publicity." Afterward, this mania only increased. Harlow reports Brodie saying to a group of reporters: "say something about me. Say I'm a crook, a faker, that I never jumped off a curbstone; anything, so you print my name." See Alvin F. Harlow, *Old Bowery Days: The Chronicles of a Famous Street* (New York: D. Appleton, 1931), 417–24.

11. See Sante, *Low Life*, 122.

12. Brodie's escapades entered the American idiom in a revealing fashion. As detailed in *The W.P.A. Guide to New York City*, 315, to "'pull' or 'do a Brodie' has come to serve as a synonym for taking a high dive, whether on the stock market, in a love affair, or in the prize ring." Interestingly, all of these uses imply failure or a hoax.

13. See John Hanners, "The Man Who Jumped Off the Brooklyn Bridge: Steve Brodie (1858–1901) and the Public/Private Persona," *Mid-Atlantic Almanac* 4 (1995), 88–95.

14. See Robert Neilson Stephens, "On the Bowery" (1894), 131, MS, Performing Arts Division, New York Public Library; McCullough, *The Great Bridge*, 546; and Harlow, *Old Bowery Days*, 419–20.

15. *The Bowery*, directed by Raoul Walsh (Los Angeles: United Artists, 1933); Sante, *Low Life*, 123.

16. David Lowenthal, "The American Way of History," *Columbia University Forum* 9 (1966), 27.

17. See especially John Bodnar, "Pierre Nora, National Memory, and Democracy: A Review," *Journal of American History* 87 (2000), 951–63. For Bodnar, as for the French historian Nora, "sites of memory" represent "hybrid places" where the competing forces of "vernacular" and "official" memory search for common ground. Equally, both authors regret that this search for common ground is often subsumed behind "official" intolerance toward dissenting or "multiple voices."

18. Christopher Isherwood, *Goodbye to Berlin* (1939; London: Panther, 1977), 11.

19. See for example Bodnar, *Remaking America*, 14–15; Paul Connerton, *How Societies Remember* (New York: Cambridge University Press, 1989), 42; John R. Gillis, "Memory and Identity: The History of a Relationship," in *Commemorations: The Politics of National Identity*, ed. John R. Gillis (Princeton: Princeton University Press, 1994), 3; George Lipsitz, *Time Passages: Collective Memory and American Popular Culture* (Minneapolis: University of Minnesota Press, 1990), 14; M. J. Bowen, "The Invention of American Tradition," *Journal of Historical Geography* 18 (1992), 3–26; and Mike Wallace, *Mickey Mouse History and Other Essays on American Memory* (Philadelphia: Temple University Press, 1996).

20. Gillis, "Memory and Identity," 3.

21. See Michael Kammen, *A Season of Youth: The American Revolution and the Historical Imagination* (Ithaca: Cornell University Press, 1978); Peterson, *Jefferson Image*; Peterson, *Lincoln in American Memory*; Blight, *Race and Reunion*; and David W. Blight, *Beyond the Battlefield: Race, Memory and the American Civil War* (Amherst: University of Massachusetts Press, 2002).

22. Quoted in Alan Brinkley, *The Unfinished Nation: A Concise History of the American People* (New York: Overture Books, 1993), 653.

23. In northern, industrial Ohio, for example, unemployment in Cleveland was 50 percent, in Akron, 60 percent, and in Toledo, a devastating 80 percent. Hoover's already damaged reputation suffered further in 1932, when he sent the army—with fatal results—to clear a veterans' demonstration in Washington, DC. In addition, he proposed a tax increase on an already impoverished population while funneling $1.5 billion into private enterprise via the Reconstruction Finance Corporation.

24. The aim of the act, to halt the fall of farm prices, was achieved through a massive reduction in farm production, coupled with the forced destruction of agricultural surpluses. As these surpluses were reduced, farm prices eventually began to stabilize before a steady rise was achieved. The promise of future stability was little comfort to the millions of Americans standing in breadlines in 1933.

25. Connerton, *How Societies Remember*, 43.

26. Mike Wallace, "Visiting the Past: History Museums in the United States," in *Mickey Mouse History*, 15, 24.

27. *New York Times*, May 21, 1933, sec. 8, 2.

28. In their evocation of American technological history, the fiftieth anniversary celebrations substantiated the claims made by Wallace: "by paying homage to machines and products, by presenting machines as the movers of the Industrial Revolution, by ignoring the fact that machines were central to the invention of the factory system and formation of the working class, by encouraging reverence towards machines for their own sake as if all machines were self-evidently good and their results progressive, by making human progress seem to depend on machines begetting machines in a process midwived by genius inventors—all this tended to imply that machines, not capitalists, were in charge. This further implied that the motives for change lay in the machines rather than the economic necessities perceived by their owners and that the social processes of factory production or the negative aspects of technology's effects on peoples' lives were not worthy of consideration." Wallace, "Progress Talk: Museums of Science, Technology, and Industry," in *Mickey Mouse History*, 79–80.

29. *Brooklyn Daily Eagle*, May 24, 1933, A2.

30. *New York Daily News*, May 21, 1933, 13. Also see *Brooklyn Times Union*, May 24, 1933, 1, which describes how extensive the re-enactment was.

31. David Glassberg, *American Historical Pageantry*, 271.

32. See, for example, *Brooklyn Daily News*, May 24, 1933, 1; *New York Post*, May 25, 1933, 4; and *New York Sun*, May 24, 1933, 11.

33. See *New York Times*, May 24, 1933, 20.

34. Harvey Douglas, "The Story of Brooklyn Bridge." This report ran serially in the *Brooklyn Daily Eagle* from May 17 to May 27, 1933. See especially *Brooklyn Daily Eagle*, May 24, 1933, A19. For Hewitt's wage claims, see Hewitt, *Address*, 9.

35. Douglas, "Story of the Brooklyn Bridge," *Brooklyn Daily Eagle*, May 20, 1933, 15. The *Eagle* supplied additional corroboration in an editorial: "there were many tragedies in connection with this undertaking, but the record is strikingly free of scandals. Those directly concerned seemed fully conscious of the fact that they were making a great contribution to human progress." The *Times* also seemed at pains to stress the civic-minded honesty of the trustees. See *Brooklyn Daily Eagle*, May 24, 1933, 16, and *New York Times*, May 24, 1933, 20.

36. *New York Times*, May 25, 1933, 21.

37. *New York Times*, May 24, 1883, 3.

38. *New York Times*, May 21, 1933, sec. 8, 2.

39. See *Brooklyn Daily Eagle*, May 24, 1933, A3, A8, A12. In addition, a majority of the interviews ended with the subjects stressing how important the *Eagle* was in their lives, and how they never missed an issue.

40. For examples, see *Brooklyn Daily Eagle*, May 24, 1933, A3, A14.

41. *Brooklyn Daily Eagle*, May 24, 1933, A3, A17.

42. *Brooklyn Daily Eagle*, May 24, 1933, A3, A12.

43. *Brooklyn Daily Eagle*, May 24, 1933, A6.

44. Davis used this phrase to describe the Constitution's bicentennial in 1987. As she continues: "corporations were clearly the historical actors who counted. . . . Large audiences were pulled in and touched by corporately sponsored imagery. A version of American history consonant with corporate and governmental interests was broadly and joyfully disseminated . . . while the past was heroic, the present is even better and getting better all the time. Today's conditions and social relations were presented as the best possible result of progress." Needless to say, these observations describe much that is pertinent to the bridge's fiftieth anniversary. See Susan G. Davis, "'Set Your Mood to Patriotic': History as Televised Special Event," *Radical History Review* 42 (1988), 128, 130, 140.

45. *Brooklyn Daily Eagle*, May 24, 1933, A6.

46. *Brooklyn Daily Eagle*, May 24, 1933, A6, A7, A15.

47. Wallace, "Visiting the Past," 8.

48. Bodnar, *Remaking America*, 15.

49. See for example "Brooklyn Bridge," *Roebling Magazine* 2 (1949), 3–5; Gilroy, "It's Art, Poetry," 26–28; Coutros, "Suspended Animation," 10–11; Hopkins, "Brooklyn's Grand Old Bridge," 197–202; Lynwood Mark Rhodes, "How They Built the Brooklyn Bridge," *American Legion Magazine* 88 (1970), 16, 18–19, 42–49; Alan Keller, "The Great Brooklyn Bridge," 4–11, 44–48; and Robert T. Murphy, "The 'Nuts' Who Built the Brooklyn Bridge Built an Epic—With Class," *The Phoenix* (Brooklyn), May 25, 1978, 18–19.

50. As Steinman further explains, "to him [the young Steinman] it was truly a 'miracle bridge'; and, as he wondered how so marvelous a work could have been created, he was fired with the ambition to become a builder of suspension bridges. In a background of poverty, this far-flung ambition seemed beyond the boy's reach; but the spirit of the Bridge, and later the story of its builders, had entered his heart—and his dream came true." See Steinman, *Builders of the Bridge*, vii; David Steinman, *I Built a Bridge and*

Other Poems (New York: Davidson Press, 1955); and David Steinman, *Songs of a Bridge-builder* (Grand Rapids, MI: William B. Eerdman, 1959).

51. The question of historical accuracy haunts Steinman's biography of the Roeblings. My own research substantiates McCullough's claim that it "was based on superficial research and contains many inaccuracies." Steinman's impressive bibliography, for example, effectively republishes large sections of A. A. Jakkula's mammoth bibliographic history of suspension bridges—published four years before Steinman's biography—with no additional material. See Steinman, *Builders of the Bridge*, 420; McCullough, *The Great Bridge*, 609; and A. A. Jakkula, "A History of Suspension Bridges in Bibliographic Form," *Bulletin of the Agricultural and Mechanical College of Texas*, 4th ser., 12 (1941).

52. Quoted in *New York Times*, May 4, 1954, 31. Wagner also went to great lengths to stress the bridge's "greatness" as a symbol of unchanging civic "unity." See Robert F. Wagner, "Symbol of Greatness," in *New/Old Brooklyn Bridge: Souvenir Presentation of Modernized Brooklyn Bridge, Official Opening May 3, 1954*, pamphlet, Brooklyn Collection, Brooklyn Public Library, no pagination.

53. See "What Happened to Brooklyn Bridge," *Architectural Forum* 102 (1955), 122–24, 76, 176, 180, 184. For an excellent illustration of the changes made to the bridge's walkway from opening to modernization, see Sharon Reier, *The Bridges of New York* (New York: Quadrant Press, 1977), 25. Of course, the span's apparent "lightness" was a major factor in public appreciation. To many, it lent the bridge an element of grace and poetry.

54. "What Happened to Brooklyn Bridge," 124.

55. Ibid., 176, 184.

56. In the wake of renovation, other complaints followed. In 1958 Pete Coutros wrote that the more the bridge is modernized, "the less it resembles the bridge thrown open in 1883." Another thirty years later, Alfred Kazin lamented that "genuine aficionados . . . have never ceased to deplore" the changes wrought by Steinman. See Coutros, "Suspended Animation," 11; Kazin and Finn, *Our New York*, 84.

57. James Huneker, *New Cosmopolis: A Book of Images* (New York: Scribner's, 1915), 63; Carl Van Vechten, *Parties: Scenes from Contemporary New York Life* (1930; Los Angeles: Sun and Moon, 1993), 142.

58. See Niklaus Pevsner, *Pioneers of Modern Design: From William Morris to Walter Gropius*, rev. ed. (Harmondsworth, UK: Penguin, 1960), 138, and Sigfried Giedion, *Space, Time and Architecture: The Growth of a New Tradition*, 5th ed. (Cambridge, MA: Harvard University Press, 1982), 178. A similar propensity can be detected in Archibald Black, *The Story of Bridges* (London: McGraw-Hill, 1936), 1–30, 86–90. Black begins his narrative with a thirty-page tribute to the Golden Gate Bridge. By contrast, the Brooklyn Bridge is accorded a mere four pages.

59. Le Corbusier, *When the Cathedrals Were White*, trans. Francis E. Hyslop Jr. (New York: McGraw-Hill, 1947), 75, 77.

60. Jeffrey Page recently put the matter succinctly: "as New York grew upward, the bridge began to shrink . . . as garish skyscrapers reached higher and higher . . . the bridge look[ed] smaller and smaller." Page, "For Sale: One Bridge; The Cost: Priceless," *Bergen County Record*, May 23, 2003, 1.

61. G.W.F. Hegel, *Introductory Lectures on Aesthetics*, ed. Michael Inwood, trans. Bernard Bosanquet (Harmondsworth, UK: Penguin, 1993), 76–97.

62. Andrei Voznesenski, "New York Airport at Night," in *Antiworlds and the Fifth Ace*, ed. Patricia Blake and Max Hayward, trans. William Jay Smith (New York: Basic Books, 1966), 149.

63. Trachtenberg, *Brooklyn Bridge*, 161.

64. Henry Miller, *Tropic of Capricorn* (1939; London: John Calder, 1964), 56.

65. Henry Miller, "The Brooklyn Bridge," in *The Cosmological Eye* (New York: New Directions, 1939), 351.

66. Bercovitch, *American Jeremiad*, 168.

67. Miller, *Tropic of Capricorn*, 49.

68. Ibid., 201–2; Henry Miller *Black Spring* (1936; London: Granada, 1974), 110–11; Miller, "Brooklyn Bridge," 347, 349; and Meyer Berger, "The Harp," in *New/Old Brooklyn Bridge,* no pagination.

69. Ed Schilders, "Dante in New York: An Analysis of Henry Miller's Writings about the Brooklyn Bridge," *Brooklyn Bridge Bulletin* 3 (1983), 35.

70. In Yusef Komunyakaa's poem "Blues Chant Hoodoo Revival," the bridge is linked to the violence inherent in African-American history: "our story is / a rifle butt / across our heads / arpeggio of bowed grass / among glass trees / where they kick down doors / & we swan-dive from / the brooklyn bridge / a post hypnotic suggestion." See Komunyakaa, "Blues Chant Hoodoo Revival," in *Copacetic* (Hanover, NH: Wesleyan University Press, 1984), 57–58.

71. Harvey Shapiro, "National Cold Storage Company," in *Selected Poems* (Hanover, NH: Wesleyan University Press, 1997), 31.

72. The title of Shapiro's American repository is significant. Singularly "National," the entity is also a corporate venture ("Company").

73. Daniela Gioseffi appears to be making a similar point when she writes, "the American Dream leapt from your cables / and fell down a deep elevator shaft / of the warehouse that hides you from view." See Gioseffi, "To the Brooklyn Bridge," in *Brooklyn Bridge Poetry Walk: A Souvenir Anthology,* ed. Daniela Gioseffi, pamphlet distributed on the Brooklyn Bridge Poetry Walk, June 25, 1972, Brooklyn Collection, Brooklyn Public Library, no pagination.

74. "The Opening of the Bridge," *Harper's Weekly,* June 2, 1883, 346.

75. William Marshall, *The New York Detective* (New York: Mysterious Press, 1988); Richard Crabbe, *Suspension* (New York: St. Martin's, 2000). In children's literature, the building of the bridge is a perennial favorite. At least six different children's histories have been published in the last twenty years. See Judith St. George, *The Brooklyn Bridge: They Said It Couldn't Be Built* (New York: Putnam's, 1982); Zachary Kent, *The Story of the Brooklyn Bridge* (Chicago: Children's Book Press, 1989); Elizabeth Mann and Alan Witschonke, *The Brooklyn Bridge: The Story of the World's Most Famous Bridge and the Remarkable Family That Built It* (New York: Mikaya Press, 1996); Elaine Pascoe, *The Brooklyn Bridge: Building America* (Woodbridge, CT: Blackbirch, 1999); Lynn Curlee, *Brooklyn Bridge* (New York: Antheneum, 2001); and Vicki Weiner, *The Brooklyn Bridge: New York's Graceful Connection* (Chicago: Children's Book Press, 2003).

76. C. Vann Woodward, "Fictional History and Historical Fiction," in *The Future of the Past* (New York: Oxford University Press, 1989), 235–36.

77. Arthur M. Schlesinger Jr., "The Historical Mind and the Literary Imagination," *Atlantic Monthly* 233 (1974), 59.

78. Dorothy Landers Beall, *The Bridge,* in *The Bridge and Other Poems* (New York: Mitchell Kennerley, 1913), 1–130.

79. For Cecelia Tichi, the professional engineer in early-twentieth-century American literature represented the "uncorruptible American surrounded by corporate and political greed." He embodies "the nation's purity of vision. The very spirit of the Republic endures in him." When applied to the characters in Beall's drama, Tichi's description more aptly fits Hilda the settlement worker. By contrast, Robert the engineer is more closely aligned to Willa Cather's bridge builder Bartley Alexander. As Tichi notes, Alexander is a dictatorial "Emperor," and his bridge is "the symbol of himself." Within this framework, Hilda's transformation from settlement worker to fiancée—from opponent to assistant—is distinctly ideological: from democracy to autocracy. See Tichi, *Shifting Gears: Technology, Literature and Culture in Modernist America* (Chapel Hill: University of North Carolina Press, 1987), 122, 176, 179, and Cather, *Alexander's Bridge* (1912; London: Virago, 1994).

80. John G. Cawelti, *Adventure, Mystery, and Romance: Formula Stories as Art and Popular Culture* (Chicago: University of Chicago Press, 1976), 265.

81. Frances Williams Browin, *Big Bridge to Brooklyn: The Roebling Story* (New York: Aladdin Books, 1956); Kathryn E. Harrod, *Master Bridge Builders: The Story of the Roeblings* (New York: Julian Messner, 1958); and F. Wenderoth Saunders, *Building Brooklyn Bridge* (Boston: Little, Brown, 1965).

82. Roy Rosenzweig, "Marketing the Past: *American Heritage* and Popular History in the United States," in *Presenting the Past: Essays on History and the Public*, ed. Susan Porter Benson, Stephen Brier, and Roy Rosenzweig (Philadelphia: Temple University Press, 1986), 22, 27, 29, 34, 37.

83. At one point, the printing business owned by Pete's father verges on bankruptcy. Although the older Schimdt decides not to bother his son, Pete finds out and is able, rather unwittingly, to bring trade to the door of his hardworking father. Needless to say, after this temporary setback, the father prospers. This train of events corresponds to Alger's formula and to Anna Davin's observations on the antirealism of children's historical novels: "poverty and illness . . . appear as temporary and individual, ended or modified by luck or personal effort, not by collective organization and struggle." See Browin, *Big Bridge to Brooklyn*, 70, 156–58, and Davin, "Historical Novels for Children," *History Workshop Journal* 1 (1976), 160.

84. Browin, *Big Bridge to Brooklyn*, 52, 134.

85. Ibid., 86.

86. Edward Countryman, "John Ford's *Drums Along the Mohawk*: The Making of an American Myth," in *Presenting the Past*, ed. Benson, Brier, and Rosenzweig, 88.

87. See Richard Harding Davis, *Soldiers of Fortune* (1897; New York: Scribner, 1919), 82, and Tichi, *Shifting Gears*, 117–32.

88. Richard King, "The Discipline of Fact/The Freedom of Fiction?" *Journal of American Studies* 25 (1991), 172.

89. Mumford, *Findings and Keepings*, 215–17; Miller, *Lewis Mumford*, 262.

90. Lewis Mumford, *The Builders of the Bridge*, in *Findings and Keepings*, 232–35.

91. Ibid., 293–94.

92. Ibid., 310.

93. Ibid., 312.

94. Ibid., 295.

95. Mumford, *Findings and Keepings*, 216.

96. See Ruth Elizabeth Everett, "The Brooklyn Novel and the Brooklyn Myth: Source Materials for the Teaching of the Urban Novel" (Ph.D. diss., Teacher's College, Columbia University, 1966), 202. Idell's moral and political commitment is evident on the dust jacket of the trilogy's first novel, *Centennial Summer* (1943). "A Message from the Author" on the back cover reads: "On page 305 of this book a wish is expressed by one of the characters on the occasion of the Centennial of American Independence. Turn back to that page, will you, and read it again. As you concur in the hope that our country's second Centennial will draw upon free American families enjoying in peace the fruits of their strivings, perhaps you will wonder what you can do to assure that future. Only one thing is required of you—to believe passionately and with a whole heart in the principles of our Declaration of Independence." The passage referred to is: "A fratricidal conflict almost extinguished this flame—a new and more terrible sort of war is dampening it at this moment. It is a war of stocks and bonds, of machines and property, against the people. It is a remorseless war, fought with starvation, exposure, and disease. . . . It is my prayer, my fervent prayer, that a hundred years from now, under this same vine [we] may celebrate a second Centennial, knowing this enemy also is dead—assured that his neighbors are also celebrating because they too have their share of the fruit of the land." Albert E. Idell, *Centennial Summer* (New York: Henry Holt, 1943).

97. Idell's use of the Philadelphia and Reading is interesting. Headed by the infamous Franklin B. Gown, described as "labor's most brilliant and remorseless enemy," the railroad company was a prime player in the machinations that led to the year's bloody

confrontations. Its strenuous efforts to smash the Engineers' Brotherhood lit "the fuse" that ignited the "year of violence." See Robert V. Bruce, *1877: The Year of Violence* (Chicago: Ivan R. Dee, 1959), 36–42.

98. Albert E. Idell, *Bridge to Brooklyn* (New York: Henry Holt, 1944), 29.

99. Ibid., 35.

100. Idell is faithful to the facts here. Just before the outbreak of the railroad strikes, the Philadelphia and Reading had become "its own principal customer by purchasing a lion's share of the Schuylkill County coal fields it served. This massive gulp gave the Reading a case of financial indigestion which in 1877 was already acute." See Bruce, *1877*, 38.

101. Idell, *Bridge to Brooklyn*, 48, 95, 99.

102. Ibid., 163.

103. Ibid., 273–74.

104. Ibid., 320.

105. Ibid., 341.

106. Ibid., 368. Rogers articulates Idell's only reference to the official opening day. After reading the reports in the newspapers, he states: "Yes, I would say that the people showed their disapproval of the trustee's dictatorial policy." Needless to say, in comparison with the opening day's press reports, this sentiment is a significant revision. See ibid., 357.

107. Kammen, *A Season of Youth*, 165, 175.

108. A young Ada Louise Huxtable captured this cultural moment in 1957. Her brief tribute to the bridge, published in *Progressive Architecture*, is equally an *assertion* of the bridge's greatness and an *appreciation* of that greatness. In essence, it is an exhortation to look afresh at the bridge, "assigning [it] a new importance" and "rediscovering [its] admirable vigor." See Huxtable, "Monograph—Brooklyn Bridge—1867–1883, New York: John A. Roebling and Washington A. Roebling, Engineers," *Progressive Architecture* 39 (1957), 157–60. A similar claim can be made for Marianne Moore's celebratory "Granite and Steel" (1966), collected in Moore, *Complete Poems* (London: Faber, 1984), 205.

109. This theme is also expressed in James Purdy's novel, *Cabot Wright Begins* (New York: Farrar, Straus and Giroux, 1964). Forced into a society marriage in Brooklyn Heights and a career on Wall Street, Cabot Wright is a young man whose life is defined by "false values, false faces, false ownership and the false feelings that fill the vacuum created by a lack of real ones." To escape his life of privilege, Wright takes to the bridge. His mother is horrified: "I say it's simply not right for Cabot to walk the bridge," she fumes, as it gives "the impression that he is not successful." Needless to say, such comments force Wright into deeper rebellion and more time on the bridge.

110. See Allen Ginsberg, "Howl," in *Collected Poems, 1947–1980* (New York: Harper and Row, 1984), 126–27, 129. In the same volume also see "Waking in New York" (339–42), "Today" (345–37), and "Hospital Window" (634). For Kerouac, see "Hymn," in *Poems All Sizes* (San Francisco: City Lights, 1992), 151–52, and *Visions of Cody* (1972; New York: Penguin, 1993), 36. On their walks over the bridge together, see *Jack Kerouac: Selected Letters, 1940–1956*, ed. Ann Charters (New York: Penguin, 1996), 101, and Robert Shelton, *No Direction Home: The Life and Music of Bob Dylan* (New York: Ballantine, 1986), 439. At a Kerouac tribute at New York University in 1995, Ginsberg read Kerouac's unfinished "The Brooklyn Bridge Blues." See Allen Ginsberg "The Brooklyn Bridge Blues," *Kerouac—Kicks Joy Darkness* (Rykodisc RCD 10329).

111. A similar observation can be made with regard to Shirley Clarke's rarely seen and thoroughly bizarre documentary film *Bridges Go Round* (1958). An attempt to translate abstract expressionism into the cinema, Clarke's short film imagines the bridge as a dancer freed from its moorings and cavorting to the jazz rhythms of the city.

112. See http://scriptorium.lib.duke.edu/dynaweb/gedney/books/bd05/.

113. Weschler is describing Hockney's photomontage, *The Brooklyn Bridge, Nov. 28 1982*. See Lawrence Weschler, "True to Life," in *Cameraworks*, by David Hockney (New York: Knopf, 1984), 26.

114. Meredith, "A View of the Brooklyn Bridge," 53.

115. Henry Nash Smith, *Virgin Land: The American West as Symbol and Myth* (1950; Cambridge, MA: Harvard University Press, 1978); Ward, *Andrew Jackson*; Leo Marx, *The Machine in the Garden: Technology and the Pastoral Ideal in America* (New York: Oxford University Press, 1964); and Christopher B. Hoskins, "From Bridge to Text: *Brooklyn Bridge*, Myth and Symbol, American/Cultural Studies," *American Studies* 40 (1999), 103–7.

116. Trachtenberg, *Brooklyn Bridge*, 7–21.

117. Walt Whitman, "Letters From a Travelling Bachelor, Number X," *New York Sunday Dispatch*, December 23, 1849, reprinted in Joseph Jay Rubin, *The Historic Whitman* (University Park: Pennsylvania State University Press, 1973), 348; Thomas Pope, *A Treatise on Bridge Architecture* (New York: A. Niven, 1811); Trachtenberg, *Brooklyn Bridge*, 23–39.

118. *Opening Ceremonies of the New York and Brooklyn Bridge*, 32; Trachtenberg, *Brooklyn Bridge*, 41–64.

119. See Trachtenberg, *Brooklyn Bridge*, 41–64.

120. Nancy Veglahn, *The Spider of Brooklyn Heights* (New York: Scribner's, 1967), vi.

121. Washington Roebling, "The Life of John A. Roebling, C.E., By His Oldest Son, Washington Roebling, Together With Some Personal Recollections of the Latter, Written Partly in 1897 and in 1907," typescript, Roebling Collection, Archibald S. Alexander Library, Rutgers University, 45–46, 187.

122. Veglahn, *The Spider of Brooklyn Heights*, 6.

123. Ibid., 174.

124. In the wider sphere of American history—especially as it relates to the construction of iconic landmarks—Gay Talese's contribution must also be acknowledged. In his classic *The Bridge* (1964), Talese documented the building of the Verrazano-Narrows Bridge between Staten Island and Bay Ridge. As he noted in the preface to the book's reissue: "We often know the names of the architects or chief engineers of renowned structures, but those men whose job it is to ascend to high and dangerous places—the kind of men who erected and connected the steel on the Empire State Building or spun the cables across the Brooklyn Bridge—are not identified by name in the books, archival materials, or other written accounts concerned with the construction of these landmarks. . . . I kept this in mind when I decided, in 1962, to write about the Verrazano-Narrows Bridge construction; it would include the names and bibliographical information about the workers, establishing their rightful place in the history of this grand undertaking." Contemporary with the work of such British historians as Christopher Hill, Eric Hobsbawm, and E. P. Thompson, Talese's book can be regarded as an exemplar of the modern "social history" movement. See Gay Talese, *The Bridge* (New York: Walker and Co., 2003), ix–x.

125. See McCandlish Phillips, "'Epitome of Knowledge' (Brooklyn Bridge) is 88," *New York Times*, May 23, 1971, 71, 90; *Municipal Engineers Journal* 59 (1973), 1–121; and Judd Tully, *Red Grooms and Ruckus Manhattan* (New York: George Braziller, 1977).

126. Bowen, "Invention of American Tradition," 4.

127. Alfred North Whitehead, *Symbolism: Its Meaning and Effect* (1927; New York: Fordham University Press, 1958), 88.

128. For Kammen, historical novelists working in the tradition of national dissent "more nearly approximate historical reality" than those concerned with assent. See Kammen, *A Season of Youth*, 223.

Chapter 5
Revision and Dissent:
The Brooklyn Bridge from Its Centennial until the Present

1. *Brooklyn Bridge Bulletin* 4 (1983), 1.

2. See *Washington Post*, May 22, 1983, B7; *Baltimore Sun*, May 25, 1983, 1; *Memphis Commercial Appeal*, May 19, 1983, 3; *New York Post*, May 24, 1983, 1; *New York Post*,

May 25, 1983, 1; *New Jersey Record*, May 25, 1983, 1; and *New York Daily News*, May 25, 1983, 1.

3. George F. Will, "Brooklyn Bridge: Form and Function," *Detroit News*, May 22, 1983, A19.

4. See John O. Fairfield, *The Mysteries of the Great City* (Columbus: Ohio State University Press, 1993), 76.

5. Hamill, "Bridge of Dreams," 30, 33. For the bridge as an exemplary immigrant symbol, see Gorde, "Bridge Is Art for Every Generation," 33; McCullough, "The Great Bridge and the American Imagination," 69, 80; and Kathy Larkin, "Parties by Land and Sea," *New York Daily News*, May 25, 1983, 31. Also see Daralice Boles, "The Brooklyn Bridge: An American Icon," *Progressive Architecture* 64 (1983), 25–26; Patrice O'Shaughnessy, "The Lore, Legends and Legacy of the Great Bridge," *Sunday News Magazine*, May 22, 1983, 15–17; "The Glory of the Brooklyn Bridge," *New York* 16 (1983), 27–47; David McCullough, "The Roeblings: Their Great Bridge Fulfilled a Dream," *Smithsonian Magazine* 20 (1983), 7, 71–83; Carl Little, "The Brooklyn Bridge," *Arts Magazine* 58 (1983), 7; Morris, "A Century Old," 565–79; and Peter Stanford, "The Brooklyn Bridge: Spanning Time and Tide," *Sea History* 28 (1983), 24–37.

6. Paul Goldberger, "Brooklyn Bridge, at 100, Embodies the Spirit of an Age: The Bridge as Symbol of the City," *New York Times*, May 24, 1983, B2.

7. Colleen J. Sheehy, "Monument and Miniature: Brooklyn Bridge and Centennial Souvenirs," *Prospects* 11 (1986), 276, and Sheehy, "The Brooklyn Bridge Centennial: Folklore and Popular Culture in a Contemporary Civic Ritual," *International Folklore Review* 5 (1987), 103. Actually, Greenberg's *Brooklyn Bridge I* also looks toward Brooklyn, although Sheehy's observation that the "isolated and deserted structure [is] unconnected to a larger urban landscape" still holds true: the borough behind the bridge is faint and barely noticeable against the romantic grandeur of the bridge.

8. See http://www.wedphotos.com/home.html. For Greenberg's images of the bridge, see http://www.wedphotos.com/bridge.html.

9. Sheehy, "Monument and Miniature," 276.

10. Bill Reed, "The Brooklyn Bridge Is an Exit," *San Francisco Sunday Examiner and Chronicle*, May 29, 1983, B11; Craig Steven Wilder, *A Covenant with Color: Race and Social Power in Brooklyn* (New York: Columbia University Press, 2000), 212.

11. "The American Bridge," *Boston Sunday Globe*, May 22, 1983, A22.

12. See Miller, *New England Mind*, 462.

13. "American Bridge," A22.

14. Martin Filler, quoting Robert Furneaux Jordan's observations on Britain's Great Exhibition of 1851. For Filler, Jordan "could have been commenting on the Brooklyn Bridge as well." See Filler, "Brooklyn Bridge at 100," 144.

15. Jimmy Breslin, "The Bridge," *House and Garden* 152 (1983), 150; Deirdre Carmody, "Brooklyn Bridge, 'the Only Bridge of Power, Life and Joy,' Turns 100 Today," *New York Times*, May 24, 1983, B1.

16. Melvin Maddocks, "Selling the Brooklyn Bridge," *Christian Science Monitor*, June 2, 1983, 22.

17. In addition, the centennial continued the ironies of 1883. The opening was formally titled the "People's Day"; the centennial celebrations were officially designated as the "People's Parade." Both events, however, were open only to invited guests.

18. Richard Eder, "Brooklyn Bridge Spans a Century," *Los Angeles Times*, June 5, 1983, calendar, 6. Of course, access to the best viewing spot was determined by economics. If one could afford a boat, the event could be watched from the East River itself. The *New York Daily News* reported the presence of many famous Americans aboard Malcolm Forbes's 120-foot yacht; they dined on "caviar, cold lobster and Nova Scotia salmon" while watching the fireworks. See Larkin, "Parties by Land and Sea," 31.

19. Davis, "'Set Your Mood to Patriotic,'" 128.

20. Donald C. Jackson, "Centennial Celebrations: Two Exhibits Commemorating

the 100th Anniversary of the Brooklyn Bridge," *Technology and Culture* 25 (1984), 287–91.

21. Filler, "Brooklyn Bridge at 100," 144–45.

22. Ibid., 151.

23. Goldberger, "Brooklyn Bridge," 1. In addition, McCullough characterized the period of the bridge's construction as a time when America "dared to be great." See McCullough, "The Great Bridge and the American Imagination," 32.

24. Breslin, "The Bridge," 150–51.

25. Ibid. The impression made on Breslin by the all-but-anonymous Seaberg was highlighted recently. Twenty years after his profile, Breslin again found reason to recall the heroism of the emergency worker: "On Friday, I rode across the Brooklyn Bridge, whose gray netting went with the sky, and as long as there was tension about the bridge, I was remembering Richard Seaberg, a big cop from Emergency One, who climbed to the top of the bridge so many times and pulled somebody down before he jumped. Seaberg protected the Brooklyn Bridge." Jimmy Breslin, "A Fate Sealed under Secrecy," *Newsday*, June 22, 2003, 2.

26. Boles, "Brooklyn Bridge," 25.

27. "Minor Mention," *Appletons' Journal* 9 (1873), 571.

28. Schuyler, "Bridge as a Monument," 332–34.

29. J. A. Mitchell, *The Last American: A Fragment from the Journal of Khan-Li, Prince of Dimph-Yoo-Chur and Admiral of the Persian Navy* (New York: Frederick A. Stokes Co., 1889), 20, 55. Profusely illustrated, *The Last American* contains two images of the bridge in ruins(pp. 24, 55–57).

30. "Buckling of Trusses on Brooklyn Bridge," *Railroad Gazette*, August 5, 1898, 564–65; Edwin Duryea and Joseph Mayer, "The Physical Condition and Safety under Present Loads of the New York and Brooklyn Bridge," *Engineering News*, October 10, 1901, 250–62; Duryea and Mayer, "The Brooklyn Bridge—Its Defects and Treatments," *Railroad Gazette*, October 25, 1901, 731; and Wilhelm Hildenbrand, *The Safety of the Brooklyn Bridge: A Review of the Report of Messrs. Edwin Duryea and Joseph Mayer on the Condition of the Brooklyn Bridge* (New York: n.p., 1902), 1, 3, 16. For the ongoing debate between Duryea and Mayer on the one hand and Hildenbrand on the other, see Hildenbrand, "Mr. Hildenbrand's Reply to the Report of Messers. Duryea and Mayer on the New York and Brooklyn Bridge," *Engineering News*, January 16, 1902, 54–60, and Duryea and Mayer, "The Safety of the Brooklyn Bridge: A Rejoinder by Messers. Duryea and Mayer to the Letters of Hildenbrand and Henning," *Engineering News*, January 30, 1902, 90–92.

31. See *New York Times*, July 4, 1922, 1, and Hyman, "This Alluring Roadway," 47.

32. See *New York Times*, May 17, 1933, 17, and *Brooklyn Daily Eagle*, May 24, 1933, A1, A3.

33. *New York Post*, May 24, 1983, 29; McCullough, "The Great Bridge and the American Imagination," 80; and *New York Daily News*, May 24, 1983, 45.

34. *New York Daily News*, October 23, 1980, 3, and *New York Times*, April 30, 1981, B3.

35. Donald C. Jackson, "Great American Bridges: Can They Stand Up to Progress?" *Historic Preservation* 33 (1981), 46–48, 50–51.

36. Wiedeman, *Why We Need Our Brooklyn Bridges*, 20.

37. Breslin, "The Bridge," 150.

38. Quoted in the *New York Times*, November 13, 1983, K36.

39. For a fine overview of the case, see Uriel Hielman, "Murder on the Brooklyn Bridge," *Middle East Quarterly* 8 (2001), 29–38.

40. *New York Law Journal*, August 29, 2001, 17.

41. See John Tierney, "Brooklyn Could Have Been a Contender," *New York Times*, December 18, 1997, reprinted in *Empire City: New York Through the Centuries*, ed. Kenneth T. Jackson and David S. Dunbar (New York: Columbia University Press, 2002), 407–21. For the bridge's role in Brooklyn's demise, see also Pete Hamill's introduction to *The

Brooklyn Reader: Thirty Writers Celebrate America's Favorite Borough, ed. Andrea Wyatt Sexton and Alice Leccese Powers (New York: Crown, 1994), xi–xiv.

42. Bascove, *Stone and Steel: Paintings and Writings Celebrating the Bridges of New York City* (Boston: David R. Godine, 1998).

43. *New York Times,* February 5, 1999, B3; *Deep Impact,* directed by Mimi Leder (Los Angeles: Dream Works, 1998); and *Godzilla,* directed by Roland Emmerich (Los Angeles: Tristar, 1998). The bridge was again pictured in ruins in *Aftershock: Earthquake in New York,* directed by Mikael Salomon (Vancouver, BC: Pacific Motion Pictures, 1999).

44. See Arthur Leipzig, *Growing Up in New York* (Boston: David R. Godine, 1995), and Burhan Dogançay, *Bridge of Dreams: The Rebirth of the Brooklyn Bridge,* introduction by Phillip Lopate (New York: Hudson Hills, 1999). Dogançay's work is reminiscent of Arthur Leipzig's International News Photos assignment in 1946.

45. *New York Times,* February 5, 1999, B3; *New York Daily News,* February 4, 1999, 1.

46. Events associated with the bridge in the spring and summer of 1999 were especially unfortunate. While "attempting to set a world record by scaling five bridges in four hours," Robert Landetta fell 500 feet from the bridge's suspension cables. Landing amid a crowd on Front Street, he died instantly. See *Newsday,* April 3, 1999, A22. Also German tourist Tilman Dohran and his sixty-four-year old father were "mugged and pistol-whipped while taking a[n evening] walk on the Brooklyn Bridge." See *New York Daily News,* August 29, 1999, 16.

47. Quoted in *New York Times,* January 2, 2001, D4.

48. *Life,* February 26, 1877, 107–8, and January 17, 1884, front cover.

49. Quoted in Linda Yoblonsky, "New York's New Watery Grave," *New York Times,* April 11, 2004, Arts and Leisure, Section 2, 28.

50. The science fiction and fantasy artist Chesley Bonestell, a major influence on Rockman, anticipated the latter's vision in 1951, when he depicted the Brooklyn Bridge almost submerged beneath the rising tides of the East River.

51. Quoted in Yoblonsky, "New York's New Watery Grave," 28. While planning his mural, Rockman was more concerned with scientific credibility than flights of the imagination. He consulted botanical, geological, and zoological experts in addition to architects, paleontologists, anthropologists, and geneticists.

52. See Kammen, *A Season of Youth,* 186–220.

53. See Turner, *Ritual Process,* 95.

54. Ibid., 96.

55. The reaggregation presented here corresponds to Perry Miller's oft-discredited claim "that the mind of the nation [in the nineteenth century] positively lusted for the chance to yield itself to the gratifications of technology. The machine has not conquered us in some imperial manner against our will. On the contrary, we have wantonly prostrated ourselves before the engine." See Miller, "The Responsibilities of Mind in a Civilization of Machines," in *The Responsibilities of Mind in a Civilization of Machines: Essays by Perry Miller,* ed. John Crowell and Stanford J. Searl Jr. (Amherst: University of Massachusetts Press, 1979), 198.

56. See Gutman, *Work, Culture and Society,* 67–73, 79–86.

57. Charles Dickinson, "Colonel Roebling's Friend," *Atlantic Monthly* 276 (1995), 74.

58. The episode also draws attention to the subjects of disability and worker compensation. Rarely broached by critics and commentators, the issue found no place in the wage-scale explications of Abram Hewitt in 1883 and Harvey Douglas in 1933. By staging this scene, Dickinson highlights the realities of permanent incapacity and inadequate reparation, while subverting the abstract heroism of labor.

59. Dickinson, "Colonel Roebling's Friend," 78.

60. Ibid., 82.

61. Ibid.

62. Ibid., 74.

63. Likewise, in the film *The Siege*, directed by Edward Zwick (Los Angeles: Twentieth Century Fox, 1998), the bridge is used to quarantine Manhattan from the Arab internment camps set up in Brooklyn. It becomes a highly liminal space: a barrier, a physical point of separation, not a passageway. The film's advertising poster featured an image of the bridge overrun with military personnel and used the promotional caption "Freedom is History." As might be expected, the film was heavily criticized by America's Middle Eastern population..

64. After his fifty-year exile, Potter "was repulsed in efforts after a pension by certain caprices of law. His scars proved his only medals." See Herman Melville, *Israel Potter: His Fifty Years of Exile* (1855; New York: Sagamore Press, 1957), 241, and Kammen, *A Season of Youth*, 225. Alston's "invisibility" is captured in the illustration drawn by Carol Benioff to accompany Dickinson's story. Alston is pictured in his wheelchair in front of the Brooklyn Bridge. He is a ghostly figure, and the lines of the bridge can be seen through his head and body. See Dickinson, "Colonel Roebling's Friend," 72.

65. See William James, "The Moral Equivalent of War," in *Memories and Studies* (London: Longmans, Green and Co., 1912), 265–96.

66. See David E. Nye, *America as Second Creation: Technology and Narratives of New Beginnings* (Cambridge, MA: MIT Press, 2003), 261–82.

67. Robert Hughes, *American Visions: The Epic History of Art in America* (London: Harvill Press, 1997), 281.

68. Leo Marx, quoted in Rob Wilson, *American Sublime: The Genealogy of a Poetic Genre* (Madison: University of Wisconsin Press, 1981), 257.

69. Don DeLillo, *Underworld* (New York: Simon and Schuster, 1997), 184.

70. Benjamin's ideas on the "angel of history" are derived from a reading of Paul Klee's painting *Angelus Novus* (1920). See Walter Benjamin, "Thesis on the Philosophy of History," in *Illuminations*, ed. Hannah Arendt, trans. Harry Zohn (London: Fontana, 1973), 249.

71. Don DeLillo, *Americana* (Harmondsworth, UK: Penguin, 1971), 118–19.

72. See Lewis Mumford, "The Pennsylvania Station Nightmare," in *The Highway and the City* (New York: Mentor Books, 1964), 152–60, and Eric E. Plosky, *The Rise and Fall of Pennsylvania Station* (Cambridge, MA: MIT Press, 2000), 49.

73. Ada Louise Huxtable, foreword to *The Late, Great Pennsylvania Station*, by Lorraine B. Diehl (1985; New York: Four Walls Eight Windows, 1996), 8.

74. Daniela Gioseffi, "To the Brooklyn Bridge," in *Brooklyn Bridge Poetry Walk*, ed. Gioseffi, no pagination.

75. Harvey Shapiro, "The Bridge (for John Wissemann)," in *Lauds and Nightsounds* (New York: Sun, 1978), 54.

76. The theme of nostalgia also informs Samuel Delany's novella *Atlantis: Model 1924* (1993), especially when set against Delany's more recent *Times Square Red, Times Square Blue* (1999), his passionate tirade against gentrification and its negative effects on social diversity and cross-class contact. A reworking of the life of Delany's own father, *Atlantis* describes the travels of Sam, a young African American, from North Carolina to New York and his first six months there. A large section of the novella is set on the bridge, where Sam meets Hart Crane and undergoes his own "New York Renaissance"; the extended interaction fuels Sam's cultural and racial awakening. See Samuel R. Delany, *Atlantis: Model 1924*, in *Atlantis: Three Tales* (Hanover, NH: Wesleyan University Press, 1995), 1–121, and Delany, *Times Square Red, Times Square Blue* (New York: New York University Press, 1999).

77. Dennis Barone, "Introduction: Paul Auster and the Postmodern Anti-Novel," in *Beyond the Red Notebook: Essays on Paul Auster*, ed. Dennis Barone (Philadelphia: University of Pennsylvania Press, 1995), 17; John Zilcosky, "The Revenge of the Author: Paul Auster's Challenge to Theory," *Critique* 39 (1998), 199; and Tim Woods, "The Music of Chance: Aleatorical (Dis)harmonies within 'The City of the World,'" in *Beyond the Red Notebook*, ed. Barone, 109.

78. Paul Auster, *Ghosts*, in *The New York Trilogy* (Harmondsworth, UK: Penguin, 1990), 207, 209.

79. Ibid., 222.

80. Ibid., 177–80.

81. Cynthia Hogue, "Crossing Brooklyn Bridge," *Southern Review* 30 (1994), 87. Significantly, Hogue's poem — dedicated "for an unknown man" — seems based on an actual event.

82. Ibid., 87.

83. Walt Whitman, "Crossing Brooklyn Ferry," in *Walt Whitman*, ed. Kaplan, 308.

84. See Conrad, *Art of the City*, 12.

85. A similar motif can be found in Geoffrey Godbert's use of Whitman in his poem *Brooklyn Bridge* (Warwick, UK: Greville Press, 1985), 6. In addition, Whitman's "age of hope" has been subject to revision in popular fiction. For historian and novelist Caleb Carr, the "benefits" of "benign industrial capitalism" hid a crucial deficit. Revising the opening-day rhetoric, Carr saw little difference between the bridge and the famed structures of antiquity. Both projected social distinction at the cost of individual human loss: "my impression of [the unfinished Williamsburg Bridge] as a temple was not far off the mark: like the Brooklyn Bridge, whose Gothic arches I could see silhouetted against the night sky to the south, this new roadway over the East River was a place where many workers' lives had been sacrificed to the faith of engineering." For Carr, the glory of Khufu, Helios, Halicarnassus, Zeus, and Artemis find a parallel in American technological progress. Both conceal subjugation and immolation behind historical greatness. See Caleb Carr, *The Alienist* (London: Warner Books, 1994), 15–16.

86. See Ron Chernow, *Titan: The Life of John D. Rockefeller, Sr.* (New York: Random House, 1998), 97.

87. For references to the bridge in the novel, see Steven Millhauser, *Martin Dressler: The Tale of an American Dreamer* (New York: Vintage, 1996), 14–17, 24, 189, 198, 225, 236, 246, 261.

88. James, *American Scene*, 79.

89. Janet Burroway, "Heartbreak Hotel: Steven Millhauser's Capitalist Hero Dreams of Bigger and Better Things, but Goes too Far," *New York Times Book Review*, May 12, 1996, 8.

90. Ibid. Also see R. Z. Sheppard, "Trump, the Early Days: A Review of *Martin Dressler: The Tale of an American Dreamer*," *Time*, June 10, 1996, 82.

91. Millhauser, *Martin Dressler*, 265.

92. The scale of the Cosmo can be sampled from the following: "on the eighteenth floor you stepped from the elevator into a densely wooded countryside with a scattering of rustic cottages, each with a small garden. The twenty-fourth floor contained walls of rugged rock pierced by caves, each well-furnished and supplied with up-to-date plumbing, steam, and refrigerated air. Those with a hankering after an old-fashioned hotel could find . . . an entire Victorian resort hotel with turrets and flying flags, a grand veranda holding six hundred rattan rockers, and a path leading down through an ash grove to a beach of real sand beside a lake. Still other levels offered a variety of living arrangements: courtyard dwellings . . . a jungle with stuffed lions, a New England village with a blacksmith and a spreading oak, an urban avenue." Ibid., 266.

93. Ibid., 275, 281.

94. Umberto Eco, "Travels in Hyperreality," in *Travels in Hyperreality* (New York: Harcourt, Brace, Jovanovich, 1986), 1–58.

95. James, *American Scene*, 65, 74.

96. Such interpretations fit squarely within the framework established by Leo Marx in "The Idea of 'Technology' and Postmodern Pessimism," in *Does Technology Drive History?* ed. Smith and Marx, 237–57.

97. See Julia Kasdorf, "Brooklyn Bridge Showing Painters on Suspenders, 1914," in *Eve's Striptease* (Pittsburgh: University of Pittsburgh Press, 1998), 68–69; Jack Agüeros,

"Sonnet for My Heart in the River Below," in *Sonnets from the Puerto Rican* (Brooklyn: Hanging Loose Press, 1996), 47; Godbert, *Brooklyn Bridge*; Marshall, *New York Detective*, esp. 258–81; and Crabbe, *Suspension*. Neither Marshall nor Crabbe depicts glorious moments in American history. The lingering divides of the Civil War, intolerance, and nativist violence ravage their New York. Where the opening day stressed unity, these authors detail national division and resentment, a nation at odds with itself and, importantly, at odds with the sentiments expressed on that day. Against the traditions of official commemoration, their depictions of the opening ceremonies are colored by deep-seated antagonisms, violence, and hatred.

98. See Bercovitch, *Rites of Assent*, 49, 65.

99. Leslie Kaplan, *Brooklyn Bridge*, trans. Thomas C. Spear (New York: Station Hill Press, 1992), 95–97. Born to American and French parents, Kaplan has lived in New York, although she publishes in French. The novel was originally published under the title *Le Pont de Brooklyn* in 1987.

100. Ibid., 91.

101. My phrasing here leans on Mick Gidley's work on the cultural incorporation of native peoples in the early twentieth century. See Mick Gidley, *Edward S. Curtis and the North American Indian, Incorporated* (New York: Cambridge University Press, 1998), 283.

102. Whitehead, *Symbolism*, 88.

Epilogue
Crisis and Change: The Brooklyn Bridge in the Wake of Terror

1. Kent Barwick of the Metropolitan Waterfront Alliance, quoted in *New York Daily News*, March 19, 2002, 5.

2. *New York Times*, June 26, 2001, B3.

3. As reported by the *New York Times*: "They walked in bewilderment and fear, some doused in ash from head to toe. . . . Some commanded their fellow citizens to calm down as the first of the two towers collapsed, and then the second, and panic spread on the Brooklyn Bridge." This panic was captured by a British expatriate: "some [were] falling to their knees on Brooklyn Bridge because they believed it was a nuclear explosion . . . others [were] mown down by panicking crowds as they knelt in the road to pray." Echoing the general fear, one woman told reporters: "I was afraid the bridge was going to go [next]." *New York Times*, September 12, 2001, 11; *Daily Mirror* (UK), September 21, 2001, 8.

4. For a graphic illustration of this point, see Page, "For Sale: One Bridge," 1.

5. The issue of safety was hardly helped when a temporary antiterrorism command center was established in the disused Purchase Building, positioned directly beside the Brooklyn Bridge. See "Is City Inviting Terrorism at the Brooklyn Bridge?" *New York Times*, March 24, 2002, B15.

6. See *Time Out: London*, November 21, 2001, 180.

7. See *New York Daily News*, May 3, 2002, 1, and *New York Times*, May 3, 2002, B8.

8. *New York Times*, May 22, 2002, 1; *Melbourne Age* (Australia), May 23, 2002, 11; *Financial Times* (UK), May 23, 2002, 9.

9. "NYPD Issues Terror Threats; What Did Bush Administration Know?" *Newsnight with Aaron Brown*, CNN, May 21, 2002, transcript # 052100CN.V84; *New York Daily News*, May 22, 2002, 3.

10. *New York Times*, May 22, 2002, 1; *New York Daily News*, May 23, 2002, 9.

11. Bill Miller and Christine Haughney, "Nation Left Jittery by Latest Series of Terror Warnings," *Washington Post*, May 22, 2002, A1; Scott Shepard, "Landmarks in New York under Alert," *Austin American Statesman*, May 22, 2002, 1; *New York Post*, May 23, 2002, 8.

12. *New York Daily News*, May 22, 2002, 4.

13. *Washington Post*, May 23, 2002, 9.

14. Ibid.

15. Joanne Wasserman, "Terrorism? We'll Cross That Bridge," *New York Daily News*, May 23, 2002, 9.

16. Ron Scherer, "Brooklyn Bridge Still Draws Visitors, Despite Terror Alert," *Christian Science Monitor*, May 28, 2002, 2.

17. *New York Daily News*, May 23, 2002, 9; *New York Post*, May 25, 2002, 8.

18. Page, "For Sale: One Bridge," 1.

19. Joyce Purnick, "Home of the Brave, or the Timid?" *New York Times*, May 30, 2002, B1.

20. James, *American Scene*, 121.

21. *New York Times*, September 12, 2002, B11.

22. Richard Pyle, "A Puzzling New Vista from the Brooklyn Bridge, One Year after Smoky Nightmare," *Associated Press*, September 12, 2002, BC cycle, http://www.lexisnexis.com/.

23. See Pierre Nora, "Between Memory and History: *Les Lieux de Memoire*," *Representations* 26 (1989), 7–24, and Bodnar, "Pierre Nora, National Memory, and Democracy," 951–63.

24. Peter Burgener, "Urban Architects Sold on Brooklyn Bridge Vision," *Calgary Herald* (Canada), November 5, 2002, B6.

25. See the World Trade Center site design archive, http://www.september11news.com/WTCPlans.htm.

26. *New York Daily News*, May 23, 2003, 1.

27. *New York Times*, May 25, 2003, 38.

28. *New York Post*, May 25, 2003, 4; *Newsday*, May 25, 2003, 21. Also see Mitch Broder, "If You've Admired the Brooklyn Bridge from Afar, Get over It," *Westchester Journal News*, June 1, 2003, E1.

29. *Newsday*, June 20, 2003, 3; *New York Times*, June 20, 2003, 12.

30. Jimmy Breslin, "A Fate Sealed under Secrecy," 2. Coincidentally, on June 22, 2003, another of New York's most renowned writers bemoaned the direction of the national errand. In the *Daily News*, Pete Hamill described a "new kind of bleakness" in American life: not only were some people trying "to knock down the Brooklyn Bridge, one of the world's glories"; but he had also begun to perceive "signs that even the tough spirit of New York is being eroded." He continued, "The resilience that followed 9/11 is being frittered away. Part of this is because our most terrible tragedy was hijacked by Washington politicians with larger schemes in mind." See Pete Hamill, "From Politics to Weather, Dark Times Gnaw the Soul," *New York Daily News*, June 22, 2003, 43.

31. Jean F. Colin, quoted in *Bergen County Record*, May 25, 2003, 4.

32. Katherine Hobson, "High and Mighty," *U.S. News & World Report*, June 30, 2003, 23.

33. Bernhardt, *Memories of My Life*, 389.

34. Colson Whitehead, *The Colossus of New York: A City in Thirteen Parts* (New York: Doubleday, 2003), 99–109.

35. Ibid.

36. E. L. Doctorow, *City of God* (London: Little, Brown, 2000), 46–47.

37. Quoted in Amy Sara Clark, "As on 9-11, Bridge a Footpath," *The Brooklyn Paper*, August 21, 2003, 1.

38. John A. Roebling, *Report of John A. Roebling, C.E., to the President and Directors of the New York Bridge Company, on the Proposed East River Bridge* (Brooklyn: Daily Eagle Print, 1867), 18, 45.

39. Quoted in *New York Daily News*, August 15, 2003, 8.

Index

About the Author

A native of Leeds in the UK, Richard Haw first came to New York in 1992. While he sat in Bryant Park he decided that he "should learn little more about this fascinating city." Thirteen years later, he's still learning. Having permanently settled in New York in 2001, he now teaches English and writing at CUNY's John Jay College of Criminal Justice. His academic work focuses on creative responses to urban America. He lives with his wife, Erica Brody, in Brooklyn. This is his first book.